EVERY DAY IN TENNESSEE HISTORY

EVERY DAY IN TENNESSEE HISTORY

Bud Miller and Bob Swan with the first legal bottle of whiskey,
Dandridge County, around 1900

James B. Jones, Jr.

JOHN F. BLAIR, PUBLISHER
WINSTON-SALEM, NORTH CAROLINA

On the cover (clockwise from top):

1. Seven logs cut from one tree—one of the last remnants
   of the virgin forest, Woodbury, 1900s
2. Nightriders (of the Ku Klux Klan) in full costume
3. Children picking cotton, Tipton County, 1904
4. Tennessee Ernie Ford, 1954.

*Unless otherwise indicated, all photos in this book were obtained
from the Tennessee State Library and Archives in Nashville, Tennessee.*

Library of Congress Cataloging-in-Publication Data
Jones, James B.
    Every day in Tennessee history / by James B. Jones, Jr.
        p.   cm.
    Includes bibliographical references (p.   ) and index.
    ISBN 0-89587-144-0 (alk. paper)
    1. Tennessee—History—Chronology.   I. Title.
F436.J666   1996
976.8'002'02—dc20   96-1760

DESIGN BY DEBRA LONG HAMPTON AND LIZA LANGRALL
PRINTED BY R. R. DONNELLEY & SONS

To my wife, Cynthia,

whose love and good cheer

encouraged me,

and our son, Boyd, who

assured me this book would

become a

Tennessee bicentennial

bestseller

Tennessee County Map

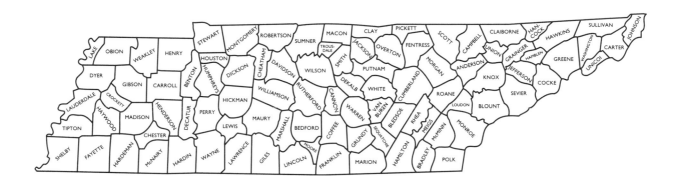

Contents

Acknowledgments

I wish to thank the staffs of the public libraries in Chattanooga, Knoxville, Memphis, and Murfreesboro. My thanks are also extended to the staffs of the Tennessee State Library and Archives in Nashville, the University of Tennessee library in Knoxville, the Beck Cultural Exchange in Knoxville, the Archives of Appalachia in Johnson City, and the Middle Tennessee State University library in Murfreesboro, as well as to Michael E. Birdwell of Tennessee Technological University, Joseph Y. Garrison of the Tennessee State Historic Preservation Office, Mr. and Mrs. Michael Darby of Nashville, and Mrs. Virginia Brock, senior editor of the *Franklin County Historical Review*.

Introduction

For many, the history of the Volunteer State is the history of its leaders. But there is more to history. As President Harry S. Truman said, "The only thing new in the world is the history you don't know." This book presents many unknown historical narratives, most of which would probably fit Truman's description.

There are no special instructions for using this book. For each day, I present a number of "true historical facts," arranged by year. All spellings are presented as they were found. These facts may concern a significant battle, the completion of a hydroelectric dam, the closing of a red-light district, a murder, a dinner party, a sermon, or a sporting event. Some events did not occur in the Volunteer State, but all involve Tennessee or Tennesseans.

It is my hope that history buffs and teachers will find in this book a means to stimulate discussions that will help reconstruct the past and lead to a better understanding of its complexities. I also hope that media professionals and writers will find a valuable reference tool. But most important, this book is meant to be user-friendly and entertaining to the general reader. If it is at all educational, so much the better.

Happy 200th birthday, Tennessee.

EVERY DAY IN TENNESSEE HISTORY

CONVICT LABOR AGAINST FREE LABOR.

Originally published in the Nashville Banner *on March 18, 1885, this cartoon depicts the effect of the convict lease system [January 1] on free Tennessee miners and their families.*

January

JANUARY I

1883, NASHVILLE

Samuel Allen McElwee, an African-American from Haywood County, took his seat in the Tennessee House of Representatives just after graduating from Fisk University. He was a tireless champion of equal rights in the state legislature and was widely respected among his white contemporaries. He died in 1914.

A Tennessee Historical Commission marker dedicated to his memory was to be placed on the Haywood County Courthouse lawn in Brownsville, but local opposition blocked its erection on April 3, 1981. The marker then was placed on the Fisk University campus on July 29, 1981.

1884, NASHVILLE

The Tennessee Coal and Iron Company became the lessee of the state penitentiary, paying rent of $101,000 a year to the state. The convict lease system was a government subsidy for business. It helped enterprises make greater profits, and more important, it cheapened the labor of free coal miners. As A. S. Colyar, a one-time vice president of TCI, said, "It was a very effective club over the heads of free labor."

In 1896, the convict lease system lapsed in Tennessee and was replaced by a state prison and coal mine known as Brushy Mountain State Prison. Significant in the system's downfall was the famous coal miners' insurrection from 1893 to 1896. The miners were "mad as hell" about low wages caused by the use of convict labor.

The gates of Brushy Mountain Prison [January 1], about 1920

JANUARY 2

1869, SHELBYVILLE

A frenzied gun battle was waged between 60 masked riders, ages 16 to 20, and freedmen defending their school and their teacher, John T. Dunlap.

Many locals feared that Dunlap was indoctrinating blacks with Radical Republican principles. He had been taken from his home and whipped by the Ku Klux Klan four months earlier.

Blacks were forewarned that their school was to be burned and so were armed. The masked riders got the worst of the five-minute battle. One of their number was killed and three were wounded.

Opinion in Shelbyville regarded the battle as "an inexcusable outrage," according to the *Nashville Republican Banner* of January 7.

1966, KNOXVILLE

A three-judge federal panel ruled unconstitutional a Tennessee law banning nudist camps.

District Judge Robert L. Taylor of Knoxville and Judge Harry Phillips of Nashville, a member of the United States Court of Appeals for the Sixth Circuit, wrote the majority opinion. The two judges held that the statute, passed in 1965, was too vague to comply with the due-process provisions of the 14th Amendment. The third member of the panel, retired federal judge Leslie R. Darr of Chattanooga, wrote a separate but concurring opinion.

The Tennessee Outdoor Club and the American Sunbathing Association went on to file suit in September 1966. Thirty years later, nudist camps are still legal in Tennessee because of this ruling.

JANUARY 3

1872, MEMPHIS

Edward Shaw, an African-American, was appointed wharf master. This was one of many political offices he held in the Bluff City. A leader of the black community, Shaw operated a successful saloon and gambling house. He was a steadfast foe of racism and the double-standard political system. He left the political arena after a frustrating public career and became an attorney a few years before his death in 1891. He was an early Tennessee civil rights champion.

1883, NASHVILLE

In his message to the general assembly, Governor Alvin Hawkins urged the legislature to appropriate money so that a stone base could be made to replace the wooden structure supporting the equestrian statue of Andrew Jackson on the State Capitol grounds: "I . . . urge upon you the importance of providing for the erection of a suitable base at as early a day as practicable."

JANUARY 4

1814, FORT STROTHER, MISSISSIPPI TERRITORY

During the Creek Indian War in what is now Alabama and Mississippi, General Andrew Jackson faced what he considered a mutiny when the men of Lieutenant William M. Kirby's East Tennessee company began to depart for home. Their 90-day volunteer enlistments had ended. As they marched by Jackson's Life Guard, Old Hickory drew his pistol and held it to Kirby's chest, swearing "by the Eternal" that he would blast a hole in the young lieutenant if he moved another inch. Fearlessly, Kirby drew his sword while his men defiantly cocked the hammers of their loaded muskets. Kirby was adamant that he was a free man and no one's servant. An army physician intervened and took young Kirby's sword. The lieutenant was subdued and placed in the stockade. Jackson immediately made preparations to have Kirby court-martialed.

After passions subsided, Jackson realized that the East Tennesseans' period of enlistment indeed had expired and that he could not legally stop their leaving. As a compromise, the general offered the soldiers honorable discharges in exchange for six weeks of additional service. The Volunteers would have none of it. Jacob Hartsell, captain of another East Tennessee company, witnessed this event. He wrote in his diary that "the men would not stay any longer on no terms. About two o'clock in the afternoon they started [out]."

Some historians have maintained that Tennessee became known as "the Volunteer State" because of the willingness of citizens to fight in the Creek Indian War. But it appears that Kirby's men cared more for their liberty than the orders of General Jackson. Later, during the Second Seminole War (1836–42), similar sentiments were expressed by other Tennessee Volunteers.

1955, WASHINGTON, D.C.

Estes Kefauver, United States senator from Tennessee, announced that America was "in the midst of a dangerous trend toward more and more monopolies. The recent trend calls for a new look at the problem and its effect on the economy and business. Every major merger movement has always resulted in a depression. The present is the third major merger movement in recent history and unless it is checked the result could be disastrous."

JANUARY 5

1886, MURFREESBORO

A primary election was held by the Rutherford County Court to fill the vacant office of sheriff. No winner was determined. The election was held because the former sheriff, Benjamin Batey, elected in 1884, had inexplicably disappeared in November 1885. He was rumored to be in Mexico, perhaps prospecting for gold.

This day also saw a telephone-service predicament in Murfreesboro. The Cumberland Telephone Company raised its rates, causing its 75 or so customers to object. CTC was a local monopoly. After the customers' protest, the managers reportedly "cut off all the telephones in Murfreesboro and [the] city is now isolated telephonically from the rest of the world." Such was the power of unregulated monopolies before the age of governmental regulation, as embodied in the late Public Service Commission.

1919, FRANCE

Colonel Luke Lea, Tennessee newspaper baron, Republican political boss, attorney, entrepreneur, and colonel in the United States Army, along with other officers and enlisted men of the 114th Artillery, attempted to visit Kaiser Wilhelm II in exile in Holland and convince him to surrender to the Allies. The mission was conceived on a whim, and as Colonel Lea later admitted at the official army inquiry, the "exact purpose of the trip is hard to define as it depended largely upon different circumstances that would develop from time to time." Lea and his entourage had conceived the idea after setting out for a drive in the French countryside on New Year's Day and making frequent stops at village taverns.

The colonel not only failed to convince the kaiser to surrender, but his actions were unlawful, breaking a number of international diplomatic sanctions. Lea and his friends faced an official army inquiry to determine if they should be court-martialed. Most likely because Lea was once a United States senator, the board of inquiry decided not to censure him.

The news of Lea's recklessness was detrimental to diplomatic initiatives at the end of the war. The entire affair was, according to the army inquiry transcripts, "amazingly indiscreet" and very embarrassing to the United States government.

It was not until 1937 that the first accurate version of the story was told in the *Saturday Evening Post*.

1988, WASHINGTON, D.C.

After picking up important endorsements for the "Super Tuesday" Democratic primaries during his campaign for the presidency, Tennessee senator Al Gore, Jr., said he was not interested in the vice-presidential slot. It was, in his opinion, a "political dead end." Gore said defiantly, "Anybody who thinks I'm in this for anything other than the presidency is going to be surprised. We're in this to win."

In the end, Governor Michael Dukakis of Massachusetts was nominated and was soundly beaten by Republican George Bush. In 1992, however, Democrat Bill Clinton defeated Bush and Gore became vice president.

JANUARY 6

1818, BRITISH FLORIDA

Nearly three years to the day after his victory at the Battle of New Orleans, General Andrew Jackson wrote President James Monroe, "Let it be signified to me through any channel . . . that the possession of the Floridas would be desirable to the United States, and in sixty days it will be accomplished."

Less than two weeks earlier, Jackson had been put in charge of American operations in Florida during the First Seminole War. His instructions were to pursue the Seminoles into Florida as far as the boundaries of the Spanish posts.

There was no answer from President Monroe, and Old Hickory regarded the silence as approval to invade Spanish Florida. Jackson marched his army into Florida and seized St. Marks on April 7 and Pensacola on May 24, even as Secretary of State John Quincy Adams was negotiating with the Spanish minister.

During the campaign, Jackson captured and executed two British traders accused of aiding the Seminoles. His actions met with the disapproval of all the president's cabinet members except Adams. Secretary of War John C. Calhoun believed Jackson's action warranted disciplinary procedures, and anti-Jackson forces in the House of Representatives proposed to censure him.

Most Americans strongly disliked the English and approved of Jackson's bringing all of east Florida under American control.

1877, NASHVILLE

Governor James Davis Porter addressed the topic of mob violence in the Volunteer State:

> It is to be regretted, that in a few localities, the County jails have been violated, by the removal and murder of prisoners by armed mobs. The power with which the Executive is clothed has been employed to bring these outlaws to trial and punishment, and the local authorities are exhibiting a commendable zeal in their efforts to discover the authors of the outrage. The provisions of the Criminal Code are adequate for the punishment of jail-breakers and murderers; all that is wanted is the development of a public sentiment that will stimulate and give courage to local officials.

Placing confidence in local officials was unwarranted. No matter how dedicated the constabulary might be in upholding the law, the power of an armed mob could seldom be thwarted, especially when public sentiment frequently took the form of mob violence in the late 19th century.

1955, NASHVILLE

Davidson County's delegation in the Tennessee House asked Governor Frank Goad Clement to call a special election as soon as possible to fill the vacant seat of State Senator Richard H. Fulton. Fulton, who later served in the United States Congress and as mayor of Nashville, had lost his seat because he was not old enough. Among the qualifications provided in the 1953 state constitution was a requirement that no one could be a state senator who was not 30 years old. Fulton was 27.

JANUARY 7

1878, KNOXVILLE

A resolution passed by a black Republican caucus was submitted to a combined black and white Republican meeting. It claimed, with considerable justification, that the role of blacks in party affairs had been ignored by white party masters. The black Republicans requested the support of white Republicans in order to exercise their right to sit on a jury. The resolution stated in part, "We ask that . . . you formally and emphatically repudiate the partial manner of transacting affairs where the whole people are interested, and say by your acts that such is not in keeping with the fundamental principles of liberty and equality—the pillars upon which the Republican party is founded."

The white Republican leaders wanted the black vote but did not support black aspirations.

In time, the black citizens of Knoxville initiated a "New Departure," in which they negotiated their votes for political spoils and support for the exercise of their rights as citizens of the United States.

1919, TROY, NEW YORK

Dorothy Lavinia Brown, M.D., the first black

woman to be elected to the Tennessee legislature, was born. She was reared in the Troy Orphans' Home. A 1948 graduate of Meharry Medical College, Brown was also the first African-American woman to practice general surgery in the South.

In the legislature, she introduced a bill to legalize abortion in the case of incest or rape. Of that bill, she said, "One of the leaders of the powerful rural bloc in the House came to me and said: 'If you don't withdraw that bill within the next hour, this will be your first and last term.'" Brown did not withdraw the bill, which ultimately failed by two votes. As predicted, she was not reelected.

Andrew Jackson, hero of the Battle of New Orleans [January 8]

GEN. ANDREW JACKSON.
THE HERO OF NEW ORLEANS.

1815, NEW ORLEANS

American forces under the command of General Andrew Jackson killed 2,500 of Britain's finest troops while losing but a handful of their own. The great irony of the battle was that it was fought after the Treaty of Ghent—completed in December 1814—had ended the War of 1812. Communications were slow in the 19th century.

The victory gave Jackson instant name recognition that aided his three presidential bids. The victory also helped sustain the hatred most American felt for the British in the early 19th century.

Twelve days later, General John Coffee wrote to his wife about the battle: "We had engaged about fourteen hundred men, and the enemy about three thousand. . . . Our whole loss . . . has been about fifty killed and twenty wounded, and about one hundred ten prisoners." He claimed that about 4,000 British enemy were slain. "Surely," he wrote, "Providence has had a hand in the thing."

1844, KNOX COUNTY

William Francis Yardley was born. Because his mother was white, he was born free and so could take advantage of opportunities other blacks could not. He was one of the first black educators in Knox County. He later became the first black attorney in Knoxville, possibly in Tennessee, and served also as a fireman, a justice of the peace, an alderman for Knoxville's Fifth Ward, and an insurance agent. In 1876, he became the first African-American to run for governor of Tennessee.

JANUARY 9

1900, BROWNSVILLE

Richard Haliburton, world-famous traveler and adventure author, was born.

After graduating from Princeton University in 1920, he traveled and wrote articles for *National Geographic* to finance his trips. He wrote many travel books, including *Richard Haliburton's Complete Guide Book of Marvels*. He was gathering material for another book while sailing a Chinese junk, the *Sea Dragon*, to San Francisco when he drowned, the victim of a typhoon on the Pacific Ocean.

1901, NASHVILLE

In his Legislative Message to the general assembly, Governor Benton McMillin recommended that the age of consent be extended two years. A growing absence of "constant parental care" left 16-year-old girls at a disadvantage when confronted by more worldly attractions. "The unwisdom and inconsistency of our present laws," noted the governor,

> are illustrated by recounting the fact that under them, if the son swaps horses and gets cheated when he is twenty years, eleven months and twenty seven days old, the irate father can go out and proclaim that his son is yet an infant . . . and revoke the trade; but if the sister of the same boy meets one of . . . worldly wisdom, and unscrupulousness, who is unprincipled enough to take advantage of her . . . and work her ruin . . . if she is sixteen years old, our law says she has reached the age of discretion, and that the crushed father, broken hearted mother, and penitent child have no remedy more potent than tears and grief. This law should

be changed from sixteen to not less than eighteen years.

Such a bill was later enacted into law, but with a number of telling conditions. One of them held that no conviction could be obtained on the unsupported testimony of the female in question. Another related to the female's reputation for chastity. If the female was age 12 or over, no conviction could be obtained if it was demonstrated that she was "a bawd, lewd, or kept female." The same rules did not apply to men.

JANUARY 10

1832, WASHINGTON, D.C.

West Tennessee congressman William T. Fitzgerald wrote to his wife about his recent dinner at the White House:

> I have just returned from dining with the President. The Hour of dining here in the fashionable circles is the same hour at which we take tea. There were about twenty there, about equal numbers of male and female. The process of eating is long and tedious and disagreeable. Your plate, knife and fork are changed more than 20 times, sometimes steel, sometimes silver and sometimes gold plates of different kinds are brought every time. . . . I have received [two dinner invitations] since I have been here—but [was only able to attend] that of the President.

1919, CHATTANOOGA

The editor of the *Chattanooga Daily Times* reacted bitterly to the passage of the 18th Amendment, which brought about Prohibition.

Tennessee, by ratifying the amendment, had dishonored "the heroes of the Confederacy who fought and died for the maintenance of rights guaranteed them under the bill of rights." The Anti-Saloon League–sponsored amendment and the Volstead Act made it evident to the editor that "the American system of representative government is a failure and that the American people are incapable of self-government, requiring the over lordship of an autocratic organization or oligarchy."

JANUARY 11

1855, NASHVILLE

The board of aldermen passed an antiprostitution ordinance that made it a "penal offense for lewd women to expose their persons at their front doors or to use vulgar language to persons passing by."

The problems that caused prostitution were present in Nashville before the Civil War and did not abate even after the conflict. The United States Army Medical Corps initiated the nation's first legalized system of prostitution during the Civil War. Based upon the licensing and regular medical inspection of prostitutes, it was introduced in Nashville (and later in Memphis) to protect Union soldiers from venereal disease. After the conflict, the system was abandoned and prostitution flourished.

1955, SMYRNA

A C-119 "Flying Boxcar" crashed and burned near Stewart Air Force Base while its load of 35 paratroopers parachuted to safety. The pilot and copilot were killed in the crash. The plane had taken off minutes earlier to ferry the troops to

Alaska for cold-weather training in "Operation Snowbird." One of the paratroopers landed in Mrs. Roy King's front yard in Rutherford County. There were many mechanical difficulties with other C-119s in Operation Snowbird, including a crash in Montana.

JANUARY 12

1869, NASHVILLE

State Senator Philip P. C. Nelson, a Radical Republican representing Carter, Johnson, Sullivan, and Washington Counties, introduced the following bill:

Whereas, A bill has been introduced into the Senate of this General Assembly looking to the enfranchisement of the female portion of our people; and,

Whereas, The present costume worn by that class to whom it is proposed to extend the elective franchise is cumbersome and entirely unsuited for the purpose of electioneering and canvassing, and is found awkward for commoner purposes; therefore

Be it enacted, etc., That the costume now worn by female citizens of Tennessee be changed from petticoats to pants, and that this act takes effect . . . after its passage.

1882, SPARTA

The editor of the *Sparta Expositor* recounted the following tale to illustrate his dislike for waltzing: "An old member of the legislature, when he saw the fashionable waltzing at the inaugural ball, made the following sensible remark: 'Well, I don't know what they call such as that now; but in my raising such wrestling was called hugging.'"

JANUARY 13

1892, NASHVILLE

Three strangers who got off the train aroused the suspicion of a city police officer named Smith. He recognized them to be wanted "second-story men" and closely followed the trio. The burglars ran and tried to steal a passing horse and buggy. Two of them managed to get on board after throwing the buggy's woman driver out. The pair got away, it was reported, after charging "several blocks at a breakneck speed." The third culprit, arrested by Officer Smith, was carrying a collection of burglar's tools, including chisels, bottles of acid, and a revolver. He was taken to the city jail and later was convicted of burglary and assault.

1979, NASHVILLE

It was announced by "sources close to the singer" that country-and-western superstar George Jones was undergoing treatment for alcoholism. The 47-year-old Jones was in an undisclosed hospital in Alabama. According to longtime friend Paul Richey, Jones was "exhausted, just completely broken down. George came to his decision of his own free will. He wasn't committed . . . but he knew he needed help. He was worn out from being on the road and he had been drinking. The doctors tell me he is suffering from exhaustion."

Jones had been on the comeback trail since a series of reversals beginning with his divorce from Tammy Wynette in 1975 and bankruptcy in 1978.

JANUARY 14

1864, OCCUPIED NASHVILLE

According to a report on "Ready-Made Houses" in the *Nashville Dispatch*, a company had been formed in the city "for the purpose of bringing to this market houses already built. All that is required to put them up is a few screws, and when you desire to move your residence to a neighboring county, all you have to do is to take it down again as you would a portable wardrobe. The scarcity of houses in the city has induced the newly formed company to commence the enterprise. The frames are being manufactured in Cincinnati, and will soon be ready for shipment."

This sort of housing remained available in mail-order catalogs throughout the late 19th and early 20th centuries. One such enterprise was the George F. Barber Company, located in Knoxville, which provided mail-order homes to clients as far away as Oregon.

1882, GALLATIN

About midnight, a fight broke out in Bill Halloran's saloon on the public square. Two men were killed outright and a third was wounded. Witnesses were unable to determine what started the altercation, although seven strangers, all of them later involved in the fight, had ridden into town on horseback about 9 P.M. Some believed that they were moonshiners and that the fight was started "by too much talking outside of the camps. Four of the men were arrested and placed in jail. There were about twenty shots fired, which caused great excitement throughout the town."

JANUARY 15

1781, FREELAND'S STATION, ALSO KNOWN AS MCGAVOCK'S SPRING

A series of deadly Indian attacks began against

white settlers. Eventually, the Indians withdrew. They returned six months later to continue their campaign against white settlers they considered intruders in their tribal domain. Such attacks were a fact of life on the Tennessee frontier five years before statehood.

1882, NASHVILLE

Continuing heavy rains swelled the Tennessee, Cumberland, Ohio, and Mississippi Rivers. In Nashville, the rainy conditions did not stop curious citizens from walking down to the Cumberland for a glance at the raging river. Many went with umbrellas and remained for hours. Some were in buggies and went from bottom to bottom. Others were in dugouts or yawls. Small boats could be seen everywhere, some being used for pleasure and others to move furniture from the many flooded houses. In one instance, a captain of police visited a woman with several children and advised her to get out of her house before the Cumberland washed it away. The captain reported, "She . . . said 'I have a canoe and I know how to paddle it.'" Eight and a half inches of rain were measured between January 1 and January 13, a record to that time.

JANUARY 16

1920, NASHVILLE

The Anti-Saloon League ran a large advertisement in the *Nashville Banner* under the title "Booze and Bolshevism." According to the ad, "Failure to enforce prohibition in Russia was followed by Bolshevism. Failure to enforce prohibition *here* will encourage Bolshevism, disrespect for the law, and *invite industrial di-*

saster. Radical and Bolshevist outbreaks are practically unknown in states where prohibition has been in effect for years. Bolshevism lives on booze."

There proved to be no Bolshevik revolution, even though many Americans continued to drink.

1967, NASHVILLE

The Vanderbilt University Commodores advanced to first place in the Southeastern Conference basketball standings after beating Auburn University 71–65. A capacity crowd exceeding 9,000 attended the game.

JANUARY 17

1886, MEMPHIS

Pauline Livingstone, the owner of a saloon at 13½ Winchester Street, known in the city by the nickname "Iron Clad," died. She was one of the most famous (and infamous) members of the Bluff City demimonde. Such women were spurned in polite society yet found a ready market for selling whiskey and sex. Iron Clad Livingstone was a Tennessee entrepreneur at a time when few women actually ran businesses.

1979, NASHVILLE

Lamar Alexander, Tennessee's 46th governor, was sworn in on his 110-year-old family Bible at 5:56 P.M., three days early to impede outgoing governor Ray Blanton from pardoning more criminals. Alexander, it was reported, appeared visibly nervous.

Blanton remarked to the press, "I am saddened and hurt for the state of Tennessee that this clandestine action has taken place this evening. There is such a thing as courtesy, and there was no courtesy extended to me today. . . . This action . . . leaves a blemish on Tennessee's record, and I have worked to promote Tennessee around the world." Blanton added that he was not bitter.

JANUARY 18

1794, NASHVILLE

Rachel Donelson Robards and Andrew Jackson were married by her brother-in-law Robert Hays and a justice of the peace. This was their "second" marriage. They were first married in Natchez, Mississippi, in 1791, mistakenly believing that Rachel's first husband had obtained a divorce in Kentucky.

Many claimed that Jackson was living with another man's wife and that the two were living in sin. The difficulty caused Andrew and Rachel embarrassment and led to duels in which Jackson defended his wife's virtue. For example, in 1803, Jackson challenged John Sevier to a duel because of a critical remark Sevier made concerning Rachel. The duel with Sevier was not fought. In 1806, Jackson killed Charles Dickinson in a duel because he was convinced Dickinson had insulted Rachel. In the 1824 and 1828 presidential campaigns, the scandal arose again. Jackson believed the accusations were so harsh that they killed his wife. His motto was "Death before dishonor."

1890, KNOXVILLE

Local elections were dramatically affected by the "Dortch Law," named after Joseph P. Dortch. The law called for use of the Australian ballot

Toon-Tua, a Cherokee Chief

for the first time in the state's history. It also forbade helping those who couldn't read the ballot, thus disfranchising many white and African-American voters.

The Democrats won most offices in Knoxville. They later won most state offices and ushered in Jim Crow laws, which prohibited the black population from mixing with whites.

JANUARY 19

JANUARY 19, 1759, CHOTEE

The Reverend John Martin, Scottish missionary to the Cherokees, noted in his diary that the Indians "had a great Dance to Night which I took for some religious Ceremony paid to the Fire, as they frequently bowed to it, but was afterwards informed by them it was only a custom they have & they don't seem to worship any Thing."

1849, MEMPHIS

An anonymous poem in the *Memphis Daily Enquirer* lamented the sad condition of the streets of the Bluff City. Entitled "Memphis Mud," it read,

> O! sad to me the luckless hour,
> When I from home did scud
> To place myself within the power
> Of awful Memphis mud.
> The thought of such a dismal scene
> Chills up my very blood;
> O! what a change from pavements clean,
> To horrid Memphis mud.
> I've heard of death by land and sea,
> By Fire and Sword and Flood
> But this will surely slaughter me,
> To dwell in Memphis mud.
> Could I this moment leave this place,
> I'd pick up every dud
> And 'gainst the fleetest, win the race,
> In 'scaping Memphis mud.
> In summer, it may fairer be,
> In Winter, O! deliver me,
> From fatal Memphis mud.

1862, NEAR MILL SPRINGS, KENTUCKY

Confederate general Felix K. Zollicoffer was killed while inspecting his lines. In the rain, he mistook the Federal force for his own. He rode up to Union colonel Speed Smith Fry, commander of the Fourth Kentucky Federal Regiment, and asked, "You are not going to fight your friends, are you?" Colonel Fry, perhaps a bit mystified, pointed over Zollicoffer's shoulder to the Confederate soldiers and said to the bewildered general, "Those are your friends." Recognizing the mistake, Zollicoffer's aide fired at Fry but killed his horse instead. Springing to his feet, the Kentucky colonel shot and killed General Zollicoffer.

After the battle, which the Confederates lost, Zollicoffer's body was laid out on a few fence rails. Soon, Union soldiers discovered his rank and cut up his uniform, hoping to claim a souvenir. According to one report, his corpse was stripped bare.

1990, NEW MARKET, JEFFERSON COUNTY

Tennessee's "Radical Hillbilly," Myles F. Horton, died.

Horton was born in Savannah, Tennessee, on July 5, 1905. His Highlander Folk School, founded in Grundy County on November 1, 1932, taught social activism. Highlander Folk School was famous for training labor-union leaders, Martin Luther King, Jr., Rosa Parks, and countless others who worked for social change through nonviolent civil disobedience.

Horton was buried next to his wife and father at Summerville in Grundy County. This Tennessean helped usher in the civil rights movement of the 1960s. Many conservatives wrongly claimed he was a communist. No such charge could be proven by the state legislature, which sought to label him with that epithet.

JANUARY 20

1869, HAMILTON COUNTY

Ewing Ogden Tade, the county's first elected superintendent of education, wrote to a friend describing a typical workday: "Up at 3:30 A.M., traveled fifteen miles on the RR; walked six miles; made up Civil District Clerk's report; examined one teacher; traveled nine miles further; and reached home by [railroad] cars at 8 P.M., eating one meal." Such was the dedication among early public educators in Tennessee.

1947, NASHVILLE

State Senator Hubert Brooks of Johnson City introduced a bill to ban nearly everything. He proposed prohibiting schools, churches, civic clubs, chambers of commerce, political parties, counties, towns, cities, taxing districts, state and federal government, fraternal organizations, and forgiveness. Brooks, who had a reputation as a prankster, said that while the bill was facetious, it had a serious purpose. It drew attention to what he considered the large number of nonessential laws in Tennessee.

1960, WILDFLECKEN, GERMANY, NEAR THE SWISS BORDER

Elvis Presley, on winter maneuvers with the 32nd Armored Division, was promoted to the rank of sergeant. His promotion put him in charge of a three-man reconnaissance team. Along with his new rank and new responsibilities, Elvis had his pay increased to a whopping $122.31 per month.

JANUARY 21

1814, EMUCKFAW CREEK, MISSISSIPPI TERRITORY

Andrew Jackson's forces battled the Redstick Creek Indians. Jackson's brother-in-law and aide, Major Alexander Donelson, was among those killed. The Tennesseans were repulsed by the Creeks.

During fighting at Enotachopco three days

later, Jackson's men were similarly repelled. They also took heavy losses at the Battle of Calibee Creek on January 27.

Jackson's army ultimately won the war at the Battle of Horseshoe Bend on March 27.

JANUARY 22

1813, NEAR FRENCHTOWN, CANADA

During action in the War of 1812, General James Winchester's invading army was surprised by a combined attack of British and Indian forces. After surrendering, wounded soldiers were summarily killed. Winchester and his army of 550 Tennesseans and Kentuckians were marched to Quebec and imprisoned for 15 months. General Winchester returned home in April 1814.

1870, CARROLL COUNTY

According to a story in the *Nashville Union and American* of January 26, county residents had been the victims of a crime wave since the previous November. The crime wave was characterized by rape, arson, and murder by "masked parties, and it was natural that there should not be a very great love entertained for this roving band of Ku-Klux going through the country."

On January 22, Colonel Coleman, a leading Carroll County citizen, was murdered at his home near King's Bridge, between Huntingdon and Trezevant. Four masked riders demanded he come to the door. As he stepped out, he was shot to death, and the riders fled into the darkness. The following morning, "a crowd of negroes rode into Huntingdon upon horses that were known to belong to parties in the neighborhood where the shooting took place, and, being closely questioned, one . . . made a full confession of the murder . . . and detailed his connection with that and other depredations and also disclosing the names of all engaged in Ku-Kluxing throughout the country."

The editor expected his readers to believe that blacks donned masks and rode through the Carroll County countryside committing various crimes just to slander the "good name" of the Ku Klux Klan. Inasmuch as the *Union and American* was a Democratic Party organ and was opposed to civil rights for African-Americans, it appears that this story was either a deception designed to discredit the Republican Party or an exaggeration of a serious crime committed under different circumstances. It is difficult to imagine that African-Americans would want to, or be allowed to, participate in Klan terrorism.

JANUARY 23

1863, NEAR MURFREESBORO

Construction began on Fortress Rosecrans, named after William Starke Rosecrans, the victorious Union general at the Battle of Stones River.

When completed, the fortress incorporated 23 miles of earthen walls, warehouses, railroad switching lines, and rail connections. Fortress Rosecrans served as the major supply center for the Union army's march to Chattanooga and through Georgia. It was abandoned in April 1866. Today, all but a few earthen walls and a cannon position remain. The fortress and battlefield are protected by the National Park Service.

1874, KNOXVILLE

A disheveled and harried Eliza Moore visited

the editorial offices of the *Knoxville Chronicle* with news that the superintendent of the county poorhouse had regularly been abusing inmates such as herself. He whipped, handcuffed, and underfed the shut-ins. Even more revolting, the facility was usually cleaned by the inmates just a few days before each quarterly inspection, then left to the vermin for three months until the next official visit.

The editor of the *Chronicle* warned the superintendent to see to it that the institution was better run, and further warned that serious consequences awaited if he did not. However, there is nothing suggesting improvements were made.

1895, MEMPHIS

The sensational evangelist Sam Jones, a former alcoholic, addressed a wildly enthusiastic crowd of over 4,000, making appeals to sin no more and follow the example of Jesus.

Evangelists were as popular in the 19th century as they are today. Jones was noted throughout the South as a fire-and-brimstone sermonizer. In many respects, his preaching was as much show business as religion. Thousands flocked to witness his sermons.

JANUARY 24

1850, MURFREESBORO

Tennessee writer Mary Noailles Murfree was born.

Because women were not supposed to write novels, she used the pen name Charles Egbert Craddock. Her first novel appeared in 1878. Her career spanned three decades. She used the Tennessee mountains and postbellum landscapes for her settings. Her work was of the "local color" school of literature. Perhaps her most famous book is *In the Tennessee Mountains*, published in 1884.

1918, CHATTANOOGA

"A rigid investigation of alleged disreputable places in various parts of the city" was being conducted by Judge McReynolds, according to the *Chattanooga Daily Times*. Bailiff Fred W. Hill and Constable George Kirklin investigated. Although most of the harlots had been run out of town, a few prostitutes discovered they could remain active if they married a soldier who would act as a solicitor. Judge McReynolds was quoted as saying, "The good women of Chattanooga are up in arms and I am going to help them. . . . The good women of Chattanooga want an example made of these women, especially mothers who are unmindful of their daughter's conduct, and we're going to help them in every way possible."

While it was never completely eliminated in Chattanooga during World War I, prostitution was strictly limited in order to protect the health of soldiers at nearby Fort Oglethorpe, Georgia.

JANUARY 25

899, RIPLEY

Tennessee blues legend "Sleepy" John Estes was born. His family soon moved to Brownsville. As a child, Estes lost one eye. His sight deteriorated until he was completely blind by 1949. His guitar mentor was "Hambone" Willie Newbern, a local blues performer.

In 1927, Estes formed a team with harmonica player Hammie Nixon that lasted for over 50 years. He began recording in 1929. In 1964,

Estes and Nixon toured Europe and Japan with the American Folk Blues Festival. A 1963 film, *The Legend of Sleepy John Estes*, brought him much fame. He died in Brownsville in June 1977.

1954, MEMPHIS

Edward O. Cleaborn, an African-American soldier, received the Distinguished Service Cross posthumously. Cleaborn was honored by an official observance in Memphis for covering the retreat of his comrades, including wounded friends, while under fire on a ridge near the village of Kuri, Korea. His parents were presented with the medal and were told how their son had destroyed the machine-gun crews threatening Company A of the 24th Infantry Regiment. While staying at his position, Cleaborn killed enemy infiltrators who had outflanked his platoon. His brave actions saved all members of the platoon but Cleaborn himself.

JANUARY 26

1821, CARTHAGE

An unnamed New York Yankee traveling in Tennessee wrote of his experience in Carthage:

> This modern Carthage is not destitute of Helots. It was my lot to fall in company with one of them a few miles from this place, who honored me with his company to town—came to lodge in my room, bringing his decanter of whisky. . . . [He] got most particularly drunk—harangued, swore & fought imaginary battles until one o'clock—then went to bed [and] repeated it all in his sleep—naked—swore a page or two—and slept again. Next morning by

sunrise he was bawling most vigorously in my ear to know if I was asleep. I found it to no avail to remain silent, nor was he satisfied with my answer in the affirmative but continued talking for an hour, altho' I was still most obstinately silent and addressing myself to sleep.

1885, NASHVILLE

The *Nashville Banner* printed an editorial entitled "Tennessee's Tewksbury." Tewksbury was an infamous hospital for the mentally ill in Massachusetts that was found to have sold the corpses of dead inmates to medical colleges for dissection. In Tennessee, the state prison system sold the bodies of dead prisoners to medical colleges. The editorial charged that Dr. Roberts, the chief surgeon for the prison system, was responsible. It asked, "Why should the state bury its insane dead and dissect its dead criminals?" The editor was curious to know if the revenue generated from the grisly practice was held in the state treasury, given to companies that leased the state's convicts, or used for charity.

Making matters worse were rape and sodomy in the state penitentiary. "No woman should be sent to the penitentiary until proper provisions shall be made for the care and protection of female prisoners," the editorial stated. As for their male counterparts, "it is said that the practice of sodomy is open and notorious and discharged male convicts are reported as leaving the state prison affected with a loathsome disease in such a way as to conclusively prove the absolutely horrifying practice referred to."

The state prison was a "school for crime" that produced "a breed of law-breakers through illegitimate intercourse of the sexes within the

JANUARY 27, 1893, CHATTANOOGA
It was reported that the Chattanooga Athletic Association's football team was beaten by the New Orleans Pelicans by a score of 48–0. Football was rapidly becoming a major sport in Tennessee in the 1890s. Harriman, for example, fielded the team shown above in 1891.

prison walls. . . . No woman should be sent to the penitentiary. . . . Rape is a common thing when necessary for the gratification of lustful desires. . . . Is the policy settled policy in Tennessee to treat all persons, after conviction for crime, as no longer human beings, but simply and purely as means for a little revenue to the state and great profit to individual and corporate greed?"

The editorial initiated an early penal-reform effort that failed because of a libel suit.

JANUARY 27

1863, NEAR CHATTANOOGA

U. G. Owen, a physician with the Confederate army, wrote to his wife that if she were to visit him she "must bring all the money that you have convenient. You can borrow some from your Pa. I have not been paid off in some time, but hope to be in next month when I will have plenty of money."

He continued, "I saw two young soldiers hung last Friday for desertion & bushwhacking our army. They were both youthful, but I suppose were dealt with according to their just deserts. I know some of my old neighbor boys would go the same way if our soldiers ever get hold of them for several of them have deserted our army & joined the Yankees."

1900, THE PHILIPPINE ISLANDS

The gunboat USS *Nashville*, it was reported, had participated in the American imperial war by throwing shells into the Filipino freedom-fighting forces. Of course, the Americans had a different view of the situation, believing that

> Underneath the starry Flag
> We'll civilize them with the Krag.

The Krag was the Swedish rifle used by United States soldiers in the Philippines.

JANUARY 28

1845, COLUMBIA

The recently elected James K. Polk left his family's ancestral home to travel to Washington, D.C., to assume the presidency. On the 30th, he stopped at the Hermitage to pay his respects to former president Andrew Jackson, who would die six months later.

During his term, Polk began a war with Mexico (1846–48). By the end of the war, America had gained all of California and many other parts of Mexico. The United States stretched from the Atlantic to the Pacific.

In all, over 1,193,000 square miles of Mexican land became American territory by force of arms.

1912, OCOEE RIVER

Ocoee No. 1, a pre-TVA hydroelectric power plant, began operations. Ceremonies and celebrations were held in Chattanooga. The plant ushered in the electric era to southeastern Tennessee. Cheap power for industrial and domestic uses created demand for such things as refrigerators, electric lights, irons, and fans. Ocoee No. 1 was listed in the National Register of Historic Places in 1989.

JANUARY 29

1834, WASHINGTON, D.C.

President Andrew Jackson ordered the War Department to put down "riotous assembly" among Irish laborers constructing the Chesapeake and Ohio Canal near Williamsport, Maryland. This was the first time in American history that federal troops were used to intervene in a labor dispute.

1888, KNOXVILLE

The calm of Sunday morning was abruptly disturbed by a catastrophe. Jim Rule, son of Captain William Rule, managing editor of the *Knoxville Journal*, was on his way to church. He was approached by John D. West, William West, and a companion. The West boys were infuriated at a letter in the *Journal* that had questioned their father's medical education. They drew pistols and knives and "commenced to crowd in on [Rule]."

Shots rang out as the three chased the editor's son, who fell wounded to the sidewalk.

In the meantime, when the choir at Rule's church concluded singing "O come, let us sing unto the Lord," the pandemonium from the street became perceptible. Mrs. Jim Rule, in "a ghastly pallor . . . flew from the choir to . . . one of the most horrible spectacles that ever fond wife looked upon." Rule was on his back and was being stabbed by John D. West while William West fired a .38-caliber Smith and Wesson revolver. Rule defended himself by firing his .38 twice at his assailants, wounding John D. West fatally.

As male members of the congregation came to Rule's rescue, the West brothers ran. John D. West subsequently made a deathbed confession. William West was soon arrested.

Despite suffering multiple stab and bullet wounds, Rule was expected to recover.

1941, MEMPHIS

The mansion constructed by Robert R. Church—an African-American entrepreneur, Republican Party activist, and power broker—sold for $4,250. Ironically, building it had cost $15,000 in the 19th century.

JANUARY 30

1835, WASHINGTON, D.C.

On his way to the funeral of a friend, President Andrew Jackson was assaulted by a man with a brace of pistols. The guns failed to fire. Jackson was assisted in wrestling the would-be assassin to the ground by David Crockett. After the affray, the two Tennesseans—political enemies—attended the funeral. The assailant, Richard Lawrence, was sent to the Maryland insane asylum. He died there in 1861.

1843, NASHVILLE

Thomas Washington, a slave, was executed for killing his master. Washington's lawyer, Return J. Meigs, had argued that the killing was justified on the grounds of self-defense. But the Tennessee Supreme Court held that it was murder and so would not stay the execution.

Meigs's son, John, later recalled that "the case excited a very wide attention on account of his vigorous defense of . . . the poor fellow. . . . The slavery debauched mind of the people could not bear the ideal of the innocence of a slave who was really defending his own life, but who dared to raise his hand against a master."

JANUARY 31

1864, OCCUPIED NASHVILLE

The *Nashville Daily Union* announced that "the distinguished young tragedian, J. Wilkes Booth" would be performing in Nashville for the first two weeks of February.

1879, KNOXVILLE

A jury of African-Americans found Newman Carter guilty of murder in the first degree with extenuating circumstances. Carter, also black, had allegedly killed his lover in 1877.

It was unusual for blacks to be on juries in the late 19th century. The jurors in the Carter case were serving because they had demanded that their right to sit in the jury box be recognized by white supremacists.

Carter was defended by William Francis Yardley, the first black attorney in Knoxville, perhaps all of Tennessee. Yardley immediately filed for a new trial.

Main Street in Memphis, [February 10] 1910

February

1825, NASHVILLE

Governor Sam Houston recommended that Matthew Fontaine Maury be appointed a midshipman in the United States Navy. Maury went on to serve in this capacity on a number of ships and had nine years of sea duty to his credit by 1839. That year, on a journey from Tennessee to New York, a stage accident in Ohio left him permanently crippled.

Abel P. Upshur, President John Tyler's secretary of the navy, assigned Maury to the Depot of Charts and Instruments in Washington, D.C., on July 1, 1842. The "Depot" evolved into the National Observatory and later the Naval Observatory. Maury's work there consisted of categorizing and indexing old ships' logbooks, from which he made observations concerning the currents and depths of the oceans and the prevailing winds. His work helped produce a series of charts that enabled American and European shipmasters to reduce their sailing times. Before his charts, it took an average of 188 days to sail the Atlantic outward passage. After this Tennessean's charts became available, crossing time was cut by nearly one-half, and sometimes more. This allowed the pace of commerce to quicken, which aided in the economic growth of America.

During the Civil War, Maury joined the Confederate cause, serving in Europe. He was given the appropriate sobriquet "the Pathfinder of the Seas." On May 31, 1946, a bust of Maury was

FEBRUARY 2, 1850, NASHVILLE
The Nashville Mechanics Manufacturing Company was incorporated by the state legislature. The intent of the company was to provide mechanics the means of becoming worker-capitalists through the establishment of a joint stock company. Even though Tennessee was primarily an agricultural state before the Civil War, there was some interest in industry, as this advertisement for the Lebanon Manufacturing Company shows.

unveiled at the State Capitol during Tennessee's sesquicentennial celebration.

1888, NASHVILLE

Reports of a conflict between the Reverend J. A. Edmonston, pastor of South Spruce Street Church, and the Reverend J. M. Carter, presiding elder of the Middle Tennessee district of the Methodist Church, reached the newspapers. Carter, with the backing of church stewards, demanded that Edmonston relinquish his parish because of charges concerning his behavior; Edmonston had supposedly behaved in a manner unbecoming a minister of the gospel. Edmonston refused and in turn charged Carter

with spreading slanderous remarks about his character. The matter was to be submitted to an ecclesiastical tribunal. The outcome is not known.

1987, KNOXVILLE

Tennessee Wildlife Resources Agency biologist Doug Scott warned of an explosion in the coyote population. The animals were first seen in West Tennessee in 1977 and then spread to East Tennessee. They thrived in an environment in which they were the largest predators. Though they threatened the fox population, they posed no risk to any livestock except sheep, which are not extensively raised in Tennessee. Coyotes are champions at adaptation. According to Scott, "You can't eradicate the coyote short of [dropping] an atomic bomb, and I have doubts about that also."

1870, NASHVILLE

In his Legislative Message, Governor Dewitt Clinton Senter addressed "with profound regret" the growing problem of mob violence in the Volunteer State. There was, he said, "frequent violence to the peace and dignity of the State . . . even atrocious murders of her citizens, by persons generally reported in disguise or unknown."

Two anti–Ku Klux Klan statutes had been enacted during the William G. Brownlow administration in September 1868 and January 1870. Governor Senter believed that these laws were honorable, but he had doubts about their efficiency in remedying the evils of lynching. Not a single arrest, claimed the chief executive, "had yet been made for violations of the law although violations were frequent. . . . The public misfortune seems not so much a want of law as a lack of power to enforce that we have."

Senter suggested that the two laws be amended so they would give the governor discretionary power to appoint special officers in counties where the KKK was active. These officers would have the power of a county sheriff "to summon posses, make arrests, and do all like things necessary to bring offenders to justice."

No such amendment was made.

1888, KNOXVILLE

The *Knoxville Daily Tribune* published two letters from readers in response to the appointment of the Reverend Job C. Lawrence, an African-American graduate of Maryville College, to the Knoxville School Board.

One stated in part, "Let parents arise in their might and nip the coming of mixed schools and mixed everything in the bud. The parents of Knoxville seeing the evil can crush it."

One father wrote, "Parents of children in the schools, especially girls, should view the pending danger in its true light, and appreciate the full significance of the situation."

1976, MEMPHIS

A quartet of rhesus monkeys escaped from the Overton Park Zoo and took up lodging on the balconies of the plush Parkway House apartment building. Zoo director Dr. Joel Wallach offered the simians biscuits laced with enough drugs to "put away three elephants." The monkeys, however, would not eat them.

About 1:30 P.M., the monkeys began darting along the walls of the balconies, causing motorists to stop and watch. Mrs. Lee Owens, the superintendent of Parkway House, was not happy

with this development. She said, "I was in my apartment last night, and suddenly I looked at my balcony door and there were four little faces pressed against the window watching me. If they don't get rid of them soon, I'll go nuts!"

The monkeys were evidently returned to the zoo later. They gave residents a novel reason to speak to one another in the hallways, something none of them had done for years.

FEBRUARY 3

1876, MEMPHIS

Victoria Woodhull, antiprostitution reformer, America's first female candidate for president, and radical advocate for equal rights, free love, and women's suffrage, spoke to a large and mixed audience. Her topics were "The Human Body, the Temple of God" and "Sexual Slavery." She wore a simple but elegant brown dress.

According to Woodhull, "For years women have been held in bondage, a bondage which has brought misery, crime and death. No woman should have to bring into the world an unwanted child. Let there be an end to forced pregnancies, to abortion, to undesired children. Let there be born love children only. This is what will end crime, degradation and poverty."

1915, CROSSVILLE

According to the *Crossville Chronicle*, Dr. J. S. Anderson, "the negro doctor who had headquarters in Bristol, passed through Crossville over the [Tennessee Central Railroad] on a special train [while] returning to Kingston."

Anderson had considerable success posing as a homeopathic doctor whose cures were from herbs and plants. Reliable physicians asserted that his medicines were little more than a "renovator" combined with a laxative. Nevertheless, he was able to convince many of his healing powers.

Anderson had been in Nashville to consult with state health authorities about sanitary conditions at his Kingston sanitarium. He had a number of patients with him on the train. One Crossville native brought his invalid daughter to Anderson for a cure.

Anderson's hospital was very popular in Cumberland County. He claimed to be a Choctaw and a graduate of Choctaw Indian Medical College, located on an island 600 miles from the African coast. Most of his patients came from Middle and East Tennessee. He was said to make an astounding $250 a day. The special train had been rented by Anderson for $670.

His medical credentials may have been dubious, but his success was not.

1990, KNOXVILLE

George Bush spoke to a crowd of 2,500. The president claimed that in 1990, 41 percent more Tennessee high-school students were taking mathematics and science classes than was the case in 1985. Bush thought this indicated educational progress in the Volunteer State.

FEBRUARY 4

1896, CHATTANOOGA

It was reported in the *Chattanooga News* that there were 693 telephones in the city. Twenty had been added in January. There were eight operators, six working the day shift and two the night shift. (The gender of the operators is not known). A total of 34 long-distance stations could be reached by outside lines. Thus, Chattanooga had "as large a number [of telephones] as is shown in any city in Tennessee." This was a point of civic pride.

1920, CROSSVILLE

It was reported in the *Crossville Chronicle* that J. S. Anderson, the African-American Choctaw doctor, had died a few days earlier in Kingston.

Anderson left his wife $1,000 and his white secretary real estate in Kingston and Harrodsburg, Kentucky.

1987, KNOXVILLE

Local education leaders and the head of the Tennessee branch of the American Civil Liberties Union were concerned over the firing of blank ammunition and the setting of mock bombs in a number of high-school auditoriums and gymnasiums, which at some schools were darkened for the opening firepower scenario. Wearing camouflaged uniforms, members of the Delta Team of the Tennessee National Guard began patriotism rallies at Doyle, Fulton, Powell, and West High Schools.

Steve Roberts, president of the Knoxville Board of Education, was concerned: "The firing of any kind of weapon unexpectedly in the dark under the guise of patriotism is inappropriate. Patriotism is something in your heart you believe. It has nothing to do with guns, with getting people fired up unexpectedly."

Pete Lotts, chairman of the Knox County Board of Education, concurred, saying he wanted to investigate the patriotism program further. He called the attention-getting measure "very inappropriate. . . . I'll just have to investigate to find out if it was unsafe. Blanks are not in themselves benign."

Hedy Weinberg, executive director of the state

ACLU, suggested other means than a mock battle could be used to instill patriotism in students: "If assemblies could be used to celebrate the Bill of Rights or the Constitution, we'd create a better atmosphere for patriotism."

Knoxville school superintendent Fred Bedelle said he had approved of the program, but the Knox County superintendent could not be reached.

Two school principals were present at the rallies and expressed enthusiasm, saying the student response was compellingly positive. Fulton High School principal W. Davis said, "We'll probably see a change [of attitude] toward the flag as a result of this." Davis said the speaker at the Fulton assembly told students that if they were not living in a free country, it could have been a foreign force walking into their school and taking over. Davis said he knew the program would be controversial: "I think in a sense it did equate guns with patriotism. You could look at it from that standpoint."

Two students at Powell High School were ebullient about the assembly. Lee Payne, a senior, said, "They started talking about how our parents and grandparents fought to save this country." Kristian Courtney, also a senior, said she liked the program but that the firing at the beginning scared her, momentarily convincing her that the school was being attacked.

The program was reportedly proposed to all the Volunteer State's high-school principals by the Tennessee National Guard. Sergeant Randy Smith of the National Guard said the rallies were not geared toward finding recruits but toward inspiring patriotism. The controversial assemblies took place against a backdrop of international terrorism and hostage-taking and the beginnings of the Iran-Contra scandal.

1991, ALAMO

Lucile Rasmussen made history as the first person to receive communion at the first Roman Catholic Mass ever celebrated in Crockett County's 120-year history. Father Joe Wiggs said that the 20 Catholic families in the county were part of his mission: "It's the only county in West Tennessee without the presence of the [Catholic] church, and it has never had a mass held in it."

Crockett County was formed in 1871 out of parts of surrounding counties. Some Catholics in the county had been celebrating Mass in Dyersburg, Humboldt, and Brownsville. Ms. Rasmussen hoped that a Catholic church would be established in Alamo.

FEBRUARY 5

1759, CHOTEE, IN THE CHEROKEE NATION

The Reverend John Martin, missionary to the Overhill Cherokees, described in his diary how he "was obliged to have myself locked up in my house for Fear of the Drunken Indians; this was a Day of Rum Drinking, and they are very troublesome then. It is a pity there is not a stop put to the carrying [of] so much Rum among them who when sober in general behave well."

1864, OCCUPIED NASHVILLE

John Wilkes Booth, thespian and future assassin of Abraham Lincoln, was performing at the Nashville Theatre on the west side of Cherry Street. His characterizations of Cardinal Richelieu and Hamlet received rave reviews.

The First Tennessee Regiment, along with the First Nebraska, began an offensive to drive the Filipino army out of the Manila environs. Colonel William T. Smith of the First Tennessee led an assault on a Filipino position but died of a heart attack during combat. The men were at first demoralized and became bogged down in a rice field, 18-inch ridges providing their only cover. Still under hostile fire, the Tennesseans rallied. Under orders from Major Benjamin F. Cheatham, they charged the Filipino lines, giving the rebel yell as they advanced and fired. After gaining their objective, the Tennesseans routed the native forces.

That night, the flames from burning Filipino villages lit the sky around Manila. James Moon, a private with the First Tennessee, wrote to his father in Nashville, "Father, I would not have missed it for the world."

1990, WARTBURG

Sixty-two-year-old James Earl Ray, convicted killer of Martin Luther King, Jr., filed for a divorce from his wife, Anna, 45. He cited irreconcilable differences. Ray's relatives intimated that he was upset because Anna hadn't visited him for several years. They were married in 1978.

FEBRUARY 6

1796, KNOXVILLE

Members of the Constitutional Convention adopted Tennessee's first constitution as a prelude to statehood.

1879, KNOXVILLE

The editor of the *Knoxville Daily Tribune* was concerned about declining morals in the city. It was estimated that a total of 5,000 drinks a day were sold in the city's 25 saloons, or 200 drinks per day per saloon. This tally did not include "the nightcaps, morning gowns, cupboard appetizers, convivial punches, and toddies, champagne suppers, dinner wine, and last but greatest, 'bottle sucking'."

1899, MANILA, THE PHILIPPINE ISLANDS

Private John F. Bright and his fellow soldiers of the First Tennessee Regiment were ordered back to Manila. For the first time, the men saw the results of the previous day's battle. Razed villages, homeless Filipinos, and hundreds of dead and near-dead littered the landscape. Bright soberly wrote in a letter of the experience: "We had not realized what war was until marching back over the battlefield and viewing the ruin and desolation on all sides."

1987, KNOXVILLE

At a rally, educators and students protested a legislative proposal by State Senator Bill Richardson of Columbia and State Representative Ben West, Jr., of Nashville that all 147,000 university and college students in Tennessee take mandatory urine tests before being allowed to attend classes.

University of Tennessee chancellor Jack Reese said, "It's absurd. This is way out of the scope of the legislature."

Representative West claimed he was serious, adding that "just merely introducing it has brought the problem to public light. That to me is the real reason for introducing it."

No such law was passed.

This cartoon, published in the Nashville Banner in 1885, illustrated a poem called "Only a Convict."

1991, MEMPHIS

It was announced in the *Memphis Commercial Appeal* that Danny Thomas, nightclub entertainer and television star, had died in Los Angeles. His passing was especially sad in Memphis because of his philanthropic work in raising funds for St. Jude's Children's Research Hospital. He had also participated in a campaign to retain the designation *street* for Beale Street at a time when it was scheduled to become Beale Avenue. Thomas was 79.

FEBRUARY 7

1860, NASHVILLE

Jeremiah George Harris, a United States Navy purser serving on the USS *Wabash*, presented the Tennessee Historical Society with a mummy from Egypt. Some 136 years later, it is still an attraction at the Tennessee State Museum.

1885, NASHVILLE

The *Nashville Banner*, in the midst of a crusade to end the convict lease system, and in the midst of a libel suit resulting from that effort, published a cartoon accompanied by a poem called "Only a Convict." The cartoon showed a convict stripped of his clothing and held defenseless on the ground by three guards. A fourth guard lashed the convict with a thick leather strop. The poem read, in part,

> Only a convict, bought body and soul;
> The price has been paid—a pitiful dole.
> Now work him and task him to the ultimate strain,
> For the harder the work, the greater the gain.

1951, NASHVILLE

African-American sculptor William Edmonson died.

Edmonson was born about 1870. He claimed God talked with him about cutting stone. A primitive artist, he began his career by working on tombstones from stone recycled from demolished city buildings. He filled his backyard with religious sculptures depicting preachers, "critters," and miracles. He was the first black Tennessean to have a one-man show at the Museum of Modern Art in New York City.

1972, NASHVILLE

Democrats in the legislature accused the Republican administration of Governor Winfield Dunn of bugging telephones in the State Capitol. State Senator Ed Gillock said it "smacked of totalitarianism and dictatorship."

Spokesmen for the governor, however, claimed that the devices were used in an effort to monitor telephone operators and ensure politeness when answering calls, and that they were vital for security. The devices had been used only twice since their installation.

Gillock was not convinced, saying that "if there's any dastardly and damnable thing, it's someone listening to you on your telephone." He added, "If the snooping is so vital how come they've only used it twice?"

It was reported that only one of the senatorial caucus, Doug Henry of Nashville, objected to an ourtright ban on the monitoring devices.

FEBRUARY 8

1882, MARYVILLE

Animosity prevailed at Maryville College be-tween faculty and members of the student Animi Cultus Society. Student associates refused to admit an African-American to the society, objecting to allegedly being forced to accept black students as members. Animi Cultus members claimed states' rights and protection under the Constitution, while the faculty maintained that the 15th Amendment and centralized power were the essentials in the argument. Many Animi Cultus members withdrew from classes in protest.

1926, MEMPHIS

Heavyweight champion "of the universe" Jack Dempsey, visiting in the Bluff City, gave an exhibition bout with his regular sparring partner and three local favorites. All were knocked to the canvas, none lasting more than one round. According to an understated comment in the *Memphis Commercial Appeal*, "Dempsey hardly knows what pulling a punch is."

FEBRUARY 9

1796, KNOXVILLE

The Constitutional Convention ended after three weeks' deliberation. A copy of Tennessee's first constitution was sent to Philadelphia, the nation's capital.

1861, ACROSS THE VOLUNTEER STATE

A statewide referendum on secession was held. The majority of voters opposed Tennessee's leaving the Union and so voted against holding a secession convention. Most white Tennesseans were pro-Union on the eve of the Civil War. By June, they changed their minds.

1990, MEMPHIS

Ken Humphreys, head of the Shelby County Historical Commission, announced that since 1989, some 10 historical markers valued at $10,000 had been stolen. The marker thieves had stolen parts of Shelby County's history when they took the markers for Marcus Winchester (the first mayor of Memphis), Isaac Rawlings, Bell Tavern, the Navy Yard, Fort San Fernando, Fort Adams, the city's first cotton gin, the city's first tavern, Catfish Bay (an early settlement), and the De Soto Mounds.

1991, KNOXVILLE

Former governor Ray Blanton was ordered to serve a 10-day jail sentence for failing to make alimony payments. The time was to be spent in the Madison County Jail on weekends, allowing Blanton (previously convicted of and imprisoned for mail fraud, conspiracy, and extortion) to return to his job on weekdays. At the time, Blanton was selling luxury automobiles at Massey Cadillac in Memphis.

FEBRUARY 10

1821, NASHVILLE

An unidentified New York Yankee wrote in his diary about the nightlife in Nashville: "Cotillions are but little understood, and the reel is therefore usually danced. A few of the most dignified ladies retire early, but the greater number seemed bent on 'Holding out to tire each other down.' The company danced till a late hour & when their exhilaration had reached its climax, the long loud laugh [and] the boisterous stamp of the foot . . . gave me so little pleasure that I retired to bed—tho' not to sleep 'till they had broken up."

He noted further that, in Nashville, "whatever is bad is sure to be attributed to the Yankees—whatever partakes of knavery, is of course, 'a Yankee trick.'"

1910, MEMPHIS

The African-American–owned Fraternal Savings Bank and Trust opened for business. This was one of the earliest such financial institutions in the city and indicates the prosperity of the black community in the Bluff City. It also demonstrates the "separate but equal" doctrine of race relations made legal by Jim Crow laws.

1920, KINGSPORT

All swine were to be removed from streets and backyards as the city's first anti-pig ordinance came into effect. Kingsport was not in the vanguard of the public sanitation movement, but it was making a beginning.

1971, MEMPHIS

Pat Boone, the popular love-ballad singer from Nashville, declared bankruptcy. The fortune he made in the music industry had been diminished by unsuccessful real-estate investments. His investments were as sound as "Love Letters in the Sand."

1987, KINGSTON

Mayor Ray Gullett had his arms pinned behind him while the just-fired chief of police, Gary Humphreys, slugged His Honor.

The city council had voted 4–2 to fire Humphreys for improper behavior. When the meeting was over, Humphreys, according to Gullett, said, "I'll get you, old boy. I'll get you for this."

Gullett suffered facial lacerations and a busted lip.

1893, CHARLOTTE, DICKSON COUNTY

Joe Vanleer and his wife, an elderly African-American couple living in the Promise Land community on Barton's Creek, were approached by a gang of masked white men. The Vanleers' daughter had recently hired out at the home of Wiltoe Mathis, one of the most respected older white citizens in the county. Mathis's sons, Cyrus and Wiltoe, Jr., suspected Ms. Vanleer of stealing $40 from them. Cyrus was convinced she was the culprit because an aged black clairvoyant had described her as the thief.

Wiltoe, Jr., said to be "of exceedingly weak mind," allegedly broke down the Vanleers' door. Joe Vanleer and his wife could not stop them. They dragged the Vanleers' daughter out of the house, took her money, and, according to reports, repeatedly raped her. They then beat her with a board so that she was "more dead than alive." Mrs. Vanleer and another woman were also attacked by the masked men.

Cyrus and Wiltoe, Jr., were identified, arrested, and incarcerated. It was said that armed blacks within 25 miles of Charlotte headed toward the jail intent on lynching the two white boys. The outcome of this alleged attack is not known, but the white perpetrators were most likely mildly rebuked and released without being tried. It is also doubtful that the Vanleers obtained compensation or justice.

Meanwhile, in Memphis, the fourth lynching of an African-American in 14 months took place. Richard Neal was forcibly taken from jail and lynched a few miles from the city limits by a mob of 200 incensed white men. Neal had allegedly raped a white woman in Forrest Hill.

1897, NASHVILLE

Robert "Our Bob" Love Taylor, the state's 25th governor, signed a bill that banned cigarettes from Tennessee. According to the law, it was a misdemeanor in the Volunteer State "for any person, firm or corporation to sell, or to bring into the State for the purpose of selling, giving away or otherwise disposing of any cigarettes, [or] cigarette papers." A fine of not less than $50 was set for guilty parties, and inquisitorial powers were granted to grand juries when considering violations of this law.

The law was overturned in 1900 by the Tennessee Supreme Court on a procedural and constitutional technicality. Governor Benton McMillin reintroduced the bill and avoided the technical obstruction. When signed into law, it was substantially the same as the bill signed by Taylor.

Ironically, it was not until 1913 that the state made the unauthorized sale of cocaine, opium, morphine, and heroin illegal.

1864, OCCUPIED NASHVILLE

The *Nashville Daily Union* said of John Wilkes Booth's final benefit performance (given, ironically, on Abraham Lincoln's birthday) that he

came amongst us as a stranger, his reputation as a rising star having preceded him, creating a general desire amongst our playgoers to get a "taste of his quality" . . . Nobly did he fulfill expectations, and establish himself as a favorite. Every succeeding performance has been but a repetition of his successes. In no part has he failed. His genius appears equal to anything the tragic muse has produced; and the time is not distant when he will attain his highest professional fame. His engagement here will not soon be forgotten by any who have attended the Theatre.

About 14 months later, Booth assassinated Lincoln.

1958, CHATTANOOGA

Tommy Sands, teenage heartthrob, came to town to promote his movie, *Sing, Boy, Sing*. He gave a performance at the Tivoli Theater. One newspaper reported, "As these affairs go, the crowd was loud but almost orderly. No hair was pulled, no clothes were torn." Sands held a news conference to which 20 high-school newspaper editors were invited.

1968, MEMPHIS

The sanitation workers' strike began. Civil rights leader Martin Luther King, Jr., later came to Memphis to demonstrate his support for the cause. He was assassinated while standing on the balcony of the Lorraine Motel. Today, the National Civil Rights Museum stands near the site of his death.

FEBRUARY 13

1836, NASHVILLE

The 21st Tennessee General Assembly reaffirmed its ban on lotteries: "All laws which authorized any person or body corporate or politic to draw a lottery for any purpose whatsoever, are hereby repealed." This sentiment has not been reversed yet.

Tennessee Ernie Ford [February 13] at Radio Station WOPI, Bristol, in 1954

1882, MARYVILLE

The faculty of Maryville College met with students protesting the entry of a black student into their Animi Cultus Society. A number of society members entered the building before discussion began and removed furniture and other property, asserting that it belonged to their society. The faculty contended it was theft of college property. Student protesters threatened to close the institution.

1919, BRISTOL

Tennessee Ernie Ford was born.

He began his show-business career as an announcer on Bristol radio station WOPI. One of his most famous hits was "Sixteen Tons."

1960, NASHVILLE

The first full-scale sit-ins in Nashville were initiated by black college students at the Kress, Woolworth, and McClellan stores on Fifth Avenue North. The protesters made small purchases

FEBRUARY 13, 1950,
WILLIAMSON COUNTY
The Forest Home covered bridge spanning the Harpeth River was destroyed by a flood. Built before the Civil War, it was the last covered bridge in Williamson County. This photo was taken around 1915.

and remained until the lunch counters closed. This marked the beginning of the nonviolent battles of the civil rights movement in Tennessee in the 1960s.

FEBRUARY 14

1882, MARYVILLE

Twenty-three students who had taken furniture from a Maryville College hall were suspended from school, and the Animi Cultus Society was disbanded. The students could return, stated faculty negotiators, if they would sign a paper expressing "regret for acts of disorder and insubordination, and promising obedience to the authorities of the College." Only two signed.

FEBRUARY 15

1858, MEMPHIS

The city council passed an ordinance prohibiting volunteer firemen from pulling their engines on the sidewalks when the streets were muddy, which was often the case. In response, the Memphis Fire Association prohibited any volunteer fire company from answering alarms until the ordinance was repealed.

On February 18, the volunteer fire companies ended their strike when the city government repealed the ordinance and remitted the fines that Companies 1 and 4 had received for running on the sidewalks. Thus, the volunteer firemen successfully held the city hostage.

Essentially the same scenario was acted out in Memphis in 1978.

1862, FORT DONELSON

Confederate general Gideon J. Pillow enthusiastically telegraphed his commanding officer, General Albert Sidney Johnston, that "on the honor of a soldier, the day is ours!"

Union general Ulysses S. Grant thought otherwise and took Fort Donelson by 1 P.M. the next day. Pillow retreated and received a censure from Jefferson Davis for allowing the fort to fall to the enemy.

To say that Pillow was incompetent would be charitable. He was later put in charge of the effort to hunt down Confederate draft evaders, a task that kept him largely out of combat.

FEBRUARY 16

1862, CONFEDERATE NASHVILLE

Louisa Brown Pearl noted in her diary,

> The congregations assembling for worship were dismissed & people were seen hurrying to & fro like crazy people not knowing what to do. [Confederate general Albert Sidney] Johnston's army which lately evacuated Bowling Green [Kentucky] commenced moving thru the city. We are informed that Nashville will make no resistance & we again hope that we may not be disturbed but everybody is on the move, hacks, carriages & drays are in requisition & by twelve nothing of the kind can be had

for love or money—thousands have left town & are still going, leaving their houses empty.

1918, CHATTANOOGA

W. J. Gladish of 503 Broad Street, the designer of a "flying torpedo," described his new military weapon:

> Starting from the ground the machine will rise at an angle of 45 degrees to a height of one or two miles, and go straight to the place of the enemy, say a distance of one or two hundred miles, when the motor is cut off and the machine drops to the ground among the enemy, causing death and destruction over a large area. This machine does not need a pilot. It will go in any direction desired. All you have to do is to get the distance [to the target], set the compass and the flying torpedo will go to the spot, it matters not how hard the wind may blow against it.

This Chattanoogan may have been on the threshold of missile warfare. The War Department was said to be interested, and, to no one's surprise, so were a number of local venture capitalists. However, there is no indication that Gladish's plans flew off the drawing board.

1928, SELMER, MCNAIRY COUNTY

Dr. Otis Floyd, the first African-American to head the university system in Tennessee, was born. He was named chancellor of the Board of Regents on June 29, 1990, after being nominated by Governor Ned McWherter.

Floyd earned his bachelor's degree in social science from Lane College in Jackson and then began his educational career as a teacher in a one-room school in Purdy. He received a master's degree at Tennessee State University and a doctorate from Memphis State University. He served also as vice president for administration at Middle Tennessee State University and was acting commissioner of education for the Tennessee Department of Education. He died on May 19, 1993, of cardiac arrest.

FEBRUARY 17

1812, WEST TENNESSEE

The most violent shock in the series of earthquakes that had begun on February 11, 1811, was felt. Reelfoot Lake is said to have been created by this geologic disturbance, called the "New Madrid Earthquake."

Legend has it that "The Prophet," an Indian leader who established a confederacy to drive the white man from Native American land, told his allies that they would know to begin fighting when he stamped his foot on the ground. The earthquake, says legend, was taken by many Indians to be the foot of The Prophet kicking the ground. Open warfare along the frontier soon commenced.

1862, NASHVILLE

As news of the surrender of Fort Donelson reached Nashville, the city experienced "The Great Panic." Many fearful Confederate officials and sympathizers found discretion the better part of valor and left the city en masse, rather than staying to defend it against the advancing Union army. They departed in railroad cars, on steamboats, by wagon, and on foot.

1868, KNOXVILLE

The city council declared it "unlawful for any female of known bad repute to walk the streets of the city of Knoxville for the purposes of soliciting or with intention of attracting attention or notice from the opposite sex after seven o'clock P.M."

Evidently, such behavior was lawful before 7 P.M.

1882, MARYVILLE

A number of students at Maryville College refused to sign a statement expressing regret for the student rebellion, and many went home. President P. M. Bartlett told the press that the students had not been suspended for rejecting the application of an African-American student but for removing furniture and defying the orders of the faculty.

FEBRUARY 18

1787, MILL CREEK, NEAR NASHVILLE

John Bell was born.

Bell served in Washington, D.C., as Speaker of the House and as a senator. He was an opponent of President Andrew Jackson. He later opposed secession, running unsuccessfully on the Grand National Union Party ticket in 1860 as a compromise candidate between Abraham Lincoln and the fire-eating secessionists in the South. Bell urged Lincoln to follow a policy of conciliation. During the Civil War, he lived with his family, moving from Tennessee to Alabama and later to Georgia. He never returned to the Volunteer State.

1862, NASHVILLE

After being repaired in 1855, the city's suspension bridge was burned down by retreating Confederate forces despite the vehement protests of local citizens. The bridge was designed by Adolphus Heiman.

1943, OAK RIDGE

Ground was broken by the Stone and Webster Construction Company at the Manhattan Engineering District.

The first "Alpha Racetrack" building at the Y-12 facility housed calutrons designed to carry out electromagnetic isotope separation of U-235, to be used in the first atomic bomb. Eventually, the Y-12 cyclotron near Oak Ridge produced 268-grade U-235, essential to America's Cold War policy of Mutually Assured Destruction, or MAD.

FEBRUARY 16, 1862, FORT DONELSON

After four days of artillery bombardment and infantry attacks, Confederate commanders at Fort Donelson surrendered 14,000 men unconditionally to General Ulysses S. Grant. Confederate general Albert Sidney Johnston retreated from Kentucky to evacuate Nashville, which would be occupied by Union forces in just nine days. Below, Fort Donelson as Union forces swept over the ramparts

1862, CLARKSVILLE

The approach of United States Navy gunboats on the Cumberland River sparked Confederate troops to burn the Memphis, Clarksville, and Louisville Railroad bridge spanning the Tennessee River. Subsequently, all rail service from Memphis to Clarksville and beyond was interrupted.

1973, LAS VEGAS

As Elvis Presley was performing his midnight show at the Hilton Hotel, four men rushed suddenly onstage. All were subdued by Elvis's bodyguards. Elvis was also a combatant in the affair, shoving one of his would-be assailants into the audience, where he landed on a table that smashed under the impact. The four men, from South America, were charged with public intoxication.

Elvis commented to his fans after the fight, "I'm sorry, ladies and gentlemen. . . . I'm sorry I didn't break his goddamned neck is what I'm sorry about! . . . If he wants to get tough, I'll whoop his ass!" The King received a seven-minute standing ovation from the audience.

1979, NASHVILLE

It was announced in *The Tennessean* that an Elvis impersonator from Lebanon was suing a California promoter for $1 million. Elvis Wade, whose real name was Wade Cummins, explained that he had been cheated out of several hundred thousand dollars. Named in the suit were promoter Steve Brodie and Elvis Wade International, a Tennessee firm the suit called Brodie's "alter ego."

FEBRUARY 20

1869, NASHVILLE

Republican governor William G. Brownlow declared martial law in Overton, Jackson, Maury, Giles, Marshall, Lawrence, Gibson, Madison, and Haywood Counties due to heavy Ku Klux Klan activity. Brownlow promised to use the 1,600-man State Guard to stop the violence and crush the Klan.

The small army was never sent, nor did the violence cease. For example, on the same day Brownlow declared war against the KKK, his hired spy, Seymour Barmore, a Cincinnatian, was found near Pulaski floating in the Duck River, a noose around his neck. Barmore had been trying to infiltrate the organization. The KKK thus maintained its reputation as a terrorist organization.

FEBRUARY 21

1828, BRAINERD, HAMILTON COUNTY

The first issue of *The Phoenix*, a Cherokee weekly, appeared in a bilingual—Cherokee and English—edition.

The new Cherokee press and newspaper greatly aided missionaries' work, allowing them to print and distribute their religious music, literature, and news to the Indians. It also allowed them to overstate the pace of Cherokee adaptation to white civilization.

1933, WASHINGTON, D.C.

President Franklin D. Roosevelt nominated Overton County native Cordell Hull to be his secretary of state.

Hull was confirmed by the Senate on March 4.

He is best remembered as the guiding force behind the organization of the United Nations. A historic museum near Byrdstown displays artifacts associated with him, including his gold Nobel Peace Prize medal. President Roosevelt claimed Hull was his right arm in the cause of peace.

1973, NASHVILLE

Tom T. Hall and Gene Dobbins won the top Songwriter's Association Award. Hall won Song of the Year for "The Year That Clayton Delaney Died," while Dobbins was honored for "Red Skies over Georgia" and "Sing Me a Love Song." Twenty-two others also won awards.

FEBRUARY 22

1865, ACROSS THE VOLUNTEER STATE

Slavery in Tennessee was officially abolished by popular vote. The 13th Amendment, banning slavery throughout the nation, was approved by the state legislature in March. The war ended in April.

1876, KNOXVILLE

The McGhee Guards, a private African-American militia unit, paraded through the streets of the city in full view of an enormous mixed crowd. According to one account, "A beautiful flag . . . was presented to the Company by Rev. Mr. LeVere. . . . Color Sergeant W. F. Yardley, Esq., received the [flag] and responded in his usual good style."

The uniformed guards marched on Gay Street and paraded on the other principal boulevards of the city. Afterwards, two white paramilitary units, the Dickinson Light Guards and the

O'Conner Zouaves, gave a separate but equal parade. Paramilitary groups such as these were important social and political organizations.

FEBRUARY 23

1778, WASHINGTON COUNTY

Two years after the Declaration of Independence, the region's first county court was held at the log-cabin house of Colonel Charles Robertson on the "east (catbird) Branch of Sinking Creek." Robertson was trustee, John Carter was court chairman, John Sevier and John McMahon were clerks, Valentine Sevier was register, and James Stuart was sheriff.

The American judicial system went west with the 18th-century pioneers.

1874, MEMPHIS

According to the Memphis *Public Ledger:* "Police raids on disreputable houses, under the direction of Captain Walsh, are all the rage at present. The unfortunates are driven through the streets to the station-house like a lot of wild Texas cattle, but they are released on payment of ten dollars, which is ruled to be the exact value of the crime supposed to have been committed."

1893, CHATTANOOGA

At the recorder's court, Judge Hope sentenced two incorrigible African-American boys to 10 lashes each. The sentence was to be administered by their mothers in the presence of a policeman. The police stables were designated as the place of punishment.

"With a cold glitter in her eyes," according to a newspaper report, "the mother seized one of the boys and then the other, and the rawhide

fell fast and furiously upon their backs and legs." The cacophony of the boys' screaming and horses' whinnying was said to have been remarkable in its intensity.

FEBRUARY 24

1817, NASHVILLE

Andrew Jackson wrote his nephew Andrew Jackson Donelson, recently appointed to West Point,

You should alone intermix, with the better class of society whose charectors are well established for their virtue and upright conduct. Amongst the virtuous females, you ought to cultivate an acquaintance, and shun the intercourse of the others as you would the society of the viper or base charector— it is an intercourse with the latter discription that engenders corruption, and contaminates the morals, and fits the young mind for any act of unguarded baseness, when on the other hand, the society of the virtuous female, enobles the mind, cultivates your manners, and prepares the mind for the achievement of every thing great, virtuous and honourable, and shrinks from every thing base or ignoble. . . . I recommend oeconomy to you as a virtue, on the other hand shun parsomony, never spend money uselessly, nor never withhold it when necessary to spend it.

1838, MARYVILLE

R. G. Williams, in a letter to the Boston-based abolitionist newspaper *The Emancipator*, requested literature that slave owners and state legislators considered subversive. "We could form a good anti-slavery society in this part of the State," he wrote, "but we choose to work in an unorganized manner a while yet, before we set ourselves up as targets."

This was probably a wise course if one was an opponent of slavery in Tennessee, for while speech was free, it wasn't free for slaves and wasn't without detrimental consequences for abolitionists.

1861, WINCHESTER

A mass meeting was held to consider Franklin County's secession from Tennessee. These "Franklinites" invited Alabama, which had already seceded from the United States, to annex them.

Tennessee seceded from the Union on June 24, making further action needless.

1892, KNOXVILLE

Henry Davenport, an aged, wealthy farmer, discovered he was the victim of a confidence game. Unsophisticated and illiterate, he "was roped by bunco steerers," according to one report.

Davenport was taken in by the "gold brick racket." One con man, going by the name Joseph Hines, said he knew of an Indian who was the sole owner of a gold mine in California. This same Indian was in possession of two gold bricks he wanted to sell for $3,500. Davenport wished to meet the mysterious Indian, so Hines drove him through the woods to a quiet spot and stopped the buggy. He called out the Indian's name, and within a minute, there appeared a man dressed as an Indian with two gold bars. Davenport was just about convinced but stressed he would like to have the gold bars analyzed. Hines readily agreed. The two men returned to Hines's hotel and soon met another con man posing as a government assayer, who pronounced the two brass bars to be gold. The gullible farmer lost all his money.

1907, KNOXVILLE

Socialists in the city met and adopted a prohibitionist position. Tennessee socialists denounced alcohol, not capitalism, as the cause of all working-class troubles. They were not alone in this contention, sharing their view with religious leaders, among others.

FEBRUARY 25

1900, NASHVILLE

William Jennings Bryan, who later became secretary of state under President Woodrow Wilson, delivered a lecture at the Tabernacle entitled "The Evils of Expansion." He was opposed to the imperialist efforts of the Republican McKinley administration to make the Philippine Islands an American colony.

Dr. Felix Adler lectured on "Perils That Threaten the Modern Family." According to Adler, two things in particular were hazardous to the family: the idea that men and women were equal and the notion that divorce was acceptable. Social problems such as divorce were not unknown in the "good old days."

1961, MEMPHIS

Governor Buford Ellington proclaimed this day "Elvis Presley Day." The day was a busy one, beginning with a $100-a-plate luncheon in Elvis's honor at the Memphis Claridge Hotel, where he was recognized for his achievement in selling 75 million records. Elvis was presented with a diamond-studded watch by RCA Victor. After a press conference, he performed two shows. Tickets cost $3, and a total of $51,607 was raised for the Elvis Presley Youth Center in Tupelo, Mississippi. Other acts on the bill included comedian "Brother" Dave Gardner, Boots Randolph, Floyd Cramer, and impressionist N. P. Nelson.

1990, MEMPHIS

The elusive midtown coyote that had outsmarted Tennessee Wildlife Resources Agency animal retrieval experts for over two years was shot and killed.

The coyote was both loved and hated by residents of the Central Gardens Apartments. Some said it had killed cats and even a poodle, while others claimed it played with neighborhood dogs. The coyote, a female, had a pup that was not captured. An 11-year-old boy who witnessed the shooting yelled to the pup to run to safety. The pup was in a litter of six found in 1989. It was the only pup to escape the lethal injections administered to the litter.

An official for TWRA explained that as cities took in more and more land for development, coyotes adapted to the urban environment.

FEBRUARY 26

1862, NASHVILLE

William Driver, born in Salem, Massachusetts, was a ship captain at age 21. He later retired from the sea. After his wife died in 1837, he came to live in Nashville with his brothers and their families. He brought with him an American flag he had received in 1831. He called it "Old Glory," a nickname that stuck. His flag was flown from the State Capitol on this day, as Federal forces occupied Nashville.

Captain William Driver died in 1883. A historical marker was later erected in his honor in Nashville.

1866, NASHVILLE

African-American males were extended the franchise by a legislature controlled by Radical Republicans.

To say that former slaves didn't appreciate what the vote meant is to say that a starving man does not appreciate bread. In August 1867, the former slaves voted for the Radical Republicans who supported their right to vote, not the Democrats who once owned many of them.

1882, KNOXVILLE

A large and zealous anti-Mormon meeting of local Protestant congregations was held at the Opera House. Pastors of various churches and hundreds of citizens attended. Resolutions condemned Mormonism for promoting polygamy, which was deemed "destructive of the social and moral well being of mankind, as well as disgraceful to our civilization."

Judge H. H. Ingersoll asked the assemblage, "Have Christian ministers and editors failed in their duty in condemning the gigantic evil?"

Colonel H. R. Gibson claimed that Mormonism wasn't really a religion but a "political scheme to possess this whole country."

The Reverend James Park of First Presbyterian Church regarded polygamy as a threat to church and society, holding that "it must be crushed."

The anti-Mormon resolutions were to be sent to all United States representatives and senators. There was little religious toleration in Knoxville this day.

1987, CHATTANOOGA

An experiment in a novel form of imprisonment began in the city. Prisoners were fitted with an ankle-bracelet transmitter that let authorities know when they entered or left their residences. It was hoped that the device, about the size of a pack of cigarettes, would reduce prison overcrowding.

FEBRUARY 27

1788, TIPTON FARM, NEAR JONESBOROUGH

This date marked the beginning of open warfare between John Sevier, governor of the state of Franklin, and bitter political opponent John Tipton, a North Carolina state senator for Washington County in what is now Tennessee. According to one source, Sevier's forces "marched within sight of the House of . . . John Tipton . . . with a party of one Hundred . . . with a drum beating, Colours flying, in Military Parade, and in a Hostile Manner . . . sent a flag demanding . . . surrender within the space of Thirty minutes . . . and submit themselves to the Laws of Franklin." Tipton had anticipated the attack and was holed up in his house with his own force.

Casualties this day included one dead horse, five captured "Tiptonites," and one wounded woman. The war began to take on comically tragic proportions.

1892, JELLICO

William R. Riley, an African-American organizer for the United Mine Workers, wrote a letter to the *United Mine Workers' Journal* expressing his views on the debilitating effect of white miners' insincere attitudes toward black miners:

I would like to know how under heaven do the white miners expect for the colored people to ever feel free and welcome in the

. . . United Mine Workers of America when their so-called brothers don't want them to get not one step higher than the pick and shovel. And yet, whenever there is anything in the way of finance these very same men will come up to the colored man and say, "Brother J. we must all stick together, for we are all miners and your interest is mine and mine is yours; we must band together." This talk . . . reminds me of the spider and the fly, the majority of the white miners only need a colored brother in time of trouble.

1897, MEMPHIS

It was reported that "Chief Moseley, on information furnished him by a woman witness of the sad accident which cost Mrs. Hattie Ward her life . . . went before Squire Garvin yesterday and swore out a warrant against Drum Major Wahlen of Primrose & West's minstrels, charging him with involuntary manslaughter by carelessly waving his baton in the face of Mrs. Ward's horse, thereby causing it to run away, resulting in Mrs. Ward's death."

A warrant was served, but Mr. Ward did not prosecute. It was learned that as the black minstrel band passed Mrs. Ward, it had struck a lively tune that caused the horse's flight.

1991, THE PERSIAN GULF

Sergeant Douglas "Lance" Fielder, 22, a Nashville native, was killed by troops of the Third Armored Cavalry Regiment. The troops mistook Fielder and four other Americans for Iraqi soldiers and fired on their disabled ammunition carrier.

The truth about the incident was finally revealed in May 1994 by the General Accounting Office. Fielder received the Bronze Star posthumously. Three decorated soldiers had their medals countermanded after former officers were reprimanded for allowing their troops to cross battle lines. None of the reprimands was placed in the officers' permanent records, on the orders of an army general.

One of the ex-officers, Captain Bo Friesen, was quoted in April 1995 as saying of the incident, "Friendly fire happens sometimes in a war, but this one could have been very easily prevented."

FEBRUARY 28

1788, TIPTON FARM, NEAR JONESBOROUGH

Hostilities between Franklinites and Tiptonites continued as John Sevier's forces laid siege to John Tipton's farm. Guns were fired sporadically at Tipton's home, but there were neither casualties nor damage to Tipton's house.

The Tipton home is open to visitors today.

1884, CHATTANOOGA

The black community was in an uproar over sensational developments at Shiloh Baptist Church. The pastor, Allen Nickerson, sold patent medicines and figured prominently in local politics. He was also a member of the Chattanooga Board of Education. The church members demanded he be a preacher, not a politician. They met and fired Nickerson, who promptly tendered his resignation.

Apparently, the congregation believed in the separation of church and state.

1945, IWO JIMA

Pharmacist's Mate First Class John Harlan Willis, 23, a navy platoon corpsman attached to the Marine Corps and a native of Columbia, was pinned down while administering plasma to a wounded marine in a shell hole. Japanese soldiers began throwing hand grenades into the hole; Willis calmly threw them back at the enemy while continuing to administer aid. His fidelity and raw courage inspired his companions in the hole so that, despite being heavily outnumbered, they launched an effective counterattack and repulsed the Japanese forces.

The last hand grenade Willis tried to throw back exploded, killing him instantly. He was awarded the Medal of Honor posthumously.

FEBRUARY 29

1788, TIPTON FARM, NEAR JONESBOROUGH

John Sevier's forces fired upon a party of men coming to the assistance of John Tipton. The guns of the State of Franklin killed Washington County sheriff Jonathan Pugh and John Webb of Sullivan County and wounded six more men, among them Captain William Delancy and John Allison. Had it not been for a blinding snowstorm, the casualties would certainly have been higher. There was no victory.

1868, MURFREESBORO

At a Radical Republican meeting, two white party bosses, William Bosson and William Yandell Elliot, spoke to a mostly African-American audience. According to a report in the *Nashville Republican Banner*, they used intemperate language, "exciting the darkies beyond measure."

When a black conservative tried to speak to the assembly, a fight started. "Pistols, guns and rocks were fired in all directions, which caused great excitement and a stampede of whites, negroes, horses and wagons." Four persons were mortally wounded and about eight seriously wounded.

The *Nashville Union and Dispatch* was of the opinion that Bosson and Elliot had provoked the audience when the black conservative was refused the podium.

Both men were scalawags. Elliot was born in Rutherford County in 1827 and was a strong Union man during the Civil War. Bosson was born in Massachusetts in 1803 but settled at the Falls of the Caney Fork in White County in 1841. He moved to Murfreesboro in 1862. During the Civil War, he was a strong Unionist, spying for Federal commanders, passing between lines, and gathering and reporting information about Confederate troop movements.

March

1788, TIPTON FARM, NEAR JONESBOROUGH

On the third day of the siege, John Sevier, the governor of Franklin, decided to fall back from the field and end the stalemate. The withdrawal took place in a blinding snowstorm. A Franklinite scouting party that included two of Sevier's sons was captured. John Tipton vowed to execute them, but cooler heads prevailed. The State of Franklin had lost its last battle.

1934, SAYRE, PENNSYLVANIA

Stephanie H. Chivers was born.

Chivers was a Republican representative in the Tennessee General Assembly from 1973 to 1975.

MARCH 2, 1902, NASHVILLE

The Fisk Jubilee Singers entertained Prince Henry of Prussia on his goodwill tour of America. Prince Henry indicated that his aunt, Queen Victoria of England, had recommended the Jubilee Singers to the Hohenzolleran side of the family because they brought her "much comfort."

In 1976, she was a delegate to the Republican National Convention. Five years later, she became political director of Lamar Alexander's election committee; she then served as an assistant to Governor Alexander from 1983 to 1986. She was appointed to the Tennessee Board of Paroles by Alexander in 1987. She also worked for the Bush/Quayle presidential campaign in 1988 and later represented District 18 of the Tennessee Republican Executive Committee.

1952, NASHVILLE

Uncle Dave Macon gave his last performance at the Grand Ole Opry. He died 21 days later.

1969, JACKSON

Elizabeth "Lizzie" Lea Miller died.

Miller was the second elected female in the Tennessee House, serving as a Democrat representing Chester, Haywood, and Hardeman Counties in 1925 and 1926. She was also a schoolteacher and a practicing attorney, following the example of Representative Marian S. Griffin of Memphis, the first female lawyer in Tennessee. Miller's father, Charles Austin Miller, was a representative in the 43rd and 45th general assemblies.

1983, NASHVILLE

It was reported that the Tennessee House of Representatives had voted 89–6 "to make teachers and their students be silent for a minute at the start of every school day." The bill, already passed in the state senate, went to Governor Lamar Alexander for his signature.

Representative Steve Cobb, a Nashville Democrat, said he voted against the measure because of constituents who were Catholics, Baptists, Methodists, Moonics, and even agnostics—people of all stripes who felt prayer was fine but didn't want "to turn our school systems into churches and turn our teachers into priests."

MARCH 2

1788, TIPTON FARM, NEAR JONESBOROUGH

John Tipton charged John Sevier's sons with taking up arms against the state of North Carolina. They were set free on bail, although their weapons were not returned.

Ironically, John Sevier's term as governor of Franklin expired on this date. There was no one to succeed him, so the State of Franklin passed from existence in a technical sense, just as it had been vanquished by force of arms.

1793, VIRGINIA

Sam Houston was born. His family later moved to Blount County, Tennessee. Young Sam had no taste for farming. Instead, he enjoyed the Cherokee way of life and spent much time living with the Indians. The Cherokees adopted him and gave him the name Co-lonneh, or "Raven."

Houston was a schoolteacher before answering the call to arms in the War of 1812, during which he was wounded. After returning to Ten-

Sam Houston [March 2]

nessee and studying law, he was appointed adjutant general in the Tennessee militia and was elected to Congress for two terms. In 1827, he was elected the state's seventh governor. Before his term ended, his wife of four months, Eliza Allen Houston, left him. Houston resigned the governorship.

Soon, he went to Arkansas to live with his friends in the Cherokee Nation, where he acquired the nickname "Big Drunk." In 1833, he wandered off to Texas. By 1836, he was commander in chief of the Texas army. From 1836 to 1846, he served as the first president of the Republic of Texas. He also served as a United States senator. In 1859, he was elected the seventh governor of the state of Texas. He was against secession and was forced from office by pro-Confederate forces. He died on July 25, 1863. His credo was written on his tombstone: "Honor."

1814, CAMP FOUR SPRINGS, MISSISSIPPI TERRITORY

In a letter to Major General Andrew Jackson, Colonel George Doherty, faced with talk of mutiny among his command, accused Major General John Cocke of the Tennessee militia of being "the chief instigator of their mutinous resolutions." Cocke had told Doherty that he would not join Jackson because "Old Hickory" had no provisions. Not only that, but General Cocke, according to Doherty, had "used every exertion, to diffuse anarchy and revolt among the troops from the Colonel down to the cook."

Cocke was later arrested and faced a court-martial. In the end, he was cleared of all charges. This was because the judges on the military tribunal were from East Tennessee; one of them was a candidate for governor.

1988, MEMPHIS

Jacquelin Smith, 37, was carried sobbing to a nearby sidewalk by two Shelby County sheriff's deputies. She had been living in the Lorraine Motel, the site where civil rights leader Martin Luther King, Jr., was assassinated in 1968. The motel had been condemned and was the centerpiece of a development effort that included the National Civil Rights Museum, a joint state and private effort. The area was designated a National Historic Landmark in 1982.

Smith, who had worked at the motel for 11 years, believed the museum would only accelerate the gentrification of the neighborhood. She said, "I'm trying to help the people who live in this area. We're being forced out. The Lorraine belongs to the people."

She remained on the street, establishing a sidewalk shelter in a makeshift plastic tent built over a folding lawn chair. On October 11, 1988, she was still there, claiming developers were trying "to force the black people out and they're using the Lorraine as a focus." She remained there until 1991, when the museum opened. She was relocated.

MARCH 3

1837, HAMILTON COUNTY

Cherokee removal began as 11 flatboats left Ross's Landing on the Tennessee River crowded with 466 Indians. They were taken west to reservations in what are now Oklahoma and Arkansas.

1875, NASHVILLE

Senator William G. Brownlow's term came to an end as Andrew Johnson, his political adversary, was elected to the United States Senate by the state legislature.

Johnson's victory has been attributed to the Irish Catholics and Methodists in the legislature. Methodists liked Johnson because of his order to turn control of their churches over to them during the Civil War; Irish Catholics liked him because of his courageous stand against the anti-Catholic force known as the American Party, or Know-Nothing Party, of the 1850s.

1956, MEMPHIS

Jackson native Carl Perkins's rock-'n'-roll classic, "Blue Suede Shoes," debuted. The song was later performed by such stars as Elvis Presley and Jerry Lee Lewis.

MARCH 4

1829, WASHINGTON, D.C.

Thousands of Americans thronged to witness the inauguration of Andrew Jackson as president of the United States. The crowd, consisting largely of laborers and farmers, followed Jackson's carriage down Pennsylvania Avenue to the White House. A public reception accessible to all was held there. The rooms were soon overflowing with people who trampled on one another, soiling the carpets and damaging the tastefully upholstered chairs and divans in their eagerness to shake the hand of the new president.

One of Jackson's political associates wrote that the people believed "General Jackson is their own President."

1861, MARIETTA, GEORGIA

African-American G. L. Nelson was born. Nelson worked in cotton fields until he was

Andrew Jackson as President [March 4]

14, when he began attending public school. His opportunities for education were meager, yet his yearning led him to Talladega College in Alabama in 1879. Due to his father's illness, he had to stop his course of study the same year. Nevertheless, he entered the Freedman's Institute in Maryville and excelled in his studies, graduating with honors in 1886. He taught for 10 years, moving to Chattanooga in 1892. His election as justice of the peace and notary public highlighted his participation in politics. His story is one of advancement against heavy odds.

1869, WASHINGTON, D.C.

President Andrew Johnson, surrounded by his cabinet, spent his last day in office. He did not attend Ulysses S. Grant's inauguration because the general had made it known that he would refuse to ride with Johnson to the ceremonies. Johnson called Grant a "faithless liar" and continued to work.

MARCH 5

1853, NASHVILLE

A letter in the *Nashville Daily Gazette* expressed working-class support for a 10-hour workday because "it not only gives the working man an opportunity of devoting more of his time to intellectual improvement, but it affords him more time for recreation after he has sweated and toiled through the labor of the day."

It was common for a white man to work 12 to 14 hours a day, six days a week. Slaves, of course, were called upon to work longer hours for considerably less pay.

1975, NASHVILLE

State Senator William Baird, acknowledged to be the general assembly's leading prankster, threw the legislature into turmoil when he managed to adjourn the Tennessee Senate until 7 A.M. the following morning. As Baird put it, "I get up early anyway." He slipped the motion through a drowsy Senate by unanimous vote.

Despite a later outcry by some senators, Lieutenant Governor John Wilder ruled that there was no way to reverse the vote. The early-morning hour threatened the presence of a quorum to vote on a bill repealing the state's fair-trade (or price-fixing) law, the first piece of major legislation in the 1975 season.

MARCH 6

1836, TEXAS

The Alamo was overrun by the numerically superior forces of Mexican general Santa Anna. All the defenders were killed, including David Crockett, who either went down swinging his rifle, was executed by Santa Anna's soldiers after surrendering, or languished in a Mexican jail. No one knows for certain.

MARCH 7

1780, ON THE TENNESSEE RIVER

On one of the flatboats carrying pioneers to the French Lick, Mrs. Ephraim Peyton gave birth to a child in what is now the Hamilton County area. The infant died a few days later when Mrs. Peyton was forced to help fend off an Indian attack.

1812, NASHVILLE

Andrew Jackson wrote a spirited plea to Tennessee men to enlist and fight the British. It said, in part, "Citizens! Your government has yielded to the impulse of a nation. . . . War is on the point of breaking out between the United States and . . . great Britain! and the martial hosts . . . are summoned to the Tented Fields! . . . A simple invitation is given . . . [for] 50,000 volunteers. . . . Shall we, who have clamored for war, now skulk into a corner?"

Many did volunteer, although their ideas about how long they had signed up for later caused Jackson much aggravation during the Creek Indian War.

1853, NASHVILLE

Journeymen carpenters met and declared that

on April 1, they would demand the initiation of a 10-hour workday and a six-day workweek. The weekend as we know it is the result of many American working-class actions such as this.

1869, CLINTON

A freedmen's school was burned to the ground. Within two days, a group of local citizens determined to rebuild the schoolhouse, raising $140 for that purpose.

MARCH 8

1780, NEAR "THE SUCK," CLOSE TO WHAT IS NOW CHATTANOOGA

The Donelson party was attacked on the Tennessee River by arrow-shooting Indians. John Donelson wrote crisply in his diary, "We immediately moved off."

1862, HAMPTON ROADS, VIRGINIA

The frigate USS *Cumberland*, named after the winding Middle Tennessee river, became the first victim of the ironclad CSS *Virginia*, better known as the *Merrimack*. Some 121 of her 376-man crew drowned as a result of the attack. It is said that many lost their lives because they stayed at their stations, firing their cannon at the Confederate ironclad as the frigate slipped into its watery grave.

1896, CHATTANOOGA

At First Baptist Church, the Reverend Dr. Garrett delivered a sermon entitled "The Worst Enemy of the Working Man." In it, he claimed the labor-organizing "demagogue" was such an enemy. Organizers never did a day's work, yet they were always "stirring up strife between [work-ing] men and their employers." Garrett contended that the Christian religion, "which was started by a working man, was the best refuge which a laboring man could find." Even worse than labor-union demagogues was liquor, which Garrett strongly advised his audience to shun. Working men should stay sober and accept Jesus, not a union demagogue, as their leader.

It is quite probable that this sermon was more widely applauded by Chattanooga's capitalist employers than the city's unionized working men.

1961, NASHVILLE

Elvis Presley attended a joint session of the general assembly. The rock-'n'-roll legend was made an honorary colonel in the Tennessee Volunteers. Later that night, Colonel Presley returned to Graceland.

MARCH 9

1882, RHEATOWN

Pete Chambers, John McCracken, and William Morgan went on trial for robbing the safe of Charles Park, county trustee. They had been arrested on the tip of Napoleon Humbard, who claimed that the crime was committed by the James Gang and that the three alleged robbers were members of that outlaw band. The prevailing view was that they most likely were not, but the local populace was excited as the trial began.

1891, NASHVILLE

The Cumberland River threatened to reach a high-water record as it flooded Sulphur Bottom, Hell's Half Acre, the lowlands of East Nashville, and a number of factories and wholesale houses on Front Street.

1892, MEMPHIS

Twenty-seven African-Americans were arrested near People's Grocery for "ambushing and shooting down four deputies who tried to arrest a negro . . . for a minor offense," according to a local newspaper.

Afterwards, a lynching occurred. Three of the four lynching victims—Thomas Moss, Calvin McDowell, and Will Stewart, the black co-owners of People's Grocery—were taken out of their jail cells by a mob of 75 masked white men who broke into the jail at 3:15 A.M. The mob took the blacks about a mile from the jail, bound them, gagged them, and shot them to death. According to one account, Thomas Moss's dying words were, "Tell my people to go west— there is no justice for them here."

This lynching prompted Ida B. Wells, editor of the *Memphis Free Speech*, to begin her antilynching campaign in this country and abroad.

1914, NASHVILLE

In a letter to *The Tennessean*, M. P. Murphy of Columbia offered the opinion that divine precepts prohibited women from participating in arguments "pertaining to prominence of leadership in the church of God, and human government. . . . Women should shrink from assuming a . . . position in government matters which . . . would subject them to adverse influences."

History demonstrated, argued another correspondent to *The Tennessean*, that even when women were confronted with an opportunity to distinguish themselves, they ultimately failed. Even in the "more important sphere of the home, the training of the child, they admit their inability by their demands for laws to help them."

It was believed that there were two spheres, one for men and another for women. The woman's place was in the home and the man's outside the home. This belief helped slow the pace of such reforms as women's suffrage.

MARCH 10

1794, NEAR HENRY'S STATION IN WHAT IS NOW BLOUNT COUNTY

Samuel Martin was killed by Indians while traveling the path to his father's home.

Near sunset, James Ferguson, his sister, and the son of David Craig were ambushed on Nine Mile Creek. James Ferguson was killed outright, but the other two rode away in great haste. They came to a fork in the road, separated, and met again when the road merged, hitting one another with such force that Miss Ferguson's horse was knocked down. Young Craig helped her remount, and they made their way to safety with the Indians in hot pursuit.

1897, NASHVILLE

It was reported that Preston Dorris had constructed a horseless carriage. It was said the homemade vehicle could attain unheard-of speeds of 15 miles per hour.

1969, MEMPHIS

James Earl Ray pled guilty to charges of murdering Martin Luther King, Jr. Ray, who was then functionally illiterate, had been captured in London, England, and brought back to the United States.

He was sentenced to 99 years. He later recanted his confession and attempted to reopen his trial.

1819, NASHVILLE

The steamboat *General Jackson* arrived in its home port for the first time. There was no heavy industry in Tennessee as of this date. The boat was built in Pittsburgh, Pennsylvania, at a cost of $16,000. It had left Pittsburgh on March 9.

It was another nine years before a steamboat reached Knoxville and another 20 before one docked in Columbia.

1882, KNOXVILLE

A comical and bloodless street encounter occurred between two newspapermen. The editor of the *Knoxville Tribune*, James W. Walker, and his counterpart from the *Knoxville Chronicle*, William Rule, met at the corner of Gay and Church Streets. Walker asked if Rule had written something insulting to him, to which Rule replied affirmatively. Walker demanded an apology but instead was hit soundly by Rule's cane. Walker then drew a pistol and fired twice at Rule, who fell to the street but soon returned to his feet and ran into a nearby drugstore. Walker then walked to the sheriff's office, gave himself up, and was released on bond. Rule, however, was not hurt, suffering only powder burns.

Perhaps Walker was a bad shot and Rule a poor editor.

1985, NASHVILLE

By a 14–13 vote, African-American state senator John Ford retained his chairmanship of the General Welfare Committee after the full Tennessee Senate refused to suspend him in an interstate shooting incident.

In February 1991, Ford was indicted on charges stemming from an incident the previous autumn in which he had fired a pistol through the sunroof of his Mercedes-Benz at a Texas trucker during an altercation on Interstate 40 in West Tennessee.

1881, MEMPHIS

Julia Hooks, an accomplished African-American pianist and socially refined young schoolteacher, found trouble when she entered a theater and sat in the white section. Hooks refused to move. She was arrested for disorderly conduct and bodily carried out of the theater by two policemen.

At her trial, both sides agreed that she had sat in the white section. The theater owner admitted that it had not been the practice to segregate whites and blacks before the 1881 season. Now, however, there was a "colored balcony" provided for blacks; sometimes, when the theater was crowded, whites also sat in the blacks-only balcony. Avoiding the larger issue of segregation, the judge declared Hooks guilty of disorderly conduct and fined her $5.

1896, NASHVILLE

According to the *Nashville Banner*, "The resolution providing for the reading of the Bible in the city schools came up again, and the report of the subcommittee . . . was read." The city council sent the report back to the school board for further study. By delaying, the councilmen were able to support the constitutional ban against the joining of church and state.

1929, ELIZABETHTON

Dissatisfaction over low wages prompted 500

female employees at the Glanzstoff Rayon Mill to quit work until Margaret Bowen, one of their number, was reinstated after having been demoted by a foreman. This action touched off the great East Tennessee textile strike. Textile operatives formed United Textile Workers Union locals.

The strike ended on May 25 without formal recognition of the unions. The German Bombery Corporation owned the mill.

MARCH 13

1795, KNOXVILLE

According to the *Knoxville Gazette*, "A tavern was opened in the town of Greeneville, in Greene County, in the territory South of the River Ohio."

In frontier America, taverns served not only as drinking places, but as news centers, trading centers, and places of lodging for travelers. Frontiersmen were not, for the most part, teetotalers.

1852, NASHVILLE

After disparaging newspaper editors as a "species of scoundrel," Reece B. Brabson, a member of the state legislature, was met by Felix K. Zollicoffer, the editor of the *Nashville Republican Banner and Whig*, near the City Hotel. Zollicoffer insulted Brabson, saying he was not a gentleman. Brabson slapped Zollicoffer's face. The editor drew a pistol and shot at the unarmed politician. Luckily, a bystander hit Zollicoffer's arm, and the ball lodged in a door. Neither editor nor politician was hurt. They parted none the worse for wear.

1969, MEMPHIS

James Earl Ray, acknowledged killer of Martin Luther King, Jr., recanted his confession. He claimed his attorney had pressured him to make a disclosure of guilt.

MARCH 14

1855, MEMPHIS

Late at night, a woman of locally bad repute was "called upon" by the men who pulled the fire engine of volunteer company No. 5. Her premises were washed out by the firemen-turned-moralists. According to the *Memphis Daily Whig* of the following day, they "abused the frail woman badly, tearing up her clothing and breaking up her property." When the police arrived, armed firemen prevented them from interfering.

Some "volunteers" were also vigilantes.

1879, NASHVILLE

The general assembly passed a law making it a misdemeanor "for any person to sell, or offer to sell, or to bring into the State for the purpose of selling, giving away or otherwise disposing of belt or pocket pistols or revolvers or any other kind of pistols except army or navy pistols." However, the proposed law "provided that this act shall not be enforced against any persons now having license to sell such articles until expiration of such present license." Governor Albert Smith Marks signed the bill into law early the following month.

Tennessee's efforts at reducing violence through gun control have roots in the 19th century.

1918, COVINGTON

Exhorting citizens to purchase more War Savings Stamps, Mayor J. J. Green declared, "Let there be no slackers in our midst. Remember that whoever is not for the government in support of the war is against it, and who is against the government now is an enemy of the people."

Mayor Green's remarks were typical on the World War I home front.

1983, NASHVILLE

The Tennessee Senate voted to make it a felony to kill a police dog.

1983, NASHVILLE

According to Dr. Jeff Harris, director of the Tennessee Department of Public Health, the state's birthrate for the first nine months of 1982 had dropped to its lowest level in 50 years. From January to September 1982, there were 51,416 births, or 14.6 per 1,000 people. In 1981, the ratio had been 15 per 1,000. Harris explained that "people are planning families. It's much more expensive to have children and people are exercising their option not to. They can have a better life style and pay more attention to the kids they do have."

MARCH 15

1767, WAXHAW, SOUTH CAROLINA

Andrew Jackson, future victor at the Battle of New Orleans and seventh president of the United States, was born.

1862, TIPTONVILLE

The United States Army's siege of the town began. It ended on April 8 after the Confederate garrison surrendered.

1946, ATHENS

A recreation center for African-American youths, given the name "Shangri-La Teen Town,"

opened. The facility was a local YWCA project. It featured a snack bar, a library, and room for dances and socials. Located on the corner of Ridge and Chestnut Streets, it was the first facility of its kind in the city.

1975, OPRYLAND

Opryland and much of Middle Tennessee were deluged by floods caused by heavy spring rains.

Even as the rain fell and the Cumberland River rose, the Grand Ole Opry celebrated its 60th anniversary at Municipal Auditorium in Nashville.

Governor Ray Blanton was certain that Tennessee would qualify for federal emergency relief.

MARCH 16

1839, COLUMBIA

The steamboat *Madison* visited town. The *Columbia Observer* ran a special edition to celebrate the arrival of the first steamboat in the city. It was front-page news.

Twenty years earlier, the *Jackson* had arrived in Nashville, the first steamboat ever in that city.

1859, NASHVILLE

Captain Dismukes and his wife were returning from the theater when they were attacked by three men. They hit Dismukes with brass knuckles and then shot him, wounding him seriously. The police were soon on the scene and exchanged shots with the thugs, who got away.

Muggings occurred in Tennessee cities long before the 20th century.

1862, OCCUPIED NASHVILLE

Andrew Johnson, the newly appointed military governor of Tennessee, appealed to Nashvillians to be peaceful citizens. He also demanded that city officials take the oath of allegiance to the United States. They refused and were quickly jailed. Governor Johnson then appointed a new board of aldermen and councilmen in their place.

Johnson allowed no challenges to Union authority.

1869, NASHVILLE

A thief who took a suit of clothes from a store on Cedar Street was recognized the next morning walking around the market house. He was arrested while wearing the stolen clothing. No doubt, this simple crook soon wore a zebra suit.

1882, NASHVILLE

Reports surfaced of the murder of Captain James W. Davis, 35, an extraordinary revenue agent.

Davis, from Lincoln County, had fought for the Confederacy. After the war, he became a detective. He came to prominence when John C. Brown was elected the state's 20th governor. Brown was impressed with Davis's abilities and persuaded him to undertake the hazardous job of arresting "various desperadoes." It was said that Davis could follow a trail as well as an Indian hunter and that he had remarkable endurance, often staying in the saddle for three days and nights without sleep. He worked as a revenue agent for Tennessee, North Carolina, Georgia, and the federal government. During his career, he arrested over 3,000 persons and destroyed nearly 700 illegal stills.

Davis was waylaid by 10 or more moonshiners in the well-settled territory near McMinnville while on his way to court. His attackers had concealed their presence with a camouflage of logs and brush. As Davis passed on his horse, he was caught in a deadly cross fire and his body was riddled with bullets.

His murderers, who apparently had the support of local citizens, were never apprehended, though liberal rewards were offered.

1925, BIRMINGHAM, ALABAMA

Archie W. Willis, Jr., was born.

From 1965 to 1969, he held the distinction of being the first African-American to serve in the Tennessee General Assembly since 1889, when Representative Monroe W. Gooden, a Democrat from Somerville in Fayette County, concluded his term.

Willis received a B.A. from Talladega College in Alabama and an LL.B. from the University of Wisconsin School of Law. He served in World War II as a corporal in the United States Army. He practiced law in Memphis from 1953 to 1971, with offices at 588 Vance Avenue. From 1971 until his death, he was a real-estate broker, a director of the Greater Memphis Race Relations Council, a member of the board of trustees at Lemoyne Owen College, and a secretary of the Tennessee Voters' Council. Willis died on July 14, 1988, after a lengthy bout with cancer.

1983, WASHINGTON, D.C.

Ronald Reagan hosted a group of country music stars at a special White House reception. The president said he believed that country music was "one of the few art forms that we can claim as truly American." Country Music Association chairman Sam Marmaduke presented the president with autographed copies of albums by every artist in the cast of the silver-anniversary special to be taped at Constitution Hall the following evening. Reagan was most pleased with his navy-blue CMA tour jacket, which, Marmaduke said, would "get you backstage anywhere you want to go."

After the awards, the president and first lady mingled with the crowd. Minnie Pearl took Roy Acuff by the arm, and the two met the chief executive. Nancy Reagan was not talkative, though she smiled politely as the country stars were introduced.

Not all the stars were Reagan supporters. Loretta Lynn said, "I didn't vote for him, and I told him I didn't vote for him." Ricky Skaggs, who had recently been opening his concerts with the line, "Reaganomics are working, are you?" said he wouldn't repeat the joke now.

As he left the bevy of country stars, the president said, "I'm looking forward to one whale of a concert tomorrow night."

MARCH 17

1775, SYCAMORE SHOALS, EAST TENNESSEE

The Transylvania Treaty was signed. Over 20 million acres of Indian land were sold for 2,000 pounds sterling and goods worth 8,000 pounds.

1886, KNOXVILLE

A special train from Nashville arrived at Erin Station on this St. Patrick's Day. On board were the first patients for East Tennessee State Hospital, characterized by the *Knoxville Daily Chronicle* as "forty-nine madmen." Hundreds of curious onlookers were the "worst disappointed crowd one ever saw." Even more troubling was that, in Knoxville, "it would be hard to get a crowd of sane men who would behave themselves as nicely as [the patients] did."

1917, NORTH ATLANTIC OCEAN

While the United States was still officially neutral in World War I, the American ship *City of Memphis*, a cargo vessel, was sunk by a German U-boat.

The ship had taken cotton to France and was on its way home when the submarine surfaced, announced its intent to sink the *City of Memphis*, and allowed the crew to abandon ship in lifeboats. The submarine then positioned itself 200 yards away and fired its deck cannon at the ship, which sank in 20 minutes. All crew members were saved.

1983, NASHVILLE

The Tennessee Education Association vowed an all-out effort to defeat Lamar Alexander's Master Teacher Plan, which it viewed as a union-busting measure. The plan would, claimed TEA spokesmen, "wipe out rights teachers have worked decades to gain." At issue were the bill's provisions that would work to erase tenure for teachers.

MARCH 18

1886, MEMPHIS

The adage holding that "hell hath no fury like a woman scorned" was dramatically illustrated on Beale Street when grocer Henry Arnold was shot to death by Emma Norman. Arnold had seduced Norman, who sought restitution.

Her trial for murder began on April 1. Large audiences attended. By April 3, Norman was found not guilty. She was released, and it was the general feeling that justice had been done.

African-American high-school and college students carried out the first sit-ins in the city, marking an acceleration of the civil rights movement in the South.

MARCH 19

1836, WASHINGTON, D.C.
George Bancroft, the so-called historian of Jacksonian democracy, began two days of interviews with Andrew Jackson, the seventh president of the United States. In his handwritten account of their talks on the 19th, Bancroft intimated that Jackson "told me he was sensible, the care of Providence had been upon him during his whole life."

He quoted Jackson as saying, "Here I am in my seventieth year, & men, cut off but half as old, that have not been exposed to half as many dangers. There is a Providence of God & I cannot deny it, it has been extended to me, & I have always endeavored to deserve it."

Jackson evidently believed God had chosen him to lead the nation.

1863, TULLAHOMA
The wife of General John C. Breckinridge presented the 20th Tennessee Infantry the famous "Wedding Dress Flag," made of material from her wedding dress. The 20th had been judged the bravest of all the units in Breckinridge's division at the Battle of Stones River two months earlier. None but the brave deserve the fair.

The interior of Paulson's Tailor Shop in Harriman, 1895

1924, LAWRENCEBURG

The Ku Klux Klan carried out a recruiting drive with a rally in a high-school auditorium. The Reverend Otis F. Spurgeon, a gifted orator who had learned his trade on the old Chautauqua podium, was the featured speaker. His remarks, according to the *Lawrenceburg Democrat*, stirred local Klansmen "to a high pitch of enthusiasm and spread alarm in the minds of many others in the huge crowd by his lurid and forceful pictures of the menace to home, church, and native land that he alleges is threatening from the Knights of Columbus, foreign-born citizens, immigrants, Jews, the League of Nations, etc." Spurgeon was convinced that the League of Nations was part of a plot hatched in the Vatican that aimed at nothing less than the destruction of the United States and Christian-American values. He called for white Protestants to join forces in a holy war against the League of Nations and all threats to America.

Seated on the stage with Spurgeon were Mayor James D. Vaughn and the Reverend John R. Morris. Morris dismissed the crowd with a fervent benediction for the success of the Ku Klux Klan.

1995, NASHVILLE

The Tennessean had as its front-page headline, "Where Illegal Drugs Hit Home."

Almost 100 years earlier, on March 23, 1895, a similar story had appeared in the *Nashville American* when Juliet Bridges of New Middleton in Smith County died from an overdose of morphine. After graduating from a leading female college, Bridges had received severe injuries in a runaway buggy accident. She suffered greatly. Morphine alone allayed her pain. She became addicted to the drug, and the habit finally grew so powerful that she was sent to the Tyson Sani-

tarium in January 1894. She escaped from the sanitarium because her doctor "wouldn't let her have enough morphine" and made her way to Nashville, where she purchased opiates from druggists' shops on South College and Broad Streets. She was later found unconscious and was returned to the sanitarium. Doctors tried to revive her but failed. She was the victim of "the deadly blight of the awful morphine habit."

One difference between 1895 and 1995 is that opiates are illegal today. One similarity is that, regardless of controls, there are still drug addicts.

MARCH 20

1836, WASHINGTON, D.C.

Historian George Bancroft's second visit with President Andrew Jackson took place. Jackson spoke of his political enemies, chief among them Henry Clay, but made no negative remark about John Adams, to whom he had lost the presidential election in 1824. He also spoke of the Ambrister and Arbuthnot affair in Florida. According to Bancroft, "Jackson is frank, open, conceals nothing."

1849, MEMPHIS

On his way to the gold fields of California, John R. Boyles, a young Fayetteville boy, wrote home to his family that the Bluff City "is about the last place in creation that I would choose to live in. A perfect hog hole now at least."

1863, MILTON, RUTHERFORD COUNTY

The Battle of Milton occurred when Confederate cavalry numbering about 2,000 attacked a ridge held by 1,500 Federals. The Confederates, commanded by General John Hunt Morgan, were beaten by the Union forces, commanded by Colonel Hall. Morgan's cavalry withdrew near the end of the day as Federal reinforcements arrived from Murfreesboro.

1956, MINNESOTA

Tennessee senator Estes Kefauver won Minnesota's Democratic primary over favored Adlai Stevenson.

Ultimately, Kefauver's effort, complete with a toothy grin beneath a David Crockett–style raccoon-skin cap, failed to gain him the party's nomination.

1960, NASHVILLE

Elvis Presley arrived from Graceland for his first recording session since being discharged from the army. The event took place at RCA's famous Studio B. It was Elvis's first stereo session. Among the songs recorded were "Stuck On You," "It Feels So Right," and "Soldier Boy." The session lasted 11 hours, beginning at 8 P.M. and ending at 7 A.M. the following morning.

Studio B is listed on the National Register of Historic Places and is a popular Nashville tourist stop.

MARCH 21

1800, KNOXVILLE

Governor William Blount died suddenly of chills and fever.

Andrew Jackson sought to occupy the vacancy in Blount's political faction. During this effort, Jackson accused John Sevier of irregularities connected with land sales, which led to hostilities between the two men.

1845, SEVIER COUNTY

Benjamin Maynard, one of the most highly respected African-Americans in 19th-century Knoxville, was born a slave.

He later accompanied his master, Colonel Horace Maynard, as a servant in the Civil War. After the war and freedom, Benjamin Maynard became a painter and paper hanger. He also worked as a custodian at the post office and later at Second Presbyterian Church.

In 1880, he moved from his home on Hill Avenue to South Knoxville, where he operated a truck farm. Later, he turned his attention to the cultivation of flowers, operating a stall in the market house. For a generation, he was the only African-American florist in East Tennessee.

Maynard was a charter member of Second Congregational Church, a trustee of Eastport Cemetery, and a charter member of First Negro Masonic Lodge of Knoxville.

1943, NEAR ABILENE, TEXAS

Cornelia Fort of Nashville became the first American female pilot to die on active military duty and the first Tennessee woman to lose her life in service to the country in World War II.

A flight instructor, Fort taught college students in the Civilian Pilots Training Program. She had witnessed the Japanese attack on Pearl Harbor. Her death came in a plane crash while on a training mission.

1979, MURFREESBORO

The husband of Debra Margaret "Maggie" Walling filed for divorce on the grounds of cruel and inhuman treatment. Maggie, an attractive socialite from Valparaiso, Indiana, had recently been involved in two armed robberies, at the Dollar General Store in Crossville on December 1 and at a First Tennessee Bank branch in

Nashville on March 1. The couple had been living in a trailer in Warren County while Walling was restoring his antebellum home in McMinnville.

1979, NASHVILLE

It was announced that country-and-western singer Porter Wagoner was suing erstwhile partner and protégé Dolly Parton for $3 million. In the contract dispute, it was claimed that Dolly owed Porter the money after she had left his television show four years earlier. According to the contract, she owed him a percentage of her income from June 1974 to June 1979. There was reportedly no animosity between the two performers. Dolly could not be reached for comment.

1844, NASHVILLE

William Carroll, the sixth governor of Tennessee, died.

Carroll won fame at the Battle of New Orleans. He was Tennessee's "Business Governor," serving as a Democrat from 1821 to 1827 and from 1829 to 1835. He is credited with putting the state's finances in order. Carroll was one of only two men to serve six terms as governor of Tennessee; John Sevier was the other.

1874, MEMPHIS

There was a parade in the Bluff City to mourn the death of United States senator Charles Sumner, a Radical Republican champion of Af-

The interior of a typical Tennessee barber shop in Waverly, 1901

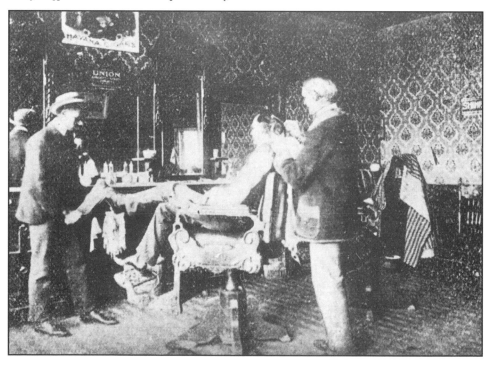

rican-American rights. Although many city officials attended, Irish-American fire chief John E. McFadden was "unable to participate because of a serious indisposition—not to turn out, despite the mandatory request of the Mayor," it was reported.

The Pole Bearers, an African-American army veterans' organization, mustered 300 and marched in the parade with shouldered muskets. Their appearance was of concern to many whites.

MARCH 23

1853, NASHVILLE

Ironworkers went on strike, parading through the streets of the city with "martial music and flying banners." They pushed for a 10-hour day and a six-day workweek. According to one report, "They were in high spirits but perfectly orderly. They were much pleased with the motto they carried at the head of their procession which read 'united to protect but not combined to injure.'"

1874, MEMPHIS

It was reported that fire had destroyed the locally famous French Garden buildings on Horn Lake Road.

During and after the Civil War, these gardens were a place of rendezvous for the fast men and faster women of Memphis. Wine drinking was common. The buildings belonged to Madame Etchevarne, a successful businesswoman. They were the last of the courtesan pleasure gardens in South Memphis.

1892, ROCKVALE, RUTHERFORD COUNTY

J. R. Puckett, a prosperous farmer, had a plantation bell on his farm. He used it to call work hands in from the fields. He had been troubled recently by pranksters who rang the bell in the middle of the night and disturbed his sleep. Finally, he threatened to kill anyone caught in the act of nocturnal signal tolling.

W. B. Neely, "in the spirit of fun," found a way to ring the bell. He tied a line of twine to the bell's clapper and hastily left the yard. His plan went awry, and he was on his way back to see why his line was not ringing the bell when he was shot in the head.

Puckett readily admitted his actions. He said he believed that Neely was a thief. It was not thought that Puckett would be prosecuted.

MARCH 24

1837, WASHINGTON, D.C.

Ex-president Andrew Jackson left the nation's capital on board the steamboat *Emigrant*. James K. Polk, who later became the 11th president, was also a passenger.

1886, MEMPHIS

Twelve homeowners were arrested for failing to obey a new ordinance requiring that houses be numbered.

1972, NASHVILLE

Z. Alexander Looby, an African-American attorney and civil rights leader, died.

Elected to the Nashville City Council in 1951, Looby helped students engaged in sit-in demonstrations. His contributions to the black community in Nashville are honored by the Z. Alexander Looby Library and Community Center.

1843, MATAMORIS, MEXICO

One-time Tipton Countian Robert Holmes Dunham, a major in the Texas army, was captured along with nearly 200 soldiers by forces of the Mexican army. Durham and the others were marched from Matamoris to Mexico City to Saltilo and finally back to Matamoris. There, they were imprisoned in the Hacienda Saluda. After briefly escaping, he and 176 soldiers were recaptured and again imprisoned.

Holmes wrote home of "the most awful feelings that a son ever addressed a mother, for in half an hour my doom will be finished by the hands of the Mexicans for our late attempt to escape. . . . [The Mexican officer in command has ordered] that every tenth man should be shot and we drew lots. I was one of the unfortunate. I can not say anything more. I die I hope with firmness. . . . May god bless you and may he in this my last hour forgive and pardon all my sins."

Eventually, the remains of Dunham and 16 others were buried at La Grange, Texas.

1942, MEMPHIS

Aretha Franklin, "the Queen of Soul," was born. Perhaps her two greatest hits were "Respect" and "Chain of Fools."

1830, RHEA COUNTY

Dewitt Clinton Senter, a member of the Tennessee House from 1857 to 1863 and the Tennessee Senate from 1865 to 1869, was born.

Senter attended Strawberry Plains College, read law, and was admitted to the bar. He was also a farmer and a politician. During the Civil War, he was arrested by the Confederate government and held prisoner for six months.

Upon the resignation of Governor William G. Brownlow on February 25, 1869, Senter, the speaker of the Tennessee Senate, became the 19th governor of the state. A Republican, he was elected to a full term soon afterwards and served until October 10, 1871. Thereafter, he lived at his home in Morristown, staying completely out of politics. He died on June 14, 1898. He was buried in the Old City Cemetery in Morristown. His remains were later removed to the Jarnagin Cemetery in Morristown, where a more substantial monument was placed to mark his grave.

1881, DAVIDSON COUNTY

W. W. Eastman, county magistrate, arrested Bill Ryan, alias Tom Hill, a ruthless and indiscreet member of the James Gang. The outlaws were hiding in a nearby neighborhood. Frank and Jesse James left early the next morning and never returned. They evidently headed west.

1883, NASHVILLE

Governor William B. Bate signed Tennessee's first antiabortion law. It provided for a prison sentence of one to five years for anyone inducing an abortion and a sentence of one to three years if the abortion was performed to save the mother's life.

1917, CAYCE, MISSISSIPPI

Rufus Thomas, Jr., a legendary entertainer, was born.

During the 1940s and 1950s, he was the organizer and master of ceremonies of the amateur shows at the Palace Theatre in Memphis.

From these shows began the careers of many notable performers, including B. B. King and Bobby "Blue" Bland.

Thomas had the first hit records for the Sun and Stax labels. As a popular personality on WDIA in Memphis, he was the first disc jockey to play Elvis Presley records on a black radio station. He was the creator of two of the biggest dance crazes of the 1960s—"the Dog" and "the Funky Chicken."

MARCH 27

1814, MISSISSIPPI TERRITORY

At Horseshoe Bend on the Tallapoosa River in Alabama, General Andrew Jackson's army surrounded a force of Redstick Creek Indians. Over 800 Indians fell that day in a total rout.

The victory helped pave the way for the eventual removal of most Indians from what are now Alabama, Mississippi, and Tennessee. The Creek Indian War was virtually over. Jackson soon turned his attention to the hated English.

1862, FORT WARREN, BOSTON

Perhaps longing for female companionship, prisoner of war Randal McGavock, a prominent plantation owner and mayor of Nashville in better days, entered in his diary that he "walked out on the parapets and met a very good looking woman, who I ascertained was the wife of the man who kept the boarding house for the laborers employed in the Ft. She broke the ice and I pitched in. She was very voluble and seemed disposed to play the agreeable, but said that she was restrained by orders. While talking with her I noticed that the eyes of the whole Ft. were upon us. . . .

Old Col. Dimmick, the Commandant . . . seemed to dislike my attentions, altho brief and casual."

1872, GALLATIN

Brigadier General William Trousdale "the War Horse of Sumner County," passed away at his home.

A courageous soldier, Trousdale had served with Andrew Jackson in the War of 1812 and in the Creek Indian War and the Mexican War. He was elected governor of Tennessee, serving from 1849 to 1851. He played a major role in the secessionist Nashville Convention of 1850. He was appointed by President Franklin Pierce as "Envoy Extraordinary and Minister Plenipotentiary to the Court of the Emperor of Brazil" in 1852. Little is known of his life from then to his death. He was buried in Gallatin.

MARCH 28

1814, OFF THE COAST OF MEXICO

A midshipman during the War of 1812, 14-year-old David Glasgow Farragut, a native of the Knoxville area, saw his first battle. It was fought between the USS *Essex* and two British ships, the HMS *Phoebe* and the HMS *Cherub*. The *Essex* lost the engagement, and Farragut and the rest of the crew were taken prisoner. The adolescent Farragut managed to escape.

1840, NASHVILLE

Tennessee's first hospital for the mentally ill—or "lunatic asylum"—was established in the city's downtown. The responsibility of caring for the mentally ill had shifted from the counties to the state. Movement toward central bureaucratic authority over local government found its roots in the early 19th century.

1859, NASHVILLE

According to Mayor Randal McGavock's diary, "A woman was arraigned before the Recorder this morning dressed in man's clothes. Her hair was cut short and she said she was from Allen Co. Ky. She was sent to the Work House."

In Nashville, it was a punishable offense for a woman to wear men's clothing.

1929, NASHVILLE

The Tennessee Department of Public Health initiated its first statewide typhoid fever inoculation drive. The responsibility of protecting the public health, previously the job of county and municipal governments, was becoming a matter for the state.

MARCH 29

1796, KNOXVILLE

John Sevier was elected the state of Tennessee's first governor. William Blount had been territorial governor.

Six years earlier on this date, Sevier had become the first member of Congress to represent a constituency in the greater Mississippi Valley.

1889, NASHVILLE

Democrat Robert Love Taylor, governor from 1887 to 1891 and from 1897 to 1899, enacted Chapter 204 and leased the entire state penitentiary to the Tennessee Coal and Iron Company. The corporation gained complete control of the

facilities and inmates, whom it used as virtual slave labor.

MARCH 30

1780, ON THE CUMBERLAND RIVER

Finding themselves out of corn, wheat, and oats, members of the John Donelson party were fed by huntsmen who, as they floated on the Cumberland, killed buffalo to sustain the hungry members of the expedition. Buffalo are usually associated with the Great Plains, not the greenest state in the land of the free.

1869, NASHVILLE

The velocipede school on Church Street was attracting novices who wished to learn to ride. Many, however, could not maintain their balance on the early bicycles, characterized by their large front wheel and smaller rear wheel, and so were battered and bruised. The streets were in such a muddy condition that tenderfoot riders began utilizing the wooden sidewalks. This annoyed and endangered many pedestrians. Police ordered velocipede riders off the sidewalks on Church and Cherry Streets.

1882, KNOXVILLE

D. B. Thompson, a foreman at the Knoxville Iron Company, was going from his boardinghouse to work when he saw smoke coming from a home in a small alley. Hearing screams, he ran into the home and found a young girl on fire. He smothered the flames. Although the girl was extremely burned about the limbs, it was said she would be all right because of the foreman's actions. Thompson's hands were burned, though not to the point of debilitation.

1905, NASHVILLE

The state legislature passed a law extending racial segregation aboard trains. This Jim Crow law helped stimulate an African-American boycott of urban transit systems in Tennessee. The boycott ultimately failed.

1914, MADISON COUNTY

John Lee Curtis "Sonny Boy" Williamson, harmonica legend, was born.

He was the most influential harmonica player of his time, a recognized master of the blues genre. His recordings included "My

The boiler crew at B. Napier Iron Co., circa 1915

Younger Days," "Nine below Zero," and "Trying to Get Back on My Feet." He died in Chicago on June 1, 1948. A Tennessee Historical Commission marker stands in his honor in Jackson.

MARCH 31

1780, MIDDLE TENNESSEE

John Donelson's flatboat fleet finally met up with Colonel Richard Henderson, the man who had sent Donelson to settle his recently purchased land in Middle Tennessee and Kentucky. Henderson assured the Cumberland pioneers that their empty grain bins would be filled once corn from Kentucky arrived from the falls of the Ohio River. In the meantime, they ate meat.

1785, GREENEVILLE

The legislature of the State of Franklin met, making it the first assembly in what was to become the state of Tennessee 11 years later. North Carolina had not granted that such a state could be formed, so the government of Franklin was an illegal one. The State of Franklin existed for three years, until early March 1788.

1828, KNOXVILLE

The steamboat *Atlas* arrived. It was the first such boat in the city.

1880, TILLMAN, MISSISSIPPI

Joseph Edison Walker was born in a cabin located near cotton fields.

He attended school in Claiborne, Mississippi, and then worked his way through Alcorn A & M in Lorman, Mississippi, and Meharry Medical College in Nashville. By 1923, the successful

Dr. Walker was in Memphis founding the Universal Life Insurance Company, which evolved into the fourth-largest black insurance company in America. In 1946, Walker founded and was elected the first president of Tri-State Bank of Memphis, which made its first loan on March 3, 1947. Before his tragic murder on July 28, 1958, he divided most of his fortune between his two children.

1964, MEMPHIS

Elvis Presley was awarded the Bluff City's "First Americanism" award. The Elks Club presented the honor, but "the King" did not attend the ceremony.

Ruins after the Clarksville fire of April 3, 1887

April

APRIL 1

1783, CUMBERLAND SETTLEMENTS

According to the minutes of the Committee of the Cumberland Association, it was the local government's decision to promote the manufacture and sale of local liquor rather than "Liquors Brought from Foreign parts; And Sold . . . here." The purchase of "foreign liquor" caused a currency drain from the Cumberland settlements. With that in mind, the committee imposed a prohibitive fee for licenses to sell all but domestic spirits, the price being set at "Two Hundred pounds Specie." No fee was required for selling domestic spirits, the price of which was set at no more than a silver dollar "for one Quart of good sound Merchantable Liquor." Failure to obtain a license resulted in confiscation of all stock.

Nashville's founding fathers were not prohibitionists, only protectionists.

1864, DALTON, GEORGIA

U. G. Owen, Tennessee medical doctor with the Confederate army, wrote to his wife, "When we get to house keeping again (if ever) I will make a handy husband for I can cook, wash dishes, milk cows, churn, &c. &c. We will not require a cook & washer woman. I will be particularly skilled in the art of cooking poor beef. We have no bacon but an old Skin & keep that for the greases. . . . Whenever we put on bread or cook anything that will stick, we get the greaser."

1867, MAURY COUNTY

Lucius Polk Brown was born.

On January 15, 1908, he was appointed by Governor Malcolm R. Patterson to the post of pure food and drug inspector for the state of Tennessee. Brown attacked the spread of narcotics and set up a system in which drug addicts could, after registering with the state, obtain their addictive substance with a physician's prescription. In 1914, he took on the responsibilities of the director of food and drugs in the New York City Department of Health.

1985, CHATTANOOGA

Tax protester Frederick Tupper Saussy III was jailed without bond after federal agents arrested him in Sewanee for failing to appear in United States District Court. The Sewanee writer-publisher and former Nashville advertising executive held that Article 1, Section 1, of the United States Constitution made it illegal to pay debts in any currency other than gold or silver.

Saussy, publisher of the *Main Street Journal*, had only recently been released from federal prison for nonpayment of federal income tax for the years 1977 to 1979. He said he was afraid to go to court and face Magistrate John Powers because the judge was prejudiced against him.

APRIL 2

1781, CUMBERLAND SETTLEMENTS

The Battle of the Bluffs took place in what is now Nashville. It was the most formidable Indian invasion ever undertaken against the white Cumberland settlements. Twenty men left the safety of their blockhouses to save friends and recover bodies as the Indians attacked the ap-

parently undefended fort. Mrs. James Robertson loosed the hounds that forced the Indians to withdraw, so saving the settlement.

1851, NASHVILLE

The second of two concerts by Jenny Lind was held. Immense preparations had been made for the event, so that the maximum profit could be made by packing people into the Adelphi Theater. New galleries were built, and the choicest seats were auctioned to the highest bidders, the best tickets going for $200.

The standing-room-only crowd at the Adelphi was wild with enthusiasm for the concert.

1899, THE PHILIPPINE ISLANDS

Young Tom Osborne, a Shelby County volunteer with the First Tennessee, wrote home describing the aftermath of a battle against Filipino freedom fighters: "Next day was quiet . . . and such sights that I saw that day will never grow old to my memory. Every house in town was burned and I saw dead women, dead horses, dead dogs, dead cows, and many burned people, and some with both legs shot off, others [with] one arm torn off their carcasses lying partly in the fire and partly out. Those [United States Navy] gunboats did most of this. . . . They are the most cruel things in existence."

One of the gunboats was the USS *Nashville*.

1936, CROSSVILLE

The *Crossville Chronicle* carried the following story: "At a meeting of the Socialist Party in Nashville, Mrs. Kate Bradford Stockton was chosen as the gubernatorial candidate for Tennessee. . . . She enjoys the distinction of being the first woman ever to be nominated for governor of the Volunteer State by any political party."

The choice of Kate Stockton as the Socialist Party candidate came about less out of concern for gender equality than from the fact that no one else was willing to run. No Socialist could have done better than her 1-percent showing in the polls.

APRIL 3

1875, KNOXVILLE

The Cumberland Street bridge over First Creek was completed. For the first time, citizens of East Knoxville weren't inconvenienced by having to drive around the Mabry Street bridge to reach Gay Street. The pace of transportation quickened.

1887, CLARKSVILLE

A fire made worse by strong winds destroyed tobacco warehouses and the three-story, brick French Building. After the fire was initially doused, it started again and razed the Elder Block, taking six houses with it, as well as the Western Union office and a number of furniture stores. It was the worst fire in the city since April 13, 1878.

1919, NASHVILLE

Albert H. Roberts, the 34th governor of Tennessee, signed into law a state-police bill. It established a police force for quelling strikes and other outbreaks of violence. The Tennessee Constitution did not allow the governor to send the state militia without the consent of the general assembly, so the state-police bill was conceived as a kind of governor's police force.

There was a "red scare" raging in the nation at the time, complete with fears of a bomb-throwing revolution led by bearded communists, reds, Bolsheviks, and anarchists. The Tennessee State Police was formed partly in response to widespread fear over this nonexistent threat.

1959, FAYETTEVILLE

Airman First Class Cole Y. Bell spoke to reporters about a unique concern he had.

He and six other soldiers, all on emergency leave, had been in Tokyo waiting to board a plane to take them home when a lieutenant colonel bumped them so he could take his wife and four children to Hawaii for a vacation. Bell could not abide this and called Lieutenant General Robert W. Burns, commanding officer of that district in Japan. After a brief investigation, Burns had called the aircraft back, bumped the lieutenant colonel and his family, and put the soldiers on board.

Bell was fearful that his chances of a successful career in the air force were now jeopardized because officers would single him out as a troublemaker.

1985, NASHVILLE

Southeastern Telecom and Communications Service Company affiliated to form the largest single business organization to supply and service cellular telephones in the Southeast. The new company also provided computer communications systems, business telephone systems, and digital radio paging.

APRIL 4

1781, NASHVILLE

According to John Cotton, the Cumberland men spent the morning after the Battle of the Bluffs digging graves near their cabins on what

Even though there were professional leagues, many towns created their own teams to play other localities. This is Hohenwald's team in the 1890s.

is now the west side of the Davidson County Courthouse. Later in the afternoon, the bodies of the Indians, from which "the stink was foul," were buried with the dog carcasses.

1862, CORINTH, MISSISSIPPI

Confederate generals William J. Hardee and Leonidas Polk and their commands marched northward toward Shiloh to engage Federal troops in one of the bloodiest battles of the Civil War.

1875, KNOXVILLE

The Riversides defeated the Cedar Bluff Baseball Club by a 19–10 score.

Cedar Bluff's uniforms consisted of a white hat with a blue band, a white shirt, and red pants. The Riversides wore cadet uniforms. "Their appearance and good playing," claimed the *Knoxville Chronicle*, "won the hearts of many of the young damsels."

1968, MEMPHIS

Martin Luther King, Jr., was assassinated while standing on the second-floor balcony of the Lorraine Motel. He was in Memphis lending his support to the sanitation workers' strike.

Today, the National Civil Rights Museum stands at the site.

1985, NASHVILLE

Sandi Patti was named the Gospel Music Artist of the Year for the third time. Accepting the Dove Award, Patti said, "I've learned a lot this year, I've learned so much from the Lord."

APRIL 5

1862, SHILOH

Joseph D. Thompson, sergeant, Company B, 38th Tennessee Regiment, wrote in his diary that in the evening advance, elements of the

Confederate and Union armies began shooting. Confederate soldiers were "laughing and huzzaing, shouting 'Hurra boys, the fun has commenced now in earnest.'"

In the end, it was far from fun, the battle winning the sanguinary sobriquet "Bloody Shiloh."

1982, GEORGETOWN, VIRGINIA

Abe Fortas, born in Memphis in 1910, died.

As a child, Abe worked in a shoe store at night to help support his parents, working-class Orthodox Jews. Not only was he an outstanding student, he was also a phenomenal violinist. He graduated from Southwestern College (now Rhodes University) in 1930. He was a noted debater. Studying under William O. Douglas, he graduated from Yale Law School and was immediately hired as a faculty member. In 1934, he was hired by the Securities and Exchange Commission, headed by Douglas. From that point, Fortas worked for the New Deal.

He subsequently met a young Texas congressman, Lyndon B. Johnson. His fortunes were closely tied to Johnson's career in the ensuing years. Fortas helped Johnson keep his name on the ballot in Texas in the notorious election of 1948. Fortas defended individual rights during the McCarthy era. He was appointed to the Supreme Court by President Johnson in 1965. When Chief Justice Earl Warren stepped down from the bench, Johnson nominated Fortas to take over the position. By this time, however, Johnson was unpopular, and a filibuster in the Senate caused Fortas to withdraw his name. In 1969, Fortas was connected with a scandal focusing upon his involvement with a convicted stock manipulator. Demands were made that he step down or be impeached. He resigned from the Supreme Court.

Fortas resumed the practice of law and played the violin in a string quartet. He became a member of Carnegie Hall and the Kennedy Center for the Performing Arts. In March 1982, he argued his last case before the Supreme Court.

APRIL 6

1790, EAST TENNESSEE

Methodist circuit rider and future bishop Francis Asbury wrote in his journal, "We reached Nelson's chapel about one o'clock, after riding eighteen miles. Now it is that we must prepare for danger in going through the wilderness. I found the poor preachers indifferently clad, with emaciated bodies, and subject to hard fare; yet I hope they are rich in faith."

1862, SHILOH

Confederate forces under General Albert Sidney Johnston attacked Union forces as the Battle of Shiloh began in earnest. The day was spent in confused fighting in which General Johnston was killed. General Benjamin Cheatham's division joined the attack, and the rebels pushed the Union force from the field.

The size and location of this force compelled Union general Ulysses S. Grant to send General Lew Wallace's division on a broad front to be ready for the attack. Wallace's men were arranged along a west-east line to meet the Confederate attack from the north or northwest. The Union forces were close to defeat but ultimately held the field.

Sergeant Joseph D. Thompson of the 38th Tennessee recorded that after the Yankees were pushed back, roving bands of Confederate soldiers, himself included, pillaged the camps the Federals had left behind. Many of them got drunk on Union wine and whiskey. Consequently, they were in sad shape for the next morning's battle.

General Grant subsequently arrived by steamboat to direct the Union's battle plan. Starting around midnight, according to Sergeant Thompson, a heavy thunderstorm began, "accompanied by peal after peal of thunder, together with the roaring of cannon and the bursting of shell. The flashes of lightning revealed the ghastly features of the dead. The groan and piteous shrieks of the wounded was most heart-rendering in the extreme. There we stood, all wet to the skin!! Oh, what a night of horrors. . . . It will haunt me to the grave."

1885, NASHVILLE

A statewide law was instituted forbidding the playing of baseball games on the Sabbath. Many fans were betting on the games, which offended some of the wealthy, pious, and conservative citizens of the city. The law stipulated a fine of from $25 to $50, with a grand-jury indictment required to prosecute. The law also forbade the playing of baseball under another name. Working-class citizens, who had only Sundays off for recreation, were outraged.

1887, SHELBYVILLE

On the night before her wedding, Carrie Sharpe was tragically killed by her fiancé's pistol.

A. H. Ruth, her intended, had put his gun on a table. Somehow, the trigger became entwined in her skirt, and the pistol accidentally fired. She died instantly.

Both Sharpe and Ruth were from locally prominent families. She was said to be "one of the acknowledged belles of Shelbyville."

1854, NASHVILLE

Architect William Strickland died at age 64. His design for the State Capitol was not yet completed. Strickland was buried in a vault hewn out of solid stone on the east facade of the first floor.

1862, SHILOH

Reinforcements from General Don Carlos Buell's Army of the Ohio and General Lew Wallace's division, sent under cover of darkness, arrived in time for the resumption of battle. The tide quickly turned.

Confederate sergeant Joseph D. Thompson, who had retrieved Yankee drawers, hats, books, a haversack, knives, forks, blankets, and India rubber the night before, was forced to drop all his loot in order to "retard [the Yankees'] flight for it was death to him who stayed behind."

On the retreat to Corinth, Mississippi, Thompson recorded in his journal, "My bed, tonight, is wet, cold ground exposed to the pitiless storm. My shivering limbs are all swollen and wracked with pain—having had nothing to eat for 24 hours. Oh, what a life is a soldier's!! Who would not be a soldier?"

About 13,000 of the 63,000 Union troops were killed or wounded, or about 21 percent of the Federal force, and nearly 11,000 of the 40,000 Confederate soldiers were killed or wounded, or about 28 percent of the rebel force. It was also at this battle that the United States Army Medical Corps instituted the first tent hospital in American martial history.

1881, NASHVILLE

Representative Thomas A. Sykes introduced a

bill in the Tennessee House of Representatives to eliminate the practice of segregation on the state's railroads. It appeared to have a good chance of succeeding until segregationist forces passed a bill that provided for "separate but equal" car facilities. The vote was 50–2, the only negative votes being cast by African-American legislators Sykes and Isaac F. Norris.

APRIL 8

1862, MISSISSIPPI RIVER

Federal forces captured Island No. 10.

Covered by Federal gunboats, Major General John Pope landed part of his army of 25,000 on Island No. 10's western shore at Madrid Bend. The Confederate defenders were outflanked. Confederate general W. W. Macula's attempt to retreat was thwarted by high tides, so he was forced to surrender to the United States Army near Tiptonville. A Tennessee Historical Commission marker in the Tiptonville Courthouse yard recognizes the event.

1897, KNOXVILLE

The "Great Gay Street fire," also known as the "Million Dollar fire," occurred.

APRIL 9

1876, MEMPHIS

Hugh McConnell made complaints before the county court about the management of the county poorhouse, where he had once been an inmate. The matter was referred to the Shelby County Grand Jury, which after thorough examination reported that McConnell had no grounds for complaint and that the poorhouse administrator, Dr. Duncan, was the right man in the right place at the right time. The investigation revealed that punishment had been inflicted on McConnell on occasion for breaching poorhouse regulations, which the grand jury thought was right and just.

County poorhouses, where poor, homeless people were sent to work and live, were very nearly prisons. They subscribed to the notion that hard work built character and would eventually lead inmates out of poverty on the path of true enlightenment.

1886, MEMPHIS

Maud Prather, the wife of a streetcar driver "and a very good looking woman," according to local sources, was assaulted by Oliver L. Racine, a clerk at Ozanne and Company.

Mrs. Prather had decided to take a trip to Texas, which infuriated Racine, who may have thought himself her lover. Grabbing a pistol, he fired but missed, whereupon "Mrs. Prather fell on her knees and plead[ed] for mercy. . . . Racine advanced on her and saying 'I had as well kill you now' fired a second shot that burned her face severely. She screamed and ran into the street without her shoes. All this time Racine's wife was pleading with him to desist . . . while he was swearing like a maniac."

Neighbors watched from their windows as the drama unfolded. The police arrived after receiving a telephone call and quieted things a bit. Mrs. Prather declined to press charges. Finally, Mrs. Racine took Mrs. Prather to an unknown location to spend the night. After Mrs. Prather left for Texas the next day, the police arrested Racine. However, he was soon out on bail. Where he went from that point is not known.

1860, MEMPHIS

According to the *Memphis Daily Appeal*, "The congregations worshipping at the various churches [had been] greatly annoyed by the cursing and shouting" of firemen and boy hangers-on rushing to a fire two days earlier. This kind of disturbance was common among volunteer fire companies in American cities at the time.

1864, OCCUPIED NASHVILLE

Concern was expressed over the appearance of an unruly juvenile gang, the Forty Thieves. Boys ages eight to 14 belonged to this band. Some were arrested for throwing rocks at city school buildings. The provost marshal sentenced them to confinement at the workhouse.

1879, FENTRESS COUNTY

A story in the *Knoxville Daily Chronicle* told of a possible revival of the feud between the followers of Tinker Dave Beaty and Champ Ferguson.

On the Cumberland Plateau during the Civil War, Champ Ferguson and Tinker Dave Beaty had carried out a guerrilla war for the Confederacy and the Union, respectively. Hatreds had developed as a result of the carnage committed by both sides, but tempers had cooled until recently.

Now, fourteen years after the war, George W. Bowles and W. C. Threel were indicted in Fentress County for the wartime murder of a Ferguson follower named Baker. Beaty followers Bowles and Threel claimed that their case should be heard at the federal court in Nashville. They were taken to the capital city, where Judge C. F. Trigg was to hear their plea for a writ of habeas corpus. Clabe Beaty, Tinker Dave Beaty's son and the principal witness in the case, went to Nashville in support of Bowles and Threel.

Meanwhile, Ferguson followers heard of the upcoming legal proceedings and determined to stop them. On the day of the hearing, Bowles and Threel were being brought out of the jail when men posing as Cumberland County sheriff's deputies "arrested" Clabe Beaty. They took him on horseback and in buggies on a circuitous route through the southern part of Middle Tennessee, into northern Alabama, and over the Cumberland Plateau to evade the United States marshals looking for them.

In Cumberland County, Beaty was arraigned before a Crossville justice of the peace on the murder charge for which Threel and Bowles stood accused. Soon, a mob gathered near the Crossville jail, headed by a Cumberland County deputy sheriff who claimed to have seen Beaty kill Baker. Seeing he was in danger, Beaty waived examination and offered to give bail. Pistols were drawn, and the crowd threatened his life. He ran out the back door and fled to the woods, where he was followed by, and protected by, his guards. A bondsman made up his bond, which was signed in the woods. From this relative safety, Beauty slipped back into Crossville to get some food and narrowly escaped with his life. He took to the woods, found a guide, and made his way across the plateau to Jamestown.

Beaty was described as a "brave, determined sort of man but says this last beats everything in his war experience." The hearing for Bowles and Threel was rescheduled for April 22, but there was a mass trial of moonshiners that day. The outcome of the matter is not known.

APRIL 11

1925, NASHVILLE

Austin Peay, the 36th governor of Tennessee, vetoed a bill that would have exempted Memphis from the 1923 law prohibiting movie shows on Sunday. Peay stated constitutional objections to special exemptions to any state law. He also stated that "when the time comes that the Sunday in this country is no longer a day of rest and worship but has become instead a day of sport and amusements, our country is headed for decay and early dissolution."

1959, CHATTANOOGA

Dr. Paul A. Witty, professor of education at Northwestern University, spoke to parents of gifted children at the last session of a two-day conference on the subject. He advised them to "listen to your child. Answer his questions as fully and patiently as you can. Accept his gifts and encourage them, but don't marvel at them unduly. On the other hand, don't be over critical. Above all, give your child the love and affection he needs."

APRIL 12

1822, WHITE COUNTY

George Gibbs Dibrell was born.

Dibrell was a Unionist at the outbreak of the Civil War, but he later joined the Confederate army and recruited and commanded brigades under Nathan Bedford Forrest and Joseph Wheeler. He and John Crawford Vaughn, a Tennessean from Monroe County, were on the last retreat from Richmond in 1865, protecting the Confederate archives. Dibrell was a member of

Congress from 1874 to 1884 and a prominent railroad and coal-mining "robber baron." He was buried in Sparta.

1824, NASHVILLE

Singing schoolteacher Allen D. Carden made known the completion of his second tune book, *The New Harmony*, with an advertisement in the *Nashville Whig*. He guaranteed that "the Book will be sold as low as any other ever published."

Kenneth Rose of the distinguished music publishing firm of Rose and Acuff has called this the first music published in Nashville with a label imprint.

1864, LAUDERDALE COUNTY

The infamous Fort Pillow Massacre occurred. Some 551 United States colored troops and another 221 white troops were killed by forces led by Confederate general Nathan Bedford Forrest. Most of the victims were massacred after desperate fighting and final surrender.

Forrest may not have specifically order a massacre, but he did issue an ultimatum to the Yankees: surrender or die. It was official Confederate policy to summarily execute any

Massacre at Fort Pillow [April 12]

Negroes found in Federal uniform. As commanding officer, the general was responsible for what followed.

1902, CHATTANOOGA

Despite the wishes of their international union, Chattanooga iron molders went on strike demanding the removal of African-American molders from the iron mills.

Racism helped to weaken the labor movement in Chattanooga and most other Tennessee cities.

APRIL 13

1790, EAST TENNESSEE

While attending his duties as a circuit rider, Methodist minister Francis Asbury noted in his journal that "we came back to Amis's [home] a poor sinner. He was highly offended that we prayed so loud in his house. He is a distiller of whiskey, and boasts of gaining 300 pounds [in currency] per annum by brewing of his poison. We talked very plainly; and I told him that it was of necessity, and not of choice, we were there—that I feared the face of no man. He said, he did not desire me to trouble myself about his soul. Perhaps the greatest offense was given by my speaking against distilling and slave holding."

1826, WASHINGTON, D.C.

Ohio congressman William Stanbery made unflattering remarks about Congressman Sam Houston when the Tennessean was absent. Houston subsequently challenged Stanbery to a duel.

The two met on Pennsylvania Avenue. Houston asked his opponent if he was indeed Stanbery. Stanbery replied in the affirmative and

bowed. It was then that Houston hit the Buckeye on his head with a stout cane. Stanbery recovered quickly and drew a pistol, which he held against Houston's chest. The pistol misfired. Houston hit Stanbery a few more times and then ended the affair by kicking the Ohioan in the groin.

Houston was mildly reprimanded by the House of Representatives.

1878, CLARKSVILLE

During a period of racial discord, a policeman arrested a black man who vigorously resisted. In the ensuing scuffle, the policeman killed the black man. Soon, the cry of "Fire!" was heard throughout the city. Flames destroyed the town's center, consisting of 63 buildings spread over 15 acres.

It was never established just who started the conflagration, but during the efforts to fight the blaze, it was noted that African-American bystanders refused to do anything to help white firefighters and store owners quell the flames.

1879, KNOXVILLE

The *Knoxville Daily Chronicle* ran an editorial praising members of the Memphis press who were lobbying for a new law prohibiting the sale of pistols in Tennessee. In Memphis, newspaper editors urged the courts to enforce the law by sending violators to jail:

> Let any man who thinks he can not go to a social party, a theater, or to any public gathering without a pistol in his hip pocket be regarded as any other outlaw. The ball is moving in the right direction now and we trust the day will soon come when human life will be considered sacred, and when murderers will be deprived of the facilities

for prosecuting . . . bloody deeds. There are more newspapers in the South now urging reform in this respect than ever before. It is a good omen. Let good people everywhere join and co-operate . . . in putting down this relic of barbarism. Let the pulpit speak out in thunder tones on the subject and society will reap a great benefit.

APRIL 14

1835, WASHINGTON, D.C.

President Jackson wrote a letter to his adopted son Andrew Jackson, Jr.: "It was well known to all that I . . . adopted you as my . . . son and you are to represent me when I am called home. How careful then you ought to be to shun all bad company, or to engage in any dissipation whatever, and particularly intoxication which reduces the human being below the brute."

Old Hickory, however, didn't practice what he preached, being known for taking a tonic now and again. For example, on August 22, 1833, President Jackson ended a month-long vacation at Old Point Comfort, Virginia. His expenses included 12 bottles each of champagne, brandy, and gin, three gallons of whiskey, wine, and six bottles of olives (at $1.50 each). The bill amounted to $118.50, or approximately a third of the average working man's annual earnings at that time.

1840, MURFREESBORO

S. H. Laughlin, a delegate to the Democratic Convention in Baltimore, departed town. He wrote in his diary, "After breakfasting at Murfreesboro, the stage proceeded on the turn-pike at the rapid rate of seven or eight miles an hour, and took us to Nashville by 4 o'clock P.M."

The trip to Nashville took probably four and a half hours.

1864, BROWNSVILLE

Sergeant Achilles V. Clark, a member of Nathan Bedford Forrest's cavalry, had participated in the decimation two days earlier at Fort Pillow. This Henry County native, small slave holder, and member of the 20th Tennessee Cavalry wrote his sisters the following:

> The slaughter was awful. Words cannot describe the scene. The poor deluded negroes would run up to our men [and] fall upon their knees and with uplifted hands scream for mercy but they were ordered to their feet and then shot down. The white men faired but little better. Their fort turned out to be a great slaughter pen. Blood, human blood stood about in pools and brains could have been gathered up in any quantity. I with several other[s] tried to stop the butchery, and at one time had partially succeed[ed], but Gen. Forrest ordered them shot down like dogs, and the carnage continued. Finally our men became sick of blood and the firing ceased.

1874, MEMPHIS

In a meeting of the common council, it was suggested that a quota system for filling municipal jobs be adopted. The percentages proposed were the following: 10 percent Italian, 20 percent Irish, 20 percent German, and 50 percent white American and African-American.

This 19th-century affirmative-action proposal was never enacted into law.

1865, OCCUPIED NASHVILLE

After hearing of the Confederate surrender at Appomattox Courthouse on April 9, military forces in Nashville prepared a victory parade.

According to Captain William H. Gay of the United States Army, "On the appointed day Nashville put on her brightest robes to shine beautiful in this hour of the nation's joy. . . . The army was to march in grand review. . . . It was a brilliant inspiring sight."

Captain Gay was at the head of a column of artillery. As it turned onto Church Street, a courier rode up to tell him that "President Lincoln and Secretary Seward were assassinated last night!" (Secretary of State William Henry Seward was attacked at his home and wounded, but not killed, the night of the Lincoln assassination.) The news spread, and enthusiasm turned to dismal muttering. The parade stopped, and the troops returned to quarters.

According to Gay, those Confederate sympathizers who were "less cautious in speech declared their satisfaction and were shot dead on the spot by an outraged soldiery."

1894, CHATTANOOGA

Bessie Smith, famous blues singer, was born.

Her career began with the Rabbit Foot Minstrels. From 1913 to 1916, she was in contact with Gertrude Pridgett Rainey, who taught her to sing the blues. Smith recorded extensively from 1923 to 1926. Leading jazzmen such as Louis Armstrong and Clarence Williams accompanied her songs. Smith had her own touring vaudeville companies, the Midnight Stoppers and the Harlem Frolic. She was featured in the film *St. Louis Blues*, and her voice was used on several soundtracks. She died in Clarksdale, Mississippi, after an automobile accident on September 26, 1937.

1964, NASHVILLE

Clayton "Rabbit" Veach, Tennessee's most elusive escape artist, was behind bars.

The 23-year-old had escaped from custody at least 17 times. Asked why he escaped, Veach said it was because of ill treatment—specifically because of leg irons and chains being put on him. He told reporters that he was tired of running but that if the authorities mistreated him again, he might make a break for it.

The next day, Veach was transferred from the Davidson County Jail to the state penitentiary. Evidently, he served his term of one year and one day without making another escape.

1877, FRANKLIN

Franklin Cumberland Presbyterian Church was dedicated, the Reverend Thomas Dale serving as the first minister.

Construction on the church had begun on June 3, 1876. It was designed by H. C. Thompson, the architect of Nashville's Ryman Auditorium. This Gothic Revival church was listed on the National Register of Historic Places in 1982.

1934, MEMPHIS

James Pinckney Alley, the first editorial cartoonist for the *Memphis Commercial Appeal*, died of Hodgkin's disease.

Alley was the creator of the nationally syndicated cartoon "Hambone's Meditations." His cartoons critical of the Ku Klux Klan were instrumental in the paper's winning a Pulitzer Prize in 1923. In the presidential campaign of 1924, one of his cartoons critical of the scandal-ridden G.O.P. was circulated to Democratic papers and was even seen in lights on Broadway in New York. His son Calvin later returned to Memphis and carried on his father's work with the *Commercial Appeal*.

1987, NEW YORK CITY

It was announced that Peter Taylor, a native of Trenton, was the winner of the Pulitzer Prize for his second novel, *A Summons to Memphis*.

APRIL 17

1809, POTSDAM, PRUSSIA

Adolphus Heiman was born.

Heiman learned architecture and the stonecutter's craft from his father. They immigrated to the United States and arrived in Nashville about 1836. Heiman's buildings included the Tennessee State Lunatic Asylum, completed in 1851. He also designed a suspension bridge across the Cumberland. His fondness for the Gothic Revival style was notable in his design for the University of Nashville's Lindsey Building, listed on the National Register of Historic Places. He also designed his own residence in Nashville, the Tennessee State Penitentiary, and Belmont, a pretentious Nashville residence.

Heiman served in the Mexican War and later in the Civil War as a lieutenant colonel in the Confederate army. He was taken prisoner at Fort Donelson and was later confined at Fort Warren in Boston. After being exchanged, he rejoined the Confederate army before dying in a military hospital in Jackson, Mississippi, on November 16, 1862.

1861, MEMPHIS

A letter "from the Ladies of Memphis" to the editor of a local paper read in part, "Though we cannot bear arms, yet our hearts are with you, and our hands are at your service to make clothing, flags, or anything that a patriotic woman can do for the Southern men and Southern independence."

1899, NASHVILLE

The *Nashville Banner* printed a letter from a soldier in the First Tennessee on duty in the Philippine Islands. Among other things, the letter complained of combat: "The boys are getting sick of fighting these heathen[s], and all say we volunteered to fight Spain, not heathen[s]. Their patience is wearing off. . . . They will be fighting [the Filipinos] 400 years, and then never whip these people, for there are not enough of us to follow them up. . . . The people of the United States ought to raise a howl and have us sent home."

1905, NASHVILLE

The state flag was officially adopted by the legislature. It was designed by LeRoy Reeves, a veteran of the Third Regiment, Tennessee Infantry, Confederate States Army.

1925, KNOXVILLE

Caledonia Fackler Johnson died.

Born a slave on October 14, 1844, Johnson made his fortune soon after emancipation. He owned saloons, brothels, racetracks, and fine horses. He served as an alderman for the mostly

Tennessee volunteers in the Philippines during the Filipino rebellion/insurrection [April 17]

black Fifth Ward in Knoxville and favored vocational education for African-Americans.

1940, CHATTANOOGA

The Hamilton County and Chattanooga Board of Health began a comprehensive venereal-disease control program. Within two years, health-care professionals treated about 2,200 people.

1968, MEMPHIS

After 65 days and the tragic assassination of Martin Luther King, Jr., the sanitation workers' strike ended. The union was fully 99 percent black. Members cheered when the contract settlement was announced.

1987, NASHVILLE

It was reported in *The Tennessean* that Frederick Tupper Saussy III, a one-time darling of Belle Meade society, was now a tax evader on the run.

In 1985, Saussy had been convicted of not filing his income tax. He denied this assertion, claiming he had filed it, he just hadn't paid his taxes. Saussy was never one to play by the rules. He sent a videotape of himself walking on the sidewalk in front of the federal prison in Atlanta, saying to the camera, "Look, I'm here, and they're not." The tape was broadcast on Chattanooga television station WRCB. His whereabouts were unknown.

Saussy was a gifted man, having been a teacher

at Montgomery Bell Academy, a songwriter, a playwright, a businessman, an artist, an author, and a pianist of high regard. He was remembered in Nashville for an ad created for Purity Dairy, the "Don't Pay No 'tention to Kangaroos" campaign. He wrote the hit song "Morning Girl." He began turning his attention to the Internal Revenue Service in the 1970s, presenting his play *The Gimmies* at his Appletree Dinner Theater in 1971. The play, as described by Saussy, was about "a miniature America where love, ambition, achievement and life itself are thwarted at every turn by officials selling licenses and collecting fines, judges issuing prison sentences and tax men auditing and harassing amidst voices muttering 'gimmie, gimmie, gimmie, gimmie, gimmie.'"

APRIL 18

1810, GILES COUNTY

Neill Smith Brown, Tennessee's 12th governor, was born.

During his administration, the first telegraph in the state was instituted. His efforts at creating a viable public-school system stand as perhaps his most important contribution to Tennessee. Brown lost the governor's chair to William Trousdale in 1849. In 1850, President Zachary Taylor appointed him the American minister to Russia. He took no part in the Civil War but was a Confederate sympathizer. As a consequence, his home was burned by Union soldiers. Brown was an influential member of the 1870 Constitutional Convention but retired from public life thereafter. He died in 1886 and was buried at Mount Olivet Cemetery in Nashville.

1847, MEXICO

Soldiers of the Second Tennessee advanced against Mexican forces at the Battle of Cerro Gordo, but the Mexicans forced them to retreat. This is no reflection on the valor of the Tennesseans, as the Mexicans numbered 3,000, while the Second Tennessee mustered only 375 strong. The odds were against the Volunteers.

1883, KNOXVILLE

What was perhaps the city's first black baseball team was formed. Named "Bank's Choice," the team was reportedly "prepared to meet any nine that shall see fit to challenge them."

1889, KNOXVILLE

Commenting on a performance of black entrepreneur Cal Johnson's minstrels, formed in 1886, the editor of the *Knoxville Daily Tribune* ironically remarked that "there was scarcely any necessity for the use of burnt cork as the 'artists' were genuine negroes."

Such were the quirks of a segregated society.

APRIL 19

1849, JONESBOROUGH

After eight years of publication, the last issue of the *Jonesborough Whig* appeared. Editor and owner William G. Brownlow moved his paper to Knoxville.

Brownlow proved to be as controversial in Knoxville as he had been in Jonesborough. At first, he supported slavery, then later called for its abolition. He later served as a Republican governor of the Volunteer State.

Because so many had been arrested by federal revenue collectors, a mass trial of moonshiners was held in the federal courthouse on Broadway. Most accepted an amnesty proposal, promising never again to make illegal whiskey. Those who did not accept the amnesty were to be prosecuted to the fullest extent of the law.

APRIL 20

1860, MEMPHIS

Memphis Volunteer Fire Department chief A. B. Jewell responded to criticism aired 10 days earlier by a writer calling himself "Z." A letter in the *Memphis Daily Appeal* from the chief claimed that firemen had been maliciously misrepresented. They served "not to destroy, but to protect and preserve both the lives and property of their fellow citizens, even at the hazard of their own health, and frequently their lives." Jewell asked how "Z" might feel if his property were ablaze and the only available water was in his neighbor's cistern. Wouldn't he think it necessary to take his neighbor's water to save his property? The chief believed all such people "should have S-E-L-F wrote in large leather letters on their foreheads. . . . If 'Z' should ever make war on the 'fire boys' he will be the worst ducked gentleman, in less than two minutes. . . . There will be far more water than blood shed."

Memphis, like many other American cities of the era, was discovering that its growth was not matched by a corresponding improvement in protection from fire. Volunteer fire companies were shortly replaced by municipally controlled and paid fire departments that utilized steam-powered fire engines.

1964, MEMPHIS

A 17-car derailment in the Louisville & Nashville switchyard resulted in $70,000 in damages. There were no injuries.

1987, NASHVILLE

Tennessee Agriculture Department spokesperson Jamie Yanes named 32 counties predicted to be heavily hit by the expected emergence of 17-year locusts. However, the plague was not anticipated to be as big an event as the swell of buzzing, red-eyed, dive-bombing 13-year cicadas that had exploded throughout the Volunteer State in 1985.

APRIL 21

1902, ATHENS

A victory at the polls for the "wets" effectively put an end to prohibitionist efforts at social control—at least for the time being. After the results were known, there was, according to one account, "a small sized deluge of drinks to celebrate the event."

1903, OLIVER SPRINGS

Miners went on strike at the Poplar Creek Mine, owned by Queener Brothers. The cause of the strike was the company's refusal to give miners a 10-percent pay advance. In fact, management demanded the miners take a 10-percent pay reduction!

After a month, the miners agreed to return to work. They took wage cuts of from 40 to 45 cents per ton of coal and from 60 to 75 cents per ton of lump coal.

1936, NASHVILLE

For the first time in its history, the Nashville City Council passed an ordinance that made it illegal to sell or possess marijuana unless prescribed by a doctor. As part of an educational effort, the council agreed to hear Earl A. Powell, an anti-marijuana zealot and lecturer, at its next session. No local record exists to indicate the gist of Powell's remarks.

1947, NASHVILLE

The executive committee of the Tennessee Historical Commission met to consider a number of matters, one of which was reportedly an appeal from "Negro Associations at Fisk [University] to aid in research for material bearing on the Negro's share in the state's development."

During the state's sesquicentennial in 1946, the commission had funded portraits, busts, statues, research, and books about the Civil War and prominent white personalities in the Volunteer State's past.

In reviewing the new appeal, the chairman of the committee agreed to provide the African-Americans with his collection of "newspaper references . . . which number quite a great many," but he did not think the commission could "compensate for research work of any sort."

1964, MURFREESBORO

Robert "Tee-Niny" Scales became the first African-American in the history of the city to win public office. Tee-Niny Scales had gotten his nickname as a baby when his sister exclaimed he was "such a tee-niny baby!"

After the results of the election were known, Scales said to the jubilant crowd, "The election is now history, the kind of history which will make Murfreesboro and America strong. . . . So,

let us all work together for the common good of our city." His voice cracked and he wept openly, but soon his face broke into a smile. He received a standing ovation from the throng.

APRIL 22

1898, THE GULF OF MEXICO, NEAR KEY WEST

The unarmed Spanish cargo vessel *Buena Ventura* was sighted by the USS *Nashville*. According to the ship's log, the *Nashville* "went to general quarters at 7:10. Fired three shells across the Spanish steamer's bow and then she stopped and hauled down her colors. Sent Ensign Magruder on board with armed crew. Found vessel to be Spanish steamer *Buena Ventura* laden with lumber from Pascagoula, Miss., bound for Norfolk, Va., for bunker coal."

The first shots of the Spanish-American War had been fired, and the news was received with great fanfare in Nashville, including a cannon salute from the State Capitol grounds. However, the entire battle was little more than routine gun practice. In fact, it was a bit ludicrous, inasmuch as a dozen American warships subdued a lone, unarmed merchantman whose captain and crew were unaware that war had been declared a day earlier.

But it was, as it later turned out, one of the more noted events in the life of the *Nashville*, which also saw service in the Filipino insurrection in 1900 and 1901, the birth of the Panamanian republic in 1903, and World War I. She was decommissioned in 1918. According to Commander A. L. Brown, her hull still had many more years of useful service.

In 1921, the *Nashville*'s entire superstructure was removed and the ship was converted to a

435-ton open barge, renamed the *Richmond Cedar Works No. 4.* As a barge, she was towed carrying logs to the ripsaws of Camden Mills, Virginia. Nevertheless, the *Nashville* had given America its first naval action in the four-month "splendid little war."

APRIL 23

1825, NASHVILLE

Anticipating the arrival of the Marquis de Lafayette, the *Nashville Whig* printed instructions for the populace to follow when he arrived. People were told to wait until the courthouse bell rang, then to assemble in the public square. There, they were to form ranks and parade for Lafayette. No one would be allowed to break ranks. Those with houses were urged to light as many candles as possible on the night of his arrival, May 4.

1886, CLARKSVILLE

The town concluded its first contract for electric lights. The generator was reportedly to be run by "the engines of the Anchor Mills, located on the rear of the city."

Wildly optimistic talk abounded that an electrical plant would "be fixed at Dunbar's Cave with sufficient power to brilliantly illuminate this great cavern, three miles underground, presenting a curious scene of the wondrous beauty of nature, unsurpassed in the world."

There is nothing to indicate that the new electrical supply allowed this potential tourist attraction to be exploited.

1968, SMITHVILLE

A tornado blasted a 350-foot path through the town, severely damaging 20 homes. One 10,000-pound mobile home was thrown an astonishing 150 yards. There were no fatalities.

APRIL 24

1802, KNOXVILLE

Archibald Roane, second governor of the Volunteer State, first used the original Great Seal of the State of Tennessee, authorized in 1796 by the state constitution. The first governor, John Sevier, had used three personal seals because of legislative failure to actually provide a seal for his three terms.

1886, NASHVILLE

It was reported that Bob Hooper, a well-known and popular African-American hackney driver, had "died . . . of pneumonia. He had for many years been engaged in the business of hacking. At the time of his death, Hooper was the owner and successful operator of four hacks. He leaves many friends, white and black who will be more than sorry to hear of his unexpected death."

1886, NASHVILLE

A report in the *Nashville American* told "the old story" of a young wife falling in love with a handsome young man.

Eight months earlier, a girl named Nannie had married John Crisp, a tall, bearded workman at a Nashville plow factory who was many years her senior. She had "barely turned sixteen, though a fully and handsomely developed woman of medium height, well rounded proportions. . . . She carried herself with the winsomeness of a girl and the ease of a woman. . . . A pair of lustrous brown eyes . . . waving chestnut hair . . . two rosy red lips, a firm chin, and the attractiveness of the young creature is fairly told." They moved to Bell Buckle, staying in a boardinghouse belonging to Crisp's relatives.

A young marble cutter, John Coleman, arrived in town and rented a room at the same boardinghouse. Coleman and Nannie soon fell in love. They left Bell Buckle for Nashville and lived in the city for about a week before the young woman's husband, with a warrant and the assistance of Constable Joe Graves, had Coleman arrested on Broad Street near First Baptist Church. Nannie declared her unyielding love for Coleman as he was taken to jail. She said of her husband, "I never loved him, but my family wanted me to marry him and I did. He was too old; they might have known I'd fall in love with a younger man. . . . Like all old men who marry young girls he was awfully jealous." According to Nannie, their "marital relations were not pleasant."

She agreed to return to Bell Buckle if Crisp would have Coleman released from jail, an act to which he would not consent. She then stayed in Nashville at the home of Coleman's mother. Nannie entertained vague notions of freeing him and divorcing Crisp. It is not known whether love conquered all, since no further information was given in succeeding papers.

APRIL 25

1834, WASHINGTON, D.C.

David Crockett, a member of the Whig Party, left for New England. It proved a memorable tour in which the "gentleman from the cane" criticized Democratic president Andrew Jackson's policies. Crockett was greeted enthusiastically everywhere he went.

Less than two years later, Crockett was slain at the Alamo.

1861, NASHVILLE

A second secret session of the state legislature was called by Governor Isham Green Harris after efforts in February had failed to lead Tennessee out of the Union.

Eventually, the session produced the "Declaration of Independence and Ordinance Dissolving the Federal Relations between the State of Tennessee and the United States of America." This declaration was not made public until May 6, with an added provision that a special referendum was to be held to ratify it.

1890, KNOXVILLE

For the first time in Knoxville's nearly century-old history, the city council passed a "cow ordinance" outlawing bovines from roaming and fouling the streets. Now that cows were outlawed, only the city's outlaws had cows.

APRIL 26

1884, CHATTANOOGA

The Almira S. Steele Home for Needy Children opened. Steele, a widow and Boston native, was the guiding force behind the facility. She said that she "came south to found a school. . . . I constantly saw destitute colored orphans compelled to beg or steal. I saw . . . the precious souls of these helpless blacks."

Within three years of her death on June 6, 1925, the building ceased to function as an orphanage and was leased to Chattanooga's school board. It has long since been demolished.

Upon learning that several of his men were isolated and engaged in heavy fire, Sergeant First Class Ray E. Duke, Company C, 21st Infantry, led a small force in a daring assault that recovered the position and the beleaguered men. During the attack, Duke was wounded by mortar fragments. Nevertheless, he bravely and calmly moved along his platoon line to coordinate firing and to urge his men to hold their position. Threatened with mounting casualities, Duke was ordered to withdraw. He was then wounded in both legs and found himself unable to walk. Realizing that he was a burden to the two comrades who were carrying him, he urged them to leave him and seek their own safety. He was last seen alive pouring devastating fire into the ranks of the enemy.

Ray E. Duke, a native of Tracy City, was posthumously awarded the Medal of Honor.

APRIL 27

1775, GUILFORD, NORTH CAROLINA

Samuel Polk Black, who served in the 7th General Assembly (1807-1809), was born. He lived in Sumner County and moved later to Rutherford County where he became the cashier of a bank in Murfreesboro in 1817. He taught at the Bradley Academy in that city, where one of his students, James Knox Polk, would become the 11th President of the United States.

1888, KNOXVILLE

A mass political meeting was held for all local voters, white and black, to gain approval for the expenditure of $75,000 by the common council to build sewers in the city. The only opposition was voiced by Dr. Thomas H. Kearney, who believed that it wasn't enough money to do a thorough job. Up to this time, the city had no sewer system.

1918, JACKSON

The case of *Dr. G. A. Hamlett v. John A. Welch* was heard. Hamlett, a resident of Pilot Oak near the Kentucky border, was suing Welch for alienation of his wife's affections. Welch, a very wealthy man, was a farmer and merchant in the community of Dukedom. The three were good friends. They had been on a trip in Paducah, Kentucky, when Hamlett drank himself to sleep. Shortly thereafter occurred the criminal intimacy of Welch and Mrs. Hamlett.

Mrs. Hamlett admitted her infidelity, and the jury found for her husband, awarding him $10,000.

APRIL 28

1793, CUMBERLAND SETTLEMENTS

A slave named Abraham, the property of Anthony Bledsoe, was plowing Bledsoe's field with

Loudon chapter of the W.C.T.U.

Jarvis, a white worker, when they were attacked by Indians. As they ran for the refuge of their cabin, the two men shot and killed an Indian apiece. In the end, Jarvis was killed and Abraham managed to escape.

1842, NASHVILLE

Former President Martin Van Buren was welcomed to the capital city. He was accompanied by James K. Spaulding, his former secretary of the Navy. He rode in an open carriage with Andrew Jackson and stayed at the Hermitage. Van Buren also visited with Governor and Mrs. James K. Polk. The Whig newspaper, the *Columbia Observer*, criticized Van Buren for wearing "a roundabout coat and striped breeches." Van Buren had a reputation as a dandy who perfumed his whiskers.

1864, OCCUPIED NASHVILLE

The *Nashville Daily Press* reported that many "ready made houses . . . are springing up . . . a striking commentary on the fast age in which we live. . . . We are glad to see them here, especially when houses are so scarce and rent so enormous."

APRIL 29

1874, NASHVILLE

The State Convention of Colored Men met. Delegates came from 20 counties. Edward Shaw of Memphis was chosen chairman. The convention protested anti-miscegenation laws, denounced United States senator William G. Brownlow for opposing supplemental civil rights legislation, urged black women to become teachers, and recommended that Tennessee blacks support political candidates who believed in the right of African-American males to serve on juries. It was a crowded agenda.

1886, MEMPHIS

The chief of police delivered his annual report. According to his figures, the following nationalities made up the annual arrest record: 17 Canadians, 14 Englishmen, six Frenchmen, 208 Germans, 594 Irishmen, 91 Italians, five Mexicans, two Norwegians, 20 Poles, 16 Swedes, eight Scotsmen, 1,851 white Americans, and 2,264 African-Americans. These encompassed the following occupations: 84 agents, 18 bakers, 35 barbers, 28 bartenders, seven bookkeepers, 74 bootblacks, 26 blacksmiths, 18 butchers, 109 carpenters, 168 clerks, four contractors, 53 cooks, 103 drivers, 39 engineers, 87 farmers, 112 gamblers, five gardeners, 444 housekeepers, nine hucksters, 46 hack drivers, 1,950 laborers, six butlers, 23 loafers, 44 lawyers, 58 machinists, 59 masons, 233 merchants, 13 newsboys, 21 peddlers, 22 plumbers, 65 painters, one runner, 123 saloon keepers, 174 household servants, 57 boatmen, 34 schoolboys, 14 tailors, 14 thieves, four tramps, 28 washerwomen, eight waiters, and 308 miscellaneous.

1887, NASHVILLE

A large crowd of all classes of citizens assembled in county court "in response to a call made by the ministers Tuesday in a meeting relative to Sunday base ball playing," according to one report. The crowd was protesting the "flagrant violation of the law as took place last Sunday in the park."

The law referred to was the state prohibition against the playing of baseball on Sunday, aimed more to stop gambling than the game itself. Nevertheless, many other citizens, mostly workers, demanded that baseball be allowed on Sunday.

1892, GOODLETTSVILLE

Henry Grizzard, an African-American, was identified as one of the two men who had assaulted Mary and Connie Bruce the night before. He was taken away from Sheriff Hill by a mob and brought to a sycamore tree on Mansker's Creek in nearby Sumner County. Grizzard maintained his innocence to the end but was finally lynched.

According to the *Nashville Daily American*, "The deed was witnessed with evident satisfaction by the assemblage of vigilantes. Someone pinned an envelope on the hanging negro's breast. On the envelope was written 'Death to the man that cuts this rope before 12 P.M.'"

A coroner's jury later rendered the following verdict on the lynching of Henry Grizzard, as reported in the *Daily American*: "That he came to his death by a party unknown to the jury." Grizzard was survived by a wife and child.

APRIL 30

1892, NASHVILLE

Eph Grizzard, accused of raping the Bruce sisters of Goodlettsville, was lynched a day after his brother Henry had suffered the same fate.

A crowd estimated at 6,000 rushed the county jail with the cry, "Remember your wives, daughters, and mothers!" Grizzard was taken to the Cumberland River bridge with a noose around his neck and dropped 15 feet. The frenzied mob hauled him up and dropped his body one more time. Afterwards, his body was taken to Goodlettsville and burned.

The *Chattanooga Times* explained that, "while everybody condemns mob law, no man can ravish a Southern girl and live a day after it is proven on him."

Unfortunately, it wasn't proven in this case.

1900, VAUGHN, MISSISSIPPI

John Luther "Casey" Jones was an engineer aboard Illinois Central Railroad Engine "Old 382" when he had a head-on collision with the IC's New Orleans Special (a.k.a. "Cannonball"). According to a ballad composed by Wallace Saunders, an African-American engine wiper in Jackson, "All the switchmen knew by the engine's moans/ That the man at the throttle was Casey Jones/ The fireman jumped but Casey stayed on/ He was a good engineer but he's dead and gone."

The Casey Jones Home and Museum is located just off Interstate 40 in Jackson, Tennessee.

Jefferson City's [May 17] first movie house, shown in 1917

May

MAY 1

1866, MEMPHIS

The Memphis race riot began as a clash between freedmen and Irish policemen.

According to one report, five black women had been raped and over 90 African-American houses, four black churches, and two schools had been burned by May 3. Forty-four blacks and two whites were killed.

1897, NASHVILLE

The opening of the Tennessee Centennial Exposition was carried off a year late. At noon, President William McKinley, in Washington, D.C., touched a button sending electricity over telegraph wires to the grounds in Nashville. The signal started the machinery at the exposition and simultaneously fired a small cannon to officially open the festivities. Attendance was 20,175.

1967, LAS VEGAS

At 9:41 A.M., Elvis A. Presley and Priscilla Ann Wagner Beaulieu were married in a second-floor suite of the Aladdin Hotel. The double-ring ceremony lasted less than 10 minutes and was performed by the Honorable David Zenoff of the Nevada Supreme Court. After the ceremony came a press conference, then a reception hosted by Colonel Thomas A. Parker, estimated to cost $100,000. Later that afternoon, the Presleys began a four-day honeymoon in Palm Springs.

The Negro Building [May 1] at the Tennessee Centennial

1971, NASHVILLE

The Southwind made its inaugural run from Chicago to Nashville on the new Amtrak railway system.

MAY 2

1855, MEMPHIS

The *Memphis Weekly Appeal* exhorted its readers to contribute to volunteer fire companies. Their annual parade was coming up, and the volunteers were demanding that they "be held in the estimation and honor that is ever grateful to the hearts of men who labor . . . for the public good."

1887, NASHVILLE

The world's largest man, weighing over 800 pounds, was engaged at the Dime Museum for one week only. It was a big show.

1917, DUNLAP

About 7 P.M., John E. Smith, the superinten-

dent of the Chattanooga Iron and Coal Corporation, shot William Davis twice, instantly killing him. The murder took place in the streets, and Smith was immediately arrested.

Smith, age 40, had taken great offense at remarks Davis made to his daughter while flirting with her. Smith was released on $10,000 bail and was to go to trial May 22.

MAY 3

1825, NASHVILLE

The Marquis de Lafayette arrived in Nashville on board the steamboat *Mechanic* at 8 P.M. He had been traveling aboard the *Natchez*, but it was too big to float in the Cumberland River.

1860, MURFREESBORO

At a meeting of the Rutherford County Medical Society, John H. Morgan, M.D., presented a paper entitled "An Essay on the Causes of Abortion among Our Negro Population." Dr. Morgan revealed that slave women were often eager to induce an abortion using remedies such as "the infusion or decoction of tansy, rue, roots and seed of the cotton plant, pennyroyal, cedar berries, and camphor, either in gum or spirits." Tansy, said the physician, was most commonly used because of its convenience. Dr. Morgan believed it was "a very rare thing for negroes to resort to mechanical means to effect an abortion, probably less than white women, on account of their ignorance."

Morgan said nothing about any motives slave women might have had for wanting abortions. Some have suggested they wanted no children born into slavery and so resorted to abortion.

The doctor's comments about white women

resorting to "mechanical means" to effect an abortion are astonishing.

1887, TULLAHOMA

A sensational seduction trial ended. Miss Lula Meadows, with a "bright bouncing child in her arms," won a $5,000 judgment against Robert Messy. Both were from locally prominent families. Meadows "had lived a good life until she was seduced by Messy," according to one source. It was a messy affair.

1916, NASHVILLE

At the second meeting of the Tennessee chapter of the National Association Opposed to Women's Suffrage, the selected topics for future debate indicated the misgivings these women felt about equality: "Feminism and Socialism," "Woman's Suffrage, a Menace to Social Reform," "Women Will Not Gain by Suffrage," and "Suffrage, Not a Natural Right."

MAY 4

1849, NASHVILLE

A letter in the *Nashville Daily American* complained that journeymen mechanics (those who made their living in the trades, such as carpentry, masonry, etc.) were earning less than before because "property holders . . . are 'taxed to death' and therefore must hold their houses and slaves at a rate sufficient to enable them to make a percentage on capitol so invested."

Most of the city's working class, said the letter, were renters and contractors and were therefore forced to bear all the burdens of taxation. "Only a few mechanics make over $10 a week,

and most with families not even one half that," the mechanics' advocate wrote.

It was difficult for free white mechanics to compete against slave labor, and they resented slave owners, who kept their wages down.

1849, KNOXVILLE

David Anderson Deaderick and party left Knoxville on a trip to the California gold fields. They arrived on May 16, 1850, their journey having taken just over a year. These Tennessee '49ers did not strike it rich.

1945, OKINAWA

Sergeant Elbert L. Kinser, serving with Company I, Third Battalion, First Marine Division, and his command came under sudden, close attack by Japanese soldiers. Kinser engaged the enemy in a fierce hand-grenade battle. A Japanese grenade landed in his unit's position and he unhesitatingly threw himself on it, absorbing the full charge of the explosion.

Kinser, a native of Greeneville, was posthumously awarded the Medal of Honor.

MAY 5

1849, NASHVILLE

Another letter appeared in the *Nashville Daily American* complaining that "it is these capitalists that advance or hold up rents and keep wages down."

White masons had to compete with slave masons rented out by their owners at much cheaper wages. In many cases, "white workmen are discharged and negroes employed." The work of slaves was shoddy, according to the letter, and put free white masons out of work. Slave owners and capitalists, argued the writer, "will soon have nothing but themselves, their money, and their negroes to look after—they are working a system which will surely drive off white mechanics and laborers because [slaves] work [for] so low [a wage] that they cannot afford to pay proper wages to a good journeyman."

Slavery was not in the interest of white working men in the urban antebellum South, but it did pay plantation owners big dividends.

1971, KNOXVILLE

University of Tennessee research scientists announced that they had successfully immunized hamsters and mice against several forms of cancer. Their finding was be studied for another two years. The work involved animal embryonic enzymes.

MAY 6

1882, CHATTANOOGA

The first electricity produced in a Tennessee city was generated when a small dynamo lit a few arc lamps downtown. It was more an advertising gimmick than a demonstration of practical lighting.

1896, NASHVILLE

A 45-foot-long, cigar-shaped airship filled with hydrogen was launched above a crowd at Centennial Park. It was driven by a propeller turned by a bicycle-like device. The airship drifted westward. The inventor, YMCA physical education instructor A. W. Barnard, tried to ride the bicycle to steer the device. Though the Associated Press later published a favorable report through out the world, unfavorable winds retarded the craft's progress, and interest from the throng fell. The device was never flown again.

1911, CHATTANOOGA

According to the *Chattanooga Daily Times*,

Alfred Taylor Markwood, the Johnson City inventor of a perpetual motion device which occasioned much comment a year ago, resulting in the sale of much stock throughout East Tennessee, and especially in Knoxville, has recently made a statement that he has not by any means abandoned the idea of making his machine a success. He declares he will be able to make the machine go, and to this end he proposes to call a meeting of the stockholders to arrange to finance the work of completion. It is said that there were but one or two minor obstacles to be overcome in the original machine.

One obstacle was friction.

1931, NASHVILLE

Police officer Michael J. Mulvihill was wounded in a shootout with members of a juvenile gang.

The gang members had stolen a car parked at Broadway and 21st Street. Herschel McGuire, one of the gang members, was evidently shot by Mulvihill. McGuire was arrested and quickly taken to a hospital, where he later died. The other gang members were arrested. Officer Mulvihill later died of his wounds.

MAY 7

1788, EAST TENNESSEE

Francis Asbury, Methodist circuit rider, wrote in his diary that at "Half-Acres and Keywoods . . . we held conference three days and I preached each day. The weather was cold; the room without fire, and otherwise uncomfortable, we nevertheless made out to keep our seats until we had finished the essential parts of our business."

Circuit riding was not for the faint of heart.

1845, NASHVILLE

The Tennessee Medical Society met at city hall to hear papers, including one by Dr. Joseph E. Manlove, who reported the particulars of a treatment "for obstructed bowels, terminating in an artificial anus, which healed without operation." Manlove's paper was well received and later appeared in the *Boston Medical and Surgical Journal*.

1855, MEMPHIS

The National Typographical Union held its fourth annual meeting. Delegates from Philadelphia, Cincinnati, New York, Buffalo, Louisville, New Orleans, Boston, Chicago, Detroit, Nashville, and Memphis attended. The economic depression, it was reported, caused a low turnout.

Founded in 1851–52, the National Typographical Union was one of America's first trade unions.

1907, RIPLEY

A large majority of the town's businesses closed in the afternoon. Local merchants and shopkeepers attended a prayer meeting at the courthouse. The meeting soon became a convention.

The following resolution was adopted: "We the citizens of Ripley in mass convention do hereby resolve that . . . we have a dry town. . . . We recognize . . . that there are three men who come here every Saturday . . . soliciting orders for whisky houses in Memphis, and we . . . earnestly request that they cease visiting this town for said purpose."

Apparently, the good people of Ripley were exercising the local option.

1917, MEMPHIS

Thirty women—true Tennessee Volunteers—showed their willingness to be of service at home for the duration of World War I. They enrolled in the National League for Woman's Service, Memphis Branch. The organization's leader insisted their ranks would eventually swell to 1,000 women. One woman attorney volunteered her time, as did a female shoe-factory manager. Many nurses volunteered their services as well.

MAY 8

1824, NASHVILLE

William Walker, the famed "Grey-Eyed Man of Destiny" was born.

An extremely intelligent man, Walker was a medical doctor, a lawyer, and a newspaper editor. But he is best known as the leader of a small band of adventurers and filibusterers known as "the Immortals" who successfully conquered Nicaragua in September 1854. Walker installed himself as president and reinstated slavery. A coalition of Costa Ricans and Nicaraguans forced him from power in 1857. Walker then toured the United States and was popularly acclaimed, especially in the South. He gathered support for other attempts to reconquer Nicaragua.

On September 3, 1860, he was captured by the British navy while making an assault on Nicaragua. He was handed over to Honduran forces, tried, and summarily executed. This Tennessean's lonely grave is said to be on the Honduran Atlantic coast.

1879, PULASKI

Gabriel Moses McKissack, one of Tennessee's first professional architects—and without doubt its most successful African-American architect—was born.

McKissack's early career was spent doing designs and details in and around Pulaski. By 1904, his practice extended to Athens, Mount Pleasant, Columbia, and Decatur, Alabama. He arrived in Nashville in 1905 to construct a residence at 24th Avenue South. From that point, he practiced architecture in the capital city. His works include the Carnegie Library and Payne Chapel at Fisk University; the A.M.E church, its Sunday-school union, and residences at Shelbyville; Lane College at Jackson; the Ovoca Apartments in Nashville; and many small residences. In 1920, he designed four residences in the fashionable Nashville neighborhood of Belle Meade. His son, Calvin Lunsford McKissack, carried on the work of his father through the firm McKissack and McKissack.

1895, NASHVILLE

At the first meeting of the Ladies' Bicycle Club, Mrs. Walter Drake was elected president. The question of wearing bloomers as proper feminine bicycling attire was answered in the negative by members.

MAY 9

1879, MEMPHIS

At 3 A.M., black patrolman Charles Wilson was shot twice by "two men who were riding in an open coach with two lewd women," according to one account.

Officer Wilson's admonishment that the party be quiet due to the lateness of the hour was answered by gunfire. He shot back but did not hit either of the men. His wounds were serious. The two men were arrested the next day and held for trial. Their companions were two prostitutes, ages 18 and 19, who were staying at a house of ill fame at 32 Hernando Street. The outcome of the trial and the recovery of Wilson are not known.

1934, NASHVILLE

Luke Lea and his son attended the Tennessee Supreme Court session that denied their plea to stop their extradition to North Carolina to face charges of bank fraud. They were then taken into custody outside the building. According to one account, "In the hallways outside the supreme court room, a cordon of Nashville and Davidson county police had been placed, but their lines were broken continuously, as the Leas marched out, by numerous friends who reached out to shake hands with the former U.S. Senator and artillery colonel."

MAY 10

1855, MEMPHIS

The National Typographical Union convention passed the following resolution: "That while, we, as working men . . . depreciate 'strikes'. . . still we believe . . . 'strikes,' like revolutions, are sometimes necessary to a proper vindication of the rights of the working man."

1885, NASHVILLE

The "Great Nashville Revival" began when evangelist Sam Jones called together at least 10,000 Christians. The revival was held in a tent, and at least 2,500 seekers had to be turned away.

Today's evangelists are following a tradition established in the 18th and 19th centuries.

1849, NASHVILLE

A letter in the *Nashville Daily American* rallied to the defense of Sarah Estell, a free black confectioner and caterer.

A letter in the same paper on May 6 had criticized her, saying in part that a "respectable class of our community have not only been slighted but insulted" because of her race, gender, and thriving business.

The May 11 letter explained that

> Sarah is peculiarly fitted for this sort of business. She makes a profession of it, it enables her to procure not only cakes and sweet meats, but everything, such as meat and vegetables. . . . [She] performs to admiration all of the other duties of the best housekeeper, all of which is out of the regular business of our confectioners. . . . As for Sarah, personally, she is industrious, neat, accommodating and unassuming . . . and anxious to perform her duties fully and promptly. In fact, she is very much a lady. . . . With the fairer proportion, she is quite a favorite and they never hesitate to encourage and respect her. Her being a negro cook is so much the better—it is the sort of thing we are all accustomed to, and most of us . . . prefer them.

Sarah Estell was a free black woman in the era of slavery, part of a tiny minority of the African-American population. She catered banquets for the city's volunteer fire department, political dinners, and a host of other occasions. She also operated an ice cream "saloon," a favorite among children after church services. From 1840 to 1860, she competed successfully with white men working in a similar line of business.

All mention of her establishment ends after the 1860 census. A Tennessee Historical Commission marker was placed in her honor on Fifth Avenue North in Nashville.

1856, MEMPHIS

The city council set the fee for having the police whip slaves at $2 a head.

1934, NORTH CAROLINA STATE PENITENTIARY

Luke Lea, Tennessee political boss and newspaperman convicted of bank fraud, entered prison. He said that he was not responsible for the failure of the banks, that it was the fault of the economy. His son, Luke Lea, Jr., also was incarcerated. Instead of bankers' pinstripes, they now wore prison "zebra" stripes. Luke Lea's convict number was 29408.

1843, GREENEVILLE

A committee of mechanics read a petition on the subject of leasing convicts to do the work of mechanics. Andrew Johnson, then a tailor and soon to be elected a United States congressman, was a member of the committee. The resolution asked employers not to hire prisoners or slaves because the practice cheapened the labor of honest working men.

1866, MCMINNVILLE

The editor of the *McMinnville Enterprise* wrote the following about African-Americans: "The colored people of this place and vicinity are industrious, well-behaved, honest, and conduct themselves in a becoming manner in their intercourse with the white people. . . . No community containing as large a population of colored people can produce a better disposed class of freedmen."

This, according to the editor, was because they had benevolent masters in the antebellum era, not because they were capable people.

1868, LINCOLN COUNTY

A four-legged child—normal from its head to its waist—was born in the western part of the county.

The father, William Corban, a Confederate veteran, took the child to Nashville the following month. There, it could be viewed at Room 32 of the Commercial Hotel. Tickets were sold at the principal drugstores and bookstores in the city.

Corban and his exceptional child did not stay in town more than a day or two. Their fates are unknown.

1918, KNOXVILLE

The city school board proclaimed its wartime patriotism by unanimously voting to exclude the study of the German language and German culture from local high schools. This decision may well have been made for practical reasons, since the American propaganda machine—the "Creel Committee"—had convinced the country that all things German were depraved. If anyone taught or studied German, he was immediately suspect and could become the victim of mob violence.

MAY 13

1914, CUMBERLAND COUNTY

A revenue officer named Tyler destroyed a large still near Glade Creek where Bledsoe, Van Buren, White, and Cumberland Counties meet. Seven men were arrested, and 700 gallons of illegal beer and the still were destroyed.

1922, MEMPHIS

Clarence Saunders, the retailing magnate who made his millions from his Piggly Wiggly food stores, announced plans for his estate, to be called "the Pink Palace."

Saunders's business reversals ultimately led the city of Memphis to utilize the mansion as a museum.

1927, NASHVILLE

Ryman Auditorium was the scene of the first Fiddler's Convention for the Southern Championship. Atlanta resident Clayton McMichen won the Best Fiddler award with his rendition of "Bully of the Town."

MAY 14

1841, JONESBOROUGH

After moving from Elizabethton to Jonesbor-

Andrew Johnson's tailor shop in Greeneville

Fiddlers were long a mainstay of Tennessee folk music. This musician, Henry Johnson, was photographed in Jackson County in 1925.

ough, newspaper editor William G. Brownlow met Landon Carter Haynes, editor of the *Tennessee Sentinel*, in the streets of Tennessee's oldest town. The two editors were bitter political and personal enemies. In the altercation that followed, Brownlow bludgeoned Haynes with a cane and Haynes shot Brownlow in the thigh.

A year later, the animosity had not subsided, as Brownlow was severely beaten by Haynes at a camp meeting.

1858, MIDWAY, WEST OF BLUE SPRINGS

Amid band music and a jubilant crowd that had gathered via a special excursion train from Knoxville, Samuel B. Cunningham of Jonesbor-

ough, president of the East Tennessee & Virginia Railroad, drove the last (silver) spike on the company's 130-mile line. The track had been laid under extremely adverse physical and financial conditions. Much credit was due the tireless efforts of Cunningham and the backbreaking, back-lashed efforts of slave construction crews.

Thanks to its connections with the East Tennessee & Georgia, the line gave East Tennessee a direct link with Washington, D.C., as well as Chattanooga, Knoxville, Nashville, Memphis, Pensacola, Augusta, Atlanta, Charleston, and nearly every other commercial center of the South.

1886, MEMPHIS

Cornelius O'Keefe, private secretary to Mrs. M. E. Conway, had a bad night, losing $600 of Conway's money in Joe Wetter's gambling house.

Conway pleaded with Judge D. P. Hadden for redress. The judge ordered Wetter to either return the money or close his establishment. Wetter kept the money. Judge Hadden then arrested O'Keefe on charges of embezzlement of Conway's funds.

On May 26, he released O'Keefe to the custody of Conway. She claimed that O'Keefe was her "business partner" and that he was needed at home.

1887, NASHVILLE

In a house just outside the city limits on the Lebanon Pike near Mount Olivet Cemetery, three women reportedly kept "an assignation house where gentlemen of wealth, birth, and high social standing are wont to resort." Though they kept their doings quiet, they had managed to offend the Wilhelms next door.

About 8 P.M., a gentlemen drove up to the house, parked his buggy, and approached Mr. Wilhelm's water pump. Wilhelm objected and threatened to shoot if the man, Benjamin Hotchkiss, dared to hitch his horse to the well. The wealthy Hotchkiss did not take the threat seriously, was shot, and managed to return fire. Wilhelm evidently vanished and was not heard from again. It is not known how long the house of assignation continued to operate.

1923, MEMPHIS

The *Memphis Commercial Appeal*, owned by publishing baron and Republican political boss Luke Lea, won a Pulitzer Prize for its editorials and its anti–Ku Klux Klan editorial cartoons by James Pinckney Alley.

1940, ZENITH, FENTRESS COUNTY

Called to arrest a drunken miner, veteran gray-haired sheriff H. E. Taylor was shot to death by C. E. Markel. Just before he fell, the sheriff managed to kill Markel with a shot from his own pistol. A wave of indignation about Taylor's murder swept over Fentress and neighboring counties.

MAY 15

1859, NASHVILLE

Dr. John Shelby died.

Shelby earned his M.D. degree at the University of Pennsylvania. In 1813, he became a surgeon in the Creek Indian War, during which he lost an eye. He served with Andrew Jackson at the Battle of New Orleans. He later practiced medicine in Sumner County and Nashville.

In politics, Shelby was a Whig and therefore an enemy of his former commander, Jackson. He served briefly in the state legislature and was postmaster in Nashville under the Whig administrations of Zachary Taylor and Millard Fillmore. He accumulated a large fortune and spent his last years pursuing his interests in real estate and animal husbandry.

1874, DAUGHTERY'S GAP, 30 MILES FROM CHATTANOOGA

During a dispute over a card game, Ben Hughes hit his father-in-law, Jesse Corn, in the head with a mallet and killed him.

Both men were known as rough characters, Hughes being noted for his skills as a moonshiner. Hughes "lit out" after the murder and was not heard of again. "The last run he made," claimed the *Chattanooga Daily Times*, "was to run away from the ghost of his father-in-law."

1898, CHATTANOOGA

At a meeting of the Chattanooga Police Commission, the matter of prohibiting the sale of whiskey on Sundays was discussed. According to one newspaper account, the commissioner stated "that there has never been a time in the history of Chattanooga that a man could not purchase a drink on Sunday."

In the end, it was decided to close all saloons on Sunday. No doubt, this was troublesome to the nearly 4,500 troops at Camp Thomas.

1946, WASHINGTON, D.C.

President Harry S. Truman, with the consent of Congress, named former Tennessee governor Prentice Cooper as the United States ambassador to Peru.

1953, GREENEVILLE

This day was "Walter Mitchell Day" in this East Tennessee town. Sergeant Mitchell, recently released from a Chinese prisoner-of-war camp, said that thoughts of Greeneville and the green mountains were what had kept him going while a prisoner. A parade was held in his honor.

1967, NASHVILLE

On his way to Florida, heavyweight boxer Muhammed Ali stopped briefly and unexpectedly at Tennessee A & I (now Tennessee State University), arriving at 10:30 A.M. in a black Cadillac. He explained his position on the draft to an impromptu crowd of 300 in front of the cafeteria.

Ali had been stripped of his world title for his refusal to be inducted into the United States Army on the grounds that he was a Muslim minister.

MAY 16

1838, KNOXVILLE

The city council passed an ordinance prohibiting bawdyhouses within the city limits. In all likelihood, this was the first antiprostitution law passed in any Tennessee city.

1846, NASHVILLE

An editorial in the *Tri-Weekly Nashville Union* entitled "Make Ready for the Call" urged Tennesseans to volunteer their services in the Mexican War: "As a state, the measure of our military glory is full—our fathers have bequeathed to us their own immortal honor won on many a battlefield. We cannot expect to eclipse the lustre of their glorious deeds, but we are bound to emulate their example and to cherish the rich inheritance of military renown handed down to us. They achieved for Tennessee the proud title of the 'Volunteer State.' We are bound to maintain the distinction thus won for us. . . . Volunteers will be in readiness to answer to the call."

The editor was referring to the War of 1812, the Creek Indian War (1813–14), and the Seminole Wars (1818, 1832–38). Ironically, many of those who volunteered to fight in the Creek Indian War returned home when their 90-day enlistment was up. Units as large as a brigade abandoned General Andrew Jackson, and patriotic speeches would not make them stay.

1868, WASHINGTON, D.C.

The Senate took its vote on one of the impeachment articles against President Andrew Johnson. Guilty vote after guilty vote was turned in. Then the chief justice called the name of Tennessee senator Joseph Smith Fowler. Fowler was the first to render a vote of not guilty, spoken in a low voice. Johnson's nemesis, Senator Charles Summer, was incredulous. He asked Fowler to repeat his response, which Fowler did.

Fowler's vote established a pattern that eventually saved Johnson from the ignominy of being the first president to be impeached.

1916, NASHVILLE

At a meeting of the Tennessee chapter of the National Association Opposed to Women's Suffrage, 200 members discussed the legal status of married women and the notion that women's suffrage would be dangerous in the South because it would mean the enfranchisement of African-American women as well. Such a state of affairs would lead to social and political equality,

Andrew Johnson, seventeenth President of the United States [May 16]

an anxiety-producing situation women of their class could not endure.

1967, NASHVILLE

The state senate passed a measure to allow the teaching of evolution in Tennessee's public schools. All it required was Governor Buford Ellington's signature.

Forty-two years earlier, the Butler Act, which prohibited the teaching of evolution, had been passed. On this day, it was overturned.

Senator Clayton Elam of Memphis, the bill's sponsor, said, "We have accomplished a great thing. We have brought Tennessee into the 20th Century."

Gary Scott, a young teacher for the Jacksboro system, was fired and later rehired by local school officials for teaching the controversial doctrine. He sought help from the National Education Association and brought suit in federal court.

1973, FRANKLIN

Roger Grace, 19, was arrested for charging telephone calls to his girlfriend in Colorado to other peoples' numbers. He was taken to the Williamson County Jail. Asked why he made the calls, he replied, "I really dig that chick." He wanted to marry her. "Man, if you've ever really been in love," Grace said, "you would know what I'm talking about."

Later, he learned that the object of his affection cared nothing for him. "Wow," he said, "I really thought she was the one for me. I guess I'll have to forget her."

MAY 17

1862, OCCUPIED NASHVILLE

Two Confederate women called on Colonel Matthews of the United States Army, yet refused to pass under Old Glory, saying they would never bow to the squalid rag of Lincoln. Aside from that, it is not known how they enjoyed their visit.

1892, TULLAHOMA

A comedy of errors began when a bungling mob of 50 furious men commandeered a Nashville & Chattanooga locomotive. Their mission was to lynch an African-American man named Everett, who was in the McMinnville jail because he had allegedly attempted burglary. However, none of the brave fellows had any idea how to operate a locomotive, and even less how to hitch it to a train. After they managed to go a few hundred feet, they were stopped by their ignorance. The crowd petered out and went home.

1911, CHATTANOOGA

A letter in the *Chattanooga Daily Times* expressed moral outrage concerning two movies, *The Nun* and *The Conflict*.

The self-chosen movie critic called *The Nun* "a disgraceful feature and a disgusting one. Anyone who saw the picture . . . felt a repulsion at the [movie] house that would consent to put on such an irreverent picture." The writer objected to scenes in the movie depicting an 80-year-old friar making improper advances on novitiate nuns.

The second movie showed young people living the high life in a bordello. "The whole program was disgraceful and disgusting and I am heartily in favor of some censuring [of] motion pictures before they are allowed to go before the public."

MAY 18

1889, TROY

After a heated campaign, the voters of Obion County decided to move the county seat from Troy to Union City. The decision may well have been made based on the fact that the Illinois Central and the Louisville & Nashville Railroads crossed in Union City, making it the county's most important transportation hub and an excellent site for the seat of county government.

1916, IN THE SKIES OVER EUROPE

Kiffin Yates Rockwell, a Newport native, be-came the first American aviator to down an enemy aircraft over France.

Rockwell had joined the French Foreign Legion in August 1914 at the outbreak of World War I. He was wounded in May 1915. After joining the French Air Forces, he helped found the famous Lafayette Escadrille. He was killed in a dogfight on September 23, 1916, and was buried in France.

1925, DAYTON

Dayton High School biology teacher John T. Scopes was indicted by a Rhea County grand jury for teaching evolution.

1933, WASHINGTON, D.C.

President Franklin D. Roosevelt signed legislation creating the Tennessee Valley Authority.

MAY 19

1831, NASHVILLE

The *Nashville Republican and State Gazette* published a letter advocating the hiring of free mechanics, not slaves, to do local construction work. Referring to the scarcity of white mechanics in the capital city, the letter suggested that "the influence of slavery may be mainly referred to as the source of this evil."

Working men in Southern cities disliked slavery not so much because it was inhumane or immoral, but because it created unfair competition for their labor.

1861, DECHERD

A troop train with 1,200 Confederate soldiers on board left the Decherd station. Though Tennessee was still technically in the Union, the soldiers shouted praise for the Confederacy and Jefferson Davis.

1886, MEMPHIS

Ida B. Wells attended her first professional baseball game and was carried away with enthusiasm. She wrote in her diary, "Lost my temper & acted in an unladylike way toward those in whose company I was."

She had obviously caught baseball fever.

1902, FRATERVILLE, ANDERSON COUNTY

The oldest coal mine in the county, opened in 1870, exploded. One of the rescuers, George M. Camp, said of the calamity, "Not a man, not a rat, not a mule came out of that mine alive. I identified 184 men, everyone who entered the mine that day."

The disaster also meant tragedy for the miners' families and the beleaguered coal companies. A plethora of damage suits resulted.

1925, CHATTANOOGA

Boosters and city leaders made an attempt to have the Scopes trial moved to Chattanooga in an effort to attract business. However, Dayton entrepreneurs made sure the trial would remain in their town.

1957, ACROSS AMERICA

Carl Perkins's "Blue Suede Shoes" peaked at number two on the charts. A rock-'n'-roll song of legendary proportions was the ultimate result.

1973, LAS VEGAS

Nashville's W. C. "Pug" Pearson won the World Series of Poker, beating his opponent's flush with a full house on the last card. Afterwards, Pug expressed his eagerness to collect his winnings and "hit the white lines for Nashville just as soon as I can."

Pearson said of gambling, "I like it, sure, I love it. It's what my life is. But, no, I wouldn't recommend it."

1993, NASHVILLE

The Tennessee Senate approved a bill to allow prayer in public schools. The bill, which passed by a vote of 27–1, later met with Governor Ned McWherter's veto on constitutional grounds.

MAY 20

1845, NASHVILLE

William Strickland submitted a plan for the State Capitol that included a Doric basement, four Ionic porticoes four feet in diameter, and a Corinthian tower rising 170 feet. He estimated the cost at $240,000 to $260,000.

1874, MEMPHIS

In a controversial move, Mayor John Logue appointed three African-Americans to the fire department. His Honor justified the move on the grounds that "the Council seemed determined to have this thing done. . . . You see, they adopted a resolution ordering me to put colored men on the police department, thinking I would not have the nerve to do it, but they will see now that I am willing to carry out their instructions."

Fire Chief John E. McFadden, an Irish-American, was strongly opposed to the action.

Irate customers of the East Tennessee Telephone Company wanted a reduction in their annual fee of $65, believing it to be unfair and exorbitant. E.T.T.C. curtly refused. Local businessmen were said to be considering the formation of another telephone company to compete with E.T.T.C.

There was no Public Service Commission in the 19th century.

1897, SHELBYVILLE

The editor of the *Shelbyville Gazette* expressed his intense antisuffrage feelings by writing,

> What more do the women want? Are they not already the bosses of everything that moves? Do they not do just as they please? Are not the men of the land bending and kneeling to them on every side? What more do they want? Why the necessity . . . to get up a hurrah! for woman's rights, equal suffrage, and such like nonsense? Women to vote! to scramble at the polls side by side with the toughs and the darkies! Pretty sight that would be. . . . They even demand a constitution provision in favor of admitting them to the ballot box. They say they will restore the ballot to its ancient purity. Bosh. Let the women vote and many of their votes would soon be for sale just as is the case with the vote of some men.

MAY 21

1866, NASHVILLE

After being destroyed by retreating Confederates on February 18, 1862, the Cumberland River suspension bridge again opened for business. Replacement costs were put at $140,000.

1902, PULASKI

The Giles County Medical Society heard a paper entitled "Trachoma." The next week's paper was on the subject of "Gastro-Intestinal Catarrh in Children under Two Years Old." Too bad if you missed it.

1908, BELLE MEADE

William Howard Taft, President Theodore Roosevelt's secretary of war, visited the mansion owned by Judge Jacob McGavock Dickinson. He attended a barbecue in his honor. Because Taft was too stout to fit in Belle Meade's bathtubs, Dickinson had installed a special shower to accommodate his guest's girth.

The moral of the story is that Taft was elected president the next year and appointed Dickinson his secretary of war.

MAY 22

1781, NORTH CAROLINA

Newton Cannon, governor of Tennessee from 1835 to 1839, was born. As a young man in Tennessee, he became a surveyor and made his fortune.

In 1811, he was elected to the state legislature. He ran unsuccessfully for governor against Sam Houston in 1827, then later ran again and became the first Whig governor in Tennessee; his victory shows just how weak and demoralized the Democratic Party was. In his second term, Cannon advocated a state bank to facilitate internal improvements. He died on September 16, 1841, and was buried at his Williamson County estate.

1886, NASHVILLE

A ceremony was held at Mount Olivet

Cemetery to honor the Confederate dead. The master of ceremonies, Colonel George B. Guild, said, "We are here to remember those gallant spirits who, forgetting self, gave their lives as sacrifice to our cause . . . and returned no more." A large crowd was in attendance and floral arrangements abounded.

1886, MEMPHIS

The cornerstone of the Schlitz Brewing Company's $65,000 warehouse at the corner of Main Street near the Louisville & Nashville depot was laid in an imposing public ceremony. The cornerstone was filled with a variety of coins and paper bills, some of them Confederate, and copies of local newspapers. The building's architect was C. G. Rosenplaenter, who practiced in Clarksville and Memphis as well as in Indianapolis.

1887, SAVANNAH

The town's first professional baseball team announced it would withdraw from the Southern Baseball League due to poor attendance at home games. This made the league a four-team association, with clubs in Atlanta, Nashville, Memphis, and Birmingham.

1908, NASHVILLE

William Howard Taft, later the 27th president of the United States, laid the cornerstone of the Academic Building at Fisk University. The structure, designed by Nashville architect Moses McKissack, was made possible by a gift from philanthropist Andrew Carnegie. It later served as the university library.

1917, CLARKSVILLE

Sheriff Walker of Montgomery County com-

plained that the daily allowance of 50 cents per prisoner for food was not enough. Wartime inflation had outpaced the limit set by the legislature. Flour, which had formerly sold for $5 to $6 a barrel, now sold for $15, and molasses had gone from 9 cents to 45 cents a gallon. If nothing was done, the sheriff predicted that the Montgomery County Jail would become a "losing proposition."

1973, OAK RIDGE

Researchers announced the "conclusive identification" of element 104, the first pinned down since element 103 had been added to the chart in 1961. Dr. C. E. Bemis, Jr., said, "We don't see any practical use for the element at the moment. But, that doesn't mean there won't be in the future."

1993, NASHVILLE

The Shelby County Commission filed suit to force the state to reinvestigate Elvis Presley's 1977 death. The suit held that Dr. Charles Harlin had failed to take late-breaking information into account.

MAY 23

1836, WASHINGTON, D.C.

President Andrew Jackson signed the Treaty of New Echota, providing for the removal of the Cherokee Nation from Tennessee and Georgia. It was to be the final solution to this particular Native American "problem."

1864, DIXON SPRINGS

David Burford, a member of the Tennessee Senate from 1829 to 1835, died at his home.

Burford had little formal education, having attended school for only six months. After moving to Tennessee in 1799, he worked as a journeyman tanner and later established his own tannery in Carthage, Smith County. In time, he moved to a farm in Dixon Springs. He served as a second lieutenant in the Seventh Regular Army in the War of 1812. He remained loyal to the Union in the Civil War and served as quartermaster at Fort Pickering in Memphis.

1973, MEMPHIS

A berserk gunman with a 30.06 rifle opened fire on Kansas Street, killing five and wounding four. The assailant, David Sanders, 30, then holed up in the Kansas Package Liquor Store.

Of the five killed, four were black and one was a police officer.

Police used tear gas to force Sanders out of the liquor store. He was then quickly killed in a barrage of shotgun fire.

MAY 24

1862, FORT WARREN, BOSTON

Confederate colonel Randal McGavock, a prisoner of war, wrote in his journal that "the notorious scoundrel and liar, Parson Brownlow of East Tennessee made a visit to the Fort today. . . . Brownlow sent for Lt. Col. White of Hamilton County, East Tennessee, and offered to parole him. . . . He also sent for Colonel Lillard and Lieutenant Colonel Odell of East Tennessee and made the same offer to them. They are not required to take the oath but to go home and not take up arms again."

Lillard and Odell did not endorse the offer.

1886, MEMPHIS

The Shelby County Court approved the payment of poll taxes owed by Richard Haynes and Lois Jones. They paid their delinquent taxes in wildcat pelts.

1887, ATHENS

Arlie Cook of Loudon County was attacked by a wild boar as she passed the home of Sam Wilson. Her screams brought men, who scared the boar off. Cook was severely lacerated and bruised and suffered a dislocated shoulder, but it was thought she would survive.

MAY 25

1866, NASHVILLE

Male African-American citizens had their right to serve as witnesses in Tennessee trials legitimated.

1887, MEMPHIS

At the annual meeting of the local chapter of the Tennessee Society for the Prevention of Cruelty to Children and Animals, it was disclosed that over the last seven years, the society had chronicled 5,628 cases of cruelty of all kinds. For 1886–87, it reported 853 cases of cruelty to animals, including cockfights, bear-baiting, and dogfights.

According to the *Memphis Daily Appeal*, "So vigorous had been the dealings of the society with some cruel parents and others that just now they had nominally little to do, and they know of none needing their care."

1917, MEMPHIS

According to a story in the *Memphis Commercial Appeal*, Mrs. W. A. Carnes, temporary chair of the Mothers Day Nursery, had announced the appointment of community chairmen to aid in the raising of funds. "It will mean a place for the women to leave their children while they are at work in the North Memphis factories," she said, "and will also be a place where children can be taken for the day when the women are forced to do the man's work when they are called to the colors."

MAY 26

1865, CUMBERLAND PLATEAU

Troops of the Fourth Tennessee Mounted Infantry, part of the United States Army in the weeks after Appomattox, captured Confederate guerrilla leader and terrorist Champ Ferguson. He was imprisoned in Nashville for later trial.

1892, KNOXVILLE

Evangelist Sam Jones gave this advice to African-American preachers: "The colored preacher ought to be the whitest man in his race. I have seen lots of good, true colored preachers but when the devil gets a hold of one in the pulpit he can make him do a lot of harm."

On political matters, Jones advised blacks, "The least you have to do with politics the better you will come out."

1935, CHATTANOOGA

The first (and last) All-Southern Conference for Civil and Trade Union Rights was scheduled to be held at a hall owned by a local African-American. But American Legionnaires, fearful of "reds," pressured the owner to stop the 100 delegates, including Myles F. Horton, from having their meeting.

MAY 25, 1987,
CHATEL-CHEHERY, FRANCE
Russell Hippe, chairman of the Tennessee Historical Commission, led a delegation of Tennesseans in placing a plaque in the small French town near the battleground where Alvin C. York had conducted himself so heroically during World War I. The photo above shows York in 1940, shaking hands with Jesse Laske, movie executive, and closing the deal for the movie of York's life starring Gary Cooper.

It was a biracial meeting as well, which only added to the fears of "red revolution." According to the *Chattanooga Daily Times*, "The debacle of the All Southern Conference was at the hands of the American Legion opposition, which radicals think will really prove a triumph for red propaganda purposes."

Conference members claimed the action by the Legionnaires was "unofficial Hitlerism."

As the meeting broke up, Horton made it known that the members would reassemble in Cleveland. It was a ruse—the All-Southern Conference continued at the Highlander Folk School in Grundy County. The Legionnaires went on a wild-goose chase through Benton and Polk Counties.

Freedom of assembly, speech, expression, and association apparently meant little to the Legionnaires, who claimed to be in support of "100-percent Americanism."

1993, NASHVILLE

The Tennessee New Gay and Lesbian Coalition brought suit in an effort to have the Volunteer State's anti-sodomy law repealed.

MAY 27

1819, HAMILTON COUNTY

At the Brainerd Mansion near what is now Chattanooga, President James Monroe visited an Indian missionary settlement and was enthusiastic in his praise. Under the guidance of the missionaries, Cherokees were taught the English language and the blessings of Western civilization.

Such niceties would no longer matter in the 1830s, when many of the same Cherokees were sent west on the Trail of Tears.

1874, MEMPHIS

The Second Circuit Court granted a writ of replevin so the remaining members of an old volunteer fire company, Invincible No. 5, could again have their fancy silver-plated hose carriage from the 1850s. The mayor had earlier made it available to a black fire company in the Ninth Ward, an action the aged white firemen could not abide. The carriage featured five silver bells and three oil paintings depicting David Crockett, former captain Joseph Holst, and the ringing of the Liberty Bell in Philadelphia.

1887, CHATTANOOGA

Mr. Woods, an employee of the Chattanooga Stove Works, was eager to end his day's work and became careless as he was filling a mold, pouring the molten iron into his boot. According to one newspaper account, "The flesh was fairly roasted from the bone while the foot was almost entirely burned off. The poor fellow's agonizing screams were heard squares away. . . . It is thought he will die."

1892, MEMPHIS

Offices and equipment of the civil rights paper published by Ida B. Wells were destroyed by an agitated white mob.

Wells was out of town when the vandalism occurred. Upon hearing the news, she was convinced that a return trip to the Bluff City would be a bad idea. She moved to Chicago, where she continued her civil rights struggles for the next 39 years.

1933, UNICOI

Two hundred white enrollees in the Civilian Conservation Corps arrived to establish Camp Cordell Hull. They pitched tents in a downpour and made preparations for their work of protecting and conserving the forests.

Company 1455 was most likely the first CCC company in Tennessee. It lived up to what became the CCC motto: "We Can Take It." The boys of the CCC built most of Tennessee's first state parks, such as Pickett, Big Ridge, T. O. Fuller, Reelfoot Lake, Norris Dam, and Cumberland Mountain, among others.

1967, NASHVILLE

Only days after the Butler Act was repealed, John T. Scopes appeared in town. He was participating in the making of a documentary about the 1925 "Monkey Trial." Scopes said, "I was a mathematics teacher and didn't teach evolution. Had they put me on the witness stand at the trial I would have had to testify that I wasn't an evolution teacher." When asked to explain a few paragraphs in a text dealing with evolution, he said, "I simply taught the students that one progressed from one order to a higher level."

The documentary was being produced by WDCN-TV and Eugene Dietz of *The Tennessean*.

1973, NASHVILLE

At a reenactment of the December 1864 Battle of Nashville, the Yankees won again, despite the

CCC [May 27] chow line at Pikeville

fact that Confederates outnumbered Federals four to one. Al Gatlin, leader of the First Arkansas, said, "We have to go up North to get outnumbered in these battles."

The event was sponsored by the National Re-Enactment Society.

1993, LEBANON

Olivia Seay, age 69, retired after 50 years of teaching in Wilson County.

Seay grew up in the Tuckers Crossroads community. Her grandmother and mother before her were teachers, as were her sisters and brother. She began teaching in a one-room schoolhouse in 1943. During that era of segregation, an old bread truck served as a school bus for the African-American children.

According to Seay, "To be a teacher you have to be a philosopher, the doctor, the mother and the father. And you are someone who has to bring in a lot of supplies."

MAY 28

1845, THE HERMITAGE

William Tyack, a visitor from New York, made the following observations concerning the moribund Andrew Jackson:

> His feet and legs, his hand and arms are very swollen with dropsy, which has invaded his whole system. Bandages are drawn tight around the parts most affected, to prevent as much as possible, the increase of water. He has scarcely any use of his hands. . . . He has not the strength to stand. His respiration is very short and attended with much difficulty, and the whole progress of the disease, accompanied by great suffering. He

gains sleep . . . by opiates. . . . When the dropsy commenced, the cough was extremely severe, and expectoration profuse. . . . This was followed by a loss of appetite and constant nausea and prostration. This change took place early in April; and about 1 May a diarrhoea commenced, which seemed to threaten an immediate dissolution. This continued for a few days, but fortunately reduced the swelling of the whole system. The abatement of the diarrhoea was succeeded by the swelling in all parts, with violent pain and extreme difficulty of breathing, when nature would again relieve itself as above described.

1869, MURFREESBORO

A group of excursionists arrived in town from Nashville. According to the *Nashville Republican Banner*, the party traveled aboard a brand-new Nashville and Chattanooga "palace car." The excursionists numbered nearly 100, including 75 girls from the Reverend W. E. Ward's seminary. After detraining, the group "formed in procession and marched through the principle streets of the town, perfectly dazzling the sober denizens of the burg, who crowded to doors to witness the novel spectacle. Amazement rested on every face."

After an hour's stroll, the party boarded the palace car and returned to Nashville.

1979, NASHVILLE

It was announced that out of over 1,800 arrests for prostitution in the capital city since 1976, only 30 had resulted in jail sentences. This was because of a metropolitan Davidson County ordinance that imposed only fines, and mild ones at that. According to Nashville police captain King Herndon, "Prostitutes come here from all over the country because they know they probably won't have to serve jail time."

Thus far in 1979, there had been 416 arrests for prostitution, with only two jail sentences handed down. In 1978, there were 484 arrests that resulted in only nine jail terms. In the preceding 2½ years, there had been just 115 arrests of men for soliciting prostitutes, resulting in only three jail terms. For 1979, there had been 33 such arrests, with no jail sentences.

"I try to give the men a break," said vice officer Ed Bartley, "because their arrest can lead to a divorce and family problems."

MAY 29

1849, NASHVILLE

The steamboat *America*, having left New Orleans on May 23, reached Nashville in the record-breaking time of five days, 15½ hours. The nautical distance between the two cities is 1,262 miles.

1882, KNOXVILLE

About 4:15 P.M., 200 African-American men gathered at the car shed to wait for the train. As it rolled in, the crowd of blacks gathered around the door of the first-class coach. A scuffle resulted as the conductor tried to hold them back. As he closed the door, two black women and one black man managed to get on board. Ten African-American men were on the platform, pressed up against the door by their comrades. Two constables arrived to enforce segregation, but their demands for order were met with yells from the crowd, which encouraged the 10 men on the platform to stand their ground.

It was feared that the crowd would become

unmanageable. Police reinforcements arrived. One resolute black was told to take the Jim Crow (segregated) car, get off the platform, or be jailed. He refused and was slammed into the car door by the policemen. The crowd of black males and their female supporters clustered close to the protesters and inspired them with shouts.

Ultimately, the train left the station with three civil rights protesters in the first-class section. Claiming victory, the crowd gave a yell as the train pulled out.

Their triumph, however, was brief, as segregation held sway until the middle of the 20th century.

1887, MURFREESBORO

The Methodist church held an auction and offered crazy quilts as premiums. Some quilts brought as much as $500, and the church was well on its way to financial success.

1895, COVINGTON

A crowd of between 3,500 and 5,000 witnessed the unveiling of a monument to Confederate soldiers from Tipton County. The monument, which symbolized the myth of the "lost cause," was placed on the south lawn of the courthouse.

1989, SHELBYVILLE

Lynchburg's favorite Irish lady, a streetwalker, died in nearby Shelbyville.

Fritz was a 16-year-old Irish setter. Technically, she belonged to Sunshine and Elwood Ervin. Most likely dropped off by a tourist, she became the town dog. She appeared in Jack Daniel's Distillery commercials and even had small parts in two movies. Once, during the filming of the movie *Starman* on the town square, she darted from behind the Confederate monu-

ment and howled so loudly that the filming was disrupted. Fritz was a favorite of tourists for years and made the rounds among the local churches, preferring the Methodists, who fed her well.

MAY 30

1806, KENTUCKY, JUST ABOVE THE TENNESSEE LINE

Andrew Jackson killed Charles Dickinson in a duel.

Dueling was strictly forbidden by law in Tennessee, but not in Kentucky. The two men stood 24 feet apart, Jackson wearing an oversized cloak. Dickinson, an expert marksman, fired first and hit Jackson in his ribs. Jackson took aim, but his piece misfired. He drew back the hammer, fired, and killed Dickinson.

Jackson carried the ball with him for many years, which caused him intense discomfort. Many in Nashville were aghast at the incident, which had started as a disagreement over a horse-racing bet between friends of the two duelists, then escalated to an alleged insult to Jackson's wife that he would not abide.

Had the duel taken place in Tennessee, Jackson would have been guilty of homicide.

1821, HARPETH SHOALS, CUMBERLAND RIVER

The *General Jackson*, Nashville's first steamboat, got snagged and sank 35 miles below the city.

1845, THE HERMITAGE

It was reported that a moribund Andrew Jackson "with considerable exertion . . . was enabled to finish the portrait. . . . After examining it, he remarked to Mr. [George Peter Alexander] Healy 'I am satisfied, Sir, that you stand at the

The Jackson-Dickinson duel [May 30] was portrayed in the "Coffin Handbill."

head of you profession; if I may be allowed to judge my own likeness, I can safely concur in the opinion of my family, this is the best that has ever been taken.'"

1886, MEMPHIS

A crowd exceeding 2,000 attended the opening of General Peter Tracy's "Toboggan," a 19th-century amusement ride that simulated a downhill toboggan ride.

1887, NASHVILLE

It was reported that Fannie Brown, a 19-year-old Middle Tennessee country girl of "German parentage, with fair hair, sparkling eyes and peach and cream complexion," had an abortion with the help of H. V. Bailey, a Vanderbilt medical student, and Drs. Patterson and Brantley. She had fallen "from the path of virtue" and become a harlot.

Abortions had been illegal in Tennessee since 1883. The townspeople were incensed. The physicians and the student left quickly.

MAY 31

1862, HAMILTON COUNTY

James J. Andrews, the leader of the famous Andrews Raid, escaped captivity but was later recaptured by Confederate forces. He was hanged in Atlanta, Georgia on June 7, 1862.

Quilting was a valued craft [May 29], as this picture of Nan Ross of Hawkins County demonstrates. Hers is a "crazy quilt."

The members of Andrews's raiding party were the first in the United States to receive the Medal of Honor. Walt Disney Studios later made a movie about this exploit.

1931, NASHVILLE

Dr. Carroll Gideon Bull died.

Bull was born in Nashville in 1884. He was a noted teacher at Johns Hopkins University, as well as an eminent immunologist whose work helped establish current theories and practices in the field. A plaque at the Johns Hopkins Immunology Department recalls his chairmanship from 1918 to 1931.

1946, NASHVILLE

As part of Tennessee's sesquicentennial celebration, the busts of Matthew Fontaine Maury and David Glasgow Farragut were unveiled. Comments were made by Vice Admiral A. S. Carpenter. In attendance were the mother of ex-governor Prentice Cooper, Judge Samuel C. Williams, Governor Jim McCord, and a host of onlookers.

1979, NASHVILLE

Claude Diehl accepted an out-of-court settlement of $1.1 million from WSM National Life and Casualty and California-based Buena Vista (Disney) Corporation on behalf of his partially paralyzed son, Dale.

In August 1976, Dale had been injured in a shooting-gallery accident at Opryland. He had originally sued for $10 million.

Interior of the James-Nelson Drug Store in Jackson, typical for its time, around 1910

June

JUNE 1

1540, IN WHAT IS NOW POLK COUNTY

Explorer and conquistador Hernando De Soto visited a Cherokee village named Canasoga, camping with his expedition in the open country near the town. A delegation of 20 villagers met his column, each person carrying a basket of mulberries as a peace offering.

This may have resulted in the first instance in Volunteer State history in which white men had to contend with the "Tennessee trots."

1796, PHILADELPHIA

Tennessee became the 16th state in the union.

The occasion is celebrated as Tennessee Statehood Day.

1827, MEMPHIS

British philanthropist Robert Dale Owen and radical female reformer Frances "Fannie" Wright visited the utopian community of Nashoba (Choctaw for "Wolf"), whose purpose was educating and freeing slaves.

On the occasion of their visit, a slave named Redrick forced sexual relations with another slave, Isabol. This was a gross violation of the mutual-consent rule practiced at Nashoba. Redrick was threatened with a flogging. Isabol had been denied a lock on her door, as Fanny Wright explained, because the mutual-consent rule was considered protection enough.

1870, KNOXVILLE

In an interview in the *Knoxville Daily Chronicle*, attorney John Baxter commented that the number of litigations was higher than ever. Commenting on the general state of neighborliness, Baxter noted that the "oldest inhabitant is unable to recall a period when East Tennessee was not disturbed by some personal, religious, or political controversy, conducted with such low and vulgar epithets and personal denunciations as to offend the refined sensibilities of every orderly and decent person."

JUNE 2

1845, THE HERMITAGE

Andrew Jackson's health continued to decline. According to William Tyack, a visitor from New York, "His distress suddenly became very great; and the water increasing to an alarming extent. An express was sent to Nashville, twelve miles, for surgical aid. An operation was performed by Dr. Evans with success: much water was taken from his abdomen, which produced great relief although great prostration."

1846, NASHVILLE

An editorial in the *Tri-Weekly Nashville Union* entitled "The Right Spirit in Tennessee" commented on the large number of men volunteering for the Mexican War. According to the editor,

> From Carter County to Shelby, the utmost enthusiasm prevailed, and we have not a doubt that more than ten thousand gallant sons of Tennessee have been disappointed in not being able to secure a reception. So

many have tendered their services that the privilege of being received was necessarily determined by ballot. The singular process has been witnessed of drafting men out of the service instead of drafting them into service. In some cases, we have heard of as much as $250 being offered by individuals for the privilege of taking the place of others who had been fortunate enough in the ballots, but we have heard of no such trade being made. The disappointment among those who drew blanks has been great. . . . We can truly say that the call has been most gallantly met—the result has proved that we are proud of the title of the "Volunteer State."

1909, KNOXVILLE

According to reports, it was decided at the 51st general assembly of the United Presbyterian Church that no Presbyterian minister was to marry a divorced person except on spiritual grounds. The "spiritual grounds" exception was more understood than defined.

1920, KYROCK, KENTUCKY

Frank Goad Clement, Tennessee's 42nd chief executive, was born.

Clement spent his childhood in Dickson and later became a famous orator. He was a three-time governor, including a two-year term beginning in 1952 and two four-year terms beginning in 1954 and 1962. He inaugurated new programs such as the Tennessee Department of Mental Health, the first state speech and hearing center, and long-range highway construction. He was also noted for providing textbooks for the public schools.

JUNE 3

1806, JONESBOROUGH

Thomas Lenoir, a wealthy landowner, noted in his travel journal that a girl age 13 or 14 had been locked in the Jonesborough jail for murdering her father. The girl sat comatose for days, not changing her position. It was said she had killed her father with an ax. Since the body was too heavy for her to drag, she cut it into pieces and put them in a nearby cellar. When neighbors began to ask about the whereabouts of her father, her little brother had indicated where the body could be found.

There would be no state facility to aid the mentally ill in Tennessee for another 24 years.

1864, OCCUPIED MEMPHIS

The editor of the *Memphis Daily Bulletin* drew his readers' attention to the great numbers of color and black-and-white pictures of nude women proliferating in the Bluff City. "We have long been accustomed to see such . . . hung on the walls of grog shops, club rooms, and places visited only by the male sex," he wrote, but gave the opinion that they shouldn't be displayed in shop windows where ladies and children might see them. The city government should, exhorted the editor, pass a law making such display illegal.

1917, CHATTANOOGA

In an effort to raise money to support striking textile operatives, young female workers wore union cards in their hatbands, solicited nickels, and tied tags bearing the slogan "Practical sympathy for locked out textile workers" to the clothing of donors. These "sympathy tags" were seen on passersby all over the downtown area, especially on the khaki uniforms of soldiers from Fort Oglethorpe, Georgia.

One striking female operative on the corner of Eighth and Market Streets explained to a reporter, "Just notice as you go down the street, and see if everybody ain't sympathizing with us. There's a few women all dressed up who can't see us girls when they go by. They're the folks we have been slaving for [for] nothing. . . . I look at some of these women and girls in their swell clothes and I wonder if they ever realize it's us that makes the money for 'em. No, they don't. We are just dirt under their feet, and they wouldn't so much as give us a nickel if they thought we was starving. But we are going to show 'em."

JUNE 4

1540, IN WHAT IS NOW HAMILTON COUNTY

Hernando De Soto broke camp at Ooltewah Gap and moved south, passing the site of what is now Chattanooga and heading around the north flank of Lookout Mountain. He then followed the Great War and Trading Path.

1861, HUNTSVILLE, SCOTT COUNTY

United States senator Andrew Johnson delivered a speech against secession at the courthouse. At the election four days later, Scott County voted against secession by the largest margin of any Tennessee county.

Later in 1861, in defiance of the state's leaving the Union, the county court passed a resolution and seceded from Tennessee to create the "Free and Independent State of Scott."

The city council passed an ordinance that made it unlawful for any male age 16 or older to accompany a prostitute through the streets or in a carriage. Additionally, the ordinance sought to control Knoxville's vice problem by decreeing that "it shall not be lawful for any woman or girl . . . to stand upon the sidewalk in front of the premises occupied by her or at the alley way door or gate of such premises, or sit up on the steps thereof in an indecent posture, or accost, call, or stop any person passing by, or walk up and down the sidewalk or strole about the . . . city indecently attired."

1981, BRUSHY MOUNTAIN STATE PRISON

James Earl Ray was stabbed by black inmates as retribution for his murder of Martin Luther King, Jr. He later recovered from his multiple wounds.

JUNE 5

1540, IN WHAT IS NOW CHATTANOOGA

Hernando De Soto set up camp at the Creek Indian village of Chiaha. Meanwhile, two scouts searched north of the town for gold. It was here that the Spanish first found fenced Indian villages.

When the Spanish left, 500 porters were provided by the Creek elders to help them on their way. Luckily for the Indians, no gold was discovered.

1817, PARIS, FRANCE

James N. Swancey, a young Tennessean from Williamson County, stood trial for blinding his landlord, a man named Bailly. Swancey, who admitted his actions, explained how the landlord had tried to cheat him out of all his money. According to the Paris newspaper *Constitutionnel*, the young Tennessean had become so "furious that he seized the [brandy] bottle which was on the table, shattered it on Bailly's face, and, by that blow, inflicted on him wounds which deprive him of his sight forever."

The jury voted to extend mercy to Swancey, whose passage home was provided by the small American community in the City of Lights. He returned to Williamson County, where he married and lived until his death in 1859. He never went back to France.

1824, THE HERMITAGE

In a letter to his nephew Andrew, Andrew Jackson mentioned the Tennessee legislature's nomination of him for president. Old Hickory said, "I never had a wish to be elevated to that station. . . . My sole ambition is to pass to my grave to retirement."

Jackson, however, made his first run for the presidency that same year. He was elected in 1828 and 1832.

1865, NASHVILLE

A law prohibiting Tennessee's ex-Confederates from voting took effect. It gave substance to white Democrats' feelings that they were being discriminated against by the pro-black forces of the Radical Republican Party. It also led to an intensification of KKK terrorism.

JUNE 6

1862, MEMPHIS

The *Memphis Daily Appeal*—lock, stock, printing press, and editors—left town after a naval battle on the Mississippi placed the Bluff City under Federal control. The editors kept printing the paper as they moved to the Mississippi towns of Grenada, Jackson, and Meridian, to Atlanta, Georgia, and to Montgomery, Alabama, until they were captured by Union forces in Columbus, Georgia, on April 6, 1865.

1887, COLUMBIA

Sam Jones, regionally famed evangelist, ended his Tennessee campaign with a sermon on the scripture "Whatever a man soweth so shall he reap."

"If you sow whisky what will you reap?" he asked. "Drunkards!" yelled a small boy on the platform. Jones continued,

> And what will you do with 'em when you've got 'em reaped? . . . If there is anything on the face of the earth that is utterly useless it is a drunkard. The devil is the only being that needs him. If you sow whisky you reap ballrooms and round dancing, and debauchery and lewd houses and gambling and broken hearts and bloody murders and damnation. Do you know how many murders in this beautiful town has been reaped from whisky sowing? One of your undertakers has buried forty-seven men who were murdered by whisky—when either the slayer or the slain was drunk. Haven't you had enough of it? I have.

He then preached separately, but no doubt equally, to the 500 African-Americans in attendance. His presentation was declared very effective. In the end, he collected $500 with which to continue the Lord's work.

Jones was a reformed alcoholic.

1900, MEMPHIS

The city council made the possession, use, and sale of cocaine illegal. News that Chattanooga had already taken action served as motivation for passing the ordinance.

Cocaine was typically retailed by dealers who could repeatedly purchase 500 ounces from a number of local drugstores. They then sold it in five- and 10-cent boxes similar to matchboxes. Cocaine boxes were commonly found in city jail cells, the police station, and the witness box at the courthouse. According to one account, "There are several street drummers who fill their pockets with the small white boxes and make a comfortable living by retailing it in the negro settlements. The use of it is not confined alone to the negro, but white people are also using it in large quantities."

The ordinance as finally passed forbade anyone to give or sell cocaine in amounts of less than one pound. It was assumed that few cocaine addicts or pushers could afford the going rate of $35 a pound, and that the problem would be largely solved. Surely, "Cocaine Joe" and "Sallie the Sniff" would find their lives dramatically changed.

1919, NEAR PALL MALL

Alvin C. York and Gracie Williams were married on a rock ledge in a ceremony performed by Governor Albert H. Roberts.

1845, THE HERMITAGE

Andrew Jackson, seventh president of the United States, hero of the Battle of New Orleans, Indian fighter, land speculator, plantation owner, slave trader, pioneer, duelist, attorney, judge, and 33rd-degree Mason, died.

1861, ACROSS THE VOLUNTEER STATE

Tennessee voted 104,913 to 47,238 (69 percent to 31 percent) to ratify the "Declaration of Independence" adopted by the general assembly. The Volunteer State had seceded from the Union.

Only four months earlier, a similar referendum had failed.

1888, KNOXVILLE

The entire city school board and an "immense audience of the elite of the colored society of the city" attended commencement exercises for the "colored department" of the school system, it was reported. The Reverend Job C. Lawrence officiated.

Major E. E. McCorskey, the president of the school board, commended the excellent work done by black students and teachers and the board itself. The industrial school established by Miss Emily Austin was not, the major said, "a white man's trick to get a nigger to work," but rather "the place where the young people can learn something that will be of lasting use and benefit to them."

Yet his closing remarks indicated the attitude of whites toward the black community in general: "There are many erroneous ideas which your race have which it will [be] your duty to aid in correcting. . . . Pattern [yourselves] after the virtues of the white man. . . . Never strive after that which the laws of nature and nature's God teach you is unattainable."

1968, LONDON, ENGLAND

James Earl Ray, a 40-year-old functionally illiterate escapee from the Missouri State Penitentiary, was arrested with an ersatz Canadian passport. He was returned to the United States to face charges of murdering Martin Luther King, Jr., in Memphis.

The wedding of Alvin C. York [June 7]. From left are Governor Albert H. Roberts, York, and Gracie Williams.

From the collection of Michael E. Birdwell

116 • *Every Day in Tennessee History*

JUNE 9

1887, CHATTANOOGA

In the so-called Bee Hive Store fire, two city firemen, Henry Ilwer and W. M. Peck, lost their lives.

Exactly one year later, the well-known Firemen's Fountain was dedicated in honor of the two. The fountain, which features an iron statue of a fireman, stands today as a testament to the bravery of the city's firemen. It is an excellent example of 19th-century public iron statuary.

1914, NASHVILLE

The nagging three-month barbers' strike ended. It was not customary for men to shave themselves in the late 19th and early 20th centuries.

1960, KNOXVILLE

Directed and managed by the Associated Council for Full Citizenship, sit-ins took place at downtown lunch counters. In time, these efforts integrated the downtown eateries, a favorite target of black protesters in the South.

JUNE 10

1785, DUMPLIN CREEK

The Treaty of Dumplin Creek was signed.

It was negotiated by John Sevier, the governor of the State of Franklin, and Ancoo, the chief of Chota. The treaty was credited with legalizing the settlement of a large area south of the French Broad and Holston Rivers by white people and their black slaves. Such settlement was now safer than before.

1846, MEMPHIS

Gaines' Guards, the Memphis Rifles, and the Jackson Avengers left for New Orleans aboard a steamboat to fight in the Mexican-American War. Many more died of dysentery than suffered glorious battlefield deaths.

1977, BRUSHY MOUNTAIN STATE PRISON

James Earl Ray, convicted killer of Martin Luther King, Jr., escaped with five other inmates.

JUNE 11

1856, NASHVILLE

In order to force the city to purchase proper fire halls and to avenge an insult they believed had been tendered by the city council, two volunteer fire companies, No. 1 and Deluge No. 3, went on strike.

The call of duty, however, led members to abandon the strike to aid in fighting a fire on July 9. Soon thereafter, the city fathers agreed to fund construction of the two fire halls.

1863, DEKALB COUNTY

Brigadier General John Hunt Morgan's cavalry raid into Ohio and Indiana began. The daring raid ended almost comically for Morgan, as the bulk of his 2,640-man force was captured at Buffington, Ohio.

Morgan was one of those officers whose career is more admired for its élan than its martial consequence. His military career was not of lasting significance to either the Confederacy or the annals of military history. He was later shot behind enemy lines in Greeneville while running from a Union patrol. The married Morgan was, some insist, visiting a lady-friend and was caught unaware by the Yankee soldiers. Had he been with his command, he likely wouldn't have died so ingloriously.

1886, SOMERVILLE

Telephone connections with Memphis were cut because Somerville authorities had assessed a privilege tax of 50 cents a year on telephones.

The telephone company was located in Memphis. Rather than submit to a local tax, it simply ended phone communication to Somerville.

There was no Public Service Commission in 1886.

JUNE 12

1887, NASHVILLE

According to the *Nashville Daily American*, "Old Miles Is Dead."

Old Miles, an African-American, had been a local sawyer for 30 years. He was found dead in a shed on Magazine Street where he had been cutting wood. "Old Miles was quite a character in his way, and he wore his long hair carefully tied up; while winter or summer, he was clad in an old overcoat, and in addition to his sawing utensils, always carried a large number of clothes strapped around his body."

The coroner found two pouches on the body, one with $30 worth of nickels, dimes, and quarters and the other with $32 in dimes. "The man dressed in rags and always had the appearance of being in the most destitute circumstances," the paper noted. The money was used to bury Old Miles at Mount Ararat Cemetery.

1887, KNOXVILLE

Captain Reeves of the Salvation Army made the following remarks at a religious service: "There is a man called Bill, but I will call him Will, a married man with three or four children, who last Thursday night took away from the altar two girls who were seeking God, and persuaded them to go to a saloon and another place of ill repute."

"The Captain," according to the *Knoxville Journal*, "then, for a few minutes used language that was so plain that the deaf might also understand, and a big sensation was caused."

After the meeting, Will McAffry accosted Captain Reeves and demanded an explanation of his scornful remarks. Reeves refused to be interviewed and proceeded to city hall to swear out warrants against McAffry and his brother John. No record of the trial is available. By July 20, however, the Salvation Army replaced Captain Reeves with the less combative Lieutenant Mark Morrison. No legal action seems to have been taken.

1900, CHATTANOOGA

It was reported that addicts were getting around the new law banning the sale of drugs without a prescription. They obtained their drugs from "drugstore doctors," charlatans whose "only claim to being a doctor lay in their having secured a physician's license to practice." Their offices were in the back of drugstores.

JUNE 13

1852, SKULLBONE, GIBSON COUNTY

William G. Randle, a traveling daguerreotypist, stopped at town on a Sunday. He was unable to get service at the local grocery store. Soon, as

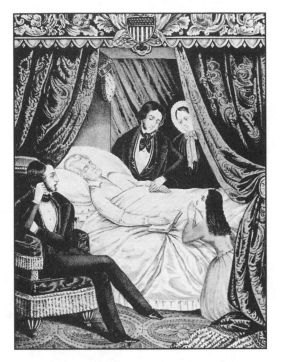

The death of Andrew Jackson [June 8]

Tennessee's chief executive: "The Ku Klux searched the train for me last night, pistols and rope in hand. Empower me to call upon the military . . . to supress all armed and masked parties. . . . I propose to fight it out."

Brownlow agreed but was not able to assemble the forces needed for such an undertaking.

1908, NASHVILLE

The Reverend H. M. DuBose, a prohibitionist, wrote a letter to *The Tennessean* suggesting a cause of black-on-white rape. The Levy Company, a maker of gin, had its major market among African-Americans. Its label featured a scantily clad white woman, with "pointed insinuations too vile to be even thought upon," according to the reverend. "This gin with its label, has made more black rape fiends, and has procured the outrage of more white women in the south than all other agencies combined. It is sold with the promise that it will bring white virtue into the brute's power."

Levy's gin was sold in Chattanooga, Nashville, and Memphis.

1953, MEMPHIS

Elvis Presley graduated from Hume High School. He soon began a 24-year career in popular music that earned him the title "King of Rock-'n'-Roll."

he reported, his party "made our way through Skullbone without seeing anything more remarkable than staring groups of women with pipes in their mouths."

1977, BRUSHY MOUNTAIN STATE PRISON

The recaptured James Earl Ray was returned to prison. He made another unsuccessful escape two years later.

JUNE 14

1868, COLUMBIA

S. M. Arnell, Governor William G. Brownlow's hatchet man, sent the following message to

JUNE 15

1849, NASHVILLE

James K. Polk died of cholera.

In his four decades of life, Polk was an attorney, a United States congressman, the ninth governor of Tennessee, the 11th president of the

United States, and the victor in the war with Mexico, when over 11 million square miles of Mexican land became United States territory. He was just 44 years old and in his 72nd day of retirement from the presidency when he died.

A large procession of firemen, students, militia, and citizens witnessed the removal of his remains from the City Cemetery to the State Capitol grounds in 1850.

JUNE 16

1838, NEAR CLEVELAND

The Reverend Evan Jones, a Baptist missionary, depicted the following scene from the removal of the Cherokee Indians, then in progress: "The Cherokees are nearly all prisoners. They had been dragged from their houses, and encamped at the forts and military places, all over the [Cherokee] Nation. . . . Houses were left as prey to plunderers, who, like hungry wolves . . . rifle houses and strip the helpless, unoffending owners of all they have on earth. Females . . . are driven on foot before the bayonets of brutal men. Their feelings are mortified by vulgar and profane vociferations. It is a painful sight."

The Cherokees probably didn't appreciate the nuances of civilization.

1941, MIDDLE TENNESSEE

Maneuvers began with elements of the regular army, the National Guard, and the Organized Reserves. George S. Patton, a commander in the maneuvers, was criticized for not coordinating better with other forces. He exhibited the same characteristic with the Third Army in France in 1944.

The exercises were popular among the people of Middle and East Tennessee, who had never seen so many troops, trucks, tanks, airplanes, and artillery pieces. The equipment destroyed land and orchards, but Patton was quoted as saying, "If there were no mistakes there would be no need for maneuvers." Farmers' wives happily cooked for the soldiers, many of whom had never been in the South before. The exercises ended June 28.

JUNE 17

1945, OKINAWA

Fitzgerald Atkinson, first lieutenant, First Tank Battalion, United States Marine Corps, and his tank crew were participating in a sweep of the enemy. Atkinson's tank had already claimed over 100 Japanese soldiers when it was hit by accurate and deadly antitank fire. Atkinson's leg was broken. He and one of his crew were burned but managed to escape the blazing tank and inch their way to a cane patch 250 yards away.

Their safety was quickly shattered by the burst of Japanese rifles. A bullet ripped through Atkinson's neck. His fellow tank man was only slightly wounded. The lieutenant's comrade could only assume Atkinson was dead and so left to find safety. In the meantime, Atkinson regained consciousness and was trying to get to his feet when another bullet hit him in the chest. He lay still for what seemed a lifetime, then tried to move his broken leg, only to have a Japanese rifleman shoot him in the shoulder.

Regaining consciousness again, he realized that eight Japanese riflemen were using him for cover as they sniped at advancing American troops.

According to Atkinson, "I decided to play dead. I shut my eyes and didn't move. I knew they were watching me for [a] sign of life, and I figured they eventually would kill me. That was what I wanted them to think. I felt like an old sieve." He moved again and was shot, this time in the hip. Atkinson managed to escape the snipers, roll into a ravine, and push himself slowly along with his good leg.

He devised a strategy for survival. Lying on his back, he lifted his good leg in hopes of attracting attention from other Americans nearby. His leg was shot at, but not hit. Finally, a fellow member of the First Tank Battalion saw the leg and recognized Atkinson's socks, which were known to be the loudest red socks in the division. However, one member of the rescuing tank crew mistook Atkinson for an enemy soldier and fired, the bullets tearing the earth near the wounded lieutenant's face. He lifted his hand in a defensive gesture, and a bullet ripped through the palm. "That," said Atkinson later, "was the last straw, my own men shooting at me! The Japs had done well enough already."

Both he and his burned comrade survived the ordeal, and navy doctors were confident they would recover.

Atkinson was the son of Mrs. Fitzgerald Atkinson of Hazlewood Avenue in Nashville. He was a graduate of Central High and had been taking classes at the University of the South when he enlisted in 1942. He was awarded the Purple Heart and was recommended for the Navy Cross and the Silver Star.

1991, NASHVILLE

Sarah Cannon, better known as Minnie Pearl, age 78, suffered a paralytic stroke. The news was not released until June 21.

She was born Sarah Ophelia Colley in Carthage on October 25, 1912. The price tag on her famous hat was for $1.98.

JUNE 18

1877, NASHVILLE

The mammoth balloon *Buffalo*, said to be the largest airship of its kind in the United States, went up with Dr. Samuel King and four others in the gondola. The crew landed in Gallatin the following day, after which another day-long flight was made that ended in Wilson County.

1958, NASHVILLE

Nashville and Davidson County voters turned down a proposal to establish a metropolitan government.

JUNE 8, 1780
William Blount was appointed Governor of the Southwest Territory by President George Washington.

1873, KNOXVILLE

John H. Ryno was born.

He began his architectural career with the firm of George F. Barber and Company in 1894 and remained there until 1908, when the partnership Barber and Ryno was formed in Knoxville.

1899, CHATTANOOGA

Chattanooga National Medical College—organized by Dr. Thomas William Haigler, an African-American, on October 3, 1898—was chartered. Haigler's facetious prescription for the ills of human existence was "grit, grace, and greenbacks."

1914, OVERTON COUNTY

Lester Raymond Flatt was born.

A bluegrass musician of great dexterity and strength, he got his first professional job on radio station KDBJ in Knoxville in 1939. He toured with Bill Monroe for a few years until 1948, when he made his first recording.

1958, MEMPHIS

A high-profit, low-overhead shoplifting racket was shut down with the arrest of Sadie Mae Draper, a 29-year-old African-American. It was a large haul for the police—in fact, the largest of its kind to that date, requiring four squad cars and a paddy wagon to cart away items of clothing. Draper had $761 in her purse, 76 sweaters, 88 silk blouses, 50 handbags, 43 pairs of curtains, uncounted stacks of men's clothing, and, it was reported, "enough sheets, towels, clocks and radios to stock a hotel." She was charged with grand larceny.

1879, KNOXVILLE

Philanthropist Emily L. Austin of Philadelphia notified the Knoxville Board of Education that generous citizens of Philadelphia, Boston, New York, Newark, and other cities in the East had donated $6,500 to aid the city in building a school for African-American children. The offer was accepted, and a seven-room brick structure named the Austin School was erected on Crozier Street (Central Avenue).

1961, KNOXVILLE

Max B. Arnstein died.

A German-born merchant, he settled in Knoxville in 1888. He opened his first dry-goods store in the city and eventually prospered. He was widely respected for his philanthropy.

1878, JERSEYVILLE, ILLINOIS

Samuel M. Shaver, Tennessee artist, died.

Shaver became recognized as East Tennessee's best representative artist about 1845. By 1851, he was a professor of drawing and painting at the Odd Fellows Female Institute in Rogersville. In 1859, he settled in Kentucky. Shaver supported the Confederacy during the Civil War; he helped establish the East Tennessee Art Association, which commissioned him to render portraits of 15 Confederate political leaders and generals. He worked in Greeneville in 1863 and in Russellville from 1863 to 1868. In the 1870s, he settled in Illinois, where he painted until he died.

JUNE 20, 1895, CHATTANOOGA
Construction began on the Lookout Mountain Incline, shown here in 1925.

1958, BOLIVAR

While campaigning for reelection to the United States Senate, Al Gore, Sr., defended his affirmative vote on civil rights legislation, saying in effect that the bill's passage was inevitable, so he did not oppose it.

1958, MEMPHIS

The press turned out to welcome Leo Seligman on his return from Hollywood, where he had been featured on a segment of the television show *This Is Your Life*.

Seligman was active in the Bluff City helping ex-convicts and parolees find employment. He managed to locate work for over 650 of them.

JUNE 22

1910, NASHVILLE

Cumberland Park was the takeoff site for the world's first night airplane flight.

1911, CHATTANOOGA

Dr. W. A. Thompson was elected president of the Tennessee Association of Colored Physicians, Surgeons, Dentists, and Pharmacists at the close of the organization's eighth annual meeting.

1925, COVINGTON

For the first time in the city's history, members of the Ku Klux Klan staged a dress parade through the streets. Attired in pointed hats and sheets, they carried burning crosses and marched silently so as to magnify the nighttime spectacle's terror.

1935, NASHVILLE

Governor Hill McAlister received the following telegram from United States congressman Walter

Chandler: "Understand you authorized changes in CCC Camp Collierview, Shelby County from White to Negro Camp. Very embarrassing to me. Please advise situation as I must act quickly."

The governor skillfully sidestepped the issue. He replied that he had no authority over the placement of Civilian Conservation Corps camps and advised the congressman to consult with the War Department.

1940, BROWNSVILLE

Elbert Williams, an African-American, attempted to register to vote. Words were exchanged and trouble developed. Later, his bullet-riddled body was found in the Hatchie River.

Williams's desire to freely participate in the American political process cost him his life.

1954, NORFOLK, VIRGINIA

Finney Thomas Carter, who represented Hamilton County in the Tennessee General Assembly from 1919 to 1921, died.

He was born in 1888 in the McMinnville area. He attended the public schools and began working as a printer's devil at the age of 13. In 1915, Carter was the cofounder of *Labor World*, the official publication of the Chattanooga Central Labor Union. He served as a linotype operator for the *Chattanooga Times* in 1926 and soon became foreman of the composing room. He left the *Times* in 1944 to become the Southern representative for the International Typographical Union, a position he held for 10 years. He returned to the *Times* in 1948 but soon left to become a newspaper publisher in Norfolk. His is a story of working-class success.

1991, MURFREESBORO

Middle Tennessee State University football fitness coach Doc Kries began using a novel approach to condition members of the team: they were fitted with special parachutes that created drag as they ran, an exercise designed to increase foot speed.

Blue Raiders senior defensive player Barry Benham said, "Doc is always coming up with something new. He'll probably have us jumping off the stadium with these things, saying it helps build up our shoulders or something."

The devices were the invention of an immigrant from Russia and were also used by the Denver Broncos, Ole Miss, the University of Maryland, and Memphis State University.

JUNE 23

1773, BRUNSWICK COUNTY, VIRGINIA

Thomas Emmerson, the first mayor of Knoxville, a judge of superior court and the Tennessee Supreme Court, a charter member of the board of trustees of East Tennessee College, and one of the founders of Knoxville Female Academy, was born.

He settled on a farm near Jonesborough and was editor of the *Washington Republican* and the *Farmer's Journal*. He died on July 22, 1837.

1863, OCCUPIED NASHVILLE

Andrew Johnson, the military governor of Tennessee, appointed Charles Davis the commissioner of abandoned property for Nashville and Davidson County. In this capacity, Davis had the power to take possession of property, collect rent, and rent or lease property as he thought proper. It isn't astonishing that most of the property the commissioner commandeered was owned by rebels.

JUNE 24

1861, NASHVILLE

Governor Isham Green Harris proclaimed the independence of Tennessee.

1886, MEMPHIS

Local African-Americans held a large and enthusiastic meeting to try to improve the general welfare of their race. The white Republican political machine was severely criticized for not appointing blacks to political offices while at the same time depending on the black vote.

1924, MEMPHIS

Forty-one prisoners broke out of the Shelby County Jail by digging a tunnel to the prison garage and knocking a hole in the wall. Their leader was appropriately nicknamed "Diggs" Nolen. Twenty-eight of the escapees were black and the remainder white. A number were apprehended immediately, while others seemed to make good their escape. Radio station WMC broadcast the news, and listeners vowed to keep a lookout for the fleeing prisoners.

1960, KNOXVILLE

African-American leaders announced a boycott of stores refusing to serve black patrons at their lunch counters. This was a step in a graduated response planned by civil rights leaders. It was hoped that, just as in the colonies before the American Revolution, concessions could be gained by economic boycott. The leaders believed that local merchants would soon feel the pinch and succumb to pressure.

1991, NASHVILLE

It was announced that 14 Tennessee counties—Campbell, Cumberland, Fentress, Grainger, Grundy, Jackson, Johnston, McMinn, Macon, Overton, Pickett, Polk, Sequatchie, and Van Buren—had populations that were 99 percent white.

JUNE 25

1855, COLUMBIA

William Banks Caperton was born.

A graduate of the United States Naval Academy in 1875, Caperton served on the USS *Brooklyn* during the Spanish-American War and was later a commanding officer in the Cruiser Squadron of the Atlantic Fleet. He conducted the Vera Cruz landing on April 21, 1914, and oversaw the American occupation of Haiti and Santo Domingo in 1915 and 1916. He was commander in chief of the Pacific Fleet in 1916. From 1917 to 1918, his diplomatic and naval operations in the South Atlantic preserved the integrity of the area for the war effort in Europe. He died December 28, 1941.

1911, CHATTANOOGA

An advertisement in the *Chattanooga Daily Times* proclaimed the availability of homes "For Colored Only." A new development in East Side Park had been set aside, claimed Wade Farrar and Company, as "the only exclusive and private Settlement for Colored People in the Entire South." The advertisement further claimed, "We are having inquiries from colored people in Atlanta, Birmingham, Nashville and Winchester and other Southern Cities, who appreciate the fact that Chattanooga was offering to her colored people advantages that no other city in the South has given them." Easy credit was offered, but readers were urged to make application soon. Whether this town or neighborhood actually developed is currently unknown.

JUNE 26

1869, MEMPHIS

An editorial in the *Memphis Daily Appeal* addressing the labor and race problems besetting the region avowed that "there is but one way out of the difficulty into which the South has precipitated by the indifference and laziness of the negro. We must employ Chinese immigrants. . . . They are just the men, these Chinese, to take the place of labor made so unreliable by Radical interference and manipulation."

The editorial also dismissed Chinese paganism, saying, "As to their heathenism, that can be readily neutralized. Destruction of their joss sticks and idols will bring ever so many converts to Christianity."

The number of Chinese immigrants was on the increase in Memphis. They worked for low wages, so they were generally welcomed by capitalist employers.

1874, MURFREESBORO

Thankful Taylor, who had been suffering from abdominal distress for five years, was relieved of her suffering when a physician pulled a snake from her mouth. It was fully 23 inches long, brown with a white belly and dark brown stripes down its sides. Quite thankful, Thankful was quoted as saying, "Doctor, I feel like a great weight has been taken from my stomach."

She had evidently ingested the reptile from a spring as she drank to cool herself while chopping cotton in the summer of 1869. She was originally diagnosed as having a large tapeworm.

1889, MEMPHIS

In the 1880s, interracial sexual relations and marriages were rigidly forbidden by law in Tennessee. However, such statutes were generally called into play in instances involving black men and white women, not the other way around.

It was reported on this day that a body of African-American men in Memphis was proposing an association to seek grand-jury indictments against more than 50 white men known to keep black mistresses. It is doubtful that these men succeeded in their "separate but equal" endeavor.

JUNE 27

1879, MEMPHIS

A group of opium smokers was arrested in Henry Wah Ying's laundry at 207 Main Street. The *Memphis Daily Avalanche* described one addict this way: "From the top of the pipe a thin blue flame ascended, and large puffs of smoke came from the lips of the girl in dreamy happiness . . . [as] she lay in transports like that of the hasheesh eater of the East."

More alarming was the reporter's contention that "the practice of opium smoking is largely on the increase not only amongst 'the gang' but also a class of people considered respectable."

Three women and Mr. Ying were dismissed from court, as there was no law against smoking opium.

JUNE 28

1846, BRAZOS ST. IAGO, MEXICO

A letter written by R. H. Smith, a Tennessee Volunteer in the war against Mexico, read in part,

"The health of the Tennesseans is comparatively good, though quite a number are indisposed on account of the bad water here."

By the end of the war, 1,721 American soldiers died of wounds, while 11,155 died of disease. No doubt, many of the latter contracted their illnesses from the bad water to which Smith referred.

1862, FORT WARREN, BOSTON

Colonel Randal McGavock, a prisoner of war since February 1862 and a roommate of fellow Tennessean Adolphus Heiman, wrote in his diary that Lieutenant Colonel Heiman became "very tight" upon the receipt of some whiskey sent by a Mrs. Thayer of Nashville.

Heiman, an architect and soldier, was reportedly "quite happy and felicitous in his remarks and singing. Just before retiring Myers [another prisoner] . . . insisted that Col. Heiman should sing the 'Old Tom Cat.' Both were undressed. The Col. commenced the song several times but without success. Finally he said; 'he would be damned if he did not sing it!' So he took one deep breath and went through it rapidly without stopping." McGavock wrote that he had not laughed so much "in an age as . . . at [Heiman's] appearance and singing."

It wasn't exactly "Jailhouse Rock," but it did relieve the boredom of captivity for a while.

1862, GIBSON COUNTY

The 12th Wisconsin Volunteers witnessed the arrival of the first train over the bridge they had constructed over a swamp near Troy Station on the Obion River.

Eight companies of the regiment had labored on the structure. Each company provided 48 men who worked a pair of two-hours shifts a day, so that between 4 A.M. and 8 P.M., there was always a 96-man crew on the job. The wooden bridge was 130 feet long. Although the trestle drooped in the middle, one proud Wisconsin soldier observed, "But such a bridge . . . ! The train got across . . . so what need we care for the looks?"

1879, MEMPHIS

The editor of the *Memphis Public Ledger* responded to talk of a pending ordinance banning the smoking of opium by writing, "Why people haven't a right to smoke opium, eat hasheesh or chew hen manure if they desire, is a question in many circles at present. Tobacco chewers, cigar smokers—especially on the street car—and bibulous people have no more right to satisfy their appetites than opium smokers."

1958, MEMPHIS

Judge John D. Martin of the United States Sixth Circuit Court of Appeals, Judge Marion S. Boyd of Memphis, and Judge William E. Miller of Nashville dismissed the suit of O. Z. Evers challenging Tennessee's segregation laws as they applied to public transportation. The effect of the ruling was to maintain segregation in all public transportation, yet this proved only a temporary setback for the civil rights movement in Tennessee.

JUNE 29

1846, BRAZOS ST. IAGO, MEXICO

A letter from a member of the volunteer Nashville Blues read in part,

> I have paid fifty cents for a cup of coffee, a dime for a small potato, fifty cents a pint for 'dog hair' [whiskey] and of all the water that was ever tasted ours is the nastiest. I could

smell it ten steps and not half try it, and before we landed we were allowed only three quarts per day. We dig a well in four or five minutes and get water that quenches thirst, but we drink more filth than is particularly agreeable. When you write as postage is so cheap I would be under obligations were you to enclose a few drinks of ice water.

The soldier's regiment was camped on an island—more of a sand bar, really. He wrote that "I . . . would be thankful once more to plant my foot on the shores of Tennessee, as this thing called being a volunteer is not the thing it is cracked up to be."

Many Tennesseans felt the same way about the Seminole Wars and the Creek Indian War.

1861, KNOXVILLE

William G. Brownlow lampooned Jefferson Davis in an editorial in the *Knoxville Whig*: "I have been expected to state in every issue of my paper that the mantle of Washington sits well on Jeff Davis! This would be a funny publication. The bow of Ulysses in the hands of a pigmy! The robes of the giant adorning Tom Thumb! The curls of a Hyperion on the brow of a Satyr! The Aurora Borealis of a cotton farm melting down the icy North! This would metamorphose a minnow into a *whale*!"

JUNE 30

1902, NASHVILLE

The Church of the Holy Family was dedicated on North College Street. It was the first Roman Catholic church in Nashville with an African-American congregation.

1908, ESTILL SPRINGS

An unusual party was given at Yellow Hammer's Nest, the home of Miss Will Allen Dromgoole. Dinner was announced by a fox horn and served under a cedar arbor. Iron-handled cutlery was used, with gourds instead of bowls. Corncob pipes were distributed after dinner. The guests included former governor Benton McMillin and his wife and Senator and Mrs. W. B. Bate. After dinner, they danced to the music of country fiddlers. Such was the social life of some of Tennessee's 19th-century rich and famous.

1914, UPPER NORWOOD, ENGLAND

The funeral of Francis Joseph Campbell was held.

Born sightless in Franklin County, Campbell was among the initial students at Tennessee's first School for the Blind, created by the general assembly in 1844. A brilliant man who worked for the cause of the disabled, Campbell even joined an expedition to climb Mount Blanc in France to demonstrate the capacities of the handicapped. King Edward VII of England bestowed knighthood upon him, making him the first Tennessean to receive such an honor.

1942, KNOXVILLE

According to African-American historian Robert J. Booker of Knoxville, Mutt, a 13-year-old Great Dane belonging to Alice Smith, the niece of well-to-do black capitalist Cal Johnson, was buried in the Johnson family plot.

Mutt was embalmed and laid out in a coffin with a plush orchid-colored satin lining. Many of the city's black citizens attended the funeral and accompanied the hearse that carried the animal to its last resting ground.

July

JULY 1

1904, MEMPHIS

Many reformers believed the city was free from vice as a result of a rigorously righteous moral-improvement movement in February. Yet when a gambling den on De Soto Street was raided by five Shelby County deputy sheriffs, 40 men and women were arrested and chained together, to be taken to the station house and booked for illegal gambling.

However, two gangsters of wide repute in the city—George Honan and Mike Haggerty—and two underlings used their pistols to disarm the deputies and set the prisoners free. Three of the deputies were fatally shot, though one lived long enough to identify Honan as his murderer.

JULY 20, 1886, COLUMBIA
A two-train wreck occurred one mile north of the Duck River station. Seven passengers and railroad employees were killed. Both locomotives were at full throttle when they met head-on in one gigantic explosion. A similar wreck would propel Casey Jones to fame on April 30, 1900. Above, a locomotive and crew in the 1890s.

Honan and Haggerty were later found guilty of murder and sentenced to death.

1909, FROM THE MIGHTY MISSISSIPPI TO THE VERDURE OF THE SMOKY MOUNTAINS

Ten years before the ratification of the 18th Amendment, statewide prohibition went into force.

The 18th Amendment, which provided for nationwide prohibition, was ratified on January 16, 1920. The 21st Amendment, which repealed the 18th, was ratified on December 12, 1933.

JULY 1, 1825, NASHVILLE

John Adams was born. He served as an officer in the First United States Dragoons during the Mexican War, just after his graduation from West Point in 1846. He was a career soldier but resigned his commission at the outbreak of the Civil War. He rose quickly through the ranks to command a brigade in the Army of Tennessee. He was killed while leading his men against a fortified Union position on the top of a hill in the Battle of Franklin on November 30, 1864. He was buried in Pulaski.

1947, MEMPHIS

The city's black cabdrivers met to discuss insurance difficulties that eventually resulted in 30 African-American cabs going out of business. They claimed that white cabdrivers were reckless, which caused the rates for black cabbies to increase. There was no corresponding rate increase for white cabbies.

1978, MEMPHIS

The Bluff City's firemen went on strike.

Forty-eight hours later, some of them stood accused of starting the unprecedented 225 fires that occurred. According to the police chief, "There is no question in my mind that [the fires] were prearranged before the strike began." Director of Fire Services Robert Walker was quoted as saying, "You just don't have spontaneous combustion just suddenly occur on July 2, 1978 and uninhabited homes all over the city suddenly burst into flames."

In the end, the firemen won their strike, just as antebellum volunteers had 118 years earlier.

1980, NASHVILLE

Tennessee House Bill 1620 became effective. It designated the square dance as the state's official folk dance.

JULY 2

1879, MEMPHIS

A letter in the *Memphis Public Ledger* wondered,

Is it not strange that [the legislative council] will allow druggists or anyone else that may desire to do so to sell morphine, opium, or any other deadly poison to anyone that may have the money to pay for it? And because the Chinese and perhaps a few others, that may wish to have an easy time for awhile by smoking their opium—something that will not kill one in five thousand to its use otherwise—morphine and opium by the mouth or skin—our city dads kick at it with both feet and say you shall not smoke your opium. We allow you, however, to take it internally or by the skin, and if it kills you, all right, we are not to blame.

1901, THE PHILIPPINE ISLANDS

During the so-called Philippine Insurrection, Allen J. Greer, second lieutenant, Fourth Infantry, charged an enemy outpost with his pistol, killing one *insurrecto*, wounding two, and capturing three with their rifles and other equipment. For his bravery, this Memphis native was awarded the Medal of Honor.

Filipino rebels were fighting to free their country from the control of the United States.

1947, MEMPHIS

Police were searching for Robert Waddy, who had allegedly dynamited a fortuneteller's house and shot two men in order to break a curse put on him by his dead wife. Frank Tetreault (a.k.a. Dr. Day, psychic reader) said Waddy had been seeing him regularly to get rid of the "evil spell." Waddy was later captured and committed to the state hospital for the mentally ill.

1966, MEMPHIS

In one of the biggest blunders in his race for the governor's chair, John J. Hooker told a small audience at the Shelby County Democratic Club that Tennesseans should try to be more like "the progressive people" in New York, California, and Illinois. He claimed Tennessee was behind in all areas of government action.

Buford Ellington won the governor's race handily.

JULY 3

1947, KNOXVILLE

On her 16th birthday, Geraldine Massengill was found chained to a bedpost at her home on 16th Street. Chief of Police Joe Kimsey said her father, a part-time fundamentalist Christian preacher, had restrained her to keep her from going outside. Geraldine claimed he beat her once a week with a belt.

She got help by writing a note on a piece of paper, crumpling it up, and tossing it out the window. A neighbor girl found it and called the police.

Geraldine had never seen a movie or been swimming. As suitable foster parents were sought, policemen took up a collection to buy her new clothes, a bathing suit, and a hairdo.

1972, MEMPHIS

"Mississippi" Fred McDowell died.

This superlative blues artist was born in Rossville on January 12, 1904. He won wide acclaim for his distinctive bottleneck slide guitar, influencing artists such as Bonnie Raitt. One of his songs, "You Got to Move," became famous after being recorded by the Rolling Stones. McDowell said of his style, "I make the guitar say what I say, if I play 'Amazin' Grace' it'll sing that too."

He was buried in Como, Mississippi. Fans contributed to provide a gravestone for this Tennessee blues legend.

JULY 4

1777, SHELBY'S FORT, NEAR BEAVER CREEK

In celebration of this, the first anniversary of the Declaration of Independence, the militia drilled and gave shooting exhibitions that included firing the fort's cannon. Then the story of the 13 colonies was told to the Cherokee guests, and the Declaration was read.

This was most likely the first Fourth of July commemoration in Tennessee history.

1805, THE CHEROKEE NATION

The Reverend Gideon Blackburn showed his Cherokee students to an assemblage of American visitors—including Tennessee governor John Sevier—and Cherokee leaders. The children were dressed in clothing donated by members of Blackburn's Presbyterian church in Maryville. They sang hymns in English and demonstrated their proficiency in arithmetic and reading.

Governor Sevier, famous for his Indian fighting, was brought to tears by the performance. He said of the ceremony, "I have often stood unmoved amidst showers of bullets from the Indian rifles . . . but this effectively unarms me. I see civilization taking the ground of barbarism, and the praises of Jesus succeeding to the war whoop of the savage."

Civilization did indeed replace barbarism, unless one counts the Trail of Tears.

1857, MARION COUNTY

The University of the South was founded at Sewanee. The first trustees, representing the Episcopal diocese in 10 Southern states, met to adopt Bishop Leonidas Polk's plan for a university sponsored by the church.

Today, the University of the South boasts Gothic Revival architecture typically associated with the Episcopal Church of the 19th century.

1868, OVERTON COUNTY

Albert Houston Roberts was born.

He was first a teacher, then a county school superintendent, and later chancellor of a division comprised of 15 county school systems.

Elected the 34th governor of Tennessee in 1919, he served for one term. Roberts is remembered for signing the bill approving the 19th Amendment to the Constitution, which allowed American women the right to vote.

1885, COVINGTON

The Covington Favorites, the town's first organized baseball team, defeated the Seaside Socials from Memphis by a 28–14 score.

While professional baseball was just getting a foothold in Tennessee, amateur contests such as this drew wide attention from fans.

1991, MEMPHIS

The National Civil Rights Museum was dedicated as a testament to the work of Martin Luther King, Jr. It was designed by an African-American architectural firm from Nashville, McKissack and McKissack.

JULY 5

1894, MEMPHIS

The violence associated with the American Railroad Union's strike against the Pullman Palace Car Company briefly spilled over into the Bluff City. A call was made to the U.S. marshal for deputies to guard mail trains. A warrant was issued for one John Phillips, an employee of the Memphis-Little Rock Railroad, who tried to cut the train's air brakes on a train conducted by H. McDonald. McDonald turned the brake on again and took the train out of the station while brandishing a revolver in his hand. He threatened to kill any man who attempted to stop him. His wife stood by his side with yet another revolver held under her apron. The train left the station under the control of Conductor McDonald.

1905, NASHVILLE

The Nashville streetcar boycott commenced. African-Americans were protesting the use of separate cars for blacks, as stipulated by state law. A similar strike also began in Chattanooga.

The civil rights movement of the 1960s was only an extension of a much longer struggle.

1905, SAVANNAH

Myles F. Horton, founder of the world-acclaimed Highlander Folk School, was born.

JULY 6

1863, OCCUPIED NASHVILLE

Lieutenant Colonel George Spalding, United States Army provost marshal, had all prostitutes rounded up and sent on a forced exile aboard the steamboat *Idahoe*. They were sent north to Cincinnati, where they were denied permission to land. By August 4, the *Idahoe*, much the worse for wear, returned to Nashville, and the prostitutes were put ashore. This led the Army Medical Corps to initiate the first system of legalized prostitution in America, complete with licenses, medical inspections, and hospitals. Prostitution was controlled by the army for the duration of the war. Afterwards, it became illegal again but did not disappear.

1886, MEMPHIS

A Shelby County financial agent by the name of Slaughter reported total receipts for the quarter to be $32,208.13, with expenditures for the same period amounting to $61,154.54.

1887, NASHVILLE

A Mr. Harwell (or Harwood) frightened Governor Robert Love Taylor. According to one newspaper account,

> The man told the governor that he was a mason and demanded to know if he was too. On being told by the governor that he was a member of that ancient order, the man said he was never in a lodge, but that his great mind had figured out all the secrets of the order. The man's eyes were flashing and his temples throbbing in a way that showed him to be in a fearful state of excitement. He told the governor that he was completely in his power, and demanded that he should devote his whole time and money to the interests of masonry, and wound up by demanding a thousand dollars from the governor.

Governor Taylor's associate, a Mr. Pearcy, "induced the man to go."

1891, NASHVILLE

The Tennessee Baptist Orphans' Home was established. It was first housed in the Hotel Delaware. In 1894, with the encouragement of Mrs. Roger Eastman, the Tennessee Baptist Convention endorsed the home as its official childcare institution, the forerunner of Tennessee Baptist Children's Homes.

JULY 7

1885, NASHVILLE

In a game between the Nashville Americans and a team from Columbus, Georgia, during the first season of the Southern Baseball League, the crowd turned surly after the umpire called a Nashville player out. Fans rushed out of the bleachers, and the situation could have gotten extremely difficult for the umpire if not for the prompt arrival of the police.

When the umpire later returned to his hotel, he was followed by a crowd of fans shouting imprecations at him.

1926, FLYNN COVE, CUMBERLAND COUNTY

"Aunt" Ezylpha Flynn celebrated her 101st birthday at her son's house. Hundreds came to pay their respects. There was only one person in the county older than "Aunt Zilph," Mrs. Hulda Eastelry, who had turned 101 in late January.

JULY 8

1865, NEW YORK NAVY YARD

The USS *Madawaska*, a steam frigate of 4,840 tons, was launched. On May 15, 1869, she was renamed the *Tennessee*.

In 1886, Rear Admiral Edward Simpson wrote, "The double decked ship *Tennessee* is the only frigate or 'first rate' that is borne on the list of vessels of the Navy as available for sea service. The ship has been for many years in commission as the flagship of the North Atlantic Station, but is now rapidly approaching that condition when the 20 per cent law will consign her to ordinary, from which she ultimately will probably [be] removed under the operation of the hammer of the auctioneer."

This, the fourth USS *Tennessee*, was sold on September 15, 1886, for $34,525.

Ezylpha Flynn at 107 years [July 7]

1897, WASHINGTON, D.C.

Isham Green Harris died.

Harris, the state's only Confederate governor, is correctly regarded as the leader most responsible for guiding Tennessee out of the Union after Abraham Lincoln's election. On April 4, 1861, in response to a request by President Lincoln for troops, Harris replied, "Tennessee will not furnish a single man for the purposes of coercion, but 50,000 if necessary for the defense of our rights and those of our Southern brothers."

After Federal forces gained control of Tennessee in 1862, Harris became a member of the staffs of Generals Albert Sidney Johnston, Braxton Bragg, and Joseph E. Johnston. When the war ended, a $5,000 bounty was offered for his capture, so he fled to Mexico, then to

England. He later returned to Memphis and practiced law before serving as a United States senator.

1898, CHATTANOOGA

An editorial in the *Chattanooga Daily Times* entitled "Vice Versus Bullets" warned that "many young fellows in the army are garnering disease and bad habits that will load them down all their future lives. The drinking places and the haunts of vice in this town are preparing more young men for invalid lives or early deaths than are Spanish bullets. . . . Remember, young soldiers that the greater number of men in the army die of disease. . . . Tens of thousands go home, wrecked, physical ruins . . . caused by reckless use of stimulants or other flagrant violations of the laws of health."

Of the 5,462 Americans who died in the Spanish-American War, only 379 were killed in battle. The rest were victims of disease.

1966, MEMPHIS

As prisoner Ernest Wells was getting his hair cut at the Shelby County Penal Farm, the barber noticed that a nail had been driven into his head. Wells said, "I don't know where it came from, but I've been having headaches." He was taken to the hospital, where a one-inch piece from an ice pick was removed from his head. Most likely, his headaches vanished.

JULY 9

1872, NEW YORK CITY

Architect George Clinton McKinzie was born.

He studied engineering at Stevens University from 1889 to 1890 and took a special course in architecture at Columbia University. He is remembered in the Volunteer State for his role in designing and erecting suburban houses for industrial workers in the newly created company town of Kingsport in 1918.

1966, NEW YORK CITY

On "Tennessee Night," Governor Frank Goad Clement addressed the 49th Lions Club International convention. The war in Vietnam was just beginning to be the target of protest, and Clement took a moment to speak his views on the topic. He said that until American fighting men were back from Southeast Asia, "they deserve to know that their country . . . [is] in back of them." He told the crowd of 20,000 that he despised draft-card-burning protesters and that "none of the three Clement boys will burn a draft card when their number is called."

"Tennessee Night" was held to honor the former mayor of Lawrenceburg, Edward M. Lindsey, who had been elected Lions Club International president. Clement told the crowd that Lindsey was "a great patriot" and that he "fit into the 'heroic mold' of distinguished men from Tennessee." Entertainment that evening was headlined by Eddy Arnold, Minnie Pearl, and Roy Acuff.

JULY 10

1817, ROBERTSON COUNTY

William Wesley Pepper, a member of the Tennessee House from 1845 to 1849, was born.

A Whig, Pepper was also a blacksmith and a judge. He is noted in Tennessee political history for a letter he sent to Democratic governor Andrew Johnson on January 25, 1854. With the letter, he included a "fire shovel of my own manufacture . . . as a memento of that fraternal regard and sympathy that should ever exist between working men, regardless of political opinion." Johnson addressed a letter to Pepper on July 17 calling the gift "the highest compliment of my life." The governor returned the gesture by sending Judge Pepper "a black cloth sack coat, which coat was drafted, cut, sewed, and pressed by my own hands." The coat made by the Volunteer State's working-class governor is on display at the Tennessee State Museum in Nashville.

JULY 11

1794, KNOXVILLE

The following advertisement by Benjamin White appeared in the *Knoxville Gazette*: "*Take Notice—Ye Whisky Drinkers.* That I, the subscriber, will positively sue every person indebted to me, in 21 days from this date, if they do not make payment."

1906, UNION CITY

The suit of Lola Montez Walker against Dick Edwards for seduction and breach of promise got under way. Walker, a theatrical performer, claimed that Edwards, a nationally known oculist and prominent gentleman, had promised to marry her when the two were on a paramours' pilgrimage to New York City.

Despite the admonition from Judge R. E. Maiden that seduction could not be proven, the jury awarded Walker damages of $21,000. Confident she would never have to work again, Walker left Union City, only to learn later that the judge had reversed the jury verdict. Since she did not return for retrial, the case was dismissed, and Edwards kept his money.

1940, TIPTON COUNTY

The Pure Oil Company mysteriously began to drill on the farm of Rob Roy McGregor. Several other oil companies were also leasing land and drilling in the county. They found nothing, however, and by July 25, all drilling operations ceased.

JULY 12

1888, KNOXVILLE

The Reverend Job C. Lawrence, an African-American graduate of Maryville College and a member of the Knoxville Board of Education, "entered the private office of Major E. E. McCorskey, sneaking in the back way." The white school-board members were having a meeting. Lawrence was told he was not welcome in McCorskey's office and was forced to leave.

It was a question of social equality. More to the point, claimed the *Knoxville Daily Tribune*, "the white people of this community could not afford to give a negro a position in which he would have the authority to exercise any degree of control over the little children, the boys and girls, the young ladies and the teachers in our public schools." Lawrence had not been legally elected by the board of aldermen, claimed the editor, and the action at McCorskey's office was valid. The editorial stated that "his action in forcing his way into the presence of five white gentlemen, seated in a private office . . . may be an indication of what he might do should he take a notion to visit the Girls High school."

Lawrence's suit to attend all such meetings ultimately failed.

1920, CHATTANOOGA

The *Chattanooga Daily Times* reported, "Every

social Bolshevik . . . and anarchistic organization in the country favors suffrage [for women]; the socialist vote in New York . . . increased more than 100 percent after women got the ballot and the freakishness of the west is largely chargeable to the same influence."

1821, BEDFORD COUNTY

Nathan Bedford Forrest was born.

As a young man, he moved to Mississippi and then to Memphis. There, he became successful in the slave trade and was elected a city councilman.

He enlisted as a private in the Confederate army in 1861. He served with distinction, rising to brigadier general by July 1862. He became a consummate cavalry commander. His clash at Brices Cross Roads was called a "perfect battle" by Nazi general Erwin Rommel.

To oppose the Union League after the Civil War, Forrest helped form the Ku Klux Klan in Nashville at the Maxwell House in April 1867. He was "Grand Wizard" of the Invisible Empire, although he never once admitted being a member.

He died heavily in debt in Memphis in 1877. The log home he is said to have lived in before leaving Bedford County at age 13 is still standing near Chapel Hill.

1862, MURFREESBORO

The Ninth Michigan, the Third Minnesota, part of the Seventh Pennsylvania Cavalry, and Kentucky troops occupied the city.

However, the presence of these units was not enough to thwart Nathan Bedford Forrest's bri-gade from capturing the town by 4 P.M. the very same day (coincidentally, Forrest's 41st birthday). Included in the capture was the garrison commander, Brigadier General Thomas T. Crittenden. As a result of this dramatic raid, Union general Don Carlos Buell's advance on Chattanooga from Nashville was temporarily abandoned.

1891, BRICEVILLE, ANDERSON COUNTY

To protest the use of convict labor in the mines, 300 armed miners surrounded Tennessee Coal and Iron's prison compound and forced the

Nathan Bedford Forrest [July 13]

40 guards to release the convicts. The miners then escorted the prisoners and guards to Coal Creek (Lake City), put them aboard a train, and sent them to Knoxville. The great Tennessee miners' rebellion of 1891 had begun.

Because of this and similar actions, the convict lease system was eventually disbanded and a state coal-mining operation was opened at Brushy Mountain in 1893.

1900, COAL CREEK, ANDERSON COUNTY

R. K. Shiflett, the Tennessee commissioner of labor, was on a coal-mine inspection tour in the region. He found that the mines had adequate ventilation, except for the Thistle Mine. He also found that Tennessee Coal and Iron and the Knoxville Iron Company had steadfastly refused to recognize organized labor and would hire no union men. In fact, both companies, determined to destroy all coal-mining unions, had fired all their employees known to have joined a union.

1909, TRACY CITY, GRUNDY COUNTY

The Tracy City nine won both games of a doubleheader against the Bridgeport team. In the second game, John Bell, the hurler for Tracy City, pitched a four-hitter. Several injuries were sustained by the victorious home team.

JULY 15

1673, IN WHAT IS NOW EAST TENNESSEE

James Needham and Gabriel Arthur, a youth in his late teens, arrived at a Cherokee settlement in what is today East Tennessee. They were most probably the first white men to set foot in what is today the Volunteer State. Their purpose was to negotiate a trade agreement between the Cherokee domain and the colony of Virginia. Virginia gained beeswax, pelts, flint and bear oil.

This business opened the Cherokee Nation to goods made by white men, such as weapons, hatchets, rum, and blankets. It also worked to change the Indians from a hunting culture to one of business and trade.

1789, NATCHEZ, MISSISSIPPI

Along with 17 other men, Andrew Jackson, 22 years old, placed his hand on the Holy Bible and took the oath of allegiance to Spain. Spanish governor D. Manuel Gayoso de Lemos administered the oath. The future seventh president of the United States thus pledged he would obey Spanish law and the Catholic king of Spain and never take up arms against His Majesty.

By 1819, the hero of New Orleans was waging an unofficial war in Florida against Spain.

1863, IN THE FIELD WITH THE ARMY OF TENNESSEE

Chaplain R. F. Bunting wrote in a letter that soldiers' interest in religion was intensifying. He said that a revival held among the infantry regiments had "resulted in the conversion of several hundred souls." Unhappily, there weren't so many proselytes among the cavalrymen—perhaps because of their greater mobility, which presumably allowed them to avoid pastors.

1898, CHATTANOOGA

Many local citizens, becoming alarmed at the number of soldiers in the area and their intemperate habits, wished restrictions put on them. However, local businessmen argued that there was a great wave of prosperity because of the soldiers' presence. The Spanish-American War was already paying dividends to merchants.

1915, CHATTANOOGA

Walden Hospital, the city's first African-American hospital, was dedicated. It was located at 612–614 West Ninth Street. According to one newspaper report, "The completion of this hospital is a work of which the colored people feel justly proud. It will be conducted by colored people, and will enable the colored physicians to render better service to patients needing the advantages which a hospital affords than has heretofore been possible."

African-Americans Dr. J. N. Wheeler and his wife, Dr. Emma R. Wheeler, were the first physicians at the hospital. A historical marker commemorates the building today.

1992, GREENLAND

Roy Shoffner, a resident of Harrogate, attended a reunion of members of a squadron of two B-17E bombers and six P-38F Lightning fighters. The veterans of the so-called Lost Squadron had been forced to land their aircraft on a glacier while caught in a blinding snowstorm on July 15, 1942.

Shoffner and two partners had already accomplished the task of salvaging a P-38 trapped in the glacier 50 years earlier. It took over 15 weeks to raise the center section of the fighter, which Shoffner hoped would never end up in a museum. "Our goal," he said, "is to restore the airplane to exactly the same way it was when it left the factory in Burbank [California] in '42. We have an excellent opportunity to bring back a World War II airplane."

That airplane is stored just over the state line in Middlesboro, Kentucky.

JULY 16

1866, NASHVILLE

J. L. Hyatt and C. M. Briggs, furniture makers, became the first businessmen in Tennessee to take advantage of a state business subsidy. The assistance was in the form of the newly inaugurated convict lease system. Renting convicts was much cheaper than hiring free working men.

1866, NASHVILLE

During the debate over ratification of the 14th Amendment, conservatives in the Tennessee House of Representatives absented themselves from the proceedings. This act forced the adjournment of the legislature because there was no longer a quorum.

The sergeant at arms, with the able (and probably eager) assistance of United States colored troops, arrested two of the conservatives, A. J.

Furniture manufacturing and retail sales were important businesses in Tennessee, as this picture of the Whitelaw Furniture Company in Jackson, shows.

Martin of Jackson County and Pleasant Williams of Carter County. They were forcibly detained at the State Capitol. Davidson County Criminal Court judge T. N. Frazier granted the legislators a writ of habeas corpus. The two prisoners were set free only after the Davidson County sheriff formed a posse that stormed the State Capitol to rescue them.

1886, STAMFORD, NEW YORK

Edward Zane Carroll Judson, a.k.a. Ned Buntline, died.

Judson spent time in Nashville as editor and publisher of the *South-Western Literary Journal and Monthly Review* and *Ned Buntline's Own*. On March 14, 1846, he killed William Porterfield, with whose wife, Mary, he had committed adultery. While awaiting a court hearing, Judson was compelled to leap from the third story of City Hotel to elude Porterfield's kin. Crippled for life as a result of his fall, he was nevertheless captured and prepared for lynching. In fact, Judson would have died had he not been cut down.

Although there was no prosecution of the case, he was defamed by the local press and left Nashville for good.

Writing as Ned Buntline, Judson did much to mythologize the West with his dime novels and his promotion of Buffalo Bill Cody.

1966, NASHVILLE

It was reported in the *Nashville Banner* that Clayton "Rabbit" Veach, locally famous escape expert, had eluded the law once again. This time, after nearly being apprehended by state troopers as he stole a car, Rabbit had found the brier patch and could not be located.

Looking for Veach was almost a routine matter for Middle Tennessee lawmen. Rabbit got his nickname in 1959.

1976, KINGSPORT

The city conferred part of the Long Island of the Holston River to the Cherokee Nation. Now, a section of this sacred island is again part of the Indians' domain.

JULY 17

1776, FORT WATAUGA, IN WHAT IS NOW SULLIVAN COUNTY

Captain James Thompson's scouts returned from a reconnaissance mission to report a great number of Indians coming toward the fort. At a hastily convened staff meeting, it was determined it would be best to meet the threat head on.

1885, MEMPHIS

Though he claimed he was not a baseball fan, Judge D. P. Hadden, president of the taxing district, had this to say about the Memphis club, as reported in the *Memphis Avalanche*: "Say, does anybody read all this here baseball stuff that's in the *Avalanche*? . . . I never read nothing but the heads [headlines] and I see every time: 'Memphis Downed Again!' I'll tell you the way that Memphis club's a-playin' is doin' this town more harm than anything else. They can't win nothing, and it's spread all over the country by telegraph that they are beat. By-and-by people will begin to think everything in the city is as no account as the baseball club."

1956, MEMPHIS

A cross burning occurred in the front yard at

1256 Azalea. The house at this address had only recently been purchased by a black couple moving into the previously all-white neighborhood. There was no mistaking the message.

JULY 18

1866, NASHVILLE

The Tennessee House ratified the 14th Amendment, which extended the franchise to all African-American men. To form a quorum, conservative legislators Pleasant Williams and A. J. Martin—under detainment in the State Capitol after having declined to participate in the proceedings—were recorded as present but also as "having failed and refused" to vote. Governor William G. Brownlow immediately telegraphed President Andrew Johnson informing him of the legislature's approval of the amendment.

The amendment was proposed on June 16, 1866, and ratified on July 28, 1868.

JULY 19

1845, BRAWLEY'S FORK, CANNON COUNTY

Baptist preacher J. M. D. Cates wrote in the journal *Baptist* that during his congregation's Monday-evening meeting, "brother John Bond was preaching the unsearchable riches of Christ, and all was peace and good feeling, and a prospect of a precious meeting, [when] the enemy of God and man influenced a pious Campbellite [a member of the Church of Christ] to arise in the congregation and greatly disturb both speaker and hearers."

1856, NEAR NASHVILLE

Edward Huffaker, aeronautical engineer and flight theorist, was born.

He graduated from Emory and Henry College in Virginia and earned his master's at the University of Virginia. After turning down a doctoral scholarship at Johns Hopkins, he taught in Mississippi for a year, then returned to his home in Chuckey City and found employment as a civil engineer.

Huffaker's interest in flight began in the 1890s. With transit and stopwatch, he made scientific observations of soaring birds. He also recorded birds' weight, wingspan, and wing area. From these observations, he developed the curved wing, an essential in heavier-than-air flight.

In early 1892, news of Huffaker's small-scale gliders prompted pioneer glider builder Octave Chanute to take note. At Chanute's urging, Huffaker wrote a well-known aeronautical paper, "On Soaring Flight," in 1893. In 1900, Huffaker arranged to construct a man-carrying glider for Chanute, an effort that proved Huffaker a better theorist than a builder. Chanute, also working with Wilbur and Orville Wright, arranged for Huffaker to join the Ohio brothers at Kitty Hawk, North Carolina. Huffaker arrived in mid-July 1901. His project was doomed from the start. He had personality clashes with the Wrights, and the structural weaknesses in his glider were of such a nature that the craft was never tested.

Huffaker returned to Chuckey City to work as a surveyor and postmaster. In 1930, he moved with his daughter to Oxford, Mississippi. He remained interested in flight, at one point contacting the Smithsonian Institution about a grant to develop a flying wing. He died in 1937 at age 81. This Tennessean made important theoretical and practical contributions to the development of heavier-than-air flight.

1868, NASHVILLE

The *Nashville Daily Press* pointed out that the city's canine population had swollen to unacceptable levels. Dogs howled at night and whelped and barked in the day. As many as 50 could be seen in the space of three city blocks. The dangerous animals disturbed sleep and threatened property and life.

JULY 20

1776, FORT WATAUGA, IN WHAT IS NOW SULLIVAN COUNTY

Just 16 days after the Declaration of Independence was issued in Philadelphia, the Battle of Island Flats, the first battle of the American Revolution in the West, was fought. Colonial militia under Captain James Thompson defeated a force of Cherokees under Chief Dragging Canoe in a short but bloody conflict. This was also the turning point in the settlers' warfare with the Cherokees, who were British allies.

1863, OCCUPIED NASHVILLE

After learning that the city's deported harlots were on their way back to town, the editor of the *Nashville Daily Press* offered the following solution to the problem of prostitution: "Send them to the Great Salt Lake city; they'd make admirable latter day saints, and old Brigham [Young] would shout gloriously at their conversion. It will require the largest fraction of a century to cure the evils they have inflicted on this community and it can never be done if they are permitted to come back."

JULY 19, 1833, SHORT MOUNTAIN, CANNON COUNTY

The camp meeting sponsored by the Caney Fork Methodist Circuit came to an end. John Kelley of the Caney Fork Circuit later reported of the event that "many were the cries for mercy. Forty professed to experience the regeneration of their hearts. . . . The slain of the Lord were many." A similar Methodist revival, shown above, occurred at Short Mountain in 1914.

1864, MOBILE BAY, ALABAMA

The First Battalion, Tennessee Heavy Artillery, participated in the Battle of Mobile Bay. Ironically, the men of the First Battalion could not stop the onslaught of Commodore David Glasgow Farragut of the United States Navy, a native of Knoxville. They were captured for the fourth and last time in the war and remained in a prisoner-of-war camp until the end of the fighting.

1925, DAYTON

The John T. Scopes "Monkey Trial" ended. Scopes was convicted of teaching evolution in high school in violation of the Butler Act.

William Jennings Bryan, a three-time candidate for president, a former secretary of state, and a fundamentalist Christian orator, was the prosecutor. Clarence Darrow, who leaned more toward secular humanism, was the defense attorney. National attention focused on Dayton. There were even national radio hookups so the trial could be followed as it happened. Local merchants profited handsomely from the curious and the press.

1946, WASHINGTON, D.C.

In a letter to United States Ambassador to Peru Prentice Cooper, a Senate hopeful, perennial United States senator and Crump-machine activist Kenneth D. McKellar wrote teasingly, "I am delighted to know you like your place. I thought that you would. Lima even attracted me. . . . August the first is my Primary date and they tell me I am going to be elected, but now, I can't say for sure."

1955, NASHVILLE

Red Ace Petroleum Company took the lead in a local price war by lowering its price for regular gasoline to 16.9 cents a gallon. James W. Perkins, the president of Red Ace, said, "This is our secret weapon to end the price war." He hoped the action would show the larger gasoline companies that small, independent shops could hold their own. Meanwhile, major companies such as Gulf, Shell, Mobil, Pan-Am, and Lion kept their prices at 24.9 cents a gallon for regular and 28.9 for premium.

Kocolene Oil Company had begun the price war on July 10, rolling its prices back to 21.9 cents for regular and 23.9 for premium.

Charles J. Sanders, a local Lion Oil dealer, said he would hold his prices until any of the major corporations dropped its price, at which time he would lower his, too.

JULY 21

1776, FORT WATAUGA, IN WHAT IS NOW SULLIVAN COUNTY

The fort was attacked at sunrise. During the battle, Lieutenant John Sevier saved Catherine Sherrill as she fled from the attacking Cherokee Indians. "Bonnie Kate" later became his second wife.

The attack, led by Chief Old Abram, was unsuccessful. This was because Nancy Ward, a Cherokee woman, warned the pioneers of the coming hostilities. One settler, Mrs. William Bean, was captured by the Indians, who were bent upon roasting her alive. Nancy Ward intervened and saved her life, as she had saved the lives of those in Fort Watauga. Some Cherokees may have considered Ward a traitor, but the white pioneers considered her a heroine.

1867, NASHVILLE

A Jewish merchant named Fessenberg who complained in court about a bordello near his house managed by a "Mrs. T." Fessenberg had her arrested for disturbing the peace. In retaliation, Mrs. T. had Fessenberg arrested for selling merchandise on Sunday.

The court held Mrs. T. responsible for court costs and dismissed the charges against Fessenberg.

1877, UNION COUNTY

Samuel Smith died.

Following the Civil War, Smith, an ex-slave and a skilled blacksmith, purchased 110 acres of

Union County land. In the 1880s, he established the only school and church for blacks in the county. He was buried on his own property, which later became part of Butcher Cemetery.

1925, DAYTON

John T. Scopes, found guilty of violating the Butler Act, the state's antievolution law, was fined $100. He left Tennessee for the University of Chicago to study geology.

JULY 22

1900, SCOTT COUNTY

A race riot occurred in the black work camp of the Cincinnati-Southern Railroad.

An African-American named Will Walker had allegedly been selling illegal whiskey to black workers. Two mounted Scott County deputy sheriffs came to arrest him. Walker's fellow blacks surrounded the lawmen in an effort to stop his arrest. Shots were fired. When the smoke cleared, two blacks were dead and the two deputy sheriffs were severely wounded, one in the head, the other in the shoulder. It is said that local mountaineers then threatened to wipe out the work camp. Will Walker escaped.

1909, TRACY CITY, GRUNDY COUNTY

At the Old Soldiers' Reunion, the following itinerary was followed during the morning session: opening exercises, followed by music from a brass band, then a bicycle race for boys, then horseback riding for ladies, then more brass-band music, then an ugliest man contest, then string-band music, then an address by the Honorable James Holman, then more brass- and string-band music, then lunch on the grounds.

In the evening, the program consisted of string-band music, a drawing contest for the old soldiers, a jumping contest for men, brass-band music, an address by the Honorable John H. McDowell, band music, a contest to determine the best gelding or mare, a largest-family competition, more band music, a bicycle race for girls under 12, an apple-nibbling contest for girls under 12, an apple-eating contest for boys under 15, and a baseball game between "the Bloomers" and "the Mother Hubbards."

Later that night at the University of the South, there was a fireworks display.

1920, NASHVILLE

J. C. McQuiddy, editor of the *Gospel Advocate*, wrote, "Everybody knows that man and woman are not equal in all respects. It is clear that in some things they are equal and like, but in other respects they are unequal and unlike. I do not believe that the good women of Tennessee want the ballot; but even if they did, the question which man must determine is not affected by what women *want*, but what they *ought* to have."

The battle over the 19th Amendment was ultimately decided in favor of women's suffrage.

JULY 23

1866, WASHINGTON, D.C.

Upon receiving Radical Republican governor William G. Brownlow's news of the passage of the 14th Amendment, President Andrew Johnson signed a congressional resolution reinstating Tennessee to its former status in the Union. Tennessee's congressional contingent expeditiously resumed its place in Washington.

1913, NEAR TOWNSEND

Three children of Mr. and Mrs. John Cooper, sent into the barn to fetch eggs, were fatally bitten by rattlesnakes. Mrs. Cooper was near the river washing clothes at the time. The long absence of the three children led her to leave her 1½-year-old infant near the bank and look for them. While she was searching, the infant fell into the river and drowned. Shortly thereafter, Mrs. Cooper discovered the four tragic deaths.

1925, ROCKWOOD

Ten miners were killed in a Roane Iron Company coal-mine explosion that occurred as they were fighting a fire more than a mile under the earth. Coal mining was indeed a dangerous occupation.

1955, CARTHAGE

Cordell Hull—father of the United Nations, Nobel Peace Prize winner, secretary of state—died at 7 A.M.

JULY 24

1794, EAST TENNESSEE

A Creek war party killed John Ish at his plow in the field and scalped him within 200 yards of his blockhouse.

White settlers and their Cherokee friends hunted and captured the chief offender, Obongphohego, or "Punk Knot." His trial was set for August 1.

1864, MECHANICSVILLE, CANNON COUNTY

A contingent of William B. Stoke's Fifth Cav-

The Rooster Gang from Cannon County, 1900. Such bands entertained at festivals like the one in Tracy City [July 22].

alry, a Federal counterinsurgency force, killed Hiram Taylor "Pomp" Kersey and Jack Neely, two infamous rebel guerrilla leaders, and arrested their gangs.

Despite their records for murder and robbery, Kersey and Neely were still beardless teenagers. Flushed from a dance on Cannell Creek, they escaped by way of Sugar Tree Knob and the north side of Dick Taylor Mountain. The Fifth caught up with them and their guerrilla bands in Mechanicsville. Unionists led by William Hathaway shot the two. Their bodies were put on a platform to be displayed in Liberty. Pomp Kersey was buried in Melton Cemetery in Mechanicsville, but there is no record of Neely's burial place.

1918, CHATTANOOGA

The new Wauhatchie Pike was dedicated. It measured only 20 feet wide where it passed around the base of Lookout Mountain. It had to be widened in 1930 to accommodate the tourist business that was increasing despite the Great Depression.

According to the *Crossville Chronicle*, there were believed to be 65 army deserters holed up in "the Gulf," a rough area around the Caney Fork River in the vicinity of Bledsoe, Van Buren, and White Counties. The stories had been circulating for several weeks "and are commonly talked [about] and generally accepted as a fact." The deserters were said to be "well supplied with money, arms and food" and "threaten death to any person who attempts to arrest them." They were "desperate deserters and are determined not to be taken alive."

The report may have been sparked by the death of Thomas Walling on July 13. After deserting the army, Walling had returned to his home near the Bledsoe and Van Buren County lines to be with his sick wife. Approached by military police demanding his surrender, he refused and "pointed a Savage automatic at the soldier, who at once fired on Walling with his rifle. . . . Death was instantaneous."

Though the *Chronicle* believed shooting and murder were expected in "the Gulf" at "almost any time," there is evidence neither to confirm nor deny the existence of so large a concentration of deserters in this remote part of Tennessee.

JULY 25

1868, NASHVILLE

The Jewish League of Nashville met at the *Union and Dispatch* building to discuss political matters. In due course, it formed the "Anti-Grant Club." This action stemmed from General Ulysses S. Grant's issuance of General Orders No. 11 five years earlier, which singled out Jews for deportation from the Western theater of the war.

The following antiprohibition communication appeared in the *Memphis Commercial Appeal*: "Prohibition is Republicanism. It is Federalism. It is Centralization. It is Paternalism. It is opposed to every principle of home rule and individual liberty. In the South it is a Trojan horse relied upon by the Republican party to divide the people on a misstated moral issue in order that Republicanism and Trustism and Protectionism and Predatory Wealth may get in their deadly work."

1913, NASHVILLE

Just after midnight, while in Nashville preparing a candidate to run against incumbent mayor Hilary E. Howse, former governor Malcolm R. Patterson was caught in a raid of Mrs. M. Ray's bordello at 466 Ninth Avenue.

According to a story in the *Nashville Tennessean and American*, the governor was apprehended in a room with eight "unusually young" women

Life for railroad construction crews was difficult at best. Food was prepared in an open tent, such as this one at McGhee Station in Hawkins County.

and three young men. "According to the police," the story said, "Governor Patterson was found in a bedroom stretched across a bed, scantily clad while playing about the place were several girls, some of whom were fully dressed, while others were strictly negligee." All those in the room were taken to the station house. Bond was paid, and the prisoners were released.

Howse was supposedly enraged because Patterson was working against his reelection. The raid was said to have been "well planned" to embarrass Patterson, who was indeed remorseful.

JULY 26

1827, THE CHEROKEE NATION

After weeks of deliberation, the eastern Cherokees adopted their own constitution. It was remarkably similar to the United States Constitution.

1847, NASHVILLE

An editorial in the *Nashville Daily Union* entitled "The Volunteer State" extolled the bravery of Tennesseans who had volunteered for wars before the clash with Mexico: "It brings back the days of the last war with England [the War of 1812], when the volunteers flocked to the standard of Jackson . . . and by their numbers in proportion to our sparse population, and gallant bearing, won for their State the enviable and deserved reputation of the Volunteer State."

1925, DAYTON

After delivering his last sermon, at Southern Methodist Church, William Jennings Bryan ate a full dinner and took a nap. He died in his sleep that afternoon.

JULY 27

1881, KNOXVILLE

John Thomas O'Connor was born. As a boy, he worked nights at the Western Union office, where he had time to read borrowed books.

By 1901, he was a machinist for the Cincinnati-Southern Railroad. He became president of the Knoxville Central Labor Union and served three terms as president of the Tennessee Federation of Labor, in which capacity he lobbied against child labor. He later took up the insurance business, served as mayor of Knoxville from 1930 to 1934, and served on the city council. He was unsuccessful as a congressional candidate.

JULY 28

1863, OCCUPIED NASHVILLE

Ms. Frank Williams, one of the prostitutes recently deported by the United States Army, returned to Nashville. She had escaped from her lodgings in Louisville, Kentucky, by jumping from a second-story window under cover of night. She then obtained a United States cavalryman's uniform and a horse, rode to Nashville, and went soldiering on her own.

According to one report, "The guards arrested her . . . at the instigation of some one who discovered that she was in disguise. She stated to the Provost Marshall that she had been on picket several days. . . . She was sent to the workhouse for a few days."

1913, NASHVILLE

Before leaving for his home in Memphis, ex-governor Malcolm R. Patterson issued a "dignified statement" concerning his arrest at a house of ill fame a few nights earlier. He explained, "I want the world to know that it is my last offense, and the weakness will never again be repeated which brought upon me and mine the deep humiliation and gave to my enemies an opportunity for revenge."

Mrs. Patterson issued a statement declaring she would stand by her man: "He has been shamefully, cruelly treated and I stand with him in his hour of trouble."

Following the affair, Patterson joined the Presbyterian Church and became a teetotaler and a prohibitionist. Before his humiliation, he had been a staunch antiprohibitionist.

1916, MEMPHIS

After a hearing presided over by Judge Tom Harsh, the eccentric son of millionaire A. S. Colyar of Tennessee Coal and Iron was committed to West Tennessee Mental Hospital in Bolivar.

The younger Colyar had enjoyed a promising career at his father's newspaper, the *Nashville American*, and at papers in Knoxville and Chattanooga. He had a long history of carrying out confidence games. His activities included entering Mexico professing to be the vice president of the United States, serving as an evangelist preacher in Kentucky, and pardoning a prisoner in West Tennessee while portraying himself as Governor Thomas Rye. He left a trail of bad checks.

He apparently remained in the hospital and died there, sparing his family any further embarrassment.

1939, KNOXVILLE

The following message was written on a picture postcard of the Great Smoky Mountains with a local postmark: "It is beautiful here in Knoxville tonite [and we are] staying at a cute tourist cabin, [which] looks just like a bungalow & the room is as nice as a hotel room, radio, rug, & everything."

Examples of these early tourist cabins are rare today, having been replaced by multistory "pleasure domes" which accommodate many more people than quaint cabins.

JULY 29

1830, GAINESBORO, JACKSON COUNTY

Alvan Cullen Gillem was born.

Gillem graduated from the United States Military Academy in 1851, served as provost marshal in Nashville during the Civil War, and later served as adjutant general of Tennessee. Promoted to major general, he commanded the expedition that found and killed Confederate general John Hunt Morgan. His last active service was in the Modoc Indian War of 1873.

1878, KNOXVILLE

The Knoxville Reds defeated the heavily favored Chattanooga Roanes 6–5, the first loss ever for the Roanes. It was said that overconfident Chattanooga baseball fans lost large sums of money on the game.

Betting on sports events played on Sunday was made illegal about 10 years later.

1924, NASHVILLE

The first airmail flight from Blackwood Field to Chicago took place.

1946, ATHENS

Around 9:30 P.M., the African-American youth center "Shangri-La" was shot up by parties unknown. Sixteen young people were enjoying the facilities at the time of the attack. Police found holes in the windows and a few spent .22 shells but said they had no idea who fired the shots.

1966, NASHVILLE

It was announced that 1.2 million Tennesseans were working, an all-time record to this date. Some 87,000 jobs had been added to the state's economy in just one year.

JULY 30

1862, COLUMBIA

United States Army general James S. Negley wrote that "the country is swarming with guerrillas."

A Union officer on cavalry patrol in Pulaski, 30 miles away, agreed, reporting that "guerrilla bands are being organized in almost every direction. They are now becoming troublesome."

1870, NASHVILLE

There was a great deal of excitement about the upcoming shooting match at the racetrack, in which the best shootist was to win a purse of $100. According to one newspaper story, "Doubtless the attendance will be large and a good deal of money will change hands on the result." The winner is not known.

JULY 31

1850, CARTER COUNTY

Two-time governor Robert Love Taylor was born. In the 1886 gubernatorial contest, "Our Bob" won the Democratic nomination and his brother Alf the Republican nomination. The election's theme was "the War of the Roses"—the Republicans used a white rose as their symbol, while the Democrats employed a red rose. Both candidates were accomplished fiddle players and often entertained the crowds at their debates with musical renditions.

Our Bob won the election and became known as "the Pardoning Governor." When evangelist Sam Jones, a reformed alcoholic, rebuked him for pardoning so many prisoners, Taylor replied by saying, "If it hadn't been for the pardoning power of God Almighty, you, Sam Jones, would have been in hell long ago."

Taylor's philosophy of life is best summed up in his comment, "I believe in the gospel of sunshine and the religion of love."

He was also Tennessee's governor from 1897 to 1899. While serving as a United States senator, he died of an attack of gallstones on March 31, 1912.

1885, MEMPHIS

Black deacons and members of Washington Street Baptist Church obtained an injunction restraining the Reverend W. A. Brinkley.

On the night of July 22, Brinkley had taken the church membership list and—without authority—read it aloud in the church, asking each member in turn whether he or she was a member of any secret or local organization, such as the Masons, in competition with the church. Upon receiving answers in the affirmative, and upon those members' declining to renounce their secret order, Brinkley struck their names from the church roll.

Several members objected to being dealt with in so summary a fashion. Brinkley, they said, was behaving like a dictator. He would not even put the question a vote. The complainants therefore asked that Brinkley be enjoined from interfering with them as members of Washington Street Baptist Church.

The outcome of the injunction is not known.

1964, DAVIDSON COUNTY

Country singer "Gentleman" Jim Reeves, his manager, and piano player Dean Manuel died when the plane they were in hit turbulent weather and crashed. Marty Robbins, Chet Atkins, Ernest Tubb, Bill Pursell, Stonewall Jackson, and Eddy Arnold all joined the search. The remains were found on August 2.

CCC Company 3464 [August 2] working on the bridge and dam at what is now Cumberland Mountain State Park

August

AUGUST 1

1794, TELLICO BLOCKHOUSE, IN WHAT IS NOW BLOUNT COUNTY

The warrior Obongphohego of the Toocauscaugee tribe was tried and found guilty of murdering John Ish. He was sentenced to die by hanging.

1867, ACROSS THE VOLUNTEER STATE

After having provided Tennessee's black males the right to vote in February 1867, William G. Brownlow, the Radical Republican candidate for governor, was reelected by a margin of 74,034 to 22,550.

Shortly afterwards, conservatives, who had failed to interest the state's African-American males in casting their ballots for the men who had previously owned them, evicted blacks from their jobs as retribution for voting for the radical platform.

1950, WASHINGTON, D.C.

In a radio address, Senator Estes Kefauver of Tennessee, the third-ranking member of the Senate Armed Forces Committee, said he was considering the introduction of a plan to permit young men to receive elementary military training without interrupting their education by universal military draft. His plan was to train boys in grades 10 through 12 during the summer. Sophomores would receive two months of training, while juniors and seniors would be in camp all summer. In this way, once the boys were drafted, they would already have learned much. According to Kefauver, "The country cannot afford to take a chance of not having trained men as they reach the age of possible military service."

Today, a similar system exists in the High School Reserve Officer Training Corps.

AUGUST 2

1885, MEMPHIS

It was reported in the *Memphis Daily Avalanche* that on July 31, African-Americans had protested police brutality in the arrest of a black by an officer named Rogers.

Hattie Manley, a 16-year-old black from Xenia, Ohio, had sat in an armchair in Court Square after a white man left it. Officer Rogers shortly thereafter yelled at her to get out of the chair. When she did not respond with the alacrity Rogers demanded, he pulled at her clothes, tearing them, and forcefully removed her from the chair. Manley objected to being so treated. She was arrested and taken to jail.

1935, CROSSVILLE

Company 3464 of the Civilian Conservation Corps was officially organized.

Its main work consisted of building what is now Cumberland Mountain State Park. In its park-building capacity, Company 3464 impounded a 30-acre lake and built a 319-foot-long combination bridge and dam. The bridge, with its 15 masonry arches and 18-foot roadway, is perhaps one of the most enduring monu-

ments of the CCC and its spirited work during the Great Depression.

1946, ATHENS

After the bipartisan GI Reform ticket was certified as the winner in the McMinn County election, goons of the corrupt Biggs-Cantrell-Crump political machine tried to falsify voting returns and declare themselves victorious. GI's who had fought for freedom and democracy in the late world war took great umbrage at the attempt to alter the returns. In retaliation, 1,000 ex-GI's and their followers engaged in—and won—a shooting battle with supporters of the Biggs-Cantrell-Crump machine. In the end, 50 McMinn County deputies and political-machine leaders holed up in the county jail were dynamited out of their temporary refuge and surrendered to the GI's. Hundreds of shots were fired, and police cars were set aflame.

According to one newspaper account, "Armed with axes, tire tools and clubs, [the GI's] hacked and bashed to wreckage a dozen automobiles that were overturned. . . . The mounting sun attracted flies to the block-long trail of blood that led from the battle-scarred jail to a little brick hospital where Drs. C. O. and W. E. Force worked wearily around the clock treating the casualties."

Governor Jim McCord initially ordered the State Guard to Athens but thought better of it and rescinded his orders. Attorney General Tom Clark was ordered to start an investigation of the gun battle.

AUGUST 3

1911, CHATTANOOGA

According to the *Chattanooga Daily Times,*

"Boys under 21 years of age are not to be allowed to visit houses of ill-fame for any purpose." This city ordinance was strictly enforced, with violations resulting in the arrest of both the boys and those who encouraged such visits.

1935, RED BOILING SPRINGS, MACON COUNTY

The *Red Boiling Springs News* described the many entertainments enjoyed by visitors at the resort, such as "tacky parties," in which participants dressed in mismatched old clothes. A prize was given to the most outrageous costume. Also popular were mock trials, scavenger hunts, and so-called womenless weddings, in which men dressed as brides and bridesmaids.

1950, ACROSS THE VOLUNTEER STATE

Tennessee's first primary election without a poll tax in 50 years took place. Many believed this "free" election deprived the Crump political machine of the power to control elections.

AUGUST 4

1794, TELLICO BLOCKHOUSE, IN WHAT IS NOW BLOUNT COUNTY

After being convicted of the murder of John Ish, the warrior Obongphohego was taken on horseback to the execution spot. Because he was so tall, it was feared his feet would touch the ground. Obongphohego was asked to stand on the horse while the noose was tightened. As the sheriff was fastening the rope over the tree limb, Obongphohego lost his balance and was hanged by the executioner, who held the other end of the rope.

Interestingly, Alexander Ish, John's son, had been informed that an Indian named Will I Omough, and not Obongphohego, was his father's murderer, but that the tribe thought it best to surrender Obongphohego because he was rather a simpleton.

1885, MEMPHIS

The Reverend R. M. Countee's house at 12 Dean Avenue was mobbed at 2 A.M.

Countee was the pastor of Tabernacle Baptist Church and the publisher of a Negro weekly newspaper called *The Living Way*. He claimed his troubles had begun at the July 24 meeting of the Memphis Lyceum, when a debate was held over the question, "Resolved, That societies as conducted in Memphis retard rather than advance the moral status of our race." Countee argued in the affirmative. Before making his argument, he stated that he had no intention of revealing the secrets of any fraternal order.

On July 31, the debate continued, the Reverend B. A. Imes arguing the affirmative. Imes, a contributing editor to *The Living Way*, tried to read from a number of books exposing some of the secrets of the Masons. His attempt was cut short when the audience rushed the podium and tore the books from his hands. The meeting ended in a fistfight.

Then, in the July 30 issue of *The Living Way*, an article appeared exposing some of the nomenclature and titles of the Masonic order.

All was quiet until the white-masked mob appeared at Countee's home. The crowd kicked at the doors and threw rocks, then began shooting. Countee returned fire, then rushed out the back door and found refuge in a house on De Soto Street. The mob shot at him as he fled, but he wasn't wounded.

The next day, Countee's house was found to

be riddled with bullet holes. It was later guarded by a detachment of police and a number of friends. Several arrests were made.

1983, WASHINGTON, D.C.

Tennessee's "rigorous standards" of refusing to distribute moldy surplus cheese to low-income families put the Volunteer State's spoilage rate at 40 times the national average, said George Braley, deputy administrator for the United States Department of Agriculture's special nutrition program. Billy Bates, a state agricultural official, responded that Tennessee authorities had put 88,000 pounds of cheese in local landfills because they wouldn't give out moldy cheese to anyone.

AUGUST 5

AUGUST 4, 1900, LAFOLLETTE

A strike began at the LaFollette mines over the company contract, which required the men to pledge not to join a union in order to work at the mines. The photo above shows the viaduct and coke ovens at LaFollette in 1911.

1882, KNOXVILLE

The mortuary report for July 1882 showed the following causes of death: consumption, one white; diphtheria, one black; diarrhea, one white; dysentery, one white; typhoid, two white, one black; gastritis, one white; heart attack, one white; inflammation of the bowels, one black; inflammation of the brain, one white, one black; jaundice, one black; acorbutus, one white; unknown causes, one white, two black; and whooping cough, one white, two black. Totals for the city that month were 19 white deaths and 15 black deaths.

1885, MEMPHIS

A large number of African-Americans assembled at Avery Chapel in the evening. The purpose of their meeting was to discuss the conduct of Officer Rogers during his recent arrest of a young black girl, Hattie Manley. One speaker claimed it was a well-known fact that Rogers did not confine his outrageous behavior to black people. He advised a respectful protest.

In the end, the protesters concluded that Rogers would not have treated a white lady the way he had treated Manley. Moreover, if he had, his actions would have been declared an outrage against Memphis society.

1950, WARTRACE

It was announced that the Medley triplets, age 19, were all engaged to be married. One of the girls, Martha Jean, was engaged to Orelle Hull Skelton of Lebanon, also a triplet. No date had been set for the weddings.

1950, OAK RIDGE

On the eve of the fifth anniversary of the Hiroshima bombing, three solemn pickets marched outside the Y-12 plant to protest the use of the atomic bomb. They held signs reading, "War Is Hitler and Stalin's Way of Peace" and "Let Us Try the Christ Way of Peace." There were no disturbances.

AUGUST 6

1848, ELIZABETHTON

Alfred Alexander "Alf" Taylor was born.

He lost the election of 1886—"the War of the Roses"—to his Democratic brother, the 25th governor of Tennessee, Robert Love Taylor. Alf Taylor served as a United States congressman and was inaugurated on January 15, 1921, as the 35th governor of Tennessee. The creation of the Tennessee Historical Commission, the passage of the Mother's Pension Fund Act, the expansion of power of the Railroad and Public Utilities Commission, and the equalization of property assessments for taxation all took place during his administration. He was the one successful candidate for governor between 1906 and 1923 who was not handpicked by political boss Luke Lea. He also helped still many labor disputes in the state. He died November 24, 1931.

1885, MEMPHIS

The Reverend R. M. Countee of Tabernacle Baptist Church was attacked near his home. His house had been mobbed two nights earlier.

He suspected it was a member of the Masonic order who accosted him, since the Masons feared he was going to reveal their secrets in his newspaper. Countee felt that secret societies retarded the "moral status" of the black race.

1885, MEMPHIS

A crowd of 200 baseball fans congregated in the lobby of the Terrace Hotel to imbibe and watch a representation of a game between Memphis and Nashville played out on a blackboard. Play-by-play results were received via telegraph in the hotel lobby, after which the news was written on the blackboard and pieces bearing players' names were placed on hooks representing the baseball field. The Nashville team won.

AUGUST 7

1760, IN WHAT IS NOW MONROE COUNTY

Fort Blount was surrendered to the Cherokee chief Oconostota, who had been conducting a siege of the British fortification.

The fort was constructed in 1756 and 1757 by provincial troops from South Carolina to check the advance of the French during the French and Indian War and to strengthen English influence in the Mississippi Valley.

1865, NASHVILLE

The State Convention of Colored Citizens met at an African Methodist Episcopal church to fight for political rights and civil equality, a dramatic demonstration of the desires of Tennessee's black population just four months after the Civil War. Obviously, the former slaves were not ignorant tools of the Republican Party.

1874, SOMERVILLE

Violence erupted in the wake of the previous day's election.

The election had been hotly contested, with Democrats shunning the black vote and Republicans soliciting it. Cash Warren, a prominent black politician, allegedly had an argument with a white man, Edgar Herndon, brother of the Democratic mayor of Somerville. Warren said that blacks had "plenty of lead" and weren't afraid to use it should whites try to block them from voting.

The day after the election, Warren was killed by Oscar Burton, a friend of the mayor. Burton was arrested, but the black community became incensed when he made bond. According to one report, "Negro runners were seen going in all directions to spread the news."

In the intense excitement that followed, white citizens established a patrol amidst reports that a force of 200 African-American miners was approaching Sommerville to avenge Warren's murder. The Memphis Chickasaw Guards, a white paramilitary organization, arrived at the request of Mayor Herndon, only to find the city in relative order.

AUGUST 8

1788, NEAR HOUSTON'S STATION ON NINE MILE CREEK

A party of 31 armed white men crossed the Tennessee River to gather apples in the vicinity of an abandoned Cherokee town, Citico. The Indians allowed them to ford the river with no interference. Soon, however, they attacked, throwing the whites into a panic. The men who were not immediately killed tried to retreat across the creek, but the Indians blocked their escape. In the end, 16 whites were dead and four wounded.

1904, NASHVILLE

The Tennessee Socialist Party held its nominating convention. John M. Ray of Rutherford County was chosen as the party's candidate for governor.

1916, CHATTANOOGA

In response to "labor sharks" who lured African-American laborers away from the South to work in Northern cities, the city commission passed an ordinance forbidding anyone from enticing contracted workers to leave their jobs. The ordinance's author, George D. Lancaster, said it was not intended to take away anyone's constitutional rights.

President J. Cohen of the Central Labor Union later said that the ordinance was meaningless because no worker in Chattanooga was under a contractual agreement with his employer.

1954, NASHVILLE

Television station WLAC, channel 5—today's WTVF—went on the air.

1983, STANDING STONE STATE PARK

The National Rolley Hole Marbles Tournament ended. National champions were Russell Collins and his partner, Doyle Rhoton.

AUGUST 9

1846, LOMETA, MEXICO

Colonel W. B. Campbell of Nashville wrote his uncle, David Campbell, former governor of Virginia, about his experiences in the Mexican War: "I have not the space or time to inform you of the great frauds that are perpetrated on the [United States] Government here in carrying out this war, the great prices given for old steamboats and other extravagant prices paid, no doubt to favorites or to persons who share with the officers the spoils."

1920, NASHVILLE

The anxieties felt by female opponents of suffrage were expressed in a form letter sent to members of the Tennessee chapter of the National Association Opposed to Women's Suffrage. The letter reminded the membership that the movement "carries with it more than white woman's suffrage. Linking with it are three deadly principles: 1st surrender of state sovereignty; 2nd Negro Woman Suffrage; 3rd Race Equality."

AUGUST 10

1760, MONROE COUNTY

The Fort Loudon garrison that had surrendered to Oconostota and other Cherokee chiefs was returning to Charleston, South Carolina, when it was attacked by Cherokees at the junction of the Tellico River and Cane Creek. Twenty-five whites were killed and the rest taken prisoner.

1874, NASHVILLE

A large and indignant crowd gathered near the railroad trestle over North Summer Street to witness a man brutally beating his overheated, broken-down ox in an effort to get it up and going after it had fallen from exhaustion. A policeman was called to stop the cruel treatment.

1882, KNOXVILLE

Typhoid fever claimed the life of Tom Clay.

A hardworking, honest man who had many friends and few enemies, Clay was one of the leaders of the city's 19th-century black community. He helped get out the black vote on Election Day. While in the delirium of fever, he repeated the names of the candidates in the late election.

1895, NASHVILLE

The *Nashville Banner* reported that over 4,000 women and girls held jobs in the city. Four hundred were retail and dry-goods clerks, 250 were secretaries, 75 were bookkeepers, 100 were cashiers, 300 were boardinghouse keepers, 1,500 were factory workers, and 1,600 held miscellaneous jobs.

1921, MEMPHIS

Four masked and armed men robbed the Ford Motor Company office on Union Avenue. Police had been alerted and were arriving on the scene as the desperadoes were making their getaway in a Cadillac. The robbers killed two police officers, wounded another five, and got away.

The police began pursuit, also in a Cadillac. As they approached Collierville, they were mistaken for the robbers by an armed group of vigilantes waiting on either side of the road. As the car passed, some 40 shots were fired. The car crashed. Lieutenant Vincent Lucarint was killed.

AUGUST 11

1862, NEAR BETHEL SPRINGS

The First West Tennessee Cavalry Regiment was formed. It later became the Sixth Tennessee Cavalry, United States Army, with Colonel Fielding Hurst in command.

The war pitted Tennessean against Tennessean. Not every soldier from the Volunteer State was committed to the Confederate cause.

AUGUST 12

1788, JONESBOROUGH

Believing his honor had been besmirched, a

young, passionate Andrew Jackson challenged Waightstill Avery to a duel. Avery, an attorney, had made sarcastic remarks in rebutting one of Jackson's arguments in court. Jackson issued the challenge.

The men met a few minutes after sundown in a hollow north of town. Proper distances were measured, the men took their marks, pistols were cocked—and both antagonists fired into the ozone. Jackson's honor was thus reclaimed, and Avery kept his intact. The two duelists shook hands and walked away.

1863, OCCUPIED NASHVILLE

By order of General Gordon Granger, the provost marshal notified all prostitutes in the city to report to his office on or before August 15. Furthermore, according to the *Nashville Daily Press*, upon "presentation of a surgeon's certificate and payment of five dollars, they will receive licenses. All such women found without certificate and license, after the specified date, will be arrested and incarcerated in the work-house for . . . not less than thirty days."

The first legalized system of prostitution in America had been initiated in Tennessee.

1881, FORT TULERSO, NEW MEXICO

During the Indian War of 1880–81, Sergeant George Jordon, part of a United States Cavalry unit at Carrizo Canyon, was commanding a detachment of 19 soldiers. Jordon stubbornly urged his men to hold their ground in an extremely exposed position, from which they gallantly forced back a superior number of enemy. Jordon, a native of Williamson County, was awarded the Medal of Honor for his bravery under fire.

1967, MCNAIRY COUNTY

Buford Pusser received a telephone call at home about 4:30 A.M. concerning a disturbance near the Tennessee-Mississippi line. His wife, Pauline, insisted on accompanying him.

A black car pulled out behind them at the church in New Hope. The car quickly came alongside the Pussers'. Pauline was shot in the head and killed. The black car sped down the road as Pusser pulled over and stopped. While he was attending to his wife's wound, the black car approached from the south. Gunfire hit Pauline again and shot off Buford's jaw.

To this day, the assailants are unknown.

AUGUST 13

1864, OCCUPIED NASHVILLE

The provost marshal's office arrested a cook with the First Ohio Regulars, only to discover "he" was really an attractive woman. She explained that she was weary of the female world and so had joined the army. She hoped eventually to find adventure with the cavalry. She was sent home.

There was no "don't ask, don't tell" policy in 1864.

1878, MEMPHIS

What became the great yellow-fever epidemic of 1878 claimed its first victim, Kate Bionda, the owner of a snack shop at 212 Front Street. Shortly thereafter, shops began to close, people grew rude to one another, and citizens began to leave the city in a seemingly endless procession of buggies, wagons, boats, and trains.

1920, NASHVILLE

Representative J. B. Summers, an antisuffragist representing Fayette and Haywood Counties, said during the debate over the 19th Amendment, "Mrs. [Mary Chapman] Catt [an activist and feminist] is nothing more than an anarchist. I heard her say in an address . . . in New York that she would be glad to see the day when negro men could marry white women. . . . This is the kind of woman that is trying to dictate to us. They would drag the womanhood of Tennessee down to a level of the negro woman."

AUGUST 14

1874, NASHVILLE

The Reverend A. G. Merry, pastor of First Colored Baptist Church, wrote a letter that appeared in the *Nashville Union and American*. It claimed that the Freedman's Bank was no longer working in the interest of the black community and that the bank's managers had taken advantage of black depositors.

He accused J. W. Alvord, a fellow African-American minister, of lying to the congregation at First Colored Baptist about the soundness of the bank. According to Merry, "Unless he repents of his sin (which is a great sin) hell will be his home."

Alvord, after filling his pockets with depositors' money, resigned as bank president when it became apparent the institution would fail. Out of Merry's congregation of 1,600, only a fourth were expected to recover their deposits.

AUGUST 15

1739, CHICKASAW BLUFFS

Fort Assumption was constructed by forces under the command of Jean Baptiste Lemoyne

de Bienville, French governor of Louisiana. It was the first edifice built by white men on the bluffs and the third such structure constructed by Europeans in all of Tennessee.

1935, SHARPS CHAPEL, UNION COUNTY

Some 206 boys from East Tennessee formed Company 448 of the Civilian Conservation Corps.

In April 1936, the company moved to LaFollette. There, it did soil-conservation work for the TVA at Lake Norris. It also constructed the largest earthen dam ever built by a CCC company. Thirty-seven feet at its highest point, 285 feet wide at its base, and 790 feet long, the dam required 40,000 cubic yards of earth fill.

1958, MEMPHIS

Elvis's mother, Gladys Presley, died of a heart attack. Elvis and his uncle mourned at Graceland.

AUGUST 16

1894, DICKSON COUNTY

The charter for the utopian socialist community of Ruskin was signed. Julius Wayland, the publisher of the socialist newspaper *The Coming Nation*, was the leader of the commune.

Dissatisfaction and bickering led to the complete abandonment of the colony in the summer of 1895. The site and its remaining buildings are listed on the National Register of Historic Places.

1977, MEMPHIS

Elvis Presley, "the King" of rock-'n'-roll, died at Graceland. The coroner's report listed heart disease as the cause of death. Other evidence indicated he was the victim of an overdose of a combination of drugs, all prescribed by his physician.

Presley, more than any other white performer, legitimized black blues and rhythm-and-blues for a white, middle-class audience. It was from black performers that Elvis drew inspiration and brought rock-'n'-roll to a prominence it has enjoyed ever since.

He was buried at Graceland. The mansion, open for visitation, is listed on the National Register of Historic Places.

Some insist that Elvis's death was an elaborate ruse and that he is living somewhere in splendid isolation.

1978, WASHINGTON, D.C.

James Earl Ray, serving 99 years at Brushy Mountain State Prison for the murder of Martin Luther King, Jr., 10 years earlier, testified before the House Select Committee on Assassinations during an investigation into King's murder.

The committee eventually concluded that although Ray acted alone, there was circumstantial evidence of a conspiracy. It believed there was "a likelihood" that Ray had been motivated by a standing offer of $50,000 from a white-supremacist St. Louis businessman who wanted King slain.

AUGUST 17

1786, GREENE COUNTY

David Crockett was born.

He fought in the War of 1812, serving as a scout for Andrew Jackson, whom he later opposed politically. Crockett is no doubt one of the most famous sons of the lost State of Franklin.

1861, RICHMOND, VIRGINIA

A report received by Confederate commander Matthew Fontaine Maury, a Tennessean, showed that the Volunteer State had furnished the Confederacy with 450,000 percussion caps. Many of these had been used at First Manassas the previous July 21.

1961, COCKRILL BEND, DAVIDSON COUNTY

An eight-hour revolt at the state penitentiary ended as an M-48 Patton tank threatened to obliterate rebel prisoners holed up in a brick building.

Twenty-five hostages had been taken, 17 of whom were prisoners. Governor Buford Ellington, reports said, directed the operation over the telephone. No one was hurt. Corrections Commissioner Keith Hampton boasted, "I didn't give an inch."

The two ringleaders, Charles Raymond Farra and Robert Rivers, had carried out another rebellion in March 1960.

AUGUST 18

1886, JACKSON

Eliza Wood, a black woman and a cook by profession, was arrested and placed in the Madison County Jail in Jackson. She was accused of poisoning her former employer, a Mrs. Wooten.

That evening, a mob in excess of 1,000 stormed the jail, captured the ill-fated woman, completely undressed her, and hanged her from a tree on the courthouse lawn. To the end, she proclaimed her innocence. Those who wanted to start a fire underneath the dangling body were dissuaded. Instead, they riddled Wood with shotgun and pistol fire. Her mangled body was left hanging until the next morning. One eyewitness, Madison County farmer Robert R. Cartmell, remarked in his diary, "She will poison no more."

1920, NASHVILLE

The 19th Amendment—the women's suffrage bill—passed in the Tennessee House of Representatives.

1994, BELLE MEADE

For the first time in its 93-year history, Belle Meade Country Club elected an African-American, Richard Sinkfield, to membership.

Bronson Ingram, the wealthiest man in Tennessee, was Sinkfield's sponsor. He justified his sponsorship this way: "I have felt for some time that in the world we live in this is the right thing to do, that there were people of other races or persuasions that were bringing a good deal to the table, and that the future was going to be that those people would be involved in everything that was going on."

Sinkfield, a successful Atlanta attorney, had attended Tennessee State University in his freshman year of college.

1994, NASHVILLE

Holding a Bible and a sign reading, "Boycott Gay Softball World Series," the Reverend Mel Perry began his latest protest. Perry, an outspoken pastor known for picketing everything from liquor stores to sex shops, stood in front of Cedar Hill Park, where the softball competition was taking place.

The 18th Gay Softball World Series drew 1,700 players and 2,500 fans and brought an estimated $2.6 million into Nashville.

1874, MEMPHIS

A story in the *Memphis Public Ledger* commented on the suicide of Dr. McDowell, the "famous tapeworm physician."

McDowell had advocated the use of tapeworms as a physic, or laxative. He was often seen on the streets selling "his wonderful tape worm physic" at 25 cents a bottle.

He was found in his room at the Commercial Hotel, dead from inhaling ether. His remains were sent to his relatives.

1903, NASHVILLE

The National Negro Business Men's League opened its annual meeting at the Tennessee House of Representatives. Official greetings were made by the mayor and white businessmen.

1969, FENTRESS COUNTY

Kate Bradford Stockton died.

She was the first woman to run for governor of Tennessee. Her campaign as a Socialist candidate in 1936 had been conducted on a red platform truck with speakers that was driven around the state. Stockton's campaign was a catastrophe—she won only 1 percent of the vote.

1852, NASHVILLE

During the election months, Felix K. Zollicoffer, the editor of the *Nashville Republican Banner and Whig*, took offense at remarks about Whig candidate Franklin Pierce made by the editor of the *Nashville Union*, John Leake Marling.

After exchanging challenges, the two editors

met in the street in front of Marling's office. Zollicoffer denounced Marling. Marling drew his pistol and fired the first shot, which went wild. Zollicoffer tried to shoot back, but his weapon misfired. While Zollicoffer was replacing the cap on his pistol, Marling fired again, hitting his antagonist in his right hand. Unfazed, Zollicoffer took aim and returned fire, hitting Marling in the head, a wound that was serious but not fatal.

The gunfight was over. Zollicoffer's wound was attended to at a nearby barbershop. Marling could not resume his editorial work for three months.

Freedom of speech was valued, as long as the speech was polite.

1874, MURFREESBORO

George Wade, 32, died suddenly. It was reported that Wade "had for some time been on a spree, and had become nervously prostrated. He complained the night before of severe stomach cramps and of an inability to sleep. He then took some morphine hoping to settle his nerves."

He settled them, all right.

Downtown Jackson in the late 19th century [August 18]

1942, COVINGTON

Isaac Hayes, known as "Black Moses" after his record album of the same name, was born.

A graduate of Manassas High School, Hayes cowrote over 200 songs with David Porter, including the soul classics "B-A-B-Y," "Hold On, I'm Coming," "Soul Man," and "I Thank You" for Stax Record Company in Memphis. His recording of the "Theme from *Shaft*" won an Oscar and three Grammy Awards. His career as an actor has included featured roles in movies and television.

AUGUST 21

1830, FRANKLIN

President Andrew Jackson met with the chiefs of the Chickasaws to begin a series of treaties that would remove the tribe to the Oklahoma Territory.

"Sharp Knife," as the Indians called Jackson, was the only American president to attend Indian removal negotiations.

1885, MEMPHIS

It was reported that over 3,000 workers in the Bluff City belonged to unions. A Knights of Labor spokesman claimed that the membership lists were growing daily. The cause was "the evident necessity of the workingmen protecting themselves from imposition." Memphis was, after New Orleans and Galveston, the best-organized city in the South.

1920, NASHVILLE

Debate on the 19th Amendment ended in the Tennessee Senate. A vote was scheduled for the next day.

1974, MCNAIRY COUNTY

After a busy day that included a press conference in Memphis, Buford Pusser was returning home when his new Corvette swerved off U.S. 64, shot over an embankment, crashed, and burned. Pusser was killed. Foul play was suspected but has never been proven.

AUGUST 22

1856, MEMPHIS

The first West Tennessee Fair played to a crowd estimated at 1,000. Local boosters were delighted with the fair and the income it generated for the city.

1878, NEAR SHELBYVILLE

A mob of 100 men lynched Dennis Beeler, a white tramp laborer, for allegedly committing rape.

Beeler had been captured by police and was on his way to jail when he was taken by the mob. He was hanged from a tree on which two black men had been lynched in 1872.

White men were occasionally lynched in 19th-century Tennessee, but hardly ever by an African-American mob.

AUGUST 23

1905, COLUMBIA

Columbia Military Academy opened.

In 1888, local residents had given 67 acres to the United States Army for an arsenal. Later, the Bowling Green buildings quartered troops during the Spanish-American War.

When the academy opened, 167 young white men from eight states were in attendance. Columbia Military Academy was designated an "Honor School" in 1935 by the federal government. Youth from all over the nation trained here to become military leaders, educators, and corporate heads. It was an upper-class preparatory facility.

AUGUST 24

1784, JONESBOROUGH

Leaders from the Watauga-Holston area met to form a new state. John Sevier, chosen the convention chairman, argued that they had a right to petition the United States Congress to accept the land that North Carolina was ceding to the federal government. He also indicated a willingness to negotiate for land in Virginia to be part of the new state. They agreed to meet again in a few weeks.

The "Lost State of Franklin" was on its way to being formed.

AUGUST 25

1868, NASHVILLE

The *Nashville Republican Banner* reported that masked horsemen had broken into the Franklin home of S. A. Bierfield, a young Russian-Jewish immigrant who owned a dry-goods store and was an active Republican. Bierfield tried to escape the Klansmen by hiding in a livery stable, but he was ultimately discovered and murdered.

A similar act of terrorism had taken place just 10 days earlier in Franklin.

1874, MEMPHIS

An article in the *Memphis Public Ledger* read,

"Every night several skiffs loaded with 'boys and girls' are pulled over to the Hopefield sandbar, and a regular Long Branch bathing is indulged in. The screams and laughter of the mixed crowd awake the echoes on both sides of the mighty river. It is rumored that the bathing suits used are of the Garden of Eden pattern. There are some queer and fast people residing on this Chic[k]asaw bluff."

1887, MEMPHIS

Despairing of her writing skills, African-American civil rights advocate Ida B. Wells confided in her diary, "I think sometimes I can write a readable article, and then again I wonder how I could have been so mistaken in myself. A glance at all my . . . productions pall on my understanding, they all savor of dreary sameness, however varied the subject, and the style is monotonous."

1920, NASHVILLE

Democratic governor Albert H. Roberts signed the certification paper and sent the 19th Amendment to the United States secretary of state. For all intents and purposes, American women finally had the right to vote.

1931, ASHEVILLE, NORTH CAROLINA

Tennessee financier and political boss Luke Lea and his son, Luke Lea, Jr., were convicted for their part in a North Carolina bank fraud. Before the verdict, Lea said, "I owe money—yes, but I will pay that. I cannot be imprisoned unless imprisoned for debt."

He was imprisoned, however, for bank fraud, and not for any debt but the one owed to society.

1874, GIBSON COUNTY

A mass murder occurred near Trenton in the midst of the preelection furor over the federal Civil Rights Bill.

On August 24, a large group of African-Americans had allegedly shot at two white men near the town of Picketsville, either as part of a quarrel over a 50-cent debt a black owed to a white or as retaliation for purported white depredations committed against blacks. The two white men managed to get to Picketsville to warn the inhabitants. A posse was formed, and 16 blacks were arrested and placed in the county jail at Humboldt.

Around 2 A.M. on August 26, some 100 masked horsemen broke into the jail and bound, gagged, and forcibly removed the 16 African-Americans. Half a mile out of town on Huntingdon Road, the nightriders shot six of their captives. Farther up the Forked Deer River, 10 miles off Picketsville Road, they hanged the remaining 10 blacks on tree branches.

Governor John C. Brown offered a $500 reward for the arrest of the nightriders. He also ordered the sheriff to form a posse and apprehend them. Despite the outrage in black (and some white) circles, no one was found culpable in the crime. Though there was some initial investigation by the United States attorney's office, a trial was never held. Rumors held that an armed force of 500 blacks was forming to visit death and destruction on all whites in the county. This seems to indicate the paranoia of the white community, since the existence of such a force of blacks was totally unsubstantiated.

This remains the greatest unsolved and unprosecuted mass murder in Tennessee history.

AUGUST 27

1874, MURFREESBORO

Monroe Fulton was killed by Sam Winston on the public square.

Upon entering Renshaw's Grocery, Winston met a man with whom he had once had difficulties. Winston decided to buy the man a drink to show that there were no hard feelings. The man declined, however, saying he did not drink. After enduring many annoying invitations to imbibe, the man hit Winston, knocking him to the ground. The man then left the store. Getting up, Winston drew his pistol and ran outside. In his haste, he mistakenly shot Fulton, an innocent bystander, killing him instantly with a bullet to the heart. Winston was arrested. It was rumored he would plead insanity, based on his attempt to commit suicide a few years earlier.

1966, MEMPHIS

George L. Holloway, Jr., became the first African-American in the South to be appointed regional director of the United Automobile Workers Union.

AUGUST 28

1846, NEAR CARMARGO, MEXICO

Colonel W. B. Campbell of Nashville wrote his uncle that "my whole regiment is . . . most sorely afflicted with sickness being near three hundred on the sick list, and every day one or

The law office of Judge T. M. Jones, said to be the place in Pulaski where the KKK was founded

two are laid away in eternal sleep. I have had 32 deaths in my Regiment and about 40 discharged from disease. So you see my Reg't. of one thousand is fast wasting away in this tropical climate."

1868, CINCINNATI, OHIO

In an interview with the *Cincinnati Commercial*, Nathan Bedford Forrest displayed a comprehensive knowledge of the identities of Ku Klux Klan members but carefully avoided his own connection with the terrorist organization. In fact, he emphatically denied he had any connection whatsoever with the Klan.

1874, PULASKI

A circus employee accidentally dropped a coal-oil lamp into a lion's cage he was cleaning. As the fire spread, the lion went to the far side of the cage. Thinking it safe to enter the enclosure to put the fire out, the man was attacked by the lion, which reportedly tore "the flesh from his face . . . breast, and . . . arm." He did not survive the mauling.

About 9 P.M., attorney Robin Cooper was called from a high-stakes card game at his stylish home. He drove away in his automobile with a stranger.

Two days later, his body was found in a creek about a mile away. There were no witnesses to the crime and no plausible suspects. A number of motives were pursued by the Nashville detective squad, centering on speculation that Cooper was heavily in debt to professional gamblers, that he had run up against bootleggers, or that he was involved in a deceitful business venture. In the end, the crime went unsolved.

AUGUST 29

1793, IN WHAT IS NOW BLOUNT COUNTY

At daylight, an Indian war party estimated at 300 made an attack on Henry's Station. Two men named Tedford and Jackson were inspecting the corn crop when the attack began. They hastened to the fort but found their access blocked by the Indians. Tedford was captured and put to death. Jackson stripped off his clothing to ensure he would not be entangled in the brush, where the Indians could kill him. His tactic worked. He soon arrived at John Craig's Station, and the alarm was spread.

1805, WYTHE COUNTY, VIRGINIA

William G. Brownlow was born.

Brownlow was editor of the *Knoxville Whig*, a staunch Unionist during the Civil War, Reconstruction governor of Tennessee from 1865 to 1869, and a United States senator from 1869 to 1875. He died in Knoxville on April 29, 1877.

Many Tennesseans were elated and many others saddened by his passing.

1851, NEAR SCHAFFHAUSEN, GERMANY

While on a tour of Europe, Tennessee resident Randal McGavock noted in his diary, "I saw for the first time two men kiss each other. They both had long moustaches and look very queer to me, although it is the custom in Germany."

1863, OCCUPIED NASHVILLE

In an impromptu speech, Military Governor Andrew Johnson affirmed that he favored the immediate emancipation of slaves. He believed this was necessary because it would help the many Tennesseans who didn't own slaves to control their destiny and their government.

According to Johnson, "The slave aristocracy had long held their foot upon the . . . necks [of those who didn't hold slaves], and exacted heavy tribute from them, even robbing them of free speech. Let the era of freedom be henceforth proclaimed to the nonslaveholders of Tennessee!"

1994, NASHVILLE

Avon N. Williams, famous civil rights attorney, state senator, and architect of the metropolitan school desegregation plan, died at age 72.

Born in Knoxville in 1921, Williams attended college at age 14. He began his law practice in Knoxville in 1949 but moved to Nashville by 1955. There, he established a partnership with Z. Alexander Looby, another black civil rights advocate. During the 1960 sit-ins in Nashville, he gave students legal advice and arranged for bail. He was also responsible for the longest civil rights suit in Tennessee history, a desegregation case that was filed in 1955 and won in 1971.

1830, KNOXVILLE

City resident Dr. John C. Gunn registered his book with the United States Court for the Eastern District of Tennessee. *Gunn's Domestic Medicine, or Poor Man's Friend in the Hours of Affliction, Pain and Sickness* was a medical self-help reference work designed for pioneers on the Southern and Western frontiers who had no access to a physician. Written in unpretentious English, it contained information about diseases and remedies for rheumatism, pox, sore legs, piles, epileptic fits, dysentery, venereal diseases, and many other afflictions. The popular book, which went through 19 printings by 1840, also supplied information on a wide range of medical matters including bloodletting, kidney stones, cramps, palsy, mumps, earaches, pregnancy, the inducement of abortion, scurvy, pleurisy, and basic anatomy. *Gunn's Domestic Medicine* taught readers about medicinal herbs and the preparation of herbal potions to help cure illnesses.

Gunn condemned tobacco as "absolutely disgusting, offensive, and *highly injurious to health*" but at the same time declared the following about the addictive drug opium: "Without this valuable and essential medicine, it would be next to impossible for a Physician to practice his profession, with any considerable degree of success; it may not improperly be called, the monarch of medicinal powers, the soothing angel of moral and physical pain."

1835, NASHVILLE

A public meeting of the "Committee of Vigilance" called for a boycott of abolitionist literature and goods sold by famed, wealthy New York merchant Arthur Tappan, who funded the abolitionist cause. Abolitionist literature, claimed the outraged and anxious members of the committee, "incites the slaves to revolt."

It is hard to imagine that abolitionist literature could give slaves reason to revolt when practically none of them could read. Perhaps they already had enough reason to want to rebel.

1846, NEAR MONTEREY, MEXICO

Writing to his uncle, former Virginia governor David Campbell, that he had orders to raise 500 men for an attack on Monterey, Tennessee colonel W. B. Campbell noted, "Out of the one thousand that I left Nashville with, I shall be hard pressed to get 500 effective men. . . . Such is the effect of disease in my camp for ten days past. My average is about a death a day and today two have died and several more are expected to die hourly."

Campbell's regiment, under the command of a fellow Tennessean, General Gideon J. Pillow, was temporarily attached to General John Anthony Quitman's Mississippians. This pleased Campbell because the Mississippi general was "far superior to Pillow in every point . . . as a man of talents and as a military man." The colonel continued, "Gen'l. Pillow is of the smallest caliber that has ever been elevated to so high a command, although he professes to be very friendly. . . . He seems not to know what to do and is often directing and interfering in matters which he . . . has nothing to do with."

Pillow's reputation followed him through the Civil War. His plantation home in Maury County is listed on the National Register of Historic Places.

1916, SANTO DOMINGO, DOMINICAN REPUBLIC

While participating in the American military

occupation of the Dominican Republic, the 14,500-ton armored cruiser USS *Memphis* (formerly the *Tennessee*) was driven ashore by a 20-foot tidal wave caused by an earthquake 150 miles away. This ship was a total wreck. Thirty-five sailors and officers were killed in the freak accident. Some of the casualties occurred when the boiler's main pipe burst, scalding them to death.

At the beginning of World War I, the *Memphis* had been sent to Europe to save Americans. It also served as the flagship of the Cruiser Division of the Atlantic Fleet. The ship's armaments included four 10-inch guns, 16 six-inch guns, 24 three-inch guns, and four six-pounders. Her top speed was 22 knots.

After the wreck, it was determined she was not worth salvaging. Her recast bell soon graced the Church of Las Mercedes, dedicated to the patron saint of Santo Domingo.

1918, NASHVILLE

Kitty Wells, "the Queen of Country Music," was born.

One of her most famous hits was "God Didn't Make Honky Tonk Angels" (1952). She was inducted into the Country Music Hall of Fame in 1972.

1919, KNOXVILLE

Whites destroyed downtown property when their anxiety about the alleged homicide of a white woman by a black man led them to strike out at the city's African-American population. Knoxville whites joined National Guardsmen in overzealously patrolling the black community. Several lives were lost, and 36 whites were arrested for rioting. After the riot, belligerent National Guardsmen searched, confined, and generally harassed members of the African-American community.

AUGUST 31

1860, MEMPHIS

It was calculated that for the year 1859–60, some 110 steamboats had sailed from Memphis to New Orleans. This averaged about one steamboat every three days.

1908, NASHVILLE

Edward Ward Carmack was hired as editor of *The Tennessean*, owned by wealthy Republican political boss Luke Lea.

Carmack's bittern denunciations of Duncan and Robin Cooper—his and Lea's political enemies—contributed greatly to the atmosphere of hatred and suspicion that resulted in the editor's death in 1909.

Main Street of Ducktown in Polk County, 1912. Ducktown was built by the copper mining industry to house its workers.

September

SEPTEMBER 1

1823, NASHVILLE

"Singing School" teacher Allen D. Carden announced that the third session of his school was to begin soon and that he would shortly have a music printer and be able to "print music of every description in this place."

"Singing Schools" were in the business of improving congregational singing. The fact that such schools were profitable ventures may say something about the quality of congregational singing in Nashville in the 1820s.

1836, MOUNT MEIGS, ALABAMA

Nashvillian Lieutenant Henry Hollingsworth, with the Second Tennessee Volunteers on their way to fight the Seminoles in Florida, noted in his journal, "There has been much discontent among the troops about going to Florida at all, and more particularly at this season of the year, on account of sickness, climate, &c. of the place. . . . I found the men in our company in a fermentation of the Florida subject, cursing everything connected with it, threatening desertion, &c."

The troops felt this way because they had volunteered strictly for service against the remainder of the Creek Nation in Alabama, not the Seminoles in Florida. Hollingsworth inquired into the legality of the orders to march to Florida.

Volunteers from Tennessee were always careful to observe their enlistment agreements and live up to their stipulated limits.

1877, NASHVILLE

The first demonstration of a telephone in the city took place. It was conducted by members of the American Association for the Advancement of Science, then meeting in Nashville. The home of Sarah C. Polk, widow of President James K. Polk, was connected with that of A. G. Adams. The battery was located at Mrs. Polk's home. The results were successful, and both parties expressed wonderment at the device invented only a year earlier.

1885, MEMPHIS

In a Southern League baseball game, an altercation developed between the Macon manager, Price, and the Memphis manager, Ted Sullivan, over an umpire's call Price believed to be prejudiced against the Macon nine. Angry words were exchanged. Price called Sullivan a "liar and a trickster!" Sullivan, the very model of forbearance, graciously replied, "You are a gentleman." Price slapped Sullivan's face with a scorecard. According to one report, Sullivan then "threw out his right fist and a knock down that would have done credit to his cousin from Boston, John L., was the sequel. Brass buttons [police] interfered and Price was lifted from the ground."

There were no arrests. It is not thought that the Memphis manager was really a cousin of champion pugilist John L. Sullivan.

1956, CLINTON

Anderson County sheriff Glad Woodward formally asked Governor Frank Goad Clement for state aid in restoring order after rioting had occurred as a result of school integration on August 24.

1811, BRUSH CREEK CAMPGROUND, WASHINGTON COUNTY

James Nelson deeded four acres and eight poles to trustees William Nelson, William Duzan, James King, and J. R. Boring. They were to be used by the Methodist Episcopal Church to build a tent for a house of worship.

For many years, this campground for religious meetings maintained a permanent meeting tent and many family tents. During the Civil War, Colonel Robert Love's 62nd North Carolina Regiment used the site as a military campground.

1814, FORT JACKSON, MISSISSIPPI TERRITORY

David Hunt, a private in Captain George Mabourn's company, was charged with posting the following bad poem on the fort gate:

> Look Below we are the Boys.
> That Fear no Noise,
> Nor Orders that we hear,
> Eighteen days more,
> And then we go,
> And you cant find us here,
> For home we go,
> Or be found in gore,
> And never come here no more,
> To Suffer as we and many others have Before,
> Liberty Street.

The hapless Hunt told two lieutenants that he and some others intended to march home on October 20, the date their 90-day tour was up. This, together with Hunt's allegedly contemptuous language to officers, led to his court-martial and death sentence. He was one of six soldiers convicted of mutiny and executed.

In 1813, mutinies had been constant, caused by low provisions and a conviction among Tennessee soldiers that they had signed up for only 90 days. During the mutinies of November and December 1813 and January 1814, General Andrew Jackson had been forced to let men march without fear of reprisal. By September 1814, he had evidently changed his mind.

The deaths of the six Tennessee militiamen were used as negative political advertising against Jackson in 1828 when he ran for president the second time. The story was printed on what is known to history as the "Coffin Handbill."

1885, CHATTANOOGA

The Chattanooga Light Infantry, an African-American militia unit and drill team, received its new uniforms. The elite paramilitary outfit was composed of 36 members.

1962, NASHVILLE

Sergeant Alvin C. York died.

SEPTEMBER 3

1844, SWEETEN'S COVE, MARION COUNTY

Jones Chamberlain Beene, State Senator in the 49th General Assembly (1895-1897), was born. He attended elementary school at Sweeten's Cove and secondary school at Jasper. During the Civil War he served in Company A, 4th Tennessee Infantry, and saw action in the battles of Murfreesboro, Chickamauga, and Missionary Ridge. He was also held as a prisoner of war in Nashville for seven months. After the war, he was a railroad depot agent, express agent, and telegraph operator. He became vice-president of the local electric light company and was a

The death of six Tennessee soldiers by order of Andrew Jackson, as depicted in the "Coffin Handbill" [September 2]

director in the First National Bank. He was the operator of the *Statesman Democrat* of South Pittsburg, a Justice of the Peace, and a postmaster.

1863, KNOXVILLE

Dr. J. G. M. Ramsey related an interesting Civil War incident from this day in his autobiography. The master of the Confederate soldiers' shoe shop in Knoxville discovered that the railroad cars carrying his supplies were stranded in Sweetwater because there was no engine to pull them. A Confederate captain suggested that the master cobbler employ muscle instead of steam to bring the cars to Knoxville. Soldiers from Tennessee, Alabama, Kentucky, North Carolina, and Georgia pushed and pulled the cars 22 miles in two days. They later found an engine that pulled the cars on to Atlanta. A Confederate soldiers' shoe shop was then established there.

1915, MEMPHIS

Peter Chapman, better known as "Memphis Slim," was born.

He began playing the piano professionally be-

Tennessee militia drilling in full uniform, late 19th century

fore the age of 16. The chief influence on his work was Roosevelt Sakes. In 1940, he joined Big Bill Broonzy, whose group included Sonny Boy Williamson, the renowned harmonica player from Jackson. He later formed his own group. In 1960, he toured Europe, eventually settling in Paris. Perhaps his most famous song was "Every Day I Have the Blues." He died in France on February 26, 1988.

1956, NASHVILLE

An article in *The Tennessean* headlined "Cold Steel, Gas Hold Off Yelling Mob" described how Governor Frank Goad Clement had sent elements of the Tennessee National Guard to patrol the streets of Clinton wearing gas masks and carrying rifles with fixed bayonets. The night before, the soldiers had quietly put down a riot and established roadblocks to search motorists for weapons and dynamite.

Many white residents were angered by court orders to racially integrate the schools in Clinton.

1957, NASHVILLE

It was announced that Charles E. Morton, a Nashville car salesman for 20 years, would head up the only Edsel dealership in the capital city. His goal was to sell 600 Edsels. His showroom was to open near the Cain-Calloutee Kaiser agency and Jim Reed Chevrolet. The Edsels, in storage in Murfreesboro, were being rushed to Nashville for the opening the next day.

SEPTEMBER 4

1813, NASHVILLE

Andrew Jackson received his second wound,

this one from a shootout at the City Hotel on the square.

His quarrel was with Jesse and Thomas Hart Benton. A dispute had arisen between Jesse Benton and friends of Jackson over the manner in which a duel should be performed. Braggadocio fed an escalating war of words in which Jackson believed himself to be challenged by Benton, even though Jesse denied it. Thomas Hart Benton sided immediately with his brother and made public remarks that Jackson interpreted as a challenge.

On September 4, Jackson and his friend John Coffee were walking from the Nashville Inn to the post office when they saw Thomas Hart Benton in the doorway of the City Hotel "looking daggers" at them. The Benton brothers were waiting. Soon, a confused shootout and knife fight began. Jackson received a painful bullet wound to his shoulder, Jesse Benton acquired several stab wounds, and Thomas Hart Benton fell backwards down a flight of stairs. Jackson carried the bullet with him for 30 years.

1835, BROWNSVILLE

Five men comprising a lynch court tried Anson Moody for being a slave stealer. Taken from his home in the dead of night, he was given 100 lashes with a "cow skin" and branded with the letter *R* on his cheek.

Moody later sued in the United States Circuit Court for West Tennessee. He won a judgment of $2,000 and costs against the five men.

1864, GREENEVILLE

Confederate general John Hunt Morgan was abruptly roused by Federal soldiers. They asked him to surrender, but having done so once previously, Morgan declined. Instead, he dashed out of the home of Mrs. Catharine Williams—whose son was serving on Morgan's staff—hastily clad in only ordinary blue pants and a calico shirt and carrying a pistol. While running toward a fence, he was seen by Union private Andrew Campbell, who fired at him and missed. Campbell's second shot killed Morgan instantly.

1876, KNOXVILLE

Knoxville Freedmen's College was dedicated. Its antecedent was the 1863 Presbyterian Crewel School, where classes were held until more substantial facilities were built on "the Hill" in West Knoxville.

The college was designed for the education of preachers and male and female teachers. It was the first institution of higher learning for African-Americans in East Tennessee. Still operating 120 years later as Knoxville College, it is listed on the National Register of Historic Places.

1886, NASHVILLE

About 1:30 A.M., former Confederate general Benjamin F. Cheatham, recovering from a protracted illness, got up from bed and reclined in a chair by the window. A wagon went by, making a rumbling sound. The old general reportedly looked up shortly before death and said, "There go the troops, bring me my horse. I am going to the front!"

More accurate accounts indicate he whispered a few words to his wife about his children, then died quietly thereafter.

1956, CLINTON

On the first day of school integration, nearly all of the white students in town boycotted classes, while nine of the 12 eligible blacks attended. Curiously, a small group of white students, mostly girls, did go to school and initiate dialogue with the blacks.

There was no hint of panic in Foley Hill, the African-American section of Clinton.

SEPTEMBER 5

1864, IN THE FIELD

In a letter to Confederate president Jefferson Davis, Nathan Bedford Forrest expressed his plans for conducting a guerrilla war in Middle Tennessee: "If permitted to do so with 4,000 picked men and six pieces of artillery of my present command, I believe I can proceed to middle Tennessee and west Tennessee, destroy the enemy's communications or cripple it, and add 2,000 men to my command."

In the end, while Forrest proved more successful than Joseph Wheeler in overrunning isolated Union blockhouses and earthworks, his prognostications were far too assured. His raiding parties picked up minimal partisan aid, and his force did little damage to the Nashville & Chattanooga rail line. He approached no closer to the Nashville & Northwest Railroad than the Duck River.

1876, NASHVILLE

Famous English man of science Thomas H. Huxley arrived in town to visit his sister. In the evening, he made his first public address in the United States at Hume Fogg High School, where he exhorted students to study and work hard.

1885, KNOXVILLE

Members of a mob tied handkerchiefs around their faces to protect themselves from future prosecution and sent runners ahead to make sure the gas lamps were turned out. Just before 11 P.M.,

they broke into the city jail and forcibly took Lee Sellers, the suspected murderer of Edward Maines. Sellers attempted to defend himself with a razor but was overcome.

He was taken to the bridge over the Tennessee River. A rope was put around his neck, and he was raised up and dropped. Suddenly, he burst the handkerchief binding his hands, climbed the rope to the bridge's crest, and ran along the trestle. Shot after shot followed him as he ran, but none could bring him down. While Sellers lay on the beams, as many as 40 shots were fired at him. Apparently, they all missed. He continued to crawl up and down the superstructure. When there was a break in the action to procure more ammunition, Sellers moved so close to a support beam that he was hidden. The marksmen in the mob waited with cocked pistols for a glimpse of him.

In the end, he called for water. A ladder was brought, and as one man went up, Sellers turned over and dropped into the Tennessee River, dead.

This lynching was rare in that the victim was a white man.

SEPTEMBER 6

1865, WASHINGTON, D.C.

Eugenia Bate Bass married Count Giuseppe Bertinatti, an Italian diplomat, becoming Tennessee's first—and probably last—countess.

She was also born on this date in 1826, at Castalian Springs.

1874, NASHVILLE

Four members of the Melrose family began to experience symptoms of poisoning at dinner. Two of the daughters—Katie, 14, and Mattie,

16—died as a result. Mrs. Melrose and son David were severely ill. Suspicion fell on son Robert, who displayed no symptoms.

In the end, however, it was determined that one of the deceased girls had accidentally spilled arsenic pills from a commercial toxin called "Rough on Rats" into the coffee grinder while preparing the meal.

1934, DYERSBURG

In the midst of a nationwide textile workers' strike, the Dyer County sheriff telegraphed Governor Hill McAlister saying he expected a "flying squad" of textile workers from Bemis to attack the Dyersburg mill and force it to shut down. McAlister was not in, but his adjutant general told the sheriff to call if there was any real trouble.

In the end, there was neither a flying squad nor trouble of any other kind.

SEPTEMBER 7

1836, ON THE MARCH IN ALABAMA

Lieutenant Henry Hollingsworth and his men of the Second Tennessee Volunteers searched the countryside for food. Coming upon a farmhouse, they volunteered to work in return for a meal. They took on the task with vigor, churning butter and taking swigs of Hollingsworth's "tickler of whiskey" as a reward for their efforts.

Hollingsworth walked away from these frivolities and "discovered a jug setting up on a shelf and thought it looked suspicious when, picking my opportunity, I slipped it down, smelt it, then tasted, and found it to be rum. I then turned it up and took a good swig—which I took care to repeat four times and gave it to two others before I left without the old fellow's [the owner's] seeing me."

1878, MEMPHIS

Charles G. Fisher, a partner in a cotton factor concern, wrote tellingly in his diary: "God help us where will the end be?" Memphis was in the midst of a calamitous yellow fever epidemic, with an average of some 200 deaths a day. Such epidemics spurred concerns for government action to protect public health.

SEPTEMBER 8

1864, OCCUPIED NASHVILLE

On this day, the citizens of Cherry Street between Broad and Cedar were "treated to a sight . . . that . . . should be allowed no mention," according to the *Nashville Daily Press* of September 10. "A fleshy . . . *fille de joie* [girl of joy], whose sense of modesty seemed wholly to have merged in the large development of her physical charms, entirely nude from her waist heavenward, in an open hack, drove rapidly up Cherry Street. . . . As she passed the Maxwell Barracks, the hundreds of soldiers . . . set up lusty and continuous shout of admiration . . . an enthusiasm so wild and hearty that it can . . . better be imagined than described."

Because the army was administering the first legalized system of prostitution in American history, there can be little doubt as to the profession of this half-naked woman. She may have done it on a bet, or maybe she was just advertising.

1866, MEMPHIS

Charles H. Mason, the founder of the African-American Church of God in Christ, was born.

One of country music's talented singer/songwriters, Virginia Patterson, was born. Her stage name was "Patsy Cline." Her entry into show business began at the age of four when she won an amateur dance competition. She won a trip to Nashville in 1948, and nine years later won the talent contest on the Arthur Godfrey show, singing her rendition of "Walking After Midnight." Her 1961 hit "I Fall to Pieces" was one of her more important hits. She bcame a member of the Grand Ole Opry and rivaled Kitty Wells as the "Queen of Country Music." Patsy died on March 5, 1963, the result of a plane crash while returning to Nashville from Kansas City, Missouri. In 1973 she was inducted into the Country Music Hall of Fame.

SEPTEMBER 9

1836, MARIANNA, FLORIDA

Lieutenant Henry Hollingsworth, a Nashville attorney, wrote in his diary that the people of Marianna had "hung out the American Flag from the top of a house and saluted us with the firing of a cannon. We are treated with much more respect and hospitality than in Alabama, [where] the people appear of another race of being altogether."

1852, NASHVILLE

Members of the Tailor's Society won their objective, higher wages, and ended their strike after one day, a demonstration of the collective action of Southern urban working men before the Civil War.

1957, NASHVILLE

Some 150 policemen stood guard as 19 black first-graders entered six previously all-white public schools.

That evening, unknown parties dynamited a wing of Hattie Cotton School, where a six-year-old African-American girl had enrolled that day.

A white-supremacist boycott of city schools lasted about a month. Nashville obeyed the procedural letter of the unpopular noncompulsory segregation law initiated by Governor Frank Goad Clement.

SEPTEMBER 10

1835, NASHVILLE

Willie Blount died.

He served as private secretary to his half-brother, William Blount, the governor of the Southwest Territory. Elected one of the judges of the Superior Court of Law and Equity in 1796, Willie Blount resigned the same year. He served in the Tennessee General Assembly from 1807 to 1809. He was elected the Volunteer State's third governor in 1809 and was reelected in 1811 and 1813. He is buried in Greenwood Cemetery in Clarksville.

1894, NASHVILLE

Caroline Meriwether Goodlett called together a group of grandes dames and organized the National Daughters of the Confederacy. A year later, the name was changed to the United Daughters of the Confederacy.

1956, CLINTON

Local desegregation began. Governor Frank

Goad Clement sent in troops to restore order after ardent segregationists reacted violently to African-American students.

1957, NASHVILLE

Policemen were ordered to clamp down on segregationist protesters. In an aggressive shift of policy, they arrested and jailed John Kasper of New Jersey and 19 others. In the end, Kasper was arrested three times, the last time on charges of inciting a riot over school desegregation. Chief of Police Douglas E. Hosse said, "Mr. Kasper has come into this city and agitated and tried to incite other people to do things to violate the law."

There were a number of incidents that night, including stone throwing by both whites and blacks and the hanging of an effigy of a black on Capitol Boulevard; the attached sign read, "This Could Be You." Police blocked a segregationist rally at the War Memorial Building; the rally was moved to Croleywood, just outside the city limits.

Chief Hosse promised that "we are going to arrest—as we did today—every person that tries to interfere with our children going to school." The matter was, the chief said, beyond segregation—it was now a matter of danger to persons and property.

There was a decrease in school attendance as well. The six integrated high schools reported that attendance had dropped as much as 75 percent.

1962, NASHVILLE

Public television station WDCN (now channel 8) began broadcasting.

1836, TURKEYTOWN, CARTER COUNTY

Thirty-one-year-old circuit rider William G. Brownlow married 17-year-old Eliza O'Brien.

Their marriage forced Brownlow to quit circuit riding and seek another means of support. He turned to newspaper publishing and eventually became governor of Tennessee and a United States senator.

1836, QUINCY, FLORIDA

Tennessee troops en route to fight the Seminole Indians marched into this small town. Lieutenant Henry Hollingsworth of Nashville wrote in his journal that the "people were in their Sunday clothes . . . [far] surpassing in appearance the South Alabamians, who are generally pale, swarthy and mean looking."

The army was 12 miles from the territorial capitol, Tallahassee. Henry Hollingsworth didn't care much for south Alabama.

1930, KNOXVILLE

City Manager George Dempster wrote Dr. M. M. Davis of the Rosenwald Fund proposing that a black hospital be built in Knoxville. On November 17, Davis replied that the agency was interested and offered a matching grant.

The first result was a black wing on the main city hospital. By November 8, 1940, a separate but equal facility was provided, one of the last vestiges of Jim Crow.

1953, NASHVILLE

At a meeting of the Tennessee Historical Commission, there was a discussion about recent setbacks in the marker program. It was proving difficult to obtain permission from some

Tennessee natives to allow historical markers on their property.

Amidst the rejections, however, was one bright spot. C. Primo Bartolini, an 80-year-old naturalized United States citizen, agreed to permit the erection of a marker commemorating William Driver, the man who gave the American flag the sobriquet "Old Glory." In a letter to the commission, Bartolini justified his decision by saying, "If we take care of our great men we will help to make people better."

For over 40 years, the marker has stood on Fifth Avenue South in Nashville.

1979, NASHVILLE

Just over two years after Elvis Presley's death, the Tennessee Department of Public Health accused Dr. George Nichopoulos of prescribing over 700 pills—painkillers, sedatives, and uppers—for the popular singer the day before he died. The drugs had been delivered to Graceland, but it was not known if Elvis consumed any of them. The complaint accused Nichopoulos of "gross negligence" that should have resulted in the loss of his license to practice medicine.

SEPTEMBER 12

1836, TALLAHASSEE, FLORIDA

Lieutenant Henry Hollingsworth of Nashville was disappointed when the Tennessee troops entered the territorial capital. He described in his journal how,

> with . . . every fellow setting straight in his stirrups, with fixed bayonets and arms at ease under the sound of three bugles, we made our entrance into Tallahassee, the seat

of the government for the territory . . . big with expectation. . . . What was our disappointment at entering the town and finding ourselves unnoticed! . . . No Governor came out to meet us. No American Flag waved. . . . No beautiful hands from windows, porticos and balconies. . . . All was one unbroken calm and as solemn as a funeral procession.

Hollingsworth booked a room in the City Hotel and was "invited to a champain drinking next door to my room, and get full of fun and frolic, and sing songs and tell jokes to the no small amusement of the company. . . . I have not seen a half a dozen ladies, or white females."

1860, HONDURAS

Freebooter William Walker, a native Nashvillian, was executed by a Honduran firing squad after being captured by members of Her Majesty's Royal Navy. He had been attempting yet another filibustering expedition into Central America.

1917, CUMBERLAND COUNTY

Officials responsible for the coal-mining and coke-production facilities in Waldensia visited the site after it had been defunct for over a decade. They wished to determine if the works could be reopened. The value of coal and coke had skyrocketed as a result of America's entry into World War I.

SEPTEMBER 13

1904, NASHVILLE

Addressing a large audience, John M. Ray, the

Tennessee Socialist Party's candidate for governor, said, "None of us is particularly anxious to work, but we are perfectly willing to produce what we consume. . . . The capitalists get 90 percent of everything produced by labor. They . . . found that wage slavery pays better than chattel slavery. . . . The capitalist government . . . [fears] that the laboring class might get thinned out and they would have to go to work, which they are too lazy to do."

Ray went on to poll only 1,109 votes in the election. James B. Frazier won, collecting 103,503 votes.

1916, ERWIN

Big Mary, said by the Sparks Brothers Circus to be the largest elephant in captivity, was executed at the Cincinnati, Clinchfield & Ohio Railroad's building and repair shops.

Big Mary had in her repertoire 25 tunes that she played on musical horns; she could "play baseball," with a batting average of .400; and she weighed five tons. But during a performance in Kingsport, she flew into a rage and killed her inexperienced handler. She then turned her attention toward the audience. Several pistol shots rang out, but Big Mary was unharmed. Her regular trainer calmed her down.

The next day, Kingsport authorities arrested the pachyderm. Finally, since there was no weapon capable of killing Big Mary, it was decided to hang her.

At 6 P.M., nearly the entire population of Erwin witnessed the event. All the circus's elephants were driven into the railroad yard, evidently to "witness" Big Mary's execution and learn an object lesson. About 8 P.M., a steel-rope noose was put around the condemned pachyderm's ample neck. She was then slowly hoisted up by locomotive crane. Big Mary struggled for five minutes, then the steel rope broke. She fell to the ground dead.

It was afterwards discovered that the elephant had two abscessed teeth, the cause of her misbehavior in Kingsport. She was buried in Erwin, although no one remembers where.

1950, MEMPHIS

A market for African-American babies was uncovered in the city. Georgia Tann, white, the head of the Tennessee Children's Home at 1556 Poplar Street, had sold as many as 1,500 babies for adoption. She had been operating the ring for as long as 10 or 15 years and made as much as $100,000 selling live human flesh.

SEPTEMBER 14

1862, BELLE MEADE

Elizabeth Harding, the mistress of Belle Meade, wrote to Military Governor Andrew Johnson that "the government has . . . taken every suitable horse I had except my carriage horses." Union soldiers had also destroyed the plantation's stone fences. The estate was "at the mercy of the stock of the neighborhood." She continued, "Either some remedy must be found for this evil or the citizens who desire to live in peace . . . will have to leave their homes . . . in an uninhabited waste."

Johnson, who had no great love for the planter class, neither answered the letter nor stopped the army from carrying out its operations.

1957, JACKSON

Amanda Whitman, Miss Tennessee for 1957, and Duncan Renaldo, TV's Cisco Kid, arrived to perform at the Western Tennessee District Fair.

1845, NASHVILLE

Dr. John S. Young, superintendent of the state penitentiary, issued a report that read in part, "I am entirely skeptical on the subject of reforming convicts by teaching the mechanical trades, little or no good comes from it." The penitentiary, he wrote, "has been made practically a State mechanic institute, fostered and sustained by the treasury of the State, and brought into direct competition with the mechanics of the country to the extent of its whole operations."

Young wanted to protect honest working men from the cheaper labor of convicts.

1851, CHEROKEE COUNTY, ALABAMA

J. W. White, a prominent Chattanooga African-American, was born.

White earned a diploma from Talladega College in Alabama and taught school in Chattanooga from 1875 to 1890. He then went into the banking business as president of Penny Savings Bank until it failed in the panic of 1902 and 1903. He served as a justice of the peace, an alderman at large, a tax assessor for the largely black Fourth Ward, and poor commissioner. He also engaged successfully in the practice of law.

1893, COLUMBIA

The editor of the *Columbia Herald* denounced Wall Street as "a band of robbers. They are not enemies of the farmers merely, they are enemies of all mankind. They are freebooters; every cussed one of them. . . . They are drones in the bee-hive of industry; they are leeches upon the body politic; they are traitors to each other; they are an enemy to mankind; they are a menace to good wholesome government for the masses of the people, and they ought to be legislated out of existence."

1903, MAYNARDVILLE

Roy Acuff, "the King of Country Music," was born in a three-room shack.

Acuff began working as a call boy for the Louisville & Nashville. He learned to fiddle and became a master of the yo-yo. Acuff recorded extensively from 1936 to 1940, when he found a home with the Grand Ole Opry. In 1940, he formed Acuff and Rose, a firm that is legendary in the music publishing business. In 1944 and 1946, he ran for governor as a Republican, though he did not win a primary until he ran again in 1948. Meanwhile, Acuff continued recording and touring. His most famous song, "Wabash Cannonball," went gold in 1942. He was inducted into the Country Music Hall of Fame in 1962.

1977, NASHVILLE

Governor Ray Blanton went on television station WSM and announced that he would pardon double murderer Roger Humphreys. The governor insisted he was not giving special treatment to Humphreys, whose father was Blanton's Washington County patronage chief.

In 1973, Humphreys had found his wife in bed with another man and killed them both with a derringer. He was convicted of second-degree murder. While a prisoner, he worked as a photographer for the Tennessee Department of Tourism on the work-release plan.

Asked why many Tennesseans were so upset about the matter, Blanton sharply replied, "Because they're stupid and didn't do their homework."

1802, NEAR JONESBOROUGH

Circuit rider Francis Asbury wrote in his diary, "I attended a camp-meeting which continued for four days; there may have been fifteen hundred souls present. . . . I crossed Nolachuckie. The heat, the restless nights, the water, or maybe, all these combined made me sick indeed."

1841, CANNON MANSION, NEAR THE HARPETH RIVER

Newton Cannon, Whig governor from 1835 to 1839, died.

Cannon was at first a saddler. Despite his poor educational background, he studied law and was elected a state representative from Williamson County in 1811. He held hard feelings for Andrew Jackson and took every opportunity to criticize the Democrat. Cannon, Tennessee's ninth governor, had no long-lasting effect on state government. The Murrell Gang, a band of outlaws, was crushed in Madison County during his term. His popularity was highest in Middle Tennessee.

1923, LAWRENCEBURG

Dr. John B. Morris, the pastor of Cumberland Presbyterian Church, was expressing a heartfelt appeal to sinners to come forward and receive God's grace when he stopped in midsentence. According to one account of the Monday-night meeting, "Four goblins, or wizards, or Cyclops, or dragons, or titans (or whatever they would properly be called in Ku Klux terminology) marched hurriedly into the . . . Church at about the close of the service . . . [and] left an envelope in passing the pulpit and quickly passed out the other aisle."

The envelope contained $50. An accompanying letter indicated that the money was a gift to Morris and his wife, given in Christ's name "in appreciation for their earnest and able service for the Master of Mankind."

The encounter was a complete surprise to the congregation as well: "It was noticeable how many in the church began to look around to see who was there and who was not." It was apparently the first time the members were aware that the Klan was active in Lawrenceburg.

1923, HERMITAGE

Daring English acrobatic pilot and skywriter Derece Shepperson crashed and died.

Engaged by the manufacturer of Lucky Strike cigarettes to write the brand's name in the sky, he was executing a dive when his propeller clipped the treetops and the aircraft crashed and burned.

1957, NASHVILLE

Local native Pat Boone and 12-year-old Brenda Lee entertained a Ryman Auditorium crowd at the United Givers Fund kickoff. They shared the stage with the Anita Kerr Singers and Owen Bradley and his orchestra. Lee sang her hit "One Step at a Time." According to *The Tennessean*, "Her throaty rendition of that bouncy tune had the audience clapping hands and stamping feet in time to the music." She also sang "Ain't That Love." Boone sang "You're Mine." He and Lee then sang a medley of tunes. Boone closed the show with his rendition of "I Believe."

1863, OCCUPIED NASHVILLE

The *Nashville Daily Press* reported that the

town was inundated by "swarms of negro women and children . . . [who] are 'lying loose' about the city. . . . There is no possible way in which this vagrant population of darkies can have adequate food, clothing, and shelter during the winter, unless the Federal military authorities help."

1900, KNOXVILLE

Two men—Jesse Hollen, black, and Jake Cohen, white—were arrested for brawling in the streets of "the Bowery." They were taken to the judge's chambers and given an opportunity to explain their behavior. Suddenly, the fire alarm sounded, and Jake Cohen, a volunteer fireman, began to chase the fire engine. As he did so, the judge shouted, "Jake! Jake! Come back, Jake!" Cohen did as the judge directed but was overheard saying, "It's a damn shame to say 'Come back Jake' when a feller want to go to a fire."

The street pugilists were fined $7.40 each.

1908, MEMPHIS

Author Robert Rylee was born.

He was educated at Phillip's Academy and Amherst College. His book *Deep Dark River*, a saga of black life in the Mississippi Delta, was the Book of the Month selection in July 1935.

SEPTEMBER 18

1846, MEMPHIS

The *Memphis Appeal* printed a letter from the commander of the Fayette Cavalry, Captain Joseph Lenow, who was on his way to fight in Mexico. According to Lenow, the men had covered 650 miles in 50 days, or about 13 miles a day. "The health of the Tennessee Regiment has not been very good," he wrote. "The surgeon, Dr. Roberts, informs me that there have been many cases of sickness among the men. . . . The horses look well, and everyone is in fine spirits."

1964, KNOXVILLE

Industrialist, inventor, city manager, Democratic Party leader, and humanitarian George Dempster died.

Born in Knoxville in 1887, Dempster was president of his graduating class at Girls' High School in 1906. At age 19, he went to Panama to work on the canal. In 1913, he and two brothers formed the Dempster Construction Company and built highways, railroads, and dams; U.S. 25W was one of the company's projects. When the Great Depression hurt the company, Dempster reorganized and began to manufacture equipment, notably the ubiquitous Dempster Dumpster. During World War II, his firm produced 15,000 pontoons for the United States Navy. He was Knoxville's city manager from 1929 to 1931 and from 1935 to 1937 and was elected mayor in 1951. Dempster served as campaign manager for Governor Henry Horton. He also established Knoxville's first paid black fire company.

SEPTEMBER 19

1824, MAURY COUNTY

George H. Gantt was born.

Gantt studied law and taught school at Williamsport. He was a delegate to the Nashville Convention of 1850, called to consider secession as a means of protecting "Southern rights." He was a member of the general assembly from 1849 to 1851 and from 1859 to 1861.

Gantt is credited with initiating the legislation that removed Memphis's city charter and made it a taxing district of the state in 1879.

1862, NEAR CHATTANOOGA

The Battle of Chickamauga began with an attack by Union forces on the Confederate right flank.

On this day 33 years later, Chicakamauga and Chattanooga National Military Park was dedicated.

1933, MEMPHIS

The notorious George R. "Machine Gun" Kelly and his wife were captured by combined elements of the FBI and local police. Wielding a sawed-off shotgun, Detective Sergeant William Ramsey led the lawmen into Kelly's hideout at 1408 Rayner Avenue, met the unsuspecting gangster head-on, and greeted Kelly by saying, "I've been waiting for you all night." Kelly surrendered peacefully.

Ironically, Machine Gun was born and raised in Memphis. Some homecoming!

SEPTEMBER 20

1782, HAMILTON COUNTY

John Sevier's raiding party against Chief Dragging Canoe routed the Indian forces. It was a severe victory over the Native Americans.

1814, ALABAMA

Some 150 Middle Tennessee militiamen marched out of Fort Jackson firing their muskets in the air, believing their three-month term of service had ended.

Their term was actually for six months. All were court-martialed in Mobile, Alabama, between December 5 and December 14, only one month before the Battle of New Orleans. Six men were executed.

1842, SHELBY COUNTY

African-American barber G. W. Sewell was born.

An active figure in Chattanooga public affairs, he was called "a thorough race man among the pioneer settlers" of the city. He was a member of the Hamilton County Court and the board of aldermen. He was also the crier for the federal court for over 20 years.

1988, RUTHERFORD COUNTY

It was reported that since Labor Day, over 100 students at Oakland High School had claimed they were bitten by the virulent brown recluse spider. Near-panic prevailed at the school.

However, one student suggested that many classmates were using the scare as a means of cutting school. Some actually took the end of their spiral notebook, heated it up, and pricked themselves in what was initially a successful ruse.

After a state entomologist carried out an inspection, school officials announced there was no significant risk. According to Dr. Robert Sanders, director of the Rutherford County Health Department, most of the "spider bites" were insect bites, acne, boils, or rashes. Six students had actually been bitten.

SEPTEMBER 21

1807, KINGSTON

The state assembly met on Race Street, then immediately adjourned to meet in Knoxville on the 23rd. This brief meeting satisfied treaty terms by which the Cherokees relinquished the site of Southwest Point, ostensibly so the capital could be located at Kingston. Thus, Kingston was capital for a day.

1876, COVINGTON

In what was his last speech, Nathan Bedford Forrest addressed veterans of the Seventh Tennessee Cavalry, saying in part, "It has been thought by some that our social reunions were wrong, and that they should be heralded to the North as an evidence that we are again ready to break out into civil war. But I think they are right to ponder, and we will show . . . by our conduct and dignity that brave soldiers are always good citizens and law abiding people."

SEPTEMBER 22

1826, SIMPSON COUNTY, KENTUCKY, JUST NORTH OF THE TENNESSEE LINE

Former United States congressman and future governor of Tennessee Sam Houston fought a duel with William A. White over slanderous remarks made about Houston. Houston fired first, hitting White in the groin. The wound was considered fatal.

It wasn't. White recovered in four months.

1879, MEMPHIS

It was reported by a local newspaper that

> our reporter visited . . . the jail at the corner of Front and Auction yesterday. . . . It can be pronounced the best patronized place in the city. The register shows a list of 148 'guests' among which are many of our most

noted local characters. The managers . . . take pride in the fact that not a single case of yellow fever has appeared. . . . Tar, lime, copperas and Wolf River Water are the preventatives used. Everything from the iron fence to the . . . cots . . . have had a thick coat of tar paint. . . . Every inmate is required to bathe once a week.

SEPTEMBER 23

1745, VIRGINIA

John Sevier, the first governor of Tennessee, was born.

His six terms covered the years from 1796 to 1801 and 1803 to 1809. He was the first member of Congress from west of the Appalachians. He died in Alabama on September 24, 1815, of a fever he contracted while negotiating with the Creeks for their land. His log home near Johnson City is a state historical site and is listed on the National Register of Historic Places.

1865, NASHVILLE

Dr. James Overton died.

Overton was born in Louisa County, Virginia, on August 12, 1785. In 1790, his family moved to Kentucky, where he attended Transylvania University, receiving a liberal education and graduating from the law department. He briefly practiced law but soon went to the University of Pennsylvania and attended lectures in medicine.

In 1818, Dr. Overton treated a woman in Nashville afflicted with what he diagnosed as an enormous ovarian tumor of eight months' growth. Before a large audience, he performed an operation to remove the tumor, which turned out to be a baby. To save face, Overton claimed he had been tricked by con men. This incident closed his career as a physician.

1923, NASHVILLE

A story in *The Tennessean* entitled "Klansmen Must Leave Masks Off, Official Advises" revealed that the KKK was planning a large ceremony to initiate 2,000 new members on the 29th of the month. According to Hal Clements, the state's assistant attorney general, "There are very drastic laws in Tennessee against Klanism. It is a misdemeanor to wear masks. It is a crime punishable with death to assault a person when the attacking person is wearing a mask, and it is a crime punishable with from 10 to 21 years in the penitentiary to destroy property while wearing a mask." Consequently, the attorney general's office was banning the wearing of hoods.

In the end, the robed ones did not break the law during their induction ceremony.

SEPTEMBER 24

1774, IN WHAT IS NOW SULLIVAN COUNTY

Chief Logan, a mixed-blood Indian, brought terror to the Reedy Creek settlement, his warriors indiscriminately seeking white blood as part of a larger Shawnee alliance aimed at driving all white men eastward. The John Roberts family was massacred when Lieutenant Christian, commander of King's Mill Fort, was away.

As news of the massacre spread, families in the lower Holston area fled to nearby forts for safety.

1869, NASHVILLE

The formal opening of the Maxwell House— 10 years in the making—took place. After its use as a barracks for Union soldiers, it had fallen into disrepair. It boasted 225 elegant rooms and an impressive rotunda. One of the best hotels in the South, it served coffee that future president Teddy Roosevelt affirmed was "good to the last drop."

1889, KNOXVILLE

The African-American population of the city celebrated the 27 years since President Abraham Lincoln had decided to free the slaves in the Confederate states. The celebration included a parade, speeches, amusements, a soldiers' reunion, and a barbecue. A reporter for the *Knoxville Daily Tribune* wrote that "the colored people of Knoxville have never before so generally observed Emancipation Day as they are this year."

1934, MEMPHIS

Police raiding squads continued their efforts to clean up illegal liquor. "Thirsty Memphians began to realize that a 'liquor drought' was really on. Whisky is now hard to get and good gin is practically off the market," claimed a newspaper account.

Moreover, according to a well-known but unidentified bootlegger, the police were "worrying us. They keep raiding us and we have to move the stuff further and further away."

Prices jumped. For example, a pint of dry gin that once sold for $1.00 now sold for $1.75, and a quart of sloe gin once worth $2.00 now sold for $3.00. To purchase whiskey, it was necessary to go to the bootlegger's outlet and pay in advance, then drive down the block. Fifteen to 20 minutes later, an attendant would deliver the booze with the terse warning, "Beat it."

1977, NEAR LEBANON

Mrs. Cliff Massa, 55, thought she had checked the fuel tanks in her Cessna 177 but had to execute an emergency landing on the westbound lane of Interstate 40.

Jim Vantrease, an incredulous trucker, picked up her distress call on his citizens band radio. He believed someone was joking—until he looked in his rearview mirror and saw the aircraft rapidly coming up behind him. He hit the brakes, got out, and stopped traffic.

Massa, a pilot for six years, managed to get some fuel from the Lebanon airport, then reloaded and made a takeoff from the interstate. She arrived safely home in Cookeville about half an hour later.

1988, READYVILLE, RUTHERFORD COUNTY

Two participants in the commemorative Trail of Tears Covered Wagon Train married. The wagon train recalled the expulsion of the Cherokees from Tennessee in 1838.

SEPTEMBER 25

1780, SYCAMORE SHOALS, EAST TENNESSEE

White frontiersmen dressed in leather hunting clothes and armed with muskets left to cross the mountains to engage the English oppressors at the Battle of Kings Mountain.

1793, NEAR KNOXVILLE

Three hundred Cherokees and 700 Creeks led by mixed-blood chief John Watts avoided detection and marched from the south to within view of Knoxville. However, the fir-

ing of the fort's morning cannon convinced the Native Americans they had been spotted, so they broke to the west. Eight miles from Knoxville, they attacked Cavett's Station, killing all the inhabitants and burning the station to the ground.

This attack was a turning point in the Indian wars because it proved to white authorities that defensive warfare must be abandoned in favor of a more aggressive strategy. Soon, John Sevier led a force of pioneers into Etowah, Georgia, and effectively eliminated the Indian menace in Tennessee. This was Sevier's last Indian battle.

1836, APPROACHING SUWANEE OLD TOWN, FLORIDA

Traveling with the Second Tennessee Volunteers toward Seminole country, Lieutenant Henry Hollingsworth of Nashville wrote in his journal, "We had many severe descriptions of this part of Florida which caused us to form very unfavorable conjectures concerning it. We now find it all that the imagination has painted it—swampy, hammocky, low, excessively hot, sickly and repulsive in all its features."

Hollingsworth was not noted for candy-coating the truth.

1862, RANDOLPH, ON THE MISSISSIPPI RIVER IN TIPTON COUNTY

The town was burned to the ground by Federal forces in retaliation for an attack two days earlier on the small steamboat *Eugene* by a band of Confederate guerrillas.

1900, SYCAMORE SHOALS, EAST TENNESSEE

A big celebration was being planned to honor the 800 Tennessee cavalrymen who had participated in the Battle of Kings Mountain during the Revolutionary War. Ex-governor Robert Love Taylor and future governor Alf Taylor were scheduled to attend. The event was engineered by Judge S. N. R. Neal, who was writing a book about the battle.

SEPTEMBER 26

1804, NASHVILLE

The following advertisement was printed in the *Tennessee Gazette*:

> Stop the Runaway. Fifty Dollars Reward. Eloped from the subscriber, living near Nashville, on the 25th of June last, a Mulatto Man Slave, about thirty years old, six feet and an inch high, stout made and active, talks sensible, stoops in his walk, and has a remarkable large foot, broad across the root of the toes—will pass for a free man, as [I] am informed he has obtained by some means, certificates as such—took with him a drab great coat, dark mixed body coat, a ruffled shirt, cotton home-spun shirts and overalls[.] He will make for Detroit, through the states of Kentucky and Ohio, or the upper part of Louisiana. The above reward will be given any person that will take him, and deliver him to me, or secure him in jail, so that I can get him. If taken out of the state, the above reward, and all reasonable expenses paid—and ten dollars extra, for every hundred lashes any person will give him, to the amount of three hundred.

The subscriber was "Andrew Jackson, Near Nashville, State of Tennessee."

On February 20, 1805, Thomas Terry Davis

of Jeffersonville, Indiana Territory, wrote to Jackson with news that he knew the whereabouts of the runaway. It is not known if the man was captured and returned, dead or alive. Forty lashes were considered the death penalty, so Jackson's urging that up to 300 lashes be administered for an extra $30 did not bode well for the fugitive.

1957, NASHVILLE

Fifty-seven toy stores were raided by public health officials. The paint on a number of Japanese-made toys was said to contain 10 times the amount of lead allowed by American standards. All toy merchants cooperated. According to Dr. John J. Lentz, Davidson County's health officer, these and other Japanese-made toys were to be tested for lead content. Such government agencies were necessary to protect the public's health.

SEPTEMBER 27

1827, JASPER, MARION COUNTY

Peter Turney was born.

The commanding officer of the First Tennessee Infantry, Turney was wounded in the throat at Fredericksburg. He later declined a promotion so he could remain with his regiment. He and his wife and children went to Salt Lake, Florida, to heal his wounds. While the family was away, Federal troops burned his home in Tennessee.

In 1870, Turney was elected to the Tennessee Supreme Court. He became its chief justice in 1886. A Democrat, he was also elected the 27th governor of the Volunteer State, serving from 1893 to 1897. He died on October 19, 1903, and was buried in Winchester.

1858, NASHVILLE

Randal McGavock noted in his diary that he had dined with filibusterer and Nashville native William Walker. He called it the "finest dinner I have ever sat down to and the company enjoyed it finely. Walker is now on his way to Nicaragua where he expects to be successful."

Walker had been overthrown in 1857 after his successful attempt at conquering Nicaragua in 1856.

1867, ATHENS

The directors of Maryville College adopted a candid statement concerning the subject of integrated education. There being no rule prohibiting integration at the college, they found no reason to exclude African-Americans then or in the future: "We deem it much to the credit of the institution that it has . . . exclude[ed] none from its benefits by reason of race or color."

Indeed, the college had been accepting African-American students since its founding in 1819.

1957, KNOXVILLE

This reputedly "bone-dry" city displayed a contradictory attribute. A reporter for *The Tennessean* visiting this Saturday night found that "the liquor flowed like a creek in spring. Under a thinly veiled sham of secrecy the people of Knoxville—and their weekend visitors from wherever—gave the numerous bootleggers scattered in and about the city a brisk business in illicit booze."

The reporter described a number of nightclubs, all illegal but tolerated. One, the swanky *C'est Bon* restaurant on the Alcoa Highway, was nearly deserted when he walked in. Soon, a "shapely, dark haired hostess" greeted his party and ushered it into the larger back room. There, he found liquor bottles and beer cans on every table and a dance floor where the "swaying bodies of couples [were] dancing to a tune of Nat King Cole." A Knoxville cabdriver said business was booming: "They really pack them in. Every night it's the same."

At a more shabby roadside bar, the patrons danced to Hank Snow instead of Nat King Cole, but the liquor bottles were still ubiquitous. Beer, which was allowed in the city, was not sold after midnight, although hard (and illegal) liquor was.

Knoxville, according to the reporter, was a "city of rear rooms" and backyard sheds where bootleggers kept their stock. Bootleggers were concentrated around Rutledge Pike on a small winding road off Magnolia Avenue just outside the city limits. It was easy to discern a bootlegger amidst the small, stylish houses by the number of cars in the driveway. Once a customer parked, a man came to take the order. A half-pint cost $2, a pint $4, and a fifth $6.

In Nashville, one had to go into town to purchase liquor, but in Knoxville, it was possible to make a telephone order that would be delivered free of charge. Private clubs such as Dean Hill County Club and the prestigious Cherokee Country Club sold mixed drinks and attracted noisy, thirsty, and big crowds.

If prohibition didn't work in Knoxville, the article concluded, it wouldn't work in Nashville. Those who were planning to campaign for a bone-dry Nashville should take heed.

1776, PENDLETON AND LOWER HOLSTON SETTLEMENT AREAS, LONG ISLAND

On this Sunday, the army that had gathered to attack the Cherokee cities held a "General Parade of Prayers," presided over by the Reverend Joseph Rhea at Fort Patrick Henry and the Reverend Charles Summers at the Long Island camps. Many in the army were "Overmountain Men."

1886, BETWEEN WAYNESBORO AND LAWRENCEBURG

On their way to Wayne and Hardin Counties, gubernatorial candidates Robert Love Taylor and Alf Taylor spun yarns at a boardinghouse to discredit each other.

George H. Armistead, an editor for the *Nashville American*, reported that in response to the question, "What kind of a boy was Bob?" Alf smiled and answered in part, "Yes, he was queer. Bob was always an artful dodger.... He was in all manner of mischief at all times, but he had a knack of getting out of the worst scrapes without a scratch, while Nat and Jim and I caught the devil."

Bob responded in part that "Alf was my favorite brother."

1918, NEAR BELLICOURT, FRANCE

Atoka native Joseph B. Atkinson, a sergeant with Company C, 119th Infantry, 30th Division, found his platoon pinned down by murderous machine-gun fire. He rushed across 50 yards of no man's land directly into the German fire, kicked the gun from the parapet into the trench, and captured three enemy soldiers at bayonet point. He was awarded the Medal of Honor.

1776, PENDLETON AND LOWER HOLSTON SETTLEMENT AREAS, LONG ISLAND

The great army of white settlers began its march toward the Indian towns, intending to destroy the Cherokee and Creek threat conclusively.

1856, GRANADA, NICARAGUA

The filibustering president of the republic of Nicaragua, Nashville native William Walker wrote diplomatic instructions to the former owner of the *Nashville Union*, John P. Heiss. Walker wanted to place the American and British governments on notice that he would allow no interference with the Mosquito Indian population, that he intended to open Nicaraguan ports to free trade, and that he would soon be in control of the entire Central American isthmus, thereby being in a position to regulate traffic from the Atlantic to the Pacific. He instructed Heiss to have both the American and British governments understand that "the present movement in Central America [i.e. Walker's imperialism] was for the advantage of those who speak the English language and who derive their laws from the institutes of Alfred."

1864, OCCUPIED MEMPHIS

The United States Army began its second experiment in the social control and medical management of venereal disease when it announced that a system of legalized prostitution similar to the one initiated in Nashville a year earlier would go into force in the Bluff City. According to the "Private Circular," which was "intended for the information of women only," all trollops were required to "be registered and take out weekly certificates" of good health. A $2.50 fee for medical examinations was charged, while a certificate cost $10.00. The money collected was to go to treating any courtesan who contracted a venereal disease.

By the end of the war, the system was proclaimed a success, like the one in Nashville. It was not continued by civilian authorities after the war.

1900, KNOXVILLE

According to a report in the *Knoxville Journal Tribune*, the University of Tennessee football team's prospects looked brighter than ever. Many of the previous season's players were back, joined by a 200-pound lineman referred to as "Mr. French," who had played for Maryville College the previous season. The team was to play King's

College at Knoxville on October 12; Vanderbilt at Nashville on October 27; the University of North Carolina at Knoxville on November 1; Centre College at Knoxville on November 5; the University of Alabama at Tuscaloosa on November 9; and Miami at Knoxville on November 19.

1950, NASHVILLE

The city's first television station, WSM, channel 4, began broadcasting. Sales of television sets increased thereafter. This was nearly 25 years after radio station WSM had gone on the air.

1987, NASHVILLE

Claiming "I want to vote," former governor and convicted felon Ray Blanton petitioned the circuit court to regain his voting privileges.

October

OCTOBER 1

1808, LIBERTY HILL, WILLIAMSON COUNTY

At a Methodist conference 12 miles from Nashville, a principle was agreed to dealing with the subject of slavery. It stated that no member or minister of the church should buy or sell a slave unjustly, inhumanely, or covetously. An ecclesiastical trial process was established for any offense to this rule.

One of the participants, circuit rider Francis Asbury, described the conference as "a camp meeting, where the preachers ate and slept in tents. We sat six hours a day, stationed eighty three preachers and all was peace."

1819, NASHVILLE

The 10th annual conference of the Methodist Episcopal Church in Tennessee was held. A protest against slavery was issued. It was decided that no slave owner could become an officer in the church. Most other Southern denominations had no such rule.

1836, 30 MILES FROM FORT DRANE, FLORIDA

Lieutenant Henry Hollingsworth of the Second Tennessee Volunteers related in his journal that the Tennesseans had killed three Seminoles: "This was good news. We go ahead and sure enough we come to the scene of death! There within one hundred yards of each other lay three of these children of the forest, all weltering in their blood, and sleeping in Death! . . . This raised the spirits of the men to the highest pitch, and their desire for a fight ran equally."

1953, NASHVILLE

It was reported in the *Nashville Banner* that Albert Dobbins, a black agricultural worker from Williamson County, had been in jail for five months for a crime he didn't commit. The charge was attempted murder, which carried a sentence of five to 10 years. A mistake had been made in the grand-jury process, and Dobbins was indicted and subsequently convicted.

When warden James Edwards told Dobbins that the mistake had been discovered, the elated prisoner said, "I didn't figure I ought to be in here in the first place." The next day, perhaps embarrassed, Governor Frank Goad Clement gave Dobbins a full pardon.

OCTOBER 2

1874, HOLLY SPRINGS, MISSISSIPPI
Edward Hull Crump, Jr., was born.

He became one of the last political bosses in America and wielded almost unlimited power in Tennessee in the 1930s and 1940s. "Boss" Crump's base of operations was Memphis.

1882, LEBANON
Robert Looney Caruthers, who was supposed to be the second Confederate governor of Tennessee, died.

Caruthers was elected as a state representative from Wilson County. He took John Bell's seat in the United States House of Representatives in 1841 and later was a justice on the Tennessee Supreme Court. When pro-Confederate governor Isham Green Harris's third term ended, Caruthers was to take his place, but the Union army's presence in Nashville made any act of Tennessee's Confederate government moot, so he was never inaugurated. He spent the rest of the war serving in the Confederate secret service. After the war, he initiated a law school at Cumberland University. He was buried in Lebanon.

1953, HUMBOLDT

The Humboldt Full-Fashion Hosiery Mill was shut down, according to plant manager Ed S. Lewis, because he feared that striking union workers might harm nonunion workers.

Workers were certain the plant was shut down because the majority of laborers were union members. They felt the strike was aimed at busting their union.

OCTOBER 3

1836, FORT DRANE, FLORIDA
Lieutenant Henry Hollingsworth confided in his journal that the Second Tennessee Volunteers "are nearly out of bread and no prospect of getting any soon. . . . The Governor [William Blount] is to a certainty guilty of unpardonable neglect. . . . Should we suffer much, the low but universal murmurs which now run through the whole crowd, will increase into a wave that will overwhelm him [General Robert Armstrong]. So he had better be on the lookout."

The lieutenant meant that the suffering soldiers might mutiny.

1865, NASHVILLE

As part of his message to the Tennessee legislature, Governor William G. Brownlow commented on the evils of alcohol: "Throughout the length and breadth of Tennessee, distilleries, wholesale and retail liquor dealers are multiplying with frightful rapidity, and increasing evils therefrom, call upon the friends of humanity and of religion to educate the public mind in opposition to this vice, and if possible, to stay the tide that now bids fair to overwhelm and degrade society."

Brownlow knew he did not have the resources to ban whiskey and destroy stills. Instead, he proposed a prohibitively high whiskey tax.

The general assembly, perhaps not sharing the chief executive's views on the subject, did not enact the tax.

1925, NASHVILLE

Twenty-five robed members of the Ku Klux Klan stood at attention around a flaming cross that had been ignited in the front yard of a large building at Carroll and Maple Streets at 8:45 P.M. They were protesting the proposed occupancy of the building by a Meharry Medical College fraternity. Blacks watched from a safe distance to the south on Maple Street, while large crowds looked on from other directions.

The house stood in the center of South Nashville's most valuable property, Carroll Street, lined with some of the most expensive buildings in the section. The members of the Phi chapter of the black fraternity Phi Alpha Phi intended to move into the building, which was owned by Universal Life Insurance Company, a large African-American concern in Memphis.

W. D. Hawkins, treasurer of the board of directors of the fraternity, declared that the organization intended to continue with the move despite Klan intimidation. Said Hawkins, "I hope that when the sane white people and the sane negroes are educated on the subject we can come to a sensible understanding."

OCTOBER 4

1847, WILLIAMSON COUNTY

John P. Buchanan, governor of Tennessee from 1891 to 1893, was born.

A member of the Farm Labor Party, he was the first farmer to serve as governor. It was Buchanan who helped negotiate an end to the miners' rebellion in 1891 and 1892, which led ultimately to the end of the convict lease system. Among his other actions were the provision of pensions for Confederate veterans and the passage of a secondary-school law that required the study of Tennessee history in the public schools.

1926, ROCKWOOD

Twenty-eight men died in an explosion in the Roane Iron Company's coal mines. Four were killed outright and another 24 were entombed and suffocated to death.

The cause of the explosion was said to be a mine-shaft fire that had been burning slowly for over 30 years. It hardly seems possible that mine owners could not have known about—or could have neglected—the fire, burning since before the Spanish-American War. There was no OSHA in 1926.

[October 4] Entrance to No. 10 mine in Rockwood, 1927

OCTOBER 5

1836, FORT DRANE, FLORIDA

Evidence mounted that the Seminoles were headed in the direction of the Withlacoochee River and Swamp. But according to Lieutenant Henry Hollingsworth, instead of attacking, the Second Tennessee Volunteers spent their time "in killing and jerking beef and eating it and shugar cane. This . . . place . . . is the most monotonous. No house, no women, no amusement or variety of any kind, nothing but the dull sameness of camp."

1880, SCOTT COUNTY

The utopian community of Rugby was founded by Thomas Hughes, the English author of *Tom Brown's School Days*. Hughes's idealistic endeavor was to provide homes and livelihood in Tennessee for the younger sons of English gentry who by British law would not inherit a cent from their fathers.

Two years later to the day, the Rugby Library opened. It became the centerpiece of the picturesque English village on the Cumberland Plateau.

Within a short span, the settlement proved financially infeasible. Nevertheless, it is listed on the National Register of Historic Places and is open for visitation nearly year-round.

1892, NASHVILLE

A movement to provide homes for girls and women who worked for low wages in the textile mills was given a boost by contributions from wealthy Nashvillians.

The concern of the wealthy class may have been as much selfish as altruistic, since efficiency and profits figured to fall if female workers couldn't afford decent housing.

1925, NASHVILLE

Radio station WSM, the country-music giant, went on the air.

1958, CLINTON

After 20 months of racial calm, three massive explosions ripped through Clinton High School late at night. They were part of a white-supremacist campaign to end the racial integration of the school system. There were no injuries.

The terrorist campaign ultimately proved ineffective.

OCTOBER 6

1885, CHATTANOOGA

Jim Howell, the baggagemaster at Union Depot, became involved in a domestic spat between a young couple on their way to Brunswick, Georgia. The wife demanded she be given her baggage to return to New Hampshire, but her husband, T. W. Brown, ignored her. Inasmuch as the husband had the claim check, her request could not be granted. Howell thus took it upon himself to negotiate a settlement. The couple ultimately kissed and made up. A curious and happy crowd had by then gathered in the depot to watch the matter unfold.

1919, CLARKSVILLE

The first bank in the United States entirely operated by women opened for business. First Woman's Bank was, according to the *Clarksville Leaf-Chronicle*, "petticoated from president to janitress." The first depositor was also female.

The bank closed on June 9, 1926, when it merged with the male-owned First Trust and Savings Bank.

1968, CHATTANOOGA

The Tennessee Archaeological Society held its first annual meeting at the Patten House Hotel. Some 150 professional and amateur archaeologists were expected to attend. Among the papers to be read was one by Chattanooga physician W. R. Buttman, Jr., entitled "What a Skeleton Has to Tell You."

Also, the Plum Nelly Art Show was held on Lookout Mountain at the studio home of printmaker Fannie Mennen. The art show was an annual event that started in 1946 as a means to showcase the work of local artists.

OCTOBER 7

1780, KINGS MOUNTAIN, NORTH CAROLINA

A Loyalist force of 1,100 led by Major Patrick Ferguson was captured on top of the mountain. Preventing its escape was the 900-member force of Americans from the Watauga settlements, led by Colonel Isaac Shelby and Colonel William Campbell. The marksmanship of the backwoods guerrillas prevailed over the spirited bayonet charges of the Tories. Some argue that this battle was the turning point of the Revolutionary War in the South.

1843, NASHVILLE

The city was chosen by the legislature as the permanent site of the state capital.

1861, NASHVILLE

Representing Fentress, Overton, Morgan, and Scott Counties, Reece T. Hildred took his seat in the 34th Tennessee General Assembly—the first Confederate assembly. Hildred was so badly crippled that he was not able to serve in the army. It was said he had been driven away from his Fentress County home by the Union Home Guard at the beginning of hostilities.

When the legislature moved to Memphis, Hildred returned home to teach school in Overton County. There, a contingent of Union Home Guards, most likely under the command of Champ Ferguson, took him either from his schoolroom or his home and executed him. His juvenile daughter, Laura, looked on helplessly.

1870, SMART STATION

"Uncle" Dave Macon, Grand Ole Opry star, was born.

Macon operated a farm near Readyville for 20 years and played the five-string banjo to amuse himself and neighbors. In 1918, he was paid by a local farmer to play at a party, and so entered the ranks of the professionals. In 1923, he formed a partnership with guitarist Sid Harkeadan. Soon, they landed a recording contract. Macon began his career on the Grand Ole Opry in 1926 with the Fruit Jar Drinker's Band. He was in the movie *The Grand Ole Opry* in 1940. He died in Readyville on March 22, 1952.

1918, CHATEL-CHEHERY, FRANCE

During the Battle of the Argonne, Private Alvin C. York attacked a fortified machine-gun position and single-handedly captured 132 German soldiers. He was awarded the Medal of Honor—and was also soon promoted to sergeant.

York provided the grateful nation a much-needed hero, but he was not the only Tennessean to win the Medal of Honor during World War I.

OCTOBER 8

1809, EAST TENNESSEE

The Reverend Francis Asbury confided in his journal that after being in the saddle a number of days and covering 200 miles, he "had the piles and pains of body." It wasn't easy being a circuit rider.

1840, JACKSON

Andrew Jackson attended a barbecue and addressed an enthusiastic audience estimated at 10,000. James K. Polk and Felix Grundy helped the aging Jackson to the podium. The former president spoke about the evils of abolitionism, the tariff, a national bank, and internal improvements.

1918, NEAR ESTREES, FRANCE

During the Battle of the Argonne, Sergeant James E. Karnes and Private John Ward of Company D, 117th Infantry, 30th Division, advanced against an enemy machine-gun nest and destroyed the German emplacement by killing three and capturing seven and their weapons. Ward hailed from Morristown, and Karnes was a native of Arlington. Both were awarded the Medal of Honor.

OCTOBER 9

1836, FORT DRANE, FLORIDA

Lieutenant Henry Hollingsworth described camp life with his fellow Tennesseans this way: "Here may be seen one group [of soldiers] singing an obscene song, there one singing a hymn, and just beyond another playing cards, and so on, every one to his particular liking, while others may be seen reading, conversing or off to themselves apparently thinking. . . . I have occupied much of my time since being here in reading and writing. *Don Quixote* is my favorite. It has an inexhaustible fund of amusement and instruction."

1901, NASHVILLE

Buffalo Bill's Wild West Show was in town. Tents were situated from West End to a point west of what is now 25th Avenue. The afternoon and evening performances featured fancy shooting by Annie Oakley and a cavalcade of cavalry from many lands.

1921, MADISON, DAVIDSON COUNTY

Mr. Summer Sanders's pig won the state's Grand Champion Hog Championship. The hog weighed in at 331 pounds.

OCTOBER 10

1788, TIPTON FARM, NEAR JONESBOROUGH

John Sevier surrendered peacefully to his foe, John Tipton, to face trial for treason against the state of North Carolina because of his central part in the formation and defense of the State of Franklin. General Charles McDowell, a fellow commander at the Battle of Kings Mountain in the Revolutionary War, signed Sevier's bail bond.

Later, as arrangements for Sevier's trial were being made, his sons and many friends were allowed to liberate him without interference. The trial was never held.

1911, NASHVILLE

The legislature adopted Tennessee's first—and current—state flag, designed by Colonel LeRoy Reeves of Johnson City. It was first raised by Company F of the United States National Guard during dedication ceremonies at East Tennessee Normal School, now East Tennessee State University.

1915, MEMPHIS

Calvin "Cal" Alley was born.

He followed in his father's footsteps, becoming an editorial cartoonist for the *Memphis Commercial Appeal* and continuing his father's popular strip, "Hambone's Meditations." He also rendered his own nationally syndicated comic strip, "The Ryatts." He died on November 10, 1970.

1915, WESTMORELAND, SUMNER COUNTY

Owen Bradley, Music City producer, musician, and executive, was born.

He was vitally important in the creation of the "Nashville Sound," which gave country-and-western music new life. He also helped Nashville gain a reputation for superb recording studios. Bradley produced such stars as Conway Twitty, Loretta Lynn, Brenda Lee, and Bill Anderson. He was inducted into the Country Music Hall of Fame in 1974.

1939, NASHVILLE

As reported in the *Nashville Banner*, M. H. Parks had an extensive collection of 20th-century firearms, including over 30 machine guns, no two of them alike—Maxims, Vickers, Marlins, Brownings, Lewis guns, St. Etienne, Hotchkiss, Schwarzloss, and Spandau. In addition, Parks had clips, drums, ammunition belts, trench helmets, bayonets, hand grenades, and artillery shells. All the weapons had been disabled so they could not fire.

The collection was housed on 10th Avenue South next to a small church with a sign that admonished passersby to follow God and be peaceful.

OCTOBER 11

1809, GRINDER'S STAND ON THE NATCHEZ TRACE

Meriwether Lewis—army officer, secretary to Thomas Jefferson from 1801 to 1803, co-leader of the famed Lewis and Clark expedition to the Pacific Northwest from 1804 to 1806, and governor of the Louisiana Territory from 1806 to 1809—died mysteriously. While no definite conclusions have been reached, it has been speculated that he either committed suicide, accidentally killed himself while cleaning a pistol, or was robbed and killed by bandits who frequented the Natchez Trace.

OCTOBER 11, 1906, PULASKI
The monument memorializing "the Boy Hero of the Confederacy," Sam Davis, was officially dedicated.

1932, MCMINNVILLE

Country-music star Dottie "Country Sunshine" West was born.

She studied music at Tennessee Technological University in the early 1950s. Her big hits included "Let Me Off at the Corner" (1963), "Here Comes My Baby" (1964), "Would You Hold It against Me?" (1966), "Country Girl" (1968), and "Country Sunshine" (1973). The tune to this last song was used in Ray Blanton's successful run for the governor's chair in 1976, to wit: "We need a Ray of Blanton sunshine."

1968, PALL MALL

Colonel William Slayden, deputy state commissioner of education, spoke at ceremonies dedicating York Grist Mill, a newly acquired state historic site. According to Slayden, "This old mill is a symbol of the peaceful life which Sgt. [Alvin C.] York preferred, the peaceful life he was willing to fight to guarantee, the peaceful life to which he returned when the fighting was over."

York's widow, "Miss Gracie," was on hand but did not speak.

OCTOBER 12

1886, NASHVILLE

Members of the Tennessee Historical Society passed a resolution to invite their wives, daughters, and sweethearts to attend meetings, especially when papers were to be read. Heretofore, only men had been allowed to attend. This did not mean that women could be members, but only that they could attend meetings if accompanied by a male member.

Today, the executive director of the Tennessee Historical Society is a woman—and a member.

1904, NASHVILLE

A crowd of 4,000 people attended the funeral service for Thomas Green Ryman.

He spent 10 years as a boy in Chattanooga learning the commercial fishing trade before returning to Nashville in 1861. During the Civil War, he sold fish to hungry Confederate and Union soldiers up and down the Cumberland and Tennessee Rivers. Around 1867, he purchased his first steamboat and soon became the foremost river man on the Cumberland and the Tennessee. He "found religion" in 1886 after hearing evangelist Sam Jones preach and decided to build Union Gospel Tabernacle, which was completed in 1892. That building, listed on the National Register of Historic Places, was the headquarters for the Grand Ole Opry from 1941 to 1974.

1912, NASHVILLE

In a letter to the *Nashville Banner*, Mrs. L. H. Hicks wrote that men had a divine right to rule the world. She used a biblical basis for her speculation, saying that God had exercised governing power from the onset and that Christ had sanctioned the existing social and political orders. She felt this way because "men have made the earth a beautiful protected home for the human race, especially the women." Women could never be the equal of men, she wrote, because it was "ordained from the first that man should be in control . . . and hysterical argument can not put them aside." Therefore, women should not have the right to vote, because they were "not logical. Women have not the power of great concentration. They easily tire. . . . They are not mathematicians. . . . They are impatient of just criticisms and their methods are devious, complicated and hard to follow. . . . We have yet to produce a woman of the first caliber, great as men are great."

OCTOBER 13

1834, DAVIDSON COUNTY

The Hermitage, the plantation mansion of Andrew Jackson, seventh president of the United States, burned to the ground while Jackson was in Washington, D.C. His adopted son had been left in charge.

1866, NASHVILLE

Near the end of the local baseball season, sports fans' attention was riveted on the contest between the Eureka club (a Jewish team) and the Rock City nine. The outcome of the game is not known.

1870, NEWPORT, COCKE COUNTY

Ben Walter Wade was born. Early an orphan, he eventually adopted the last name of Hooper.

A Republican, he served as Tennessee's 32nd governor from 1911 to 1915. During his progressive administration, a law was passed stipulating that working women's pay should be issued to them and them alone, and the Pure Food and Drugs Act was enacted. In his second term, a compulsory school law was passed, and the method of carrying out the death sentence in Tennessee was changed from hanging to electrocution.

1978, BRUSHY MOUNTAIN STATE PRISON

Anna Sandhu, a courtroom artist for a Knoxville television station, married James Earl Ray inside the prison. Ironically, the ceremony was performed by the Reverend James Lawson, an associate of Martin Luther King, Jr., the civil rights leader Ray had assassinated in April 1968.

OCTOBER 14

1803, EAST TENNESSEE

The Reverend Francis Asbury, Methodist circuit rider, wrote in his journal about the flood of pioneering immigrants from North and South Carolina settling in Tennessee. Typically, the

> men, women, and children, [were] almost naked, paddling bare-foot and bare-legged along, or labouring up the rocky hills, whilst those who are best off have only a horse or two for two or three children to ride at once. If these adventurers have little or nothing to eat, it is no extraordinary circumstance, and not uncommon, to camp in the wet woods after night: in the moun-

tains it does not rain, it pours. . . . But the people it must be confessed, are amongst the kindest souls in the world. But kindness will not make a crowded log cabin twelve feet by ten, agreeable: without are cold and rain; and within, six adults, and as many children, one of which is all motion; the dogs too, must sometimes be admitted.

1886, DYERSBURG

Mat Washington, an African-American, was taken from jail about 10 A.M. by 250 men and brought to the courthouse square. He was about to be lynched when some of the town's leading citizens persuaded the mob's leaders that such an action would reflect badly on Dyersburg. In other words, they convinced the mob to take him out of town.

A mile or so away, Washington allegedly confessed to rape, the crime he stood accused of; he also confessed his guilt in four other crimes.

The Hermitage, plantation home of Andrew Jackson [October 13]

He was hanged from a tree. The good name of Dyersburg was thus saved from reproach.

OCTOBER 15

1882, PUTNAM COUNTY

The last stagecoach robbery in Tennessee took place on what is now U.S. 70. "Bug" Hunt and his accomplices, described as the "two Edward boys," held up the Cookeville-to-Nashville stagecoach, driven by Joby Rayburn. They robbed the mail and the passengers but missed the registered pouch and a quantity of money on one passenger.

Hunt was later apprehended, tried, and given a prison sentence. The "two Edward boys" escaped and were never heard from again.

1895, KNOXVILLE

Tom Breene, a young man of Irish descent and reputedly the best mechanic on the Cincinnati-Southern Railroad, was shot and killed on Central Avenue, the city's famous red-light district. His killer was allegedly Charles Rich, also an employee of the Cincinnati-Southern.

Breene, generally a good-hearted man, had become intoxicated and gotten into a quarrel at Emma Clark's bordello, loudly berating her. When Madam Clark could tolerate no more, she left the house to search for her lover, Rich. Returning to her place of business, they were confronted by Breene. Rich drew his pistol and fired point-blank at Breene, killing him instantly with a shot through the heart.

Breene's body was taken to DeArmond's Saloon shortly after the shooting. His father came to identify the body and fell prostrate at the sight of his dead son. Rich was nowhere to be found.

1836, DAVIESS COUNTY, KENTUCKY

Albert Smith Marks, governor of Tennessee from 1879 to 1881, was born.

Marks began his career as an attorney. Despite his Union convictions, he fought for the Confederacy. A colonel with the 17th Tennessee Regiment, he lost a leg at the Battle of Murfreesboro. Marks refused to quit soldiering and became a judge advocate with Nathan Bedford Forrest.

As a Democratic governor, he tried unsuccessfully to reduce the state's debt. He died on November 4, 1891.

1853, BAJA CALIFORNIA

Having led an assault on Sonora, Nashville native William Walker declared himself president of Lower California. The newly installed president, however, was shortly chased out of the country by Mexican authorities.

Undaunted, Walker would attack and ultimately control all of Nicaragua in a few years, though his rule was short-lived.

1973, NASHVILLE

Roy Clark, mainstay of *Hee Haw*, won the Country Music Association's coveted top award for Entertainer of the Year. Charlie Rich received an award for his hit single "Behind Closed Doors." Loretta Lynn, 1972's Entertainer of the Year, shared an award with Conway Twitty for their duet "Louisiana Woman, Mississippi Man."

1788, BLOUNT COUNTY

James Gillespy's fort was attacked by 300 Indians led by John Watts. The defenders held out until their ammunition was spent. Thirty-one were taken prisoner and 28 slaughtered. Their bodies were burned. Thereafter, the site was called Burnt Station.

John Sevier, former governor of the State of Franklin, soon followed the Indians and took an equal number of prisoners for exchange.

Note: Some sources say this event occurred on October 13.

1819, ADAIR COUNTY, KENTUCKY

William Palmer Jones was born.

Before settling in the Volunteer State, Jones earned a medical degree in Ohio. He served in the Tennessee General Assembly from 1873 to 1875 as a Republican senator representing Davidson County. He was on the board of editorial managers of the *Southern Journal of Medical and Physical Sciences* from 1853 to 1857; he also assisted in organizing Shelby Medical College.

During the Civil War, Jones was in charge of the first hospital established in Nashville after the Federal occupation in February 1862. That same year, Military Governor Andrew Johnson appointed him superintendent of the Tennessee Hospital for the Insane. Jones was instrumental in establishing the Tennessee Negro Asylum, the first such institution in the United States. He wrote a number of pioneering articles on mental illness, among them "Necessities of the Insane in Tennessee" and "Adequate and Impartial Provisions for the Insane of the State." He held a chair at Nashville Medical College and served as president of the faculty of the medical department at the University of Tennessee until his death on September 25, 1897. He was buried in Mount Olivet Cemetery in Nashville.

OCTOBER 18

1813, NEAR DITTO'S LANDING ON THE TENNESSEE RIVER

Captain James Raulston wrote Major General Andrew Jackson, "With Reluctance and Disgrace I have to Inform you that after I Brought my company of Volunteers to Dittoes Landing I could not Prevail with more than six of them to Cross the river to preform the campaign[.] I Do not Pretend to Vindicate aney thing about the Business. Onley state that this is the last command that I shall Ever Pretend to take. The Excuse was they had Enrold themselves for a tower [tour] of three months and they would not go the campaign."

This was most likely the earliest instance of such insubordination in Jackson's force. There were similar actions by Tennessee soldiers from November 1813 to January 1814.

1856, BLEDSOE COUNTY

James B. Frazier was born in Pikeville.

He was the state's 29th governor, serving from 1903 until he resigned in 1905 upon his appointment as a United States senator following the death of incumbent William B. Bate. Frazier served in the Senate until 1911, when he was defeated for another term. He then practiced law in Chattanooga until his death in 1937.

1956, MEMPHIS

Elvis Presley was involved in an altercation with service-station attendants Aubrey Brown and Ed Hopper.

Elvis had driven his Lincoln Continental to Hopper's gas station. When a crowd of fans began to gather, Hopper three times asked Elvis to leave, but the performer did not comply. Hopper then shoved Elvis back into the Lincoln, and Elvis retaliated, hitting Hopper in the eye.

All three men were charged with disorderly conduct and assault and battery and posted a bond of $52. The next day in city court, Elvis was acquitted, while Hopper and Brown were fined $25 for assault.

OCTOBER 19

1818, NEAR WHAT IS NOW TUSCUMBIA, ALABAMA

Andrew Jackson and Isaac Shelby induced Chief Levi Colbert to sign a treaty giving up all Chickasaw land in Tennessee and Kentucky. This transaction is known as the Jackson Purchase.

In order to protect the Indian signers from Chickasaws who did not like the terms, Jackson stipulated that the treaty minutes be kept secret. They remained concealed until 1930, when historian Samuel Cole Williams wrote *Beginnings of West Tennessee and Kentucky, the Land of the Chickasaws, 1541-1841*. Williams exposed the underhanded means by which Jackson and Shelby tricked the Indians into signing the Jackson Purchase.

1832, NASHVILLE

The state legislature enacted a law that made the sale of lottery tickets illegal in Tennessee.

Antilottery sentiment is still strong, as witnessed nearly 163 years later when a move to create a lottery was defeated in the state senate.

1895, CHATTANOOGA

As reported in the *Chattanooga News*, the common council had received a petition from parents who were concerned that the school board had banned the reading of the Bible in many city schools. The parents wanted Bible reading reinstated.

There was a similar movement in Nashville. Eventually, both petitions were denied.

1896, KNOXVILLE

Reports surfaced in the city that Forest Oil Company had struck oil in the western portion of the Rugby tract. The *Fentress Gazette* of October 15 had claimed, "A reliable man living in the vicinity was at the well when the tools were pulled for the last time, and states that oil followed the tools out. This man says . . . that the well was immediately plugged, sand thrown on the oil which was scattered around and the sand thrown into the well, which was immediately plugged again. The Forest company acknowledges that a show of oil was found."

In the end, however, little oil was discovered, and Tennessee did not experience an oil boom.

1910, JOHNSON CITY

Trying to avoid the divisive issue of prohibition, United States senator Robert Love Taylor, the Democratic Party's last-minute nominee for governor, told a crowd, "I come to you today with a harmonicon in my mouth, with an olive branch in one hand and a bowie knife in the other, and with a heart full of good will to my fellow-man, provided that my fellow-man votes for me for governor."

1797, KNOXVILLE

Reacting to complaints from Tennessee's frontier counties about Indian raids and the continual depredations of squirrels, crows, and wolves, the general assembly passed the following law: "Each county in this State is authorized to lay a tax, to be paid in squirrels' or crows' scalps, on every person subject to a poll tax in their respective counties, not exceeding twenty-five squirrels to each poll."

One crow's scalp (or skin) equaled two squirrels' scalps. Each man who failed to supply his quota of scalps had to pay a penny for each undelivered scalp. The animal skins were to be delivered to the respective county justices—who held the lists of taxable property—and were then to be burned after a proper accounting had been made. Each county court was authorized to pay as much as $2 for wolf hides, which were also to be incinerated.

1865, NASHVILLE

Confederate guerrilla chief Champ Ferguson was hanged at the state penitentiary. Many felt it was too good for him.

1941, HONOLULU, HAWAII

Samuel R. Maples died.

Born in Sevier County in 1860, he was the son of Edward Maples, who had come to Knoxville soon after the Civil War and opened a prosperous grocery business on East Vine Avenue at State Street. In 1888, Samuel R. Maples was elected a city magistrate; he was later re-elected for a term of six years. Soon afterwards, he was elected vice chairman of the Knox County Court by his fellow magistrates. He did a large business as a city magistrate and was said to average $6,000 to $7,000 in annual income from his office.

In 1899, he went to the Hawaiian Islands with a group of fellow Knoxville African-Americans. Both the racial and natural climates appealed to him, and he never returned to Knoxville.

1944, THE PHILIPPINE ISLANDS

About 15 minutes before a scheduled amphibious assault, General Douglas MacArthur went to the bridge of the USS *Nashville* to watch the attack. Then, after an early luncheon, MacArthur made preparations for going ashore. With him were the Filipino president and American and Filipino generals. The party boarded a landing craft, MacArthur sitting upright at the stern. Soon, he made his famous walk onto the shore of Moratri Island, honoring his promise to return. However, because the landing craft had run aground 150 yards from the beach, the party had to wade in through waist-deep water. Not satisfied that it was a Kodak moment, MacArthur ordered a number of subsequent takes until the landing craft was much closer to shore. He evidently had anticipated such a problem and brought extra pairs of dry pants.

MacArthur later paid this tribute to the cruiser that served him in the Pacific theater: "The *Nashville* carried me in many amphibious operations. She proved herself a gallant ship, under a gallant Captain and officers served by a gallant crew. May she be preserved safely to the end."

On this date 49 years earlier, the original USS *Nashville*, then the navy's newest gunboat, had been christened. She later fired the first shots of the Spanish-American War and figured prominently in the war against the Philippines from 1898 to 1901 and the Panamanian revolt in 1903.

OCTOBER 21

1869, UNION CITY

The first monument in the United States dedicated to the memory of the Confederate war dead was erected. Twenty-nine Confederates who had died of measles at a nearby training camp and some who rode with Nathan Bedford Forrest's Seventh Cavalry in an engagement with the Union army's Seventh Tennessee Cavalry were among those memorialized.

Disease killed more men than did bullets in the Civil War.

OCTOBER 22

1805, JEFFERSON COUNTY

According to county records, David Crockett was licensed to marry Margaret Elder. However, she refused to have him.

Crockett married Polly Finley in August 1806. He left her for Texas in 1835.

1836, FLORIDA

Lieutenant Henry Hollingsworth of the Second Tennessee Volunteers wrote the following advice in his diary: "Go to town and get ½ dozen bottles of liquors. Live well and from the contrast of our late starving condition enjoy it!"

1882, NASHVILLE

Mrs. Baker and Mrs. E. I. Roach from McKenzie and Mrs. Johnson, Mrs. Sam Watson, and Mrs. Hawks from Memphis met with female temperance leaders from other states and formed the Tennessee Temperance Union.

1916, KNOXVILLE

Marie Cline of Crossville, a student nurse at Knoxville General Hospital, was killed in a freak accident. At 4 P.M., she boarded an elevator and fell so that her head was caught between the third and fourth floors and her skull was crushed. "Her body," read the report in the *Crossville Chronicle*, "remained wedged so tight in the elevator shaft that quite a portion of the elevator floor had to be cut away before the body could be removed." Her funeral in Cumberland County was widely attended.

1948, MEMPHIS

During a political rally for Estes Kefauver on Court Square, African-Americans were chased out by police. There was concern that their presence would disrupt the festivities.

OCTOBER 23

1790, CARTER COUNTY

William Blount arrived to take up residence at Rocky Mount. He quickly assembled the local gentry to inform them of the provisions of the ordinance of 1787 and North Carolina's act of cession in 1789. He also related the acceptance by Congress of the territory that was to become the state of Tennessee, declared all appointments under North Carolina law void, and gave the names of newly appointed officials.

Over the next 10 days, he repeated his message in Greene, Hawkins, and Sullivan Counties.

1889, CHATTANOOGA

The *Chattanooga Times* had a lower-court judgment of $2,000 reversed in its favor.

James A. Allen had brought suit against the newspaper for commenting on his public conduct and slandering his name while he was chief of police.

The Tennessee Supreme Court thus upheld the freedom of the press in criticizing the conduct of public servants.

1937, ACROSS THE UNITED STATES

A *Saturday Evening Post* story revealed that when Tennessee politician and newspaperman Luke Lea was a colonel in the United States Army in France in 1919, he had made an unauthorized visit to Kaiser Wilhelm II and tried to persuade the former German leader to submit to a trial for war crimes.

The story was written by T. H. Alexander, a columnist for *The Tennessean*, a paper owned by Lea before his conviction for bank fraud in North Carolina. Lea had given Alexander the first accurate account of his escapade so Alexander could sell the story in order to pay for an operation for his polio-stricken son.

1968, VIETNAM

Lieutenant Raymond G. Clark, 21, a graduate of Brainerd High School in Chattanooga, was killed in combat. Clark was a platoon leader with Company A, Third Battalion, 60th Infantry, Ninth Infantry Division.

Over 49,000 Tennesseans served in Vietnam from 1961 to 1975. Of those, 1,289 were killed.

OCTOBER 24

1843, NASHVILLE

S. H. Laughlin, Democratic state senator representing Warren, Coffee, Cannon, and DeKalb

Counties, wrote in his diary, "Slept late and soundly, got up and went to the Senate. I introduced a Bill to tax Gold watches, plate, paintings, and jewelry at 5 pr. cent on value over $50—and to tax pianos [at] 2 per cent on value, except where used in schools, Academies, and by teachers . . . giving music instruction."

Another tax-and-spend Democrat.

1864, OCCUPIED NASHVILLE

Surrounded by American flags, burning torches, and flying banners, Military Governor Andrew Johnson spoke to African-Americans in front of the State Capitol to proclaim freedom for every man in Tennessee, saying, "I will be your Moses and lead you through the Red Sea of Bondage."

The large crowd of blacks applauded his remarks vigorously, while the music of trumpets, drums, and fifes enlivened the gathering.

1973, WASHINGTON, D.C.

Republican congressman Dan Kuykendall of Tennessee displayed a hangman's noose to members of the House of Representatives after warning them not to become a "legislative lynch mob" in their rush to begin impeachment proceedings against President Richard M. Nixon.

OCTOBER 25

1860, MURFREESBORO

William Anne Dromgoole was born. Inasmuch as her father wanted a boy and had already chosen the name William, it was given to her.

She was an author of prose and poetry, writing under the pseudonym of Will Allen Dromgoole. Her work depicted the lifestyle of

hill folk on the Cumberland Plateau. Her first novel was *The Sunny Side of the Cumberland* (1886). Perhaps her best work was *The Heart of Old Hickory and Other Stories of Tennessee* (1895). She died September 1, 1934.

1878, MEMPHIS AND CHATTANOOGA

Reports surfaced of continued outbreaks of yellow fever, prompting many to leave the cities in panic.

Businessmen found that yellow fever drastically curtailed their transactions. Many died of the fever nicknamed "Bronze John."

1900, NASHVILLE

According to an article in the *Nashville Banner* entitled "Short Skirts," women were boldly wearing ankle-length skirts on clear days. The ladies claimed they did so because it made it easier to get on and off trolley cars.

Apparently, the sight of a woman's ankle was considered scandalous in the last year of the 19th century.

OCTOBER 26

1919, KNOXVILLE

During a streetcar workers' strike, dissidents surrounded a number of streetcars, severed trolley ropes, and pulled motormen and conductors off the vehicles following a massive union meeting. Trolleys were vandalized, rails were greased, and boulders were placed on tracks.

Since many Knoxville policemen were in sympathy with the protesters, Adjutant General Edward B. Sweeney sent in 800 National Guardsmen from the Fourth Tennessee Infantry to maintain order.

1957, NASHVILLE

Governor Frank Goad Clement officiated at a ceremony honoring the crew and officers of the USS *Tennessee*.

The silver punch service handed down from the ship's 1906 precursor and namesake was taken to the Governor's Mansion, where it remained until it was transferred to the Tennessee State Museum for the enjoyment of all.

OCTOBER 27

1832, FRANKLIN COUNTY, ALABAMA

William Wallace Guy was born. His parents moved to Hardeman County in 1836, where he was privately educated. He engaged in farming until the Civil War.

Guy was a member of the Tennessee House from 1859 to 1861. In 1861, he was made associate commissary general with the rank of major of infantry, serving under General Lucius Polk. By 1863, he was acting commissary officer for the Army of Tennessee. He surrendered in 1865 in Montgomery, Alabama.

After the war, he moved to Memphis and engaged in the cotton and wholesale grocery businesses. He died on August 19, 1879, a victim of the yellow-fever epidemic. He was buried at Elmwood Cemetery in Memphis.

1877, MEMPHIS

Nathan Bedford Forrest died in the home owned by his brother, Jesse. Poor financial circumstances had left him deeply in debt.

Forrest is deservedly known as one of the greatest commanders of light cavalry among English-speaking peoples. He also has another, darker reputation as founder and first "Grand Wizard" of the Ku Klux Klan, formed in Pulaski in 1866. Forrest, however, never publicly admitted to being a member of the Klan.

OCTOBER 28

1859, NASHVILLE

The first Louisville & Nashville passenger train and two other locomotives crossed the newly completed railroad drawbridge and entered the capital city.

1859, LOUISVILLE, KENTUCKY

Knoxville industrialist Willis P. Davis, leader of the movement to create Great Smoky Mountains National Park, was born.

His work on behalf of the park was recognized by giving the name Mount Davis to a 5,020-foot elevation on the main crest between Siler's Bend and Thunderhead. He died in 1931.

OCTOBER 29

1799, NORTH CAROLINA

Miles Darden was born.

Darden, who moved to the Volunteer State at about age 30, was perhaps the biggest Tennessean of all time. Estimates of his height range up to eight feet, five inches, and he weighed at least 850 pounds in 1845. A typical Miles Darden breakfast consisted of a dozen eggs, two quarts of coffee, a gallon of water, and 30 buttered biscuits. Three ordinary-sized men could be buttoned inside his coat. He weighed about 1,000 pounds when he died on January 27, 1857. He was buried near the community of Life. A Tennessee Historical Commission marker was erected in his memory in Henderson County.

1809, WILSON COUNTY

James Chamberlain "Lean Jimmy" Jones, the 10th governor of Tennessee, was born.

Jones stood over six feet tall and weighed a scant 125 pounds. He defeated the aristocratic James K. Polk for governor in 1841, largely by mocking him during debates while wearing a coonskin cap. "Lean Jimmy" Jones usually routed "Little Jimmy" Polk in these debates. The coonskin cap became a symbol of the Whig Party in Tennessee during that race.

In his second term as governor, Jones settled on Nashville for the site of the State Capitol and the State Institute for the Blind and Deaf.

In 1851, he was elected by the state legislature to the United States Senate, where he served until March 3, 1857. He died while in the midst of negotiating a substantial railroad deal in Memphis, his place of residence.

Jones was the first native-born Tennessean to fill the governor's chair.

1836, CAMP LANE, FLORIDA

Lieutenant Henry Hollingsworth wrote in his daily journal, "We are now out of liquor—out of, in fact, everything but meat and bread."

After selling his saddle for $4, Hollingsworth purchased food and other necessaries "and return[ed] to camp rich as a lord." Several men under his command were sent out "striking"— searching for food—and returned with a small pig. The resourceful Tennesseans then enjoyed an excellent meal, including a soup made by Hollingsworth.

He noted in his journal, "We all done justice to the brandy meantime."

1878, KNOXVILLE

Workmen erected telephone poles on Clinch Street for the system being established for the firm of William R. Caswell and Company. Knoxville's first telephone system was designed to connect the company's storerooms to its steam works at the Maryville railroad crossing.

OCTOBER 30

1773, NORTH CAROLINA

Hugh Lawson White was born.

His family later moved to Knoxville, where he began his study of law. White was a judge on the Tennessee Supreme Court from 1801 to 1807, a state senator, a United States district attorney, and president of the Bank of Tennessee from 1811 to 1827. He served with Andrew Jackson during the War of 1812. He was a United States senator from 1825 to 1840; a disagreement with Jackson led him to run as an independent in the 1836 election. He later bolted the Democratic Party and became a Whig. He died on April 10, 1840.

1861, NASHVILLE

Governor Isham Green Harris sent a telegram to Jefferson Davis. Harris believed a Federal attack from Kentucky was inevitable and wanted to know if the Confederate president would return the troops Tennessee had sent earlier. Davis evidently did not reply.

In just four months, Nashville was occupied by Union troops.

1897, NASHVILLE

In a speech at the ceremonies closing the Nashville Centennial Exposition, orator Tully

Brown asked rhetorically if the people of the city would yield to plans to tear down the Parthenon: "Who will be the man that will strike the first blow at the Parthenon?"

His windy rhetoric was instrumental in the move to save the building for the "Athens of the South." It stands today at Centennial Park and is utilized as an art museum.

1959, NASHVILLE

Hill McAlister, governor of Tennessee from 1933 to 1937, died.

As a progressive state legislator, McAlister initiated reforms in the Pure Food and Drugs Department and introduced a bill establishing

James Chamberlain "Lean Jimmy" Jones [October 29]

Davidson County's tuberculosis hospital. He lost both his 1926 and 1928 bids for the governor's seat but won in 1932. As governor, he launched a severe cost-cutting program that even reduced the annual cost of running the Governor's Mansion from $35,000 to $1,000. A sober governor, he seldom made jokes. He won distinction for granting pardons to many convicts. During McAlister's administration, Norris Dam was completed and the first commercial airports in the state were built in Chattanooga, Memphis, and Nashville. After his term, McAlister was appointed a field counsel for the Bituminous Coal Commission in Washington, D.C.

OCTOBER 31

1794, IN WHAT IS NOW BLOUNT COUNTY

James Greenway, future member of the Tennessee General Assembly, was reportedly licensed to trade with the "Southern Indians for horses at Tellico Blockhouse."

After statehood was granted to Tennessee, Greenway's wealth was established as three slaves and 950 acres of land. He was appointed a justice of the peace by Governor William Blount on August 3, 1795, and was elected a delegate to the Tennessee Constitutional Convention in 1796.

1888, CHATTANOOGA

The funeral of Madam Rosa Walker, described as the "proprietor of the bagnio on Florence street," was held. The hearse was followed by 12 carriages filled with women, "all inmates of houses of similar character in the city." The service was brief. According to the *Chattanooga Daily Times*, it was "attended only by women who display their devotion one to another even until death." A sense of professional community was evident in the large number of courtesans who attended.

Walker had inherited the Florence Street house from her mother and "maintained it as her mother had done . . . in order to gain . . . a livelihood."

1891, BRICEVILLE, ANDERSON COUNTY

Hundreds of armed miners surrounded the state prison stockade and forced the release of convict miners. Like a guerrilla army, they then melted into the hills and hollows of the Cumberland Plateau.

The legislature had failed to address the grievances of the miners, who wanted the state to abolish the convict lease system, which cheapened their wages.

1895, NASHVILLE

Between 5:00 and 5:15 A.M., the city was shaken by an earthquake. According to one newspaper account, "The quaking was preceded by a low rumbling sound, as of distant thunder. . . . The vibrations were strong enough to wake people . . . and rattle windows and bric a brac."

Judge John H. Henderson of Franklin wrote in his diary, "This morning shortly after 5 o'clock there was an earthquake of from ½ to one minute. I at first thought it was Mrs. Perkins moving about upstairs, but finally concluded it was an earthquake."

The quake was felt in other Southern cities as well.

1923, LAWRENCEBURG

The Ku Klux Klan marched up and down the main streets of the city in their ghostlike outfits singing religious songs. Approximately 100 Klansmen attended the event. They did their trick, but it is not known if they got a treat.

1958, KNOXVILLE

A number of fistfights broke out during a football game between the University of North Carolina and the University of Tennessee. According to the *Knoxville News-Sentinel* of November 1, "[The] sod looked more like a boxing ring than a gridiron. The gladiators swapped punches." Other minor altercations occurred in and out of the stadium. Tennessee lost the game 21–7.

1971, STRAWBERRY PLAINS

A United States Navy A-4 Skyhawk on a routine training mission accidentally dropped a 900-pound Walleye missile 5,000 feet onto the home of Judge James Parrot. The bomb went through the roof, tore a 30-foot hole in the attic floor, demolished the master bedroom, and came to rest in the basement of the $40,000 home. All but two family members were at church when the accident occurred. Miraculously, no one was hurt, but the home was a total wreck. Naval investigators made no comment to the press.

November

Coca-Cola's popularity [November 12] spread throughout the state, as this 1915 picture attests.

1835, MEMPHIS

Former congressman David Crockett and three companions arrived in town, put up at the Union Hotel, and engaged in a farewell drinking soiree just before leaving the Volunteer State for Texas.

After a few libations, Crockett toasted those who had not voted for him in the recent congressional election, "Since you have chosen to elect a man with a timber toe [Adam Huntsman, who had a peg leg] to succeed me, you may all go to hell and I will go to Texas."

According to one account, as he crossed the Mississippi River the next morning, he was wearing a coonskin cap. Four months later, he was killed at the Alamo.

1878, NASHVILLE

Alex Ament, it was reported, bet $50 that Charles Deschaw couldn't eat 30 quail eggs on each of 30 consecutive days.

Deschaw performed his gastronomic task between 8 A.M. and 9 A.M. each morning. Despite some digestive disorders caused by the fowl eggs, he won the bet.

Deschaw claimed that on January 1, 1879, he would resume eating 30 eggs per day, and increased the stakes by betting $500 he could do it for 90 consecutive days. There is no record to indicate if anyone took the bet.

1880, GALLATIN

For nearly a month, the number of vagabonds in the area had been increasing, as hobos from the North made their way south on freight trains. "People all along the line complain of their annoying presence," it was reported. "Many [tramps] . . . are desperadoes of the worst class."

Today, J. W. Brown, editor of the *Gallatin Examiner*, was badly beaten by a band of eight tramps while on his way to work. Brown was passing through the south tunnel of the Louisville & Nashville when the attack occurred. He drew his pistol, killed one of his attackers, and seriously wounded another. The remaining thieves overpowered him and robbed him of $900, a gold watch, and an emerald stickpin.

While Brown was expected to recover, it was also believed he would lose his right arm. The Sumner County sheriff organized a posse. Armed citizens scoured the area for the culprits.

1932, GRUNDY COUNTY

The famous Highlander Folk School was opened by social and political activist Myles F. Horton in the Summerfield community.

Horton taught many labor leaders and civil rights activists the essentials of nonviolent resistance. His pupils included Martin Luther King, Jr., and Rosa Parks.

Reactionary Tennesseans were fearful of Horton, thinking he must be a communist. In the 1950s, the school was confiscated by anxious state legislators who trumped up a liquor-law violation against Horton. The school mysteriously burned to the ground in December 1961.

Highlander Folk School continues to function in New Market, Tennessee.

1795, MECKLENBERG COUNTY, NORTH CAROLINA

James K. Polk, the 10th governor of Tennessee and the 11th president of the United States, was born.

Oddly enough, Polk lost his own state when he won the presidency in 1844. He led the United States in a war against Mexico and gained approximately 1.2 million square miles of territory by conquest or treaty, at a cost of only $15 million—or about $12.50 per square mile. The Mexican cession included the present states of Arizona, Nevada, California, and Utah, as well as parts of New Mexico, Colorado, and Wyoming.

When his term ended, he kept a campaign promise that he would not run again. Polk died of cholera in Nashville on June 15, 1849.

1875, NASHVILLE

At a meeting of the Tennessee Historical Society, the discussion between Colonel J. B. Killebrew and Judge J. M. Lea was about the "pigmies," short-statured ancient people believed to have lived on the slope of the Cumberland Mountains or at the foot of the mountains in White County. Some early ethnologists and archaeologists were said to have found stone graves with small skeletons in them, each face down.

1903, THE CARIBBEAN, NEAR NORTHERN COLOMBIA

In order to protect his upcoming orchestrated Panamanian revolution, President Theodore Roosevelt ordered American warships, the most significant of them being the USS *Nashville*, to maintain the "free and uninterrupted transit" guaranteed by the Treaty of New Granada (1846).

The *Nashville* served notice to Colombian forces that as the "revolution" on their northernmost soil began, they were not to interfere with the Panamanian insurrection.

The successful revolt allowed the plucky Panamanians to realize a dream they hardly knew they had. By November 6, the United States recognized the newly independent nation of Panama. By November 18, a treaty was signed giving the United States permission to construct the Panama Canal.

NOVEMBER 3

1803, KNOXVILLE

The Tennessee legislature passed a law forbidding any white person to incite slaves by making inflammatory speeches about freedom and the equality of humankind. Such talk would, they believed, cause slaves to desire their freedom.

1813, MISSISSIPPI TERRITORY

General Andrew Jackson ordered General John Coffee and his mounted rifles to destroy the Native American town of Tallushatchee.

Early in the morning, nearly 1,000 Tennessee soldiers attacked systematically. David Crockett said of the subsequent massacre, "We shot them like dogs; and then set . . . [a] house on fire with forty six warriors in it." The next day, claimed Crockett, famished soldiers returned to the burnt house and found potatoes in the cellar. The soldiers ate the potatoes, not minding that "the oil of the Indians we had burned the day before had run down on them, and they looked like they had been stewed with fat meat."

It was at Tallushatchee that an Indian infant, Lincoya, was found on the battlefield alive but unclaimed by any of the Indian women who were prisoners. Moved, Jackson, once an orphan himself, took Lincoya to serve as a companion for his adopted son, Andrew Jackson, Jr. In a letter to his wife, Jackson wrote, "Charity and Christianity says he ought to be taken care of and I send him to my little Andrew and I hope will adopt him as one of our family." Later, Jackson wrote his wife that she must "keep Lincoya in the House—he is a Savage [yet]. . . . He may have been given to me for some Valuable purpose—when I reflect that he as to his relations is much like myself I feel an unusual sympathy for him—tell my little Andrew to treat him well."

Lincoya often ran away to look for his people. He was taught the harness-making trade. He died in 1828, having lived at the Hermitage 15 or 16 years. His grave is unmarked.

1864, ON THE TENNESSEE RIVER

Confederate forces captured two United States Navy ships, the *Undine* and the *Venus*, near New Johnsonville. After cruising the river to create diversion, the *Venus* was run aground and the *Undine* was sunk by order of Nathan Bedford Forrest. The next day, Forrest attacked New Johnsonville.

In 1992, the Tennessee Division of Archaeology initiated a project to find and possibly raise the *Undine*.

NOVEMBER 4

1854, NASHVILLE

The old oak bridge over the Cumberland River collapsed just after workmen assigned the job of razing it had left work and gone home. No injuries were reported.

After blocking the river approaches to Johnsonville Landing, General Nathan Bedford Forrest's cavalry captured Federal boats and destroyed the base at Johnsonville with artillery. Losses were placed at four United States Navy gunboats, 14 steamboats, 12 barges, and 95,000 tons of quartermaster stores. Some 150 Union soldiers were taken prisoners. Forrest's force lost but two dead and nine wounded.

NOVEMBER 5

1794, CUMBERLAND SETTLEMENTS

Colonel Isaac Tittsworth and his brother John decided to move their families to Double Licks, Kentucky, away from the danger of Creek Indian attacks. As they slept in the forest that night, they were attacked by Indians. Eight whites were killed and five taken prisoner. The neighboring militia gave chase but could not catch the war party. It was said that the three children taken prisoner could not keep up with the warriors and were scalped by "the Indians holding them by the hair and dragging them along until their heads were entirely skinned."

1884, HAMILTON COUNTY

William C. Hodge was elected to the state legislature. He was the first African-American from the county in the general assembly.

1901, NASHVILLE

After repeated warnings to contain their bovines at home, many house and cow owners were indicted by a grand jury for letting their animals roam freely in East Nashville. The city meant to enforce its anti-cow law.

1912, NASHVILLE

The 51-million-gallon municipal reservoir sustained a rupture in its east wall at 12:10 A.M. Many were inconvenienced by the sudden rush of water, but there were no fatalities.

The facility was repaired and operates today. It is listed on the National Register of Historic Places.

1947, KNOXVILLE

Sallie Rebecca "Pattie" Boyd, newspaperwoman, died.

A Knoxville native, Boyd was educated in the public schools. On her own initiative at age 18, she landed a job with the *Knoxville Tribune* and wrote a social/gossip column as society editor, a position she held for half a century. Pattie Boyd was the first woman on the editorial staff of any Knoxville newspaper.

1948, KNOXVILLE

Residents of West Knoxville were thrown into a near-panic when several hundred pounds of ammonia gas escaped from a nearby ice plant. Many were forced to vacate their homes to avoid the poisonous fumes. No one was hurt.

1948, NASHVILLE

Country-and-western legend Roy Acuff, recently defeated in his bid for the governor's chair, was, as he said, "tired and run down." He entered Midstate Baptist Hospital for a checkup and rest.

NOVEMBER 6

1794, KNOXVILLE

An advertisement in the *Knoxville Gazette* read, "Notice is given that Mary Parker hath absconded from my bed and board and I hereby warn all persons to have no dealings with her on my account."

1861, ACROSS THE VOLUNTEER STATE

Eligible male voters chose their representatives and senators for the Confederate Congress.

1863, BIG CREEK

The Big Creek skirmish occurred when Confederate general Sam Jones arrived at a site outside Rogersville. His subordinate, Colonel Henry Gilmer, was riding from Surgoinsville. Federal forces caught between them were the Second Mounted Infantry and elements of the Seventh Ohio Cavalry. The entire Union force was captured.

1958, KNOXVILLE

A front-page story in the *Knoxville News-Sentinel* told how Princess Sophia of Greece, on a goodwill tour of America, had turned down an invitation to attend a football game so she might visit TVA facilities. It was a good thing, too, as the football game in question ended in a riot.

NOVEMBER 7

1794, TELLICO

Whites and 400 Cherokees had a powwow to discuss the recent massacres at the Indian settlements of Nickajack and Running Water Town. The Cherokees, under duress, seemed to agree that they had gotten what they deserved.

1835, BRADLEY COUNTY

At the last home of the Cherokee Nation east of the Mississippi River, John Ross, principal chief of the Cherokees and the man who led the battle against removal, and John Howard Payne, author of the song "Home, Sweet Home," were illegally arrested by Georgia soldiers and imprisoned at Spring Place, Georgia. Both were to be held until "about Christmas," it was reported.

The illegal arrests made possible the "Christmas trick of New Echota," so named because without John Ross to negotiate for them, the Cherokees agreed to leave their ancestral grounds.

After his release, Payne spoke and wrote extensively on the plight of the Cherokees. It did little good, because United States Army rifles and bayonets made a more convincing statement.

1836, CAMP LANE, FLORIDA

Lieutenant Henry Hollingsworth of the Second Tennessee Volunteers confided in his diary that "General [Robert] Armstrong left here a few days since for Ft. Drane, after having been drunk for a week at this place."

Armstrong was more a close friend of President Andrew Jackson than a soldier.

1903, NASHVILLE

African-American physicians, dentists, and pharmicists attended the first of three days of meetings of the National Medical Convention, held at First Baptist Church. Nashville's F. A. Stewart, head of the NMC, presided.

1905, MOUNTAIN CITY

Finley Preston, a notorious murderer, was hanged. A large crowd of spectators came to have a picnic and witness the execution.

1964, MEMPHIS

Archie W. Willis, Jr., became the first African-American from the Bluff City to be elected to the state legislature since the 1880s.

Finley Preston, being made ready for hanging [November 7]

1809, KNOXVILLE

The legislature passed an act forbidding private lotteries because "it has been represented to this General Assembly, that the drawing of private lotteries hath become a serious and alarming evil, relaxing the sinews of industry and encouraging habits of idleness and dissipation."

1833, NASHVILLE

Tennessee declared its supremacy and jurisdiction over the Cherokees.

The problem was that the Indians owned land that the state wanted to sell for pennies an acre to speculators, who would in turn sell it for dollars an acre to white settlers.

1861, EAST TENNESSEE

While nominally under the control of Confederate forces, five major railroad bridges were burned by Union sympathizers.

It was thought by many secessionists that William G. Brownlow was involved in the plot. He was not, but as he said to a friend later, "I thought . . . that the affair was beautifully planned and executed, and I enjoyed it considerably in my own quiet way."

1890, NEAR WOODBURY, CANNON COUNTY

James H. Cummings was born. Known as "Mr. Jim," he was a lifelong Democrat and a political legend.

Cummings was first elected to the state legislature in 1929. After that, he served continuously in the House and the Senate except for the years from 1949 to 1952, when he was Tennessee's secretary of state. During the 85th general assembly, he was speaker of the House. A strong advocate of rural education, he is credited with saving Middle Tennessee State Teachers' College and Agricultural and Industrial State College, today Middle Tennessee State University, from destruction during the Great Depression.

1920, CHATTANOOGA

Dr. Philander Davis died.

Davis was born in what is now Putnam County in 1828. He attended the Alpine Institute and received his M.D. from the University of Nashville in 1856. He then moved to Chattanooga, where he stayed the rest of his life. In 1873, he was elected Chattanooga's first Democratic mayor since the Civil War. During the 1878 yellow-fever epidemic, he was active in organizing the fight against the disease. He was president of the Medical Society of Tennessee for the year 1887–88.

1958, KNOXVILLE

A riot took place after the Chattanooga Moccasins defeated the Tennessee Volunteers 14–6. According to a banner headline in the *Knoxville News-Sentinel* the following day, "1000 Riot at U-T for 1½ Hours."

The rioting began soon after Chattanooga fans succeeded in uprooting the goalpost at the north end of Shields-Watkins Field. It spread outside the stadium, where Chattanooga mayor P. R. Ogliati pleaded in vain for calm.

The crowd witnessing the execution of Finley Preston [November 7]

In the end, police were forced to use tear gas and water hoses to quell the football fans' anarchy. Eight policemen and one civilian were injured, and 10 arrests were made.

NOVEMBER 9

1813, MISSISSIPPI TERRITORY

At the Battle of Talladega, Andrew Jackson's forces killed 300 Creek Indians, versus 15 American dead and 85 wounded.

This was the last victory for Jackson's army until the early spring of 1814. Disagreements about the length of enlistment and the steady shortage of food and clothing led many Tennessee soldiers (at one point an entire brigade, or about 1,000 soldiers) to leave Jackson and head home. The enraged Jackson considered the legally departing soldiers mutineers.

1861, HAMILTON COUNTY

In the early morning, bands of Union sympathizers burned two railroad bridges over Chickamauga Creek, cutting Chattanooga's rail connection with Knoxville and Atlanta. This was part of a coordinated effort by East Tennessee's Unionist guerrillas, who hoped to clear the way for a Federal invasion from Kentucky.

The offensive, however, never materialized. Confederate forces executed several guerrillas elsewhere in East Tennessee for similar attacks.

1908, NASHVILLE

On the corner of Union Street and Seventh Avenue, where the Holiday Inn Crown Plaza stands today, Edward Ward Carmack was killed by newspaper publishers Duncan and Robin Cooper.

The Coopers, father and son, were jailed and later indicted for murder. The testimony indicated that Carmack had fired the first shot and hit Robin Cooper, who then fired three shots at Carmack, two of which hit his heart and one his spinal column.

The incident stirred up the prohibition movement in Tennessee, inasmuch as Carmack was a teetotaler.

Both the Coopers were sentenced to 20 years. Upon appeal, the charges against Robin were dropped, and his father was pardoned by Governor Malcolm R. Patterson.

Robin Cooper was mysteriously murdered 11 years later.

NOVEMBER 10

1860, MEMPHIS

The *Memphis Daily Appeal* announced that one of the two steam-powered fire engines the city had purchased would arrive from Cincinnati in January 1861.

These were to be an instrument of change for the fire department. The volunteers' penchant for lawlessness had created a demand for a paid and municipally controlled fire department. However, the Civil War halted delivery of the new fire engines.

1862, ON THE MISSISSIPPI RIVER

Covered by Federal gunboats, Major General John Pope landed part of his force of 25,000 on the western shore of Madrid Bend, a maneuver that outflanked Confederate defensive positions.

Confederate brigadier general W. W. McKall, retreating south, found his egress blocked by gunboats and high water. He surrendered the remnants of his force on the northern outskirts of Tiptonville.

1898, MEMPHIS

A representative of the prestigious landscape architectural firm of Frederick Law Olmsted, Jr., arrived to discuss the design of the future Overton Park.

1973, GOODLETTSVILLE

Banjo virtuoso David "Stringbean" Akeman and his wife, Estelle, were tragically murdered at their home.

Born in Annville, Kentucky, in 1915, Stringbean began playing the banjo before he was in his teens and started performing professionally before he was in his 20s. He worked with Charles and Bill Monroe on the Grand Ole Opry in 1942. His banjo style closely mimicked that of "Uncle" Dave Macon. Stringbean appeared on the county-music show *Hee Haw*.

NOVEMBER 11

1794, MONTGOMERY COUNTY

The stone blockhouse built by Colonel Valentine was attacked by Indians. Six persons were killed, including his son, James. His daughter, Rebecca, was scalped but survived.

1813, MISSISSIPPI TERRITORY

While marching to Andrew Jackson's relief at Fort Strother during the Creek Indian War, Captain Jacob Hartsell of Tennessee wrote in his diary that he saw in a Cherokee village "all kinds of squaws with their children on their backs, one little girl with one almost as large as herself on her back asleep. I laughed as hearty as ever I did at the sight."

1842, PERSON COUNTY, VIRGINIA

Sawney Webb, founder of the world-famous Webb School in Bell Buckle, was born.

Webb was a stalwart Democrat and served briefly as a United States senator.

1878, MEMPHIS AND CHATTANOOGA

Both of these river cities reported that the recent infestation of yellow fever had ended. Promoters glibly predicted that business, severely hurt by the epidemic, would soon resume its normal pattern.

1878, KNOXVILLE

William Francis Yardley, a black attorney and politician, was seeing a lady friend off on the noon train. He lingered with her a bit too long, however, and the train started moving toward the Broad Street crossing. Yardley jumped off and was thrown down and badly bruised, striking the crossties with his left foot, tearing his shoe to pieces, and cutting his flesh. He also received a gash above his right eye and knocked a few teeth loose. He received medical attention and was sent home.

Love is a many-splendored thing.

1885, MEMPHIS

Forty-two moonshiners were convicted in federal court, illustrating that United States marshal Freeman's September 14 threat to rid West Tennessee of illegal stills was not an idle one.

NOVEMBER 12

1895, NIOTA, MCMINN COUNTY

Harry Thomas Burn was born.

Burn was a Republican representative in the

Tennessee House from 1919 to 1923. He played a crucial role in the struggle for women's suffrage, casting the deciding vote on August 18, 1920, to pass the 19th Amendment, which gave American women the right to vote.

1899, CHATTANOOGA

Benjamin F. Thomas and J. F. Johnston started the world's first Coca-Cola bottling plant. They initially delivered their product in a two-mule wagon.

1994, NASHVILLE

Wilma Rudolph, the first woman and the first African-American Tennessean to win three Olympic gold medals, died of brain cancer.

Rudolph overcame polio, scarlet fever, and pneumonia in her early life to become one of the world's most distinguished athletes and role models for black youth. She was a graduate of Tennessee State University and a member of the famous Tiger Belles, directed by Coach Edward Templeton. Her achievements were extraordinary and exemplary.

NOVEMBER 13

1847, MECHANICSVILLE, CANNON COUNTY

Confederate guerrilla leader Hiram Taylor "Pomp" Kersey was born.

Kersey was only 13 when the Civil War began and 16 when he was tracked down and killed by elements of the Fifth Cavalry on July 24, 1864. His body was put on display in Liberty.

1902, NASHVILLE

The city council passed its first million-dollar budget.

1958, NEW YORK CITY

Governor Frank Goad Clement and his wife began a five-week cruise on the HMS *Queen Mary* that would take them to Europe—including the Nobel Prize ceremonies in Norway—and the Middle East. Clement said he was "particularly anxious to visit the Middle-East. As a Christian I am interested in seeing Israel, which I consider a real bastion of democracy to which the United States of America can look in these troubled times."

The Clements expected to return to the United States by December 17.

NOVEMBER 14

1785, JONESBOROUGH

The legislative body of the "Lost State of Franklin," met for the first time. Those who formed the state mistakenly believed that North Carolina had released its western provinces from its laws and authority.

1823, NORTH OF TREZEVANT, CARROLL COUNTY

The town of Christmasville was founded at John Christmas McLemore's bluff on the South Fork of the Obion River.

Goods were shipped to and from this spot until 1854. The town spring furnished water for the early inhabitants and a tanning yard. A post office operated in Christmasville from 1827 to 1902.

1894, NASHVILLE

George K. Whitworth, the clerk and master of the chancery court, shot and killed Chancellor Allen, the man who had appointed him six years earlier. Soon thereafter, he discarded his pistol, replaced it with a shotgun, and shot himself.

According to the *Nashville Banner*, "Never in its history has Nashville been so profoundly shocked." Whitworth died of his wounds on November 22.

1934, NASHVILLE

The African Methodist Episcopal Ministers Alliance of Nashville protested the planning of the 398-unit Andrew Jackson Courts, a public housing project in the black section of the city.

"Standing on Fisk University Campus look west and observe two square miles of Negro homes whose owners' prayers for sewers and city improvements go unanswered[,] where the death rate exceed[s] the birth rate with typhoid fever and tuberculosis playing the leading roles," the alliance noted in a letter to Secretary of the Interior Harold L. Ickes. "Might does not make right in the housing scheme of white promoters that cannot vote the endorsement of a single Negro organization."

The plea for streetlights, sewers, and paved streets in the black section of town went unheeded. The Jackson housing project was carried out according to plan.

NOVEMBER 15

1879, MEMPHIS

A mass meeting called to consider the sewer question was moved to the Mississippi River bluff when a crowd of approximately 2,000 shouted down opponents. Thoroughly frustrated, meeting organizers appointed a committee to select an appropriate plan for a citywide sewer system.

1880, MORGAN AND SCOTT COUNTIES

The formal opening of Rugby, the English utopian colony, took place. The colony was intended for second and third sons of the British gentry, who could not by law inherit their fathers' wealth.

1888, SHELBYVILLE

The editor of the *Shelbyville Gazette* addressed the issue of the corset: "Let us say, for example, suppose a woman is flat where she should show the curve of beauty, suppose a plumb-line dropped from her neck, back or front elevations. . . . What is she to do? Without going into indecorous particulars it is easy to show why few women would be doing themselves justice in rejecting the aid of art. . . . The first duty of a woman is to make herself attractive. When flesh and blood fail, art must supply the deficiency."

1913, THE TENNESSEE RIVER

The pre-TVA hydroelectric facility at Hale's Bar first transmitted electrical power to Chattanooga. The dam across the river had taken years to build. A lock operated on the western side.

The huge facility's remains can be seen from the Interstate 24 bridge over Nickajack Lake.

1989, NASHVILLE

Representative Tommy S. Burnett, a spokesman for Fentress, Overton, and Morgan Counties in the general assembly since 1971, was indicted on 10 felony charges for conspiracy, mail fraud, and illegal gambling during the Rocky Top investigation into bingo operations and corruption in public office.

He was convicted on nine counts on July 6, 1990. On November 1, he was ordered to pay

$48,000 in restitution and was sentenced to five years' probation after his prison sentence was completed at a federal detention facility. His term began on January 2, 1991.

Burnett had been chosen the Tennessee Jaycees' Outstanding Young Man in 1975, was listed in *Who's Who among Students in American Universities and Colleges*, and was a former president of the Rotary Club and a member of the Church of Christ. In 1984, he had served 15 months at the federal prison camp at Maxwell Air Force Base in Alabama for tax evasion.

While serving his 15-month sentence on the charges brought in 1989, he was reelected from jail, so popular was he among his constituents.

NOVEMBER 16

1873, FLORENCE, ALABAMA

African-American W. C. Handy was born.

Handy moved to Memphis and found overnight fame in 1909 after being hired for Edward H. Crump's first mayoral campaign. Handy wrote "Mr. Crump," a blues-style campaign song, for the Memphis politico. Not only did Crump win the election, but Handy's band achieved wide popularity in the Bluff City.

Handy soon operated a chain of bands and began to write and publish music. Among his better-known titles are "Beale Street Blues" and "Harlem Blues." In 1931, Handy was honored with a parade in Memphis. A city park was also named after him. He died in 1958.

1946, LIMA, PERU

Ambassador Prentice Cooper, former governor of Tennessee, organized an American relief expedition to help Peruvians in outlying districts after the monumental earthquake of November 10. He was praised for his genuine efforts to help the suffering victims.

NOVEMBER 17

1788, JONESBOROUGH

Although 20-year-old Andrew Jackson had not been in this village of 60 log cabins for long, he purchased his first slave. A bill of sale in the Washington County Court's minute book for the years 1783 to 1793 shows that Jackson purchased an African-American, Nancy, who was 18 or 20 years old. It is not known if the gender of his newly acquired asset was a consequence of supply or demand.

Unlike her owner, Nancy's fate is not known.

1814, GREENE COUNTY

Sam Milligan, a member of the general assembly from 1841 to 1847, was born.

An attorney in Greeneville, Milligan served with the Quartermaster Department during the Mexican War. He taught school, served as editor of *The Spy*, and was a delegate to the Democratic Conventions at Charleston and Baltimore in 1860. He was offered the associate judgeship of the Nebraska Supreme Court by Abraham Lincoln, but refused. He was also offered positions as solicitor of the treasurer, consul to Cuba, and minister to Bolivia by President Andrew Johnson, all of which he declined. He did accept an appointment to the Tennessee Supreme Court but resigned after four years when he became a judge on the Court of Claims in the nation's capital. He remained a civilian during the Civil War. He died April 7, 1874, in Washington, D.C., and was buried in Oak Grove Cemetery in Greeneville.

1878, KNOXVILLE

It was announced that the city's most prolific sausage manufacturer, Ignaz Fanz, was shipping a total of 1,200 pounds of sausage every day.

1896, MEMPHIS

Two world records for bicycling were established at the Memphis Coliseum.

Jimmie Michael, "the Welsh Wonder," shaved 13 seconds off his previous record for five miles.

John "the Terrible Swede" Lawson slashed 13 minutes and 27 seconds off the 50-mile unpaced record. The Terrible Swede began at 3 P.M. and averaged two minutes and 40 seconds per mile for the first 25 miles. To keep up his strength, he drank beef soup from a mug handed to him by his trainer. Lawson completed the 50 miles in two hours, six minutes, and three seconds, averaging just under 25 miles an hour, an outstanding speed even today.

1914, BULL'S GAP

Archie Campbell, star of the Grand Ole Opry and *Hee Haw*, was born. A Tennessee Historical Commission marker now stands in remembrance of him.

1958, WASHINGTON, D.C.

Senator Al Gore, Sr., of Tennessee recommended to President Dwight D. Eisenhower that the United States seize the initiative at the Geneva talks by offering to halt the atmospheric explosion of nuclear weapons for a minimum of three years. Gore had just returned from failed talks with the United Kingdom and the Soviet Union on nuclear test bans. "We can act to stop further contamination of the atmosphere without cumbersome inspection systems," Gore said.

It seems that future vice president Al Gore, Jr., got much of his concern for the environment from his father.

NOVEMBER 18

1859, NASHVILLE

After eight days of editorial warfare between George G. Poindexter of the *Nashville Union and American* and Allen A. Hall of the *Nashville News*, a political controversy became a personal clash.

Following a scurrilous comment by Poindexter in the *Union and American*, Hall had let it be known that he resented the calumnies printed in that paper and that "I shall go on with a thorough exposure of all misstatements, misrepresentations, and falsehoods which may appear in the *Union and American* . . . and [I am] fully able and prepared to protect my person against assault and to punish the assailant."

On the morning of the 18th, Poindexter, carrying an umbrella that concealed a navy pistol, walked toward the offices of the *News*. When he got within 30 feet, Hall stepped out with a double-barrel shotgun and shouted three times for Poindexter to halt, commands his rival did not obey. Hall raised the shotgun, took deliberate aim, and emptied one of the two chambers into Poindexter's torso, killing him instantly.

NOVEMBER 19

1847, NASHVILLE

The *Nashville Daily Republican* contained an advertisement for "Taylor's Celebrated Female Bitters." Among other things, this compound was a "remedy in all cases of Deranged Menstruation, bringing about regular, easy, and healthy Menstrual Evacuations."

Taylor's Bitters were purchased by women primarily for their effect in inducing abortion in the first trimester.

1873, NASHVILLE

An intoxicated C. H. Collins was behaving rudely and brandishing a large knife on the corner of Deaderick Street and the public square. Officer John Allison asked him to put down the knife but was instead severely cut by the blade, sustaining a seven-inch gash. Allison was then stabbed again and knocked down. His right arm was so badly cut that he could not draw his pistol, so a bystander gave him the weapon, which he held in his left hand.

Officer Allison chased Collins on foot down Deaderick Street, firing four shots. Collins was running up Cherry Street toward Union when two other policemen managed to subdue him. He was taken to the station house and then to the workhouse.

Collins, on a binge for a number of days, had been arrested for assaulting John O'Malley just the day before. Officer Collins was ordered not to report for duty until his wounds healed.

1932, FENTRESS COUNTY

Company A of the 109th Cavalry arrived in Wilder-Davidson to suppress starving, striking miners and protect company property. The soldiers stayed until December 24, then returned from January 5 to February 2 the following year.

NOVEMBER 20

1857, BLOUNTVILLE

While on a business trip, Randal McGavock stopped at Snapp's Tavern. There, he shared a room with Thomas A. R. Nelson. According to McGavock's diary, "This morning Col. Nelson rose as is his custom, made a fire and commenced his work but it being rather cold he took a drink of apple brandy and before breakfast he took five drinks which made him drunk. I was pained to see this, for he is a man of the first order of intellect and an ornament to the State."

1865, NASHVILLE

William Heffran was dragged out of his carriage and killed by ruffians.

His murderers were executed on January 26, 1866. Today's carjackings had a 19th-century counterpart.

1895, WARTBURG

Charles Hurd, an African-American charged with killing a white man, was taken from his cell in the Morgan County Jail by masked men. The mob dragged him about 100 yards to an oak tree and swung him up. Hurd managed to free his hands and climb to a limb. He was knocked down, and a second attempt at hanging him was successful.

The owner of the oak demanded that the body be removed. It was then hanged from another tree 1,000 feet from the first one. A sign was pinned to the corpse's chest threatening death to anyone removing the body until the next day.

1922, MICHIGAN

Benton E. Dubbs of Michigan wrote the Tennessee Historical Society describing his experiences in Nashville during the Civil War. According to Dubbs, "They had an old saying that no man could be a soldier unless he had gone through Smoky Row[.] They [Dubbs's friends] started through Smoky Row . . . and I went with them and of all the sights you could see I dare not tell you, but I believe the street was three-quarters of a mile long and Every house or shanty [on] Both sides was a house of Ill fame[.] Women had no thought of Dress or Decency. They said Smoky Row killed more soldiers than the war."

NOVEMBER 21

1813, ALABAMA TERRITORY

While in camp with John Cocke's East Tennessee relief force, Captain Jacob Hartsell witnessed the execution of a Creek Indian by Cherokees. According to Hartsell,

They took him to the Indian fire. . . . One of the Cherokee Indians took his knife out and cut [the prisoner's] hair . . . off close to his head. Immediately they took him towards the guard. . . . One of the Indians struck his tomahawk into his head, no sooner then that was five or six more in his head. He fell to the ground. One of the Indians stepped up and scalped him and took his scalp in his hand and jumped and hollered "aleway, aleway" and seemed to rejoice much. One of the others stripped him; another put a piece of rope around his neck and drawed him around the neck. . . . Several of them stuck their knives in him.

1815, GREENE COUNTY

During a meeting at Lick Creek Friends' Meeting House, the assorted abolitionist societies of East Tennessee formed an association named the Tennessee Manumission Society.

While better organized than previous abolitionists, these opponents of slavery were no more effective.

1852, LAWRENCEVILLE, ALABAMA

African-American attorney S. L. Hutchinson was born.

Because his father was a successful artist, Hutchinson enjoyed educational opportunities that most blacks—even most whites—did not have. He studied law at the University of South Carolina and practiced in that state and in Georgia until 1881, when he moved to Chattanooga. Just one year after arriving, he entered politics and with other black citizens established an African-American newspaper, *The Independent Age*, for which he served as editor. In 1896, Hutchinson was nominated by the Hamilton County Republican Convention to run for a seat in the Tennessee House. He won election and held his seat until 1898. Thereafter, he practiced law until at least 1905.

1992, STANTON

This tiny West Tennessee town where health insurance and physicians were nearly unknown participated in a novel experiment in which the National Guard provided health-care services.

Governor Ned McWherter visited and had his blood pressure checked. According to the governor, "Now that the cold war is over, the [Berlin] Wall is down, we need to utilize the military in the country to improve the quality of life, try to help control health care costs and, more than anything, help this next generation of young boys and girls be a healthy generation."

United States congressmen Bob Clement and John Tanner were also on hand. Both credited McWherter with the idea. Having seen how

National Guardsmen in Honduras helped the sick, the governor thought the same services could be afforded to the poor in Tennessee.

NOVEMBER 22

1878, ONE MILE FROM NEWPORT, COCKE COUNTY

At 3 P.M., Stephen Griffey was hanged for the rape of a nine-year-old girl, Eveline Clark. A crowd of 2,000 witnessed his execution for what was called "one of the most atrocious and brutal crimes in the criminal annals of this County."

In his last remarks, Griffey claimed that whiskey had led him to commit the transgression. He admitted his guilt. His father and some cousins climbed the gallows to shake his hand and say a final good-bye. He was dead in seven minutes, and his body cut down 23 minutes later.

This was the first legal hanging in Cocke County, as well as the first hanging of a white man there. Griffey had violated Section 4624 of the Tennessee Code, which stated that "any person who shall unlawfully and carnally know and abuse a female under the age of ten years, shall be punished as in a case of rape." The prescribed punishment was hanging.

NOVEMBER 23

1856, MONTGOMERY COUNTY

A cache of arms was reportedly found at the Louisa Iron Furnace. It was alleged that these arms were to be used by slaves to begin a revolt. The report proved false but indicated the paranoia of slave owners.

1863, HAMILTON COUNTY

Major General William T. Sherman ordered four Federal divisions across the Tennessee River prior to attacking Missionary Ridge the next day.

Because mountains veiled Sherman's activity, Confederate forces briefly lost contact with the United States Army. This led to inadequate reconnaissance. Confederate leaders were persuaded that Sherman was en route to Knoxville, moving north to relieve the pressure that Confederate forces under General James Longstreet were imposing on a beleaguered General Ambrose E. Burnside.

1867, MCMINNVILLE

The morally outraged editor of the *McMinnville Enterprise* wrote, "The city papers of Nashville contain daily the following notice: 'Ladies Restaurant. The only Restaurant in the city for Ladies is A. Texler's, 141 Church street (opposite the Gas office.) The best brands of Wines and Liquors will be served in this saloon. Also egg-nogg every day.' This," fulminated the editor,

speaks but little in favor of the morals of the ladies of Nashville. The very fact that a ladies restaurant exists in the city is evidence that it is patronized by ladies. Think of it—well educated, well dressed and well-to-do ladies visiting a drinking saloon, where "the best brands of wines and liquors are served" with "egg-nogg every day." Then think of them returning to their homes in a state of partial intoxication. What must be the feeling of the husband, grown up sons and daughters, and even little children when the wife and mother come home drunk! Shame! shame! that the ladies of Nashville should patronize one of these cinques of destruction.

Roy "I'm Proud to Be a Hillbilly" Acuff died. Acuff sold 50 million records, established a lucrative music publishing house, and made a fortune on real estate. He was the undisputed "King of Country Music."

NOVEMBER 24

1813, KENTUCK, 10 MILES SOUTH OF WINCHESTER

David Crockett arrived home before his 90-day enlistment for the Creek Indian War had been served.

David Crockett [November 24]

Crockett was a private in Captain Francis Jones's company, part of Colonel Newton Cannon's regiment of the Tennessee Mounted Rifles, commanded by General John Coffee. Two days earlier, near Huntsville in the Mississippi Territory, General Coffee had allowed his command to return home early with the proviso that they get fresh horses and winter clothing and rendezvous at Huntsville by December 8.

Like his fellows in the Mounted Rifles, Crockett did not attempt to return as promised, remaining at Kentuck for nine months. He therefore may technically have been guilty of desertion and/or mutiny. Neither was uncommon among Tennessee soldiers in late 1813 and early 1814.

Crockett later served as a sergeant in Captain John Cowan's company from September 1814 to March 1815. During this period, he was in the backwoods of Alabama, where he scouted for remaining pockets of hostile Creeks and foraged for provisions and food for the army. He did not participate in the Battle of New Orleans.

1863, HAMILTON COUNTY

The Battle of Lookout Mountain raged. Some 3,000 United States infantry troops crossed Lookout Creek in a thick fog at dawn. In the fashion of the linear warfare practiced in that day, they lined up at the creek base under the cliffs and charged north along the mountainside over slashed timber and deep ravines, completely collapsing the Confederate left.

1923, MEMPHIS

The annual Thanksgiving-season football game between the Memphis Athletic Club and the University of Mississippi was played. Ole Miss fans gathered on the north side of the field and were exceedingly loud. According to one newspaper report, "On the south side were lined up the Memphis partisans. Several hundred strong who did all they could to offset the noisy demonstration on the other side. The result was that for about two hours there was a conglomeration of contentious sound that made people uptown wonder if a lynching had been in progress, a prize fight, or just a football game."

The Athletic Club won 6–2.

1926, NASHVILLE

Radio station WLAC (Life and Casualty), billed as the "new super power broadcasting station," went on the air.

A year or so after the battle, a Union officer and his date enjoy the view at Lookout Mountain [November 24]

1857, SCOTT COUNTY

The population of the Welsh colony of Brynyffynon ("the Hill with a Spring"), located near the Kentucky line, was down to four.

In Wales, social and political reformer Samuel Roberts had been the guiding conscience for many of his countrymen. In 1855, the Reverend Roberts met land speculators Evan B. Jones and William Bebb, the former governor of Ohio, when they were on a trip to Europe. Seeing the destitute condition of the people and the Welsh countryside, Jones and Bebb promoted the sale of supposedly surveyed land in Tennessee through Roberts. The promotional brochure that circulated in Wales in 1856 told of land on a "minor tributary of Pine Creek known as Nancy's Branch."

Roberts and a band of Welsh immigrants arrived at the site in Scott County in July 1856. The village they had been led to believe would greet them was nowhere in sight. They built two log cabins and gave their settlement its distinctive name.

By the summer of 1857, a new group of settlers arrived. They, too, were shocked at the lack of accommodations. By September, families were leaving.

Roberts stubbornly remained at Brynyffynon until 1867, when he returned to Wales a bitter and disillusioned man.

1863, HAMILTON COUNTY

Missionary Ridge, named for its nearness to the Brainerd Mission to the Cherokees, was the scene of the final and conclusive action in the series of battles that drove Confederate forces from the Chattanooga area. After clearing a line of rifle pits at the foot of a ridge, Union troops charged up the slopes, driving the rebels from their entrenchments at the summit.

1939, NUTBUSH

Annie May Bullock, better known as singer, actress, and show-business legend Tina Turner, was born.

Her song "Nutbush City Limits" describes the town as a community so quiet that the corn can be heard growing.

1958, KNOXVILLE

"Granny" Harriet Hill turned 100. According to Mrs. Hill, "I took care of myself and never went in for any kind of devilment, like swimming or keeping late hours."

1991, ACROSS THE UNITED STATES

Who Killed Martin Luther King? The True Story of a Convicted Assassin, the book by James Earl Ray, went on sale.

NOVEMBER 26

1895, NASHVILLE

The *Nashville Banner* reported the suicide of Willie Rundles, "a pretty girl . . . in a house of ill fame on Front street. . . . In a moment of depression she ended her existence. At 11:30 o'clock last night she took her morphine; and at 7 o'clock in the morning breathed her last." Her fellow harlots summoned a physician, but Willie "never awoke from the stupor in which she was found."

Rundles had "boarded in a house run by Ethel Flowers, at 706 North Front street. About a week ago she was married, but continued to live in the disreputable house. A former lover contin-

ued to visit her, and the two men quarreled. It was the quarrel of the men that brought on the poor girl's despondency."

NOVEMBER 27

1836, NEAR VOLUSIA, FLORIDA

Lieutenant Henry Hollingsworth of the Second Tennessee Volunteers wrote in his daily journal, "O these wars, and the soldier's life! They unhinge a fellow. . . . [It] is a picture of dirt and toil, privation and vexation, and the poorest pay in the world $6 per month!"

1863, NEAR PULASKI

Legend has it that, a noose around his neck, 23-year-old accused spy Sam Davis spoke these last words when asked to divulge the name of his contact: "I would die a thousand deaths before I would betray a friend."

There are three monuments to Sam Davis, one on the State Capitol grounds and two in Pulaski. His family home near Smyrna is listed on the National Register of Historic Places and is open year-round for visitation.

Sam Davis, "the Boy Hero of the Confederacy," was executed by hanging after a military court found him guilty of espionage. A decoding device was found on his person and he was not wearing a uniform.

1864, OCCUPIED NASHVILLE

Elements of the 13th Regular Infantry and the combined forces of the Ninth Pennsylvania and the Fourth Michigan Volunteer Infantry got into a dispute on Smoky Row over which unit was the best at fighting. Angry words escalated to the use of weapons, and a serious affray began at Mat Carson's saloon. In the "Battle of Smoky Row," the 13th was driven back to Dutch Lizzie's bordello. Over 100 shots were fired.

1885, MEMPHIS

The largest cast of iron ever made in the city was manufactured at John E. Randle's Chickasaw Iron Works. A shaft for Merchant's Cotton Press and Storage Company, it weighed nine and a half tons, required the labor of 40 men, and was three weeks in the making.

1895, NASHVILLE

A Thanksgiving Day football game between Vanderbilt and the University of the South—"the game of the season," according to the *Nashville Banner*—was played. A hundred fans from Sewanee accompanied their team, but in the end Vanderbilt won 18–6.

1925, NASHVILLE

The Grand Ole Opry began radio broadcasting. "Uncle" Jimmy Thompson, a 77-year-old fiddle player, was the first act.

NOVEMBER 28

1864, MCMINNVILLE

Overton County native and Federal soldier John B. Allison wrote his sweetheart, Martely "Martha" C. Smellage, who lived near Livingston,

> I have bad news to tell you, we are now ordered to march at 4 o'clock this evening. It is reported that Hood is in the vicinity of Pulaski. I was aiming to start home in the morning but I am sadly disappointed. I may never see home again. . . . Martha you must be a good girl. That if we never see each other on earth that we may meet in heaven. . . . Dearest girl as I have towled you before that you have long since been the object of warmest and truest love, and though I remain one thousand miles from you I shall ever remember you and recognize you as a lady and true friend. . . . Martha, Peas excuse my bad writing for I am in such a hurey. Write every chance you have.

John and Martha later married, farmed, and raised a family in Overton County.

NOVEMBER 29

1807, DUNLAP

Josiah McNair Anderson was born in what was then Bledsoe County.

Anderson served in the Tennessee House from 1833 to 1839. He practiced law and farmed in Marion County, where he owned large tracts of land on Coop's Creek. A Whig, he served in the United States House of Representatives from 1849 to 1851. He was thereafter twice defeated for reelection. Anderson was later a delegate to the Peace Convention, which tried to prevent civil war. He was named a colonel in the Provisional Army of Tennessee in 1861. On November 8 of that year, he was killed at Looney's Creek, near Whitwell in Marion County, after making a speech in favor of secession.

1863, KNOXVILLE

The assault on Fort Sanders began. Confederate general James Longstreet ordered his forces to make a bayonet charge at dawn. The onrushing Confederates were stopped by a deep ditch and cannon fire from the Federal position. This ended Longstreet's failed siege of Knoxville.

A bungling attempt was made to rob the safe of T. J. Mooney, a plumber who lived near the Vendome on Church Street. The burglars were evidently new to the trade. They entered at the rear door and built a wall of boxes between the front door and the safe, shutting off the view from the street. The blasting powder they left behind indicated that the burglars meant to blow the safe up. Using a hammer and chisel, they managed only to break the safe's handle.

When the attempted crime was discovered on the morning of the 30th, it was too late to find many clues. As it turned out, there was little money in the safe, as Mooney had deposited the day's receipts at a bank.

1895, NASHVILLE

The city council, after due consideration, sent back to the school board a request to allow Bible reading in the public schools, so dodging the issue of the separation of church and state, which remains controversial a century later.

1953, NASHVILLE

Television station WSIX, channel 8, went on the air. In 1973, it became WKRN, channel 2.

NOVEMBER 30

1864, FRANKLIN

The Battle of Franklin was fought.

Through the night and day, a steady stream of dead and wounded was brought to Randal McGavock's mansion. By the next day, the back porch displayed the bodies of four dead Confederate generals. More important, fully 40 percent of the Confederate force was decimated. Losses were approximately 2,000 Union and 6,000 Confederate.

The Union forces held the high ground, one of the most fundamental lessons in military science. Confederate general John Bell Hood had already been wounded twice, at Gettysburg and Chickamauga, where his leg was amputated. It has been suggested that the opiates that surgeons most certainly gave him to manage his pain severely affected his judgment. Hood may well have been addicted to the medicine.

His Union counterpart, General John M. Schofield, withdrew to Nashville after the battle.

One participant, Private Sam R. Watkins of Company H, First Tennessee Regiment, wrote about the battle from a common Confederate soldier's viewpoint:

> As [we] marched through an open field to the rampart of blood and death, the Federal batteries begin to open and move down. . . . "Forward, men," is repeated all along the line. A sheet of fire is poured down into our very faces. . . . "Forward, men!" The air [is] loaded with death dealing missiles. Never . . . did men fight against such . . . odds. . . . "Forward, men!" And the blood spurts in a perfect jet from the dead and wounded. The earth is red with blood. . . . The death angel shrieks and laughs. . . . I had made up my mind to die—[it] felt glorious. We pressed forward. . . . I passed on until I got to their [the Yankees'] works, and got over on their side. But in fifty yards of where I was, the scene

. . . seemed like hell itself. . . . Dead soldiers filled the entrenchment. . . . It was a
grand holocaust of death.

1919, CHATTANOOGA

The Reverend Billy Sunday, evangelist, lectured men and boys with a sermon entitled "The
Devil's Boomerang, or, Hot Cakes Right off the
Griddle." Apparently, the sermon dealt with illicit and premarital sexual relations.

1925, SPARTA

The Sparta Transportation Company announced its one-day round-trip bus service between Crossville and Nashville. For the first time,
residents of either city could travel to the other,
conduct business, and be home for the evening
meal.

Boats such as the Avalon, *a Tennessee River packet, aided commerce along Tennessee's rivers.*

December

DECEMBER 1

1795, KNOXVILLE

Meeting in its second session, the territorial assembly set fees for various services. It was decreed that a constable was to receive 33 cents for whipping an African-American by order of any court or justice of the peace.

1847, NASHVILLE

Dorothea Dix, the famous New England reformer, spoke to the state senate on the deplorable treatment of the mentally ill at Tennessee's lunatic asylum. She recommended that a new asylum building be constructed at once because the "highly excited patients . . . [in] those wretched cells in the cellar" were living in inhuman conditions.

1856, DOVER

After being tortured, nine slaves confessed that they were involved in planning an attack on white people. All were summarily hanged.

The revolt was neither real nor planned, but only a figment of slave owners' imaginations. Fearful of even a rumor of rebellion, owners sometimes took murderously extreme measures.

1864, MIDDLE TENNESSEE

On the retreat with John Bell Hood's army just after the slaughter at the Battle of Franklin, Confederate captain S. T. Foster wrote in his diary that "General Hood has betrayed us. This is not the kind of fighting he promised us at Tuscumbia and Florence, Ala. when we started into Tenn. This was not a 'fight with equal

Private charity was one way to help the poor, as were poor houses. Above is the home of the Cannon County Poor House manager in 1901.

numbers and choice of the ground' by no means. And the wails and cries of widows and orphans made at Franklin, Tenn Nov 30th 1864 will heat up the fires of the bottomless pit to burn the soul of Gen J B Hood for Murdering their husbands and fathers at that place that day. It can't be called anything but cold blooded Murder."

1873, KNOXVILLE

The Knoxville Benevolent Association was formed to give help to the so-called worthy poor. The unworthy poor apparently had to help themselves.

Private charity organizations were one response to the problems posed by the urban poor.

1925, CROSSVILLE

The Tennessee Electric Power Company finished work on streetlights in the town, making it possible for citizens to walk down Main Street at night without the use of pocket flashlights.

The power line extending to Cumberland Mountain School was finished during the holidays.

DECEMBER 2

1940, FOREST HOME, WILLIAMSON COUNTY

Thelma C. Harper, Tennessee's first black female to be elected to the state senate, was born.

She served on the Metropolitan Nashville/ Davidson County Council from 1983 to 1991. As a councilwoman, she led a movement against the continued operation and expansion of the Bordeaux landfill. She served in the general assembly from 1991 to 1995.

DECEMBER 3

1813, FORT STROTHER, MISSISSIPPI TERRITORY

General Andrew Jackson replied to a November 20 letter from the Reverend Gideon Blackburn, saying in part, "The influence you have over the minds of men is great and well founded; and can never be better applied than in summoning volunteers to the defence of their Country. . . . I want volunteers, and I want them immediately."

A little over a week later, an entire brigade of volunteers whose 90-day enlistments had ended left Jackson and headed for Tennessee.

Colonel William Carroll, in the Volunteer State to raise troops, wrote to Jackson on December 15 about the clergyman's efforts: "Mr. Blackbourne is doing what he can, himself and most of his students have turned out."

On December 28, while Blackburn was encamped near Huntsville with General John Coffee, the men of a rifle regiment expressed their desire to return home because their enlistment periods had ended. According to General Coffee, the soldiers were exhorted by "an animated address from the Revd. Blackburn, but all to no effect."

Apparently, Jackson's belief that Blackburn had great power over the minds of men was unfounded.

1894, MEMPHIS

New horseless wagons were being seen around the city. One such truck was described this way: "It weighed eight tons and can travel nine miles per hour."

It was a speed demon in anybody's book.

1935, POWELL'S STATION

Company 4497 of the Civilian Conservation Corps, composed entirely of African-American youths, was formed.

After working on highway beautification projects between Knoxville and Norris Dam, Company 4497 was moved to Burns. There it remained until 1941, cooperating with Public Works Administration personnel in the construction of Montgomery Bell State Park.

DECEMBER 4

1820, EAST TENNESSEE

Elihu Embree died.

Embree, an early iron manufacturer, converted to the Society of Friends (the Quakers) in 1815 and freed all his slaves. Thereafter, he became the editor and driving force behind the Tennessee abolitionist paper *The Emancipator*.

1887 CHATTANOOGA

J. A. Hodge, an African-American from the city's Fourth Ward, began his last term on the city council, having been first elected in 1878.

Hodge was born into slavery about 1846 in North Carolina. A longtime Chattanooga resident, he was self-employed as a contractor, stonecutter, and house mover. In 1882, he served as the city jailer and was the night mail-transfer agent for the East Tennessee, Virginia & Georgia Railroad. From 1885 to 1887, he served as the first African-American state legislator from Hamilton County. His date of death and place of burial are not known.

1956, MEMPHIS

Elvis Presley and his girlfriend, Marilyn Evans, stopped by Sun Studios and found that Carl Perkins was in the middle of a recording session. Also there was Jerry Lee "the Killer" Lewis, whose first single, "End of the Road," had just been released by the legendary recording company.

Elvis, Jerry Lee, and Carl, later joined by Johnny Cash, sang a series of popular and gospel songs. A reporter and a photographer for the *Memphis Press-Scimitar* were called to cover the extraordinary unscheduled event.

The unplanned gathering of the four entertainers later came to be labeled "the Million Dollar Quartet."

DECEMBER 5

1814, MOBILE, ALABAMA

The court-martial of 150 Tennessee militiamen for mutiny began. The charges had been brought September 20. The militiamen had been under the impression that their enlistments were over in three, not six, months.

The trial concluded December 14. Five Tennesseans—a sergeant and four privates—were sentenced "to death by shooting."

The executions plagued Andrew Jackson's bid for the presidency in 1828 and were depicted in the infamous "Coffin Handbill."

1887, CHATTANOOGA

According to a report in the *Chattanooga Daily Times*, there existed "a City of Negroes" near town. This phenomenon was considered "an anomaly."

A recent real-estate boom had forced a large number of African-Americans from their homes on the "valuable hilltops," after which they decided to settle on a strip of ground in a grove of trees about a mile north of McCallie Avenue. Other blacks migrated to the area, and a building boom took place, as many as 30 houses being built at once. About 110 houses, a church, a schoolhouse, four stores, and a number of two-story buildings were erected in this community, which had a population of 800. Streets were laid out, and the interurban belt railway made a stop not too far away. Another 50 houses were scheduled to be built within six months, and it was estimated the population would swell to 1,500. The African-American community planned to

incorporate the town, which would be "the first negro city on American soil." All government officials, schoolteachers, storekeepers, and ministers would be black.

According to the *Daily Times*, "The progress of the community will be watched with great interest, as it will demonstrate . . . whether or not negroes can successfully administer the affairs of a large community without the assistance of the whites."

The fate of this special town is not known.

1901, NEAR DEL RIO, COCKE COUNTY

Grace Moore was born.

She was educated at Ward-Belmont College in Nashville and later studied music in Washington, D.C., and New York. She became one of the outstanding operatic sopranos of her day. She was killed in an airplane crash near Copenhagen, Denmark, on January 26, 1947.

DECEMBER 6

1856, SPRINGFIELD

Thirteen frantic men sent a letter to Governor Andrew Johnson asking him to send arms to put down an anticipated slave revolt. According to the letter, the Springfield Vigilance Committee thought that "about 100 Muskets, 60 Brace of Pistols & 60 Swords would answer our purposes." Johnson granted the request.

Fear was rampant that a major slave insurrection was about to take place that would result in wholesale slaughter. Any such threat was imaginary.

1856, MEMPHIS

The *Memphis Daily Appeal* ran an editorial

advocating that "an energetic plan should be devised, and carried out to expel . . . all free colored persons who have not done some signal service to the State or community."

It was feared throughout the South that free blacks would incite their enslaved brothers to revolution.

DECEMBER 7

1864, NEAR OCCUPIED MURFREESBORO

The Battle of the Cedars took place.

Hoping to protect Confederate general John Bell Hood's flank while he prepared to advance on Nashville, General Nathan Bedford Forrest's cavalry rode south to conduct a reconnaissance of Fortress Rosecrans and secure stores. Forrest's attacks were repulsed near Murfreesboro by Federal troops from New York, Illinois, Ohio, and Minnesota under General Lovell H. Rousseau, a veteran of the Battle of Stones River nearly two years earlier.

As the Federals executed their battle plan, seasoned rebel troops began to run. According to eyewitness W. A. Galloway of the Columbus (Georgia) Artillery, Forrest ordered the color bearer to halt his retreat. When the command was not obeyed, Forrest "drew his pistol and shot the retreating soldier down," according to Galloway. Forrest then took up the colors and managed to rally his men.

It was too late to do more than retreat in an orderly fashion. The rebels were forced to yield the field.

The Battle of Nashville would soon prove even more disastrous to the Confederate cause.

1900, LYNCHBURG

At a meeting of the city council, the "town marshal was instructed to vigorously enforce the ordinance as to hogs running at large in the town," it was reported.

1900, CROSS BRIDGES, NEAR COLUMBIA

The remains of Confederate soldier Patrick H. Cooke were disinterred and carried to Franklin for reburial.

A Maury County resident, Cooke enlisted in Nashville in 1861. He was subsequently captured by Union forces and sent to a prisoner-of-war compound in Chicago. He died there in 1862, after which his remains were sent to Cross Roads in a metallic casket.

According to one report, "After remaining in the ground here for thirty four years, little change is noticeable in the features." Little change in the casket, that is, not Cooke's remains.

1941, PEARL HARBOR

The USS *Tennessee*, whose guns had not seen action in 20 years, downed four enemy aircraft during the infamous Japanese sneak attack. Berthed alongside the USS *West Virginia*, the *Tennessee* was hit by two armor-piercing bombs, only one of which exploded. The *Tennessee* was effectively put out of action until repairs were made. One Nashvillian, pilot Cornelia Fort, was an eyewitness to the attack.

The *Tennessee* began extensive patrol duties in early June 1943, serving throughout the Pacific theater from the Aleutians to Layette Gulf. At Saipan, enemy gunners hit the ship, killing eight and wounding 24.

1849, MEMPHIS

The slaves of Dr. Caesar A. Jones were freed upon his death. His will requested that his brother establish a trust fund of $2,000 for the "use and benefit of my negroe woman Matilda, and her children." Matilda had five children ranging in age from one to 12, all presumed to have been fathered by Jones.

1900, NASHVILLE

The Meharry Medical College squad won the black Southern College Football Team Championship. Also in the league were Roger Williams University, Fisk University, and the City Giants.

1933, MEMPHIS

"Law took a holiday on the third floor of the county courthouse," it was reported, "while more than a score of enthusiastic members of the Holiness Church arrived and hailed a court decision with a strenuous 'meeting' which completely stopped the legal proceedings of all courts in the building for more than 15 minutes. . . . [Members of the Holiness Church] stamped the floor, praised the Lord and sang out in a joyful abandon that nearly caused court attendants to send in a hurry-up riot call."

The court had dismissed the divorce bills of Thomas O'Neil, 61, and his wife, Minnie, 53, and admonished them to kiss and make up. The O'Neils were longstanding members of Holiness Church, and the African-American congregation could not bear to see them separate.

1982, NASHVILLE

Country-music star Martin David Robinson, better known as Marty Robbins, died.

This Arizona-born performer was influenced by Gene Autry to become a "singing cowboy." He played at first in nightclubs in Phoenix. Little Jimmy Dickens recommended that he sing on the Grand Ole Opry, and he became a regular in 1953. A two-time Grammy winner, he was inducted into the Country Music Hall of Fame in 1982. He was also a skillful stock-car racer.

1813, FORT STROTHER, MISSISSIPPI TERRITORY

Convinced that their period of enlistment was up, and having endured weeks of inadequate rations and clothing, the men of General William Hall's Tennessee brigade were rumored to be in a rebellious temper. The fact that, almost to a man, they marched to Nashville indicates that they did indeed want to leave the army.

Andrew Jackson wrote to his wife that "the Phisic of the indian prophet must have worked upon them to ocassion, once so brave, to conduct so strangely and disgracefully to themselves and country."

Factors other than cowardice, however, led the Tennesseans to forsake Jackson.

1831, WASHINGTON, D.C.

Congressman William T. Fitzgerald, a Jacksonian Democrat from Dresden, wrote his wife that "this city [Washington] is the most servile and prostituted place. . . . It is the resort of the vile and dissolute from every portion of the world. . . . The ex-President [John Quincy] Adams is as you know a member of our house. He sits in front of me not far from me. He is an awkward looking man. He is Low. . . . He has a small dull eye. The common civilities of life seem to burden him. He has an honest face but not the first indication of talent."

1891, NASHVILLE

A city "cow-raider," whose responsibilities included rounding up stray livestock within the town limits, was reportedly confiscating cows illegally and taking them to the cow pound. One editorial suggested that putting him on salary rather than paying him piece rate might cut down on his eagerness to "arrest cows."

DECEMBER 10

1862, LA GRANGE

Major General Ulysses S. Grant commanded his chief of staff, General Joseph D. Webster, to "give orders to all the conductors on the [rail]road that no Jews are to be permitted to travel on the railroad southward from any point. They may go north and be encouraged in it; but they are such an intolerable nuisance that the department must be purged of them."

The "department" was the military administrative area known officially as the "Department of the Tennessee." It included those portions of northern Mississippi, Tennessee, and Kentucky west of the Tennessee River. Grant also wrote the assistant secretary of war in Washington informing him of his actions.

1932, CHESTNUT MOUND, SMITH COUNTY

Gentry Crowell, a representative in the general assembly from 1969 to 1977 and Tennessee secretary of state, was born.

In the legislature, Crowell was chairman of the Democratic caucus, the General Welfare Committee and the Rules Committee and a member of the Education Committee, the Ways and Means Committee, and the Transportation Committee. He sponsored and supported bills for education, transportation, mental health, vocational education programs, and unemployment compensation. He assisted local governments with financing of sewer and water lines in rural and urban areas. Crowell was elected secretary of state by the 90th, 92nd, and 96th assemblies.

In the summer of 1989, his administrative assistant, Mary Sue Wright, was indicted by a federal grand jury for embezzling thousands of dollars from the Democratic caucus campaign fund. Crowell had served as treasurer of the caucus from 1973 to 1988 and was thus called twice to testify before the grand jury in the ongoing Rocky Top investigation into bingo and corruption.

On December 12, 1989, Crowell attempted suicide. Eight days later, suffering from a bullet wound to the head, he died in Vanderbilt Hospital in Nashville. He is buried in Cedar Grove Cemetery in Lebanon.

It seems that the Rocky Top investigation ceased after his act.

1979, MEMPHIS

Truckdriver and professional-wrestling fan Malcolm McClain was sentenced to five days in jail for attacking a pair of wrestlers. Police, accustomed to the excesses of fans, were baffled at first as McClain entered the Mid-South Coliseum ring. According to the police report, McClain "jumped into the ring with the wrestlers and began beating on Tojo Yamamoto and Sonny King and a free for all ruckus broke out. At this time we were informed the defendant was not a part of the show. The defendant had to be physically restrained."

McClain, 27, said he was only having fun: "I watch wrestling every Saturday [on television] and I wanted to be a wrestler. I didn't think the fans or the coliseum would mind."

He was released by Judge Ann Pugh after serving three days of his term.

DECEMBER 11

1877, KNOXVILLE

Black citizens met to demand representation on juries and to consider the question of equal school facilities for their children. A number of resolutions were passed that revealed the existence of racial discrimination. For example, one read,

> While we do not claim any extra privileges, we respectfully but earnestly call attention to the uniform practice of being excluded from the jury-box. . . . It does not look reasonable that out of the hundreds of jurors summoned to every court, that no colored men are put on the jury unless it was the wish . . . of those who summon juries. This certainly is no ordinary coincident. We think the law demands juries to be taken from the body of the county of the good and lawful men. . . . It will hardly be said in this enlightened day that colored men are not good and lawful.

These words were spoken a decade after Negro males' right to sit on juries had been established by Tennessee statute.

1903, NASHVILLE

An establishment called "The Southern Turf"

was raided by police at 4 P.M. Twenty-five arrests were made in the pool room, the first floor, and the rear of the building for the crime of loitering around a gambling establishment. Ike Johnson, the manager, insisted that his customers be taken to the police station in carriages, which he provided. One of the detainees, a city councilman, escaped. Bail, set at $40 per man, was signed by Johnson and others.

1911, NASHVILLE

Socialists met to condemn the use of violence as a means of obtaining a socialist government. They promised to inaugurate a five-part lecture series on socialism, free to the public.

1992, ACROSS AMERICA

After the votes of postage-stamp consumers had been tallied, commemorative stamps featuring a young Elvis Presley went on sale. Sales were phenomenal.

Bumper stickers later appeared reading, "Don't blame me, I voted for the old Elvis."

DECEMBER 12

1911, CHATTANOOGA

An attempt was made to rid the Third Ward of its red-light district. Depositions in the case of *Weidner v. Friedman* were taken from two local madams.

Irene Friedman testified that the city fathers had agreed to recognize "bawdy houses as a social evil, which should be regulated by confining their operations to a given district in the city. . . . The red light district was selected as the proper place for carrying on and indulging in this social, necessary evil."

Nellie Hood testified that "some of the complainants in this bill were liberal patrons of the bawdy houses. . . . The truth is that this district . . . [has] been under strict police surveillance, all the time, and no persons are permitted to visit these houses in the day time, except the clerks with bills to collect and persons having business transactions with the owners or occupants of the houses."

In the end, the Tennessee Supreme Court ruled that the prostitutes had to exit the Third Ward. The court did not rule on the question of prostitution, only the matter of the prostitutes' leaving.

1917, CHATTANOOGA

A partially clad Baroness Lona Shope Wilhelmina Sutton Zollner was arrested in the Hotel Patten just after midnight. It was thought she was a German spy, a suspicion that took on an added dimension when Lieutenant J. W. Spaulding of the Sixth Infantry was found under her bed, unclothed.

The baroness, a wealthy, dazzling free spirit from New York who smoked and drank whiskey, was later arraigned on charges of violating the Espionage Act. After nearly a month of incarceration and interrogation by federal officials, she obtained bail and returned to her home.

The press in Chattanooga and Knoxville made much of her case, printing jail-cell interviews and stories about her exciting life. Her relationship with the 22-year-old lieutenant was never adequately explained. The 44-year-old baroness said he was a family friend.

1993, LONDON

A British newspaper, *The Observer*, reported that an anonymous Tennessee business executive, still alive, had given statements to a Memphis jury saying he had hired a black man to assassinate Martin Luther King, Jr.

The information did not lead to a reopening of the James Earl Ray case.

DECEMBER 13

1813, MISSISSIPPI TERRITORY

General John Cocke and 2,000 East Tennessee soldiers joined Andrew Jackson in the future state of Alabama. Jackson had experienced mass abandonments as a result of near-famine among his troops and the end of their three-month enlistment period.

With these fresh troops, complete with their longer enlistment periods, Jackson went on to defeat the Creek Indians and later the British at the Battle of New Orleans.

1850, NASHVILLE

Tennessee No. 1, the state's first steam locomotive, arrived at the wharf on the steamboat *Beauty* from Cincinnati. The locomotive had been ordered by the Nashville & Chattanooga Railroad. Its first trip from the wharf to South Cherry Street was on a hastily improvised set of tracks. Mules, not steam power, moved the engine over the course of four days.

Tennessee No. 1 made a successful one-mile test run on December 27.

1856, NASHVILLE

All the members of a Springfield vigilance committee that had urgently requested arms from Governor Andrew Johnson to put down a slave revolt signed a letter in the *Nashville Union and American*. Under the headline "Stop the Falsehood," they acknowledged that the whole story of a slave revolt "was a fabrication."

In his "Assessment for Relief of the Poor," Military Governor Andrew Johnson singled out wealthy Confederate planters to be taxed to aid the poor. Johnson wrote, "There are many help-less widows, wives and children in the city . . . [living in] wretchedness in consequence of their husbands, sons and fathers having been forced into the armies of this unholy and nefarious re-bellion. . . . Their wants for the necessaries of life [are] so urgent, that all the laws of justice and humanity would be grossly violated unless something is done to relieve their destitute and suffering condition."

1887, PALL MALL

Alvin C. York was born.

1944, THE PHILIPPINE ISLANDS

Having sustained only minor damage in both the Atlantic and Pacific theaters, the USS *Nash-ville* was attacked by a kamikaze at about 1 P.M. Some 133 sailors and officers were killed and another 190 wounded.

The *Nashville* was back in action on June 20, 1945, in time to participate in the conclusion of the war.

DECEMBER 14

1784, JONESBOROUGH

Leaders of the Watauga settlements met to de-clare the formation of the State of Franklin. The move was later disputed by North Carolina.

1895, NASHVILLE

W. P. Trent spoke to a meeting of the South-ern Historical Society at Vanderbilt. According to the *Nashville Banner*, Trent "said history in 1895 is very different from what it was in 1795; it had lost some of its beauty, but the light was there."

Trent, a history professor at the University of the South, also called for government support of historical study in the South.

1960, FAYETTE COUNTY

A milestone in the modern Tennessee civil rights movement occurred when the famous "tent cities" were erected.

The movement began as a result of a black voters' initiative in 1959 that had added 9,000 blacks to the voting list and interdicted the county's all-white primary system.

Soon thereafter came harsh retributions against the black community, including a trade ban against African-Americans. There were whole-sale evictions of black workers, sharecroppers, and tenant farmers—but only after the crops had been harvested. This action violated the local custom in which white planters provided life-time housing for favored blacks.

John and Viola McFerren and the Fayette County Civic and Welfare League fought back. On land donated by a black philanthropist and landowner from Somerville and black farmer Shephard Towles, Sr., the league erected surplus army tents to relieve the suffering of those evicted.

A similar tent city, also called "Freedom Vil-lage," was established in Haywood County. Yet another camp was secretly initiated near Mos-cow on Gertrude Beasely's land. In the end, the Freedom Villagers were triumphant.

1978, HENNING

Author Alex Haley's boyhood home was

listed on the National Register of Historic Places. It is a state-owned historic house and museum today.

Ironically, Haley paid approximately $650,000 in an out-of-court settlement to terminate a plagiarism suit the same day. He also apologized to the offended writer, Harold Courlander, who contended that Haley had copied passages from Courlander's 1967 novel, *The African*, published nine years before Haley's *Roots*. Haley blamed friends who had sent him the passages when he was writing his book. According to Courlander, the tip-off was a "field call" in *Roots* that had appeared in *The African*: "Yooo-hooo-ah-hoo, don't you hear me calling you?"

Haley's reputation in literary circles plummeted, never to rise again. He died in 1993.

DECEMBER 15

1807, NEAR NASHVILLE

William Bowen, a pioneer and a successful plantation owner, died at age 65.

His two-story brick house, built in 1788, was restored in the 1970s and 1980s with funds provided by the National Park Service. It is listed on the National Register of Historic Places.

1856, NICARAGUA

After the successful siege of Granada, some of the men under Tennessee's William Walker, nearly starved after 15 days of scant rations, ate too much and died.

"Some of the men, when liquor, tobacco, and cigars gave out lived on opium until it killed them," wrote Mrs. Elanore Callaghan Rattermann, an American eyewitness.

1864, OCCUPIED NASHVILLE

The Battle of Nashville began as Union general John M. Schofield's infantry forced John Bell Hood's army two miles to the foot of Brentwood Hills.

Sergeant Edmond T. Eggleston of the Confederate artillery wrote in his diary, "We went to the left this evening and lost our guns & horses. The infantry ran like cowards and the miserable wretches who were to have supported us refused to fight and ran like a herd of stampeded cattle. I blush for my countrymen and despair of the independence of the Confederacy if her reliance is placed in the army of Tennessee to accomplish it." He also related that all his company's papers were lost and that he had lost all his rations and blankets. "Expect to freeze this winter," he wrote.

DECEMBER 16

1831, NASHVILLE

The Tennessee legislature passed a law severely restricting the movement of free blacks.

Fear of blacks, free or slave, was high after Nat Turner's revolt in Virginia had demonstrated to the slave-owning minority that African-Americans really didn't like slavery and could stage rebellions to free themselves. Laws on slavery also became much harsher in the ensuing decades.

1864, OCCUPIED NASHVILLE

General John M. Schofield's cavalry and infantry completely broke Confederate resistance and sent the remnants of John Bell Hood's rebel army in a hasty retreat south.

The Battle of Nashville was the last significant military contest in Tennessee during the Civil War.

Two heroes of the Spanish-American War, Washburn Maynard, captain of the USS *Nashville*, and Lieutenant Richard Hobson, were given a reception and banquet at the Tabernacle and a banquet at the Maxwell House. Maynard enthralled the audience with details of the beginning of the "splendid little war" with Spain.

DECEMBER 17

1862, MEMPHIS

General Ulysses S. Grant issued General Orders No. 11, stating in part, "The Jews, as a class, violating every regulation of trade established by the Treasury Department and also department orders, are hereby expelled from the department within twenty four hours from the receipt of this order."

Nashville's Jewish community thereafter reviled Grant.

There is little to indicate that the order was fully executed.

1875, RED BOILING SPRINGS, MACON COUNTY

John Washington Butler was born.

Butler was a member of the Macon County Election Commission, a member of the Primitive Baptist Church, and clerk of the Round Lock Association of Primitive Baptists. While serving in the Tennessee House of Representatives, he authored the state law prohibiting the public-school teaching of "any theory which denies the story of the Divine creation of man as taught in the Bible and [teaching] instead that man is descended from a lower order of animals."

The so called Butler Act set the stage for the "Monkey Trial" in Dayton, in which John T. Scopes was found guilty of teaching evolution. The law was not repealed until 1967.

1955, MEMPHIS

Carl Perkins recorded the rock-'n'-roll classic "Blue Suede Shoes."

DECEMBER 18

1836, CAMP DADE, FLORIDA

Lieutenant Henry Hollingsworth of the Second Tennessee Volunteers visited the site of the Dade massacre of December 28, 1835, the incident that sparked the Second Seminole War.

Hollingsworth thought that, in the future, "the patriotic and brave . . . [will] pause for a moment on the spot reflecting on the sublime associations of the place and let fall the tear of sympathy."

The site is now a Florida historic park.

1919, MEMPHIS

Twenty-six county prisoners, all serving short terms for minor crimes, decided to quit the roadwork they were engaged in. They undertook their strike because rain had made the materials they were working with quite heavy.

All but seven changed their minds when the attending deputy informed them that strikers would have to eat bread and water instead of the usual holiday fare.

1919, NASHVILLE

Police discovered that a well-organized burglary ring had been operating in town for the past month. The gang had hit other Southern cities, moving when the police got close.

No arrests were made, and the ring most likely got away to burglarize another city.

DECEMBER 19

1895, MEMPHIS

The manslaughter case against Christian Science practitioner Laura B. Aikin was dropped.

Seven months earlier, Caddie Wade had been under Aikin's care when she died of excessive bleeding. Aikin was arrested, but it later came to light that Wade may have expired because of an attempt at self-induced abortion, not as a result of Christian Science healing. According to her husband, J. H. Wade, "I was told by my wife that she took some drugs before any trouble ever came on. I knew nothing about the drugs, and neither did my wife. I told Mrs. Aikin that I heard my wife had used instruments before the trouble, but I do not believe it now. I am sure that my wife would not try to commit an abortion."

The drugs referred to were abortifacients. When such measures failed, a woman might procure medical instruments and perform an abortion on her own.

Abortion had been illegal in Tennessee since 1883.

1934, SHELBYVILLE

Armed with tear gas, rifles with fixed bayonets, and machine-gun emplacements, the National Guard staved off a mob intent on rushing the courthouse where the trial of E. K. Harris was taking place. Harris, an African-American, was accused of attacking a 14-year-old white girl.

Judge J. T. Coleman declared a mistrial and set the retrial date for January 21, 1935. At 3 P.M., Harris was smuggled out of Shelbyville disguised as a National Guardsman wearing a gas mask. The crowd had no idea he had slipped through its fingers.

After the National Guard left town, the mob swarmed over the courthouse looking for the accused criminal. The men assumed he was hidden away somewhere in the 63-year-old building and so set fire to it, thinking that if they couldn't hang him, they would incinerate him. The building was totally ruined.

One of Harris's attorneys was future governor Prentice Cooper.

The editor of the *Bedford County Times*, embarrassed by the sordid, senseless affair, wrote on December 27, "Let us bury the past, it is history now; make the best of the present, and press forward to a brighter and better future."

DECEMBER 20

1917, CHATTANOOGA

While delivering his "All Mankind Must Be Judged after Death" sermon at the Baptist Tabernacle, the Reverend Billy Sunday was attacked by a German-American named Beuterbaugh, who had become enraged after the celebrated preacher made disparaging remarks about Germany and things German. He and Sunday traded a few punches. At one point, Beuterbaugh had his hands around the preacher's neck, choking him.

The crowd swarmed around Beuterbaugh, and shouts of "Lynch him!" echoed in the auditorium. The police whisked the Teutonic assailant off to jail, where he was charged with assault and battery.

1919, CHATTANOOGA

During the second day of a child-molestation trial, it was established that two defendants, Tom Snyder and Ed Martin, had taken sexual liberties with young girls. According to a newspaper report, "Even the most callous who sat in the courtroom . . . were sickened by the evidence produced and the questions asked."

In the end, the court had to establish the age of one of the victims, Mabel Dillard, who claimed she was 11. "Under the arrest law," reported the *Chattanooga Daily Times*, "no girl is entitled to protection who can be proved a common character and is over 12."

The two defendants were convicted of "lewdness" and received sentences of 11 months and 30 days each.

DECEMBER 21

1862, GIBSON COUNTY

Moving north from Trenton with his entire brigade, Nathan Bedford Forrest captured two companies of Federals and destroyed stores.

His men spent the next two days capturing garrisons and supplies along the railroad, wrecking 15 miles of track, and destroying trestles in the Obion River bottoms.

1885, KNOXVILLE

The city witnessed its first display of electric lighting, courtesy of a power plant located at 88 Gay Street. According to the *Knoxville Daily Chronicle*, "The novelty of the new deal in lighting brought out hundreds of people, many of whom promenaded up and down the streets. . . . The front of nearly every business house lighted by electricity had a constant throng of callers

during the evening. . . . It is safe to say that but very few people are disappointed."

1923, DAYTON

A gas explosion in the Dayton Coal Mine killed 22 workers. According to F. P. Clutch, the state superintendent of mines, a miner had strayed beyond the "danger zone," and the flame from his carbide lamp had set off the blast.

DECEMBER 22

1813, FORT STROTHER, MISSISSIPPI TERRITORY

Captain Jacob Hartsell of Tennessee wrote in his diary that "on this Evening there was news that General Jackson head Received orders from the Governor that he meant to keep us Six months. [T]here was more confusion In the Camps then I ever Saw in my Life. I cold not help lafing tell my Sides Did ack, Concerning the Deferent opinions of the Captains and the opinions of the privates. Some Swore that before they wold Stay three monthes they would kill General Jackson. Some Swore that they wold desert, Some one thing, Some another thing."

1921, KNOXVILLE

Avon Nyazna Williams, Jr., an African-American Democrat in the Tennessee Senate from 1969 to 1991, was born.

An attorney, Williams used his skills in the case of *Gray v. University of Tennessee*, which sought to desegregate the university. He moved to Nashville in 1953 and began practicing with famous civil rights attorney Z. Alexander Looby. Williams was involved in the landmark 1977 case of *Geier v. Blanton*, which merged Tennessee State

University into the University of Tennessee. He died on August 29, 1991.

Thelma Harper was later elected to the seat in the legislature, becoming the first black woman in the Tennessee Senate.

DECEMBER 23

1837, DAVIDSON COUNTY

Four men attempting to follow a submerged section of the Gallatin Turnpike decided to swim the Cumberland River, rather than wait for a ferry. Only two survived.

1850, CHATTANOOGA

The steamboat *Chattanooga* arrived in the river town for which it was named.

1862, OBION COUNTY

Nathan Bedford Forrest's raid into West Tennessee had by this date captured the Federal garrison in Union City and ravaged railroad tracks north and south of Dresden.

1887, KNOXVILLE

A mass meeting of the Colored Political League at the Knox County Courthouse was well attended. Candidates for mayor had been interviewed about their positions toward blacks by a committee of leading African-American citizens, whose reports were made to the assembly.

One mayoral candidate, a Mr. Clark, a Republican, had not impressed the committee. As the Reverend Job C. Lawrence, pastor of Logan Chapel, divulged,

> Mr. Clark reminds me of the old dog Tray, who was a very good dog, but alas! he got into bad company, and the trouble began. . . . I know my people, and I know all to[o] well the treatment they have received at the hands of their Republican clique of this city. They have been long suffering and freely forgiving people. . . . They have been fondled and . . . then cast aside and their rights and liberties trampled upon by the party . . . they supported. . . . Then came apologies and explanations . . . until Sambo gets confused and his mouth begins [to] say, "dat's so." They have him then. He freely forgives, is soaped anew, fired into a Republican ballot box and forgotten until the next election.

DECEMBER 24

1863, JEFFERSON COUNTY

The Battle of Dandridge, a critical point in the cavalry combat that plagued Confederate general James Longstreet's withdrawal from Knoxville to winter quarters near Morristown, took place. Approaching from the northwest, elements of the Army of the Cumberland were attacked by the Confederate men of Russell's Brigade at Hays Ferry and driven back through Dandridge to New Market.

1881, KNOXVILLE

After a day of betting on cockfights, racing, fighting, and drinking, Will Mabry and Don Lusby, the constable for Knox County's Second District, headed to a favorite saloon. Words were exchanged, and the two proceeded to fight. Mabry threw a heavy plate at Lusby and cut him on the forehead, causing him to bleed profusely. Mabry ran outside, followed closely by Lusby, who drew his pistol and shot Mabry dead on Gay Street.

This murder led to a blood feud in which Lusby, his father, Mabry's father and brother, and wealthy industrialist Thomas O'Conner all suffered similar fates in the summer and fall of 1882.

The last of the shootouts was described by a writer for the *Knoxville Tribune* on October 20, 1882:

> The reverberations from wall to wall of a few successive explosions, the curling up of a little sulphurous cloud upon this and that side of a narrow street and forms prone upon the wet and slippery flagging [pavement], then the hurried tramp of curious feet and pale lips are busy with eager questions. The dead are carried to houses upon either side of the street, which is made dismal by rain and the gathering throng of funeral umbrellas that block the way. The first palsey over, . . . fragmentary explanations are given while the curious throng gather around the bullet hole in the wall and the horrid pool of blood on the pavement that is mingling with the descending rain.

1917, NASHVILLE

Allen Watson, the son of a well-known Chattanooga family, was pardoned by Governor Thomas Rye. He left his prison cell immediately to join his family for the holidays.

As editor of the *Knoxville Citizen*, Watson had been a reformer and muckraking journalist who was especially critical of Mayor Samuel G. Heiskell's administration. Acknowledged by friend and foe to be an excellent writer and a progressive reformer, he was not so talented with financial arrangements. When his paper failed, he had been successfully prosecuted for embezzlement.

DECEMBER 25

1779, FRENCH LICK

James Robertson's party of 200 settlers arrived at the Cumberland River. Finding it frozen, they crossed to the opposite side to what later became Nashville.

1836, TAMPA, FLORIDA

Tennessee's First and Second Regiments boarded a steamboat for New Orleans. Their six-month enlistments had ended, and they were impatient to return home. Among them were newspaper editor and future Confederate general Felix K. Zollicoffer, future two-time mayor of Nashville Henry Hollingsworth, and two future governors, Neill Smith Brown and William Trousdale.

1901, JACKSON

This day saw the opening of the new YMCA, housing a 250-seat auditorium, a parlor, a reception room, reading and writing rooms, and a gymnasium. The erection of the facility was thanks in large measure to the work of the Reverend Mark Allison Matthews, who was heavily influenced by the Social Gospel, which held that the church should actively help reform society.

1985, PARIS, FRANCE

African-American jazz musician Peter "Memphis Slim" Chapman received France's highest award for cultural attainment.

DECEMBER 26

1847, NASHVILLE

The editor of the *Nashville Republican Banner*

was amazed at the artistic work being done at the State Capitol: "The work . . . has been done at our Penitentiary . . . superintended by the architect [William Strickland] himself. . . . We are inclined to doubt the possibility of such a specimen of art being produced in our neighborhood; and having been produced, we are grieved and surprised to find our citizens so silent upon the subject."

The editor was referring to the Ionic columns at the State Capitol, made by prisoners.

1863, NEAR DALTON, GEORGIA

Assistant surgeon John Kennerly Farris, a native of Winchester serving with the 41st Tennessee Infantry Regiment, wrote to his wife, Mary, about the demoralized condition of Confederate camp life:

Christmas day is past, & I am truly glad it is so, for such a day as we had yesterday is by no means agreeable. The drunk men in our Regt. & Brig. could not be numbered. I had thought that the Army had, to some extent, got over its demoralization, witnessed in the retreat from Missionary Ridge & immediately after, but I was badly mistaken. This Army is yet disgracefully demoralized.

Nothing could have afforded more evidence of this fact than yesterday's events. . . . The Col. commanding the brigade was beastly drunk, & so was the Col. commanding the Regt. & the Officer of the Day. Some of the guards were drunk, & many men & officers throughout the Brigade were the same. Oh, the scenes of yesterday were awful to contemplate. . . . Guards & officers were cursed & abused by drunken officers. . . . No regard was payed to any law or regulations whatever.

Before yesterday I had a very faint hope that something might turn . . . the course of events to gain for us our independence, but now I have no such a hope. Our cause is lost, certain, and I would just now say that I do not know but it will be as well otherwise. I am of the opinion that, should we gain our independence, that we would have a totering of aristocrat government, & many are of this opinion. . . .

. . . If I had known at the beginning of the war what I now know, I today would have been in Canida making an honest living. God knows I wish I was there now.

1901, PULASKI

Tennessee's black teachers met at Campbell's Chapel A.M.E. Delegates were from Nashville, Murfreesboro, Pulaski, Chattanooga, Franklin, Clarksville, Lexington, Athens, Cleveland, Columbia, and Memphis. The papers presented at the meeting accented the need for an industrial and a normal school for blacks in Tennessee.

Although it rained heavily, the banquet was described as "the grandest and most elaborate social affair ever given by the colored people of Pulaski."

1911, ON THE WATAUGA RIVER NEAR ELIZABETHTON

The hydroelectric facility at Horseshoe Bend operated by Doe River Light and Power Company (later Watauga Power Company) produced electricity for the first time.

1970, ARLINGTON, SHELBY COUNTY

Mabel Hughes, a state senator from 1951 to 1956 and the 10th woman to serve in the Tennessee General Assembly, died.

An educator and civic leader, she was superintendent of the Shelby County schools from 1905 to 1915, postmaster of Arlington from 1921 to 1949, president of the National Parent-Teacher Association in 1946, a delegate to the Pan American Child Congress in Caracas, Venezuela, and a member of the National Commission for United Nations Educational, Scientific, and Cultural Organization. She was also the director of *P.T.A. Magazine*, a delegate to the White House Conference on Education, and a recipient of the Award of Merit, given by the Daughters of the American Revolution.

Her husband, Louis W. Hughes, was a representative in the 65th, 66th, and 67th general assemblies.

DECEMBER 27

1806, MIDDLE TENNESSEE

Following his last visit to Tennessee, Aaron Burr was seen on a flatboat flotilla on the Stones and Cumberland Rivers, bound for the Mississippi River and New Orleans.

The vessels had been built on the Stones River at the Clover Bottom racetrack. Some have said the construction was carried out under contract with Andrew Jackson.

Burr was arrested in Natchez, Mississippi, within a few months on charges of treason.

1915, NASHVILLE

Mary Frances Doyle, a representative from Davidson County in the general assembly from 1969 to 1973, was born.

Upon the death of her brother, William Patrick Doyle, in October 1959, Mary Frances Doyle succeeded him as a Democratic representative on Nashville's city council. She was the first woman

to serve on the Nashville/Davidson County Metropolitan Council. She joined the Republican Party in 1973, after her service in the Tennessee House. She served as assistant chaplain at Central State Hospital for the Criminally Insane (now Middle Tennessee Mental Health Institute) in Nashville. Doyle died on July 8, 1981, and was buried in Woodlawn Memorial Park.

DECEMBER 28

1818, THE HERMITAGE

In a letter to his nephew Andrew Donelson, a cadet at West Point, Major General Andrew Jackson gave this advice about discipline and punishment: "If your superior forgets what he owes you & his station, & attempts to insult you or maltreat you . . . you have my permission to resign—but if the Superior attempts either to strike or kick you, put him to instant death. . . . Never . . . outlive your honour."

1831, CANNON COUNTY

Henry Jefferson St. John, a member of the Tennessee House from 1857 to 1859, was born.

St. John practiced law in Woodbury and was mustered into the Provisional Army of Tennessee as captain of Company D, 18th Tennessee Infantry, in May 1861. Taken prisoner at the surrender of Fort Donelson, he was exchanged at Vicksburg in September 1862. He was re-elected captain of Company D during its reorganization, only to be honorably discharged because of poor health. After returning home, he spent a great deal of time buying cattle for the Confederate army. The Union victory at the Battle of Stones River in late 1862 and early

1863 put an end to his cattle business.

In his application for a pension after the war, St. John revealed that "in the latter part of 1863, or first of 1864, I was arrested by a Squad of Yankee Bush Whackers . . . and given my choice to take the Oath or be Shot and of course I took the oath. . . . But when I got away from them . . . I felt no obligatory obligation as to the enforced Oath, but I did not violate my oath."

1925, ALCOA

Over 1,400 children, all the progeny of ALCOA workers, received Christmas presents from the company. Three enormous trees were situated at different locations, two for white children and one for black children. Black youngsters went to the Commercial Building, while white children went to the Springbrook and Bissel communities.

The festivities were financed by local businessmen.

DECEMBER 29

1758, CHOTEE, IN THE CHEROKEE NATION

The Reverend John Martin, missionary to the Overhill Cherokees, described in his diary how he

> went to their Town-house where a great many were met & were dancing round a cane Fire, going from West to East; their young Peo. [people] seemed very active & brisk; was filled with pity for them in their present state of Heathenism; was surprised in them after they were all in a Leather with sweat, having Danced an Hour together, run out into the cold Air and cool themselves & sometimes in the River, which occasions great colds among them. Their Town houses are built in the Form of a Sugar Load & will hold 4 or 500 peo.; they are supported by ten Pillars; at the Foot of most of them are seats for the great Men among them. . . . Here they sit & talk & smoke & dance sometimes all night.

1808, RALEIGH, NORTH CAROLINA

Andrew Johnson was born.

He briefly attended school and was apprenticed to a tailor at the age of 10, at which time he learned the rudiments of reading and writing. His wife later taught him mathematics.

He moved to Greeneville about 1825 and took up the tailor's trade. In 1828, he began his public career as a political organizer by putting together the Working Man's Party, which propelled him to the position of alderman in Greeneville. He was mayor of that town from 1830 to 1834.

Johnson served in the United States House of Representatives from 1834 to 1853 and was elected the 15th governor of Tennessee, holding that office from 1853 to 1857. He then served in the United States Senate from 1857 to 1862. Johnson was appointed military governor of Tennessee by Abraham Lincoln, holding that office from 1862 to 1865 with the rank of brigadier general. He was elected vice president of the United States and served until Lincoln's assassination on April 15, 1865, when he took the oath of office as president. He continued as president until March 3, 1869, after which he was again elected to the Senate, where he remained until his death in 1875.

1835, NEW ECHOTA, GEORGIA

Cherokees under Chief John Ross signed a removal treaty with the United States.

The Treaty of New Echota was ratified by the United States Senate on May 23, 1836. In time, some of the signers—namely, Chiefs John Ridge and Elias Boudinot—were executed by other Cherokees.

1950, WASHINGTON, D.C.

The Kefauver-Celler Act was passed. It amended Section 7 of the Clayton Act to prohibit corporate acquisitions where the effect would tend to substantially lessen competition, thus granting the federal government power to tackle incipient monopolies. The law was inspired by the Senate Special Committee to Investigate Interstate Crime, headed by Tennessee senator Estes Kefauver.

DECEMBER 30

1862, NEAR BLOUNTVILLE

Coming south through Moccasin Gap, Union brigadier general Samuel P. Carter's task force captured 30 wounded Confederates from the Fourth Kentucky Cavalry, then sent detachments to Bluff City and Carter's Depot, where more captures were made and stores and railroad facilities were destroyed.

Toward evening, a Confederate colonel was captured aboard a railroad train by members of Carter's task force. Carter's men dispersed or captured the Confederate garrison and destroyed the railroad bridge over the Watauga River.

Crossing to the south bank of the river while being pursued on their flanks and from the rear,

the outmaneuvered Confederates moved northwest to Kingsport.

1901, GILES COUNTY

The Reverend A. J. Brooks, a Baptist minister, was murdered near the Enterprise neighborhood by Elihue Wisdom, an arrant drunk and bully.

Wisdom had been arrested a year or so earlier for shooting into Brooks's house. In court, he had threatened that if Brooks ever spoke to him again, he would kill the minister.

Brooks was returning from a visit to Mount Pleasant in Maury County when he met Wisdom on the road. Brooks politely said "Good evening" as he passed. Wisdom quickly turned around, drew his pistol, and fired three shots, one of which killed the Baptist cleric. Wisdom then remarked, "I told you if you spoke to me again I would kill you, and now I have kept my word."

Authorities were unable to locate Wisdom.

DECEMBER 31

1862, MURFREESBORO

At dawn, Confederate general Braxton Bragg attacked the forces of General William Starke Rosecrans, pushing them in a northeasterly direction.

After three days of fighting, neither army could claim victory. Of the 83,000 men on both sides, nearly 33 percent were killed or wounded. The battle demonstrated the deadly power of cannon against human-wave assaults, as practiced in the linear warfare of that time.

1862, NEAR NOLENSVILLE, WILLIAMSON COUNTY

Confederate general Joseph Wheeler's cavalry

brigade left its overnight bivouac and, having passed completely around Union general William Starke Rosecrans's army, rejoined General Braxton Bragg's Army of Tennessee in time to screen its left flank during the Battle of Stones River.

1927, JOHNSON CITY

Ruth C. Montgomery was born.

She served in the Tennessee House from 1981 to 1989, during which time she was assistant minority leader, chair of the VET caucus, secretary of the Upper East Tennessee (Republican) caucus, and a member of the Fiscal Review Committee, the Transportation Committee, the Commerce Committee, and the General Welfare Committee. While serving in the state senate from 1989 to 1991, she was secretary of the General Welfare, Health, and Human Resources Committee, secretary of the State and Local Government Committee, and secretary of the Government Operations Committee. She either sponsored or supported legislation for nursing-home reform, alternative treatment for juvenile delinquents, and durable power of attorney for health care of the elderly. She was the 31st woman to serve in the Tennessee General Assembly.

Bibliography

Abernathy, T. P. *From Frontier to Plantation in Tennessee*. Memphis: Memphis State University Press, 1955.

Allen, Alberta K. *Once upon a Time in Rives: A History of Rives, Obion County, Tennessee*. Union City: H. A. Lanzer, 1969.

Allen, Jack, and Herschel Gower, eds. *Pen and Sword: The Life and Journals of Randal W. McGavock*. Nashville: Tennessee Historical Commission, 1959.

Alvarez, Eugene. *Travel on the Southern Antebellum Railroads, 1828–1860*. University, Ala.: University of Alabama Press, 1974.

Atkinson, George Wesley. *After the Moonshiners, by One of the Raiders*. Wheeling, W. Va.: 1881.

Banks, Frank, coordinator. *Memphis African-American '93 Historical Calendar*. Memphis: African-American Historical Calendar Partnership, 1992.

Bayer, Linda. "Roadside Architecture." *Historic Huntsville Quarterly of Architecture and Preservation* 9 (Fall 1982/Winter 1983): 3–39.

Beach, Ursula S. *Montgomery County*. Tennessee County History Series, ed. Robert B. Jones. Memphis: Memphis State University Press, 1988.

Beard, Mattie Duncan. *The W.C.T.U. in the Volunteer State*. Kingsport: Kingsport Press, 1962.

Beard, William E., comp. *It Happened in Nashville, Tennessee: A Collection of Historical Events Which Occurred in Nashville, Are Commemorated There, or in Which Nashville People Were Actors*. Nashville: Davie, 1912.

Berg, Walter E. *Buildings and Structures of American Railroads: A Reference Book for Railroad Managers, Superintendents, Master Mechanics, Engineers, Architects, and Students*. New York: C. E. Wiley and Sons, 1893.

Bergeron, Paul H. *Paths of the Past: Tennessee, 1790–1970*. Knoxville: Tennessee Historical Commission and the University of Tennessee Press, 1979.

Biggs, Riley Oakes. "The Development of Railroad Transportation in East Tennessee during the Reconstruction Period." Master's thesis, University of Tennessee, August 1934.

Black, Robert C., III. *The Railroads of the Confederacy*. Chapel Hill: University of North Carolina Press, 1952.

Bledsoe, Thomas. *Or We'll All Hang Separately: The Highlander Idea*. Boston: Beacon Press, 1969.

Bowen, J. W. *History of Smith County*. Carthage: Smith County Record, 1887.

Braden, Beulah Brummett. *When Grandma Was a Girl*. Oak Ridge and Clinton Courier-News, 1976.

Brand, Robert R. "Personal Reminiscences of a Northern Farmer in Sherwood, Tennessee, 1883–1885." On file at Tennessee State Library and Archives Manuscript Division.

Bryant, Keith L. "Cathedrals, Castles, and Roman Baths: Railway Station Architecture in the Urban South." *Journal of Urban History* 2 (February 1976): 195–230.

Burns, Frank. *Davidson County*. Tennessee County History Series, ed. Robert B. Jones. Memphis: Memphis State University Press, 1989.

Byrum, C. Stephen. *McMinn County*. Tennessee County History Series. Memphis: Memphis State University Press, 1984.

Camp, Henry R. *Sequatchie County*. Tennessee County History Series, ed. Robert B. Jones. Memphis: Memphis State University Press, 1984.

Capers, Gerald M., Jr. *The Biography of a River Town: Memphis, Its Heroic Age*. Chapel Hill: University of North Carolina Press, 1932.

Cartwright, Joseph H. *The Triumph of Jim Crow: Tennessee Race Relations in the 1880s*. Knoxville: University of Tennessee Press, 1976.

Carver, Martha. *Historical and Architectural Inventory File Jacket for the S.R. 33 (U.S. 411) Project from the Georgia Line to Madisonville, Property No. H-11, Surveyed July 21, 1989*. On file at the Tennessee Department of Transportation in Nashville.

Chattanooga and St. Louis Railway. *Before Railroads: A Contemporary View of Agriculture, Industry, and Commerce of the South in the Forties*. Louisville, Ky.: Nashville, Chattanooga & St. Louis Railroad, 1929.

Civil War Centennial Commission. *Guide to the Civil War in Tennessee*. 3rd ed. Nashville: Civil War Centennial Commission, 1977.

Clark, Thomas D. *The Beginning of the L & N: The Development of the Louisville and Nashville Railroad and Its Memphis Branches from 1836 to 1860*. Louisville, Ky.: Standard, 1933.

———. *A Pioneer Southern Railroad: From New Orleans to Cairo*. Chapel Hill: University of North Carolina Press, 1936.

Clayton, W. Woodford. *History of Davidson County, Tennessee, with Illustrations and Biographical Sketches of Its Prominent Men and Pioneers*. Philadelphia: J. W. Lewis, 1880.

Connelly, Thomas L. *Civil War in Tennessee: Battles and Leaders*. Knoxville: Tennessee Historical Commission and the University of Tennessee Press, 1990.

Corlew, Robert E. "The Negro In Tennessee, 1870–1900." Ph.D. diss., University of Alabama, 1954.

———. *Tennessee: A Short History*. 2d ed. Knoxville: University of Tennessee Press, 1981.

Corliss, Carlton J. *Main Line of Mid-America: The Story of the Illinois Central*. New York: Creative Age Press, 1950.

Council, Bruce R., and Nicholas Honerkamp. *The Union Railroads Site: Industrial Archaeology in Chattanooga, Tennessee*. TVA Publications in Anthropology, no. 38. Chattanooga: 1984.

Cowan, Samuel K. *Sergeant York and His People*. New York: Funk, 1922.

Crawford, Earle E. *One of Those Tall Tennesseans: The Life of G. S. W. Crawford, 1849–1891*. Maryville: Maryville College Press, 1988.

Creekmore, Betsy Beeler. *Knoxville*. Knoxville: University of Tennessee Press, 1959.

Creighton, Wilbur Foster. *Building of Nashville*. Nashville: privately printed, 1969.

Cresswell, Stephen. *Mormons, Cowboys, Moonshiners and Klansmen: Federal Law Enforcement in the South and West, 1870–1893*. Tuscaloosa: University of Alabama Press, 1991.

Deaderick, Lucile, ed. *Heart of the Valley: A History of Knoxville, Tennessee*. Knoxville: Knoxville History Committee, East Tennessee Historical Society, 1976.

Dickinson, W. Calvin. *Morgan County*. Tennessee County History Series, ed. Frank B. William, Jr. Memphis: Memphis State University Press, 1987.

Doyle, Don H. *Nashville in the New South, 1880–1930*. Knoxville: University of Tennessee Press, 1985.

Durham, Walter T. *Nashville, the Occupied City: The First Seven Months, February 16, 1862, to June 30, 1963*. Nashville: Tennessee Historical Society, 1985.

Egerton, John. *Visions of Utopia: Nashoba, Rugby, Ruskin and the New Communities in Tennessee's Past*. Knoxville: Tennessee Historical Commission and the University of Tennessee Press, 1988.

Eller, Ronald D. *Miners, Millhands and Mountaineers: Industrialization of the Appalachian South*. Knoxville: University of Tennessee Press, 1982.

Environment Consultants, Inc. *An Inventory and Evaluation of Architectural and Engineering Resources of the Big South Fork National River and Recreation Area, Tennessee and Kentucky*. Cultural Resources Report 82-4. Lexington, Ky.: Environment Consultants, Inc., 1982.

Ferguson, Edward A. *Founding of the Cincinnati Southern Railway*. Cincinnati, Ohio: Robert Clark Company, 1905.

Fishback, Price V. "Did Coal Miners 'Owe Their Souls to the Company Store?' Theory and Evidence from the Early 1900s." *Journal of Economic History* 46 (December 1986): 1011–29.

Folmsbee, Stanley John. *Sectionalism and Internal Improvements in Tennessee, 1796–1845*. Knoxville: East Tennessee Historical Society, 1939.

Freytag, Ethel, and Glena Kreis Ott. *A History of Morgan County*. Specialty Printing Company, 1971.

Fuller, Justin. "History of the Tennessee Coal and Railroad Company, 1852–1907." Ph.D. diss., University of North Carolina at Chapel Hill, 1966.

Gillenwater, Mack Henry. "Cultural and Historical Geography of Mining Settlements in the Pocahontas Coal Field of Southern West Virginia, 1880 to 1930." Ph.D. diss., University of Tennessee, 1972.

Ginger, Ray. *Age of Excess: The United States from 1877 to 1914.* 2d ed. New York: Macmillan, 1975.

Glenn, L. C. *The Northern Tennessee Coal Field Included in Anderson, Campbell, Claiborne, Fentress, Morgan, Overton, Pickett, Roane, and Scott Counties.* Bulletin 33-B, Tennessee Department of Education, Division of Geology. Nashville: 1925.

Goodspeed Publishing Company. *A History of Tennessee from the Earliest Times to the Present.* 6 vols. Nashville: Goodspeed Publishing Company, 1886.

Goodstein, Anita Shafer. *Nashville, 1780–1860: From Frontier to City.* Gainesville: University of Florida Press, 1989.

Govan, Gilbert E., and James W. Livingood. *The Chattanooga Country, 1540–1951: From Tomahawks to TVA.* New York: Dutton, 1952.

Harper, Herbert L., ed. *Houston and Crockett, Heroes of Tennessee and Texas: An Anthology.* Nashville: Tennessee Historical Commission, 1986.

Hawkins, A. W. *Hand-Book of Tennessee.* Knoxville: Knoxville Whig and Chronicle Steam Book and Job Printing Office, 1882.

Herr, Kincaid A. *The Louisville and Nashville Railroad, 1850–1959.* Louisville, Ky.: L & N Magazine, 1959.

Hindle, Brooke. *America's Wooden Age: Aspects of Its Early Technology.* Terrytown, N.Y.: Sleepy Hollow Restorations, 1975.

Holt, Edgar A. *Claiborne County.* Tennessee County History Series, ed. Joy Bailey Dunn. Memphis: Memphis State University Press, 1981.

Howell, Benita J. *A Survey of Folklife along the Big South Fork of the Cumberland River.* Report of Investigation no. 30, Department of Anthropology, University of Tennessee. Knoxville: 1981.

Hudson, Kenneth. *Industrial Archaeology.* 2nd rev. ed. London: John Baker, Publishers, 1966.

Huehls, Betty Sparks. "Life in the Coal Towns of White County, Tennessee, 1882–

1936." Master's thesis, Tennessee Technological University, 1983.

Huizinga, Johan. *America: A Dutch Historian's Vision from Afar and Near.* Translated by Herbert H. Rowan. New York: Harper and Row, 1972.

Humes, Thomas William. *The Loyal Mountaineers of Tennessee.* Knoxville: Ogden, 1888.

Jackson, Andrew. *The Papers of Andrew Jackson.* Vol. 1. Edited by Sam B. Smith and Harriet Chappell Owsley. Knoxville: University of Tennessee Press, 1980.

Johnson, Andrew. *The Papers of Andrew Johnson.* Edited by Leroy P. Graf and Ralph Haskins. 6 vols. Knoxville: University of Tennessee Press, 1967–73.

Johnson, LeLand R. *From Memphis To Bristol, a Half Century of Road Building: A History of the Tennessee Road Builders' Association.* Nashville: Tennessee Road Builders' Association, 1978.

Jones, Shirley Farris, and John Abernathy Smith, eds. *Letters to Mary: The Civil War Diary of John Kennerly Farris.* Winchester: Franklin County Historical Society, 1994.

Josephson, Matthew. *The Robber Barons: The Great American Capitalists, 1861–1901.* New York: Harcourt Brace and Company, 1934.

Keating, John M. *History of the City of Memphis and Shelby County, Tennessee, with Illustrations and Biographical Sketches of Some of Its Prominent Citizens.* Syracuse, N.Y.: D. Mason, 1888–89.

Keith, Jean E. "The Role of the Louisville and Nashville Railroad in the Development of Coal and Iron in Alabama, Tennessee and Kentucky." Master's thesis, Johns Hopkins University, 1959.

Kelly, Cameron. *A History of South Pittsburg, Tennessee.* South Pittsburg: Hustler Printing Company, 1973.

Killebrew, J. B. *Introduction to the Resources of Tennessee.* Nashville: Tavel, Eastman, and Howell, 1874.

King, Duane H., ed. *The Cherokee Nation: A Troubled History.* Knoxville: University of Tennessee Press, 1979.

Kirk, Stephen. *First in Flight: The Wright Brothers in North Carolina.* Winston-Salem, N.C.: John F. Blair, Publisher, 1995.

Lamon, Lester C. *Blacks in Tennessee, 1791–1970.* Knoxville: Tennessee Historical Commission and University of Tennessee Press, 1981.

Lawrence, Randal Gene. "Appalachian Metamorphosis: Industrializing Society on the Central Appalachian Plateau, 1860–1913." Ph.D. diss., Duke University.

Leonard, Charles. *A Pictorial History of Sparta-White County, Tennessee.* Cookeville: Anderson Performance Printing, 1984.

Lewis, Ronald L. *Black Coal Miners in America: Race, Class, and Conflict.* Lexington: University Press of Kentucky, 1987.

Life in the Company Towns. Part 1 of *The Wilder-Davidson Story: The End of an Era.* Upper-Cumberland Institute and WCTE, 1987. Educational video.

Lillard, Roy G. *Bradley County.* Tennessee County History Series, ed. Joy Dailey Dunn. Memphis: Memphis State University Press, 1980.

Livingood, James W. *A History of Hamilton County, Tennessee.* Tennessee County History Series. Memphis: Memphis State University Press, 1981.

Lloyd, Ralph Waldo. *Maryville College: A History of 150 Years, 1819–1969.* Maryville: Maryville College Press, 1969.

Lowenthal, David. *The Past Is a Foreign Country.* Cambridge: Cambridge University Press, 1985.

Lowenthal, David, and Marcus Binney, eds. *Our Past before Us: Why Do We Save It?* London: Temple Smith Limited, 1981.

Martin, Charles E. *Hollybush: Folk Building and Social Change in an Appalachian Community.* Knoxville: University of Tennessee Press, 1984.

Mason, Robert L. *Cannon County.* Tennessee County History Series, ed. Joy Bailey Dunn. Memphis: Memphis State University Press, 1982.

McCormack, Edward Michael. *Slavery on the Tennessee Frontier: Tennessee in the Eighteenth Century.* Bicentennial Series, ed. James C. Kelly and Dan E. Pomeroy. Nashville: American Bicentennial Commission, 1977.

McDonald, Michael J., and William Bruce Wheeler. *Knoxville, Tennessee: Continuity and Change in an Appalachian City.* Knoxville: University of Tennessee Press, 1983.

McGuffey, Charles D., ed. *Standard History of Chattanooga, Tennessee, with Full Outline of the Early Settlement, Pioneer Life, Indian History, and General and Particular History of the City to the Close of the Year 1910.* Knoxville: Crew and Dorsey, 1911.

Meeks, Carroll L. V. *The Railroad Station: An Architectural History.* New Haven, Conn.: Yale University Press, 1956.

Miller, William D. *Mr. Crump of Memphis*. Baton Rouge: Louisiana State University Press.

Mills, Jesse C. "A Short History of Briceville." Paper on file at the Tennessee Valley Authority Technical Library in Knoxville. 1973.

Moore, Elwood S. *Coal: Its Properties, Analysis, Classification, Geology, Extraction, Uses and Distribution*. New York: John Wiley and Sons, 1922.

Morgan, John T. "The Decline of Log House Construction in Blount County, Tennessee." Ph.D. diss., University of Tennessee, 1986.

Morton, Dorothy Rich. *Fayette County*. Tennessee County History Series, ed. Charles W. Crawford. Memphis: Memphis State University Press, 1989.

Murfree, Mary Noailles [Charles Egbert Craddock, pseud.]. *In the Tennessee Mountains*. Boston: Houghton Mifflin, 1884.

Nelson, Wilbur A. *The Southern Tennessee Coal Field Included in Bledsoe, Cumberland, Franklin, Grundy, Hamilton, Marion, Putnam, Rhea, Sequatchie, Van Buren, Warren, and White Counties*. Bulletin 33-A, Tennessee Department of Education, Division of Geology. Nashville: 1925.

Nicholson, James L. *Grundy County*. Tennessee County History Series, ed. Robert E. Corlew. Memphis: Memphis State University Press, 1982.

O'Neal, Michael R. "Historic Railroad Depot Architecture in Middle Tennessee." Master's thesis, Middle Tennessee State University, 1983.

———. "A History of the Glenmary Coal and Coke Company." On file at the Tennessee Historical Commission/State Historic Preservation Office planning section in Nashville. 1988.

Patten, Z. C., and Carter Patten. *So Firm a Foundation*. Chattanooga: by the authors, 1968.

Peters, Kate Johnston, ed. *Lauderdale County, Tennessee*. Ripley: Sugar Hill–Lauderdale County Library, 1957.

Phillips, Margaret I. *The Governors of Tennessee*. Gretna, La.: Pelican Publishing Company, 1978.

Pierce, Dean. "The Low-Income Farmer: A Reassessment." *Social Welfare in Appalachia* 3 (1971).

Polk, James K. *The Correspondence of James K. Polk*. Edited by Wayne Cutler and James P. Cooper, Jr. 7 vols. Nashville: Vanderbilt University Press, 1969–89.

Prince, Richard E. *The Nashville, Chattanooga & St. Louis Railway: History and Steam Locomotives*. Salt Lake City, Utah: Wheelwright Lithographing Company, 1967.

————. *The Southern Railway System: Steam Locomotives and Boats*. Rev. ed. Green River, Wyo.: Richard E. Prince, 1970.

Pulliam, Walter T. *Harriman: The Town That Temperance Built*. Maryville: Marion R. Mangrum Brazos Press, 1978.

Remini, Robert V. *Andrew Jackson and the Course of the American Empire*. New York: Harper and Row, 1971.

————. *The Election of Andrew Jackson*. New York: J. B. Lippincott, 1963.

Riedl, Norbert F., Donald B. Ball, and Anthony Cavender. *Survey of Traditional Architecture and Related Material Folk Culture Patterns in the Normandy Reservoir, Coffee County, Tennessee*. Report of Investigation no. 17, Department of Anthropology, University of Tennessee. Knoxville: 1976.

Ringwalt, J. L. *Development of Transportation Systems in the United States: Comprising a Comprehensive Description . . .* Philadelphia: by the author, 1888.

Rogers, David, comp. *Reflections in the Water, Coal Creek to Lake City: A History of Lake City, Tennessee*. 1976.

Rothrock, Mary U., ed. *The French-Broad-Holston Country: A History of Knox County, Tennessee*. Knoxville: East Tennessee Historical Society, 1946.

Rule, William, George F. Mellen, and J. Wooldridge, eds. *Standard History of Knoxville, Tennessee, with Full Outline of the Natural Advantages, Early Settlement, Territorial Government, Indian Troubles and General and Particular History of the City down to the Present Time*. Chicago: Lewis, 1900.

Satz, Ronald N. *Tennessee's Indian Peoples: From White Contact to Removal, 1540–1840*. Knoxville: Tennessee Historical Commission and University of Tennessee Press, 1990.

Scofield, Edna. "The Evolution and Development of Tennessee Houses." *Journal of the Tennessee Academy of Sciences* 11 (October 1936).

Scott, Mingo, Jr. *The Negro in Tennessee Politics and Governmental Affairs, 1865–1965*. Nashville: Rich, 1965.

Shapiro, Henry David. *Appalachia on Our Mind: The Southern Mountains and Mountaineers in the American Consciousness*. Chapel Hill: University of North Carolina Press, 1978.

Shifflett, Crandall A. *Coal Towns: Life, Work, and Culture in Company Towns of Southern Appalachia, 1880–1960*. Knoxville: University of Tennessee Press, 1991.

Slaughter, G. H. *Stagecoaches and Railroads: Or, the Past and the Present*. Nashville: Haaslock and Ambrose, 1894.

Smallfrank, Fedora. *Beginnings on Market Street: Nashville and Her Jewry*. Nashville: by the author, 1976.

Smith, Ross. *Reminiscences of an Old Timer*. By the author, 1930.

Soule, Andrew M. *A Visit to the Cumberland Plateau, Tennessee*. New York: Meyer Brothers, 1901.

Southern Pine Association. *Homes for Workmen*. New Orleans: Southern Pine Association, 1919.

Speer, William S., comp. and ed. *Sketches of Prominent Tennesseans: Containing Biographies and Records of Many of the Families Who Have Attained Prominence in Tennessee*. Nashville: A. B. Tavel, 1888.

Stahl, Ray. *Greater Johnson City: A Pictorial History*. Norfolk, Va.: Donning Company, 1983.

Sulzer, Elmer G. *Ghost Railroads of Tennessee*. Indianapolis, Ind.: Vane A. Jones Company, 1975.

Tennessee Department of Transportation. *Truss Bridge Survey*. On file at TDOT in Nashville.

Tennessee Division of Archaeology. Site file no. 40GY78. On file at TDOA offices in Nashville.

——. Site file no. 40MI17. On file at TDOA offices in Nashville.

Tennessee Historical Commission. *Biographical Directory of the Tennessee General Assembly*. 7 vols. Nashville: Tennessee Historical Commission, 1975–90.

——. *Tennessee Historical Markers Erected by the Tennessee Historical Commission*. Nashville: Tennessee Historical Commission, 1980.

Tennessee Historical Commission/State Historic Preservation Office. *Historic Architectural Survey of Blount County, Tennessee*. 1984. On file at THC/SHPO in Nashville.

Tennessee Mining Department. Annual reports no. 1–36 (1895–1930). On file at Tennessee State Library and Archives.

Tennessee Railroad Commission. Annual reports, 1897–1920, in *The Coal Field Directory*. Pittsburgh, Pa.: Keystone Consolidated Publishing Company, 1903, and Cupola, 1920.

Turner, William Bruce. *History of Maury County, Tennessee*. Nashville: Parthenon Press, 1955.

United Motor Courts, Inc. *United Motor Courts: A Guide*. 10th ed. Houston, Tex.: United Motor Courts, Inc., 1942.

U.S. Army Corps of Engineers, Nashville District. *Draft Feasibility Report, Oneida and Western Railroad*. October 1981.

————. *Structural Treatment Plan for National Register: Eligible Architectural Structures of the Big South Fork National River and Recreation Area*. March 1986.

U.S. Department of Labor, Bureau of Labor Statistics. *Housing by Employers in the United States*. Bulletin no. 263. Washington, D.C.: GPO, 1920.

U.S. Department of the Interior, Bureau of Mines. *Houses for Mining Towns*. Prepared by Joseph H. White. Washington, D.C.: GPO, 1914.

U.S. *House Journal*. 39th Cong., 2d sess. Report no. 34. *Affairs of Southern Railroads*.

Walker, Nancy Wooten. *Out of a Clear Blue Sky: Tennessee's First Ladies and Their Husbands*. Cleveland, Tenn.: 1971.

Waller, William, ed. *Nashville in the 1890s*. Nashville: Vanderbilt University Press, 1970.

Way, William, Jr. *The Clinchfield Railroad*. Chapel Hill: University of North Carolina Press, 1931.

Webb, Thomas G. *DeKalb County*. Tennessee County History Series, ed. Robert B. Jones. Memphis: Memphis State University Press, 1986.

Weidner, Maude. *Nashville Then and Now, 1780–1930*. Nashville: Hermitage Publications, 1930.

White, John H., Jr. "Tracks and Timber." *Industrial Archaeology* 2 (1976): 35–46.

White, Robert H., and Stephen V. Ash, eds. *Messages of the Governors of Tennessee*. 10 vols. Nashville: Tennessee Historical Commission, 1952–90.

Wight, E. M. *A People without Consumption and Some Account of Their Country, the Cumberland Table-land*. Nashville: Tavel, Eastman, and Howell, 1876.

Williams, Emma Inman. *Historic Madison: The Story of Jackson and Madison County, Tennessee, from the Prehistoric Moundbuilders to 1917*. Jackson: Madison County Historical Society, 1946.

Williams, Frank B., Jr. *Tennessee's Presidents*. Knoxville: Tennessee Historical Commission and University of Tennessee Press, 1981.

Wilson, Samuel Tyndale. *The Southern Mountaineers*. New York: Presbyterian Home Missions, 1915.

Womack, Walter. *McMinnville at Milestone, 1810–1960: A Memento of the Sesquicentennial Year of McMinnville, Tennessee, and Warren County, Tennessee, 1958*. McMinnville: Standard, 1960.

Woodward, Comer Vann. *Origins of the New South, 1877–1913*. Baton Rouge: Louisiana State University Press, 1951.

Wust, Klaus G. *Wartburg: Dream and Reality of the New Germany in Tennessee*. Baltimore: Society for the History of the Germans in Maryland, 1963.

In writing this book, I consulted back issues of over 15 historical journals and magazines and over 45 19th- and 20th-century newspapers, most of them on file at the Tennessee State Library and Archives. Likewise utilized were both the vertical files and the manuscripts collection of the Tennessee State Library and Archives, the National Register listings files deposited at the State Historic Preservation Office in Nashville, and the local-history sections of the public libraries of Nashville/Davidson County, Chattanooga, Knoxville, and Memphis.

Index

USS *Nashville*, 19, 81–82, 204, 212–13
USS *Tennessee*, 134, 207, 237
USS *Wabash*, 27

Van Buren County, 94, 125, 146
Van Buren, Martin, 85
Vanderbilt Hospital, 239
Vanderbilt University, 12, 190, 230, 242
Vanleer, Joe, 30
Vanleer, Mrs. Joe, 30
Vantrease, Jim, 186
Vaughn, James D., 56
Vaughn, John Crawford, 73
Veach, Clayton "Rabbit," 76, 140

"Wabash Cannonball," 180
Waddy, Robert, 131
Wade, Caddie, 245
Wade, Elvis, 35
Wade Farrar and Company, 125
Wade, George, 162
Wade, J. H., 245
Wagoner, Porter, 58
Wahlen (drum major), 40
Walden Hospital (Chattanooga), 139
Waldensia, 178
Walker, James W., 50
Walker, Joseph Edison, 63–64
Walker, Lola Montez, 136
Walker, Robert, 130
Walker, Rosa, 209–10
Walker, Will, 144
Walker, William, 91, 178, 188, 189, 201, 243
Wallace, Lew, 70
Wallach, Joel, 23
Walling, Debra Margaret "Maggie," 57
Walling, Thomas, 146
Walsh, Captain, 37
War Memorial Building (Nashville), 177
"War of the Roses, the," 149
Ward, John. *See* Medal of Honor, Tennessee recipients
Ward, Nancy, 143
Ward, W. E., 107
Ward-Belmont College, 236
Warren, Cash, 155–56
Warren County, 58
Wartrace, 154
Washington County, 41, 170, 180
Washington, George, 121
Washington, Mat, 200
Washington Street Baptist Church, 149–50

Washington, Thomas, 20
Watauga Power Company, 249
Watauga settlements, 242
Watson, Allen, 248
Watson, Mrs. Sam, 204
Watts, John, 201
Wauhatchie Pike, 145
Wayland, Julius, 159
WDCN, 106, 177
WDIA, 61
Webb, Sawney, 219
Webster, Joseph D., 239
Weidner v. Friedman, 240–41
Weinberg, Hedy, 24
Welch, John A., 84
Wells, Ida B., 49, 100, 105, 164
Wells, Kitty, 168, 176
West, Dottie, 198
West High School (Knoxville), 24
West, John D., 19–20
West Tennessee Fair, 163
West Tennessee Mental Hospital, 148
West, William, 19–20
Westmoreland, 197
Wheeler, Emma R., 139
Wheeler, J. N., 139
Wheeler, Joseph, 73, 174
Whig Party, 83
White, Benjamin, 136
White County, 42, 94, 146, 212
White, Hugh Lawson, 208
White, J. W., 180
White, William A., 184
Whitelaw Furniture Company, 139
Whitman, Amanda, 179
Whitwell, 230
Whitworth, George K., 220–21
Wiggs, Joe, 25
Wilder, John, 47
Wilder-Davidson, 224
Wilhelm II, 6
Williams, Avon Nyazna, Jr., 166, 246–47
Williams, Catharine, 173
Williams, Elbert, 124
Williams, Gracie, 115, 116
Williams, Ms. Frank, 147
Williams, R. G., 37–38
Williams, Samuel Cole, 110, 202
Williamson County, 32, 101, 114, 158, 191, 192, 193, 252–53
Williamson, John Lee Curtis "Sonny Boy," 63, 172

Williamsport, 182
Willis, Archie W., Jr., 53, 215
Willis, John Harlan, 41
Wilson, Charles, 92
Wilson County, 121, 208
Wilson, Sam, 103
Winchester, 38, 227, 249
Winchester, James, 15
Winston, Sam, 165
Wisdom, Elihue, 252
Witty, Paul A., 73
WKRN, 231
WLAC (channel 5). *See* WTVF
WLAC (radio), 228
WMC, 125
Wood, Eliza, 160–61
Woodbury, 216, 250
Woodhull, Victoria, 23
Woodlawn Memorial Park, 250
Woods, Mr., 105
Woodward, Glad, 170
Wooten, Mrs., 160–61
WOPI, 331
Working Man's Party, 251
WRCB, 78
Wright, Frances "Fannie," 111
Wright, Mary Sue, 239
Wright, Orville, 141
Wright, Wilbur, 141
WSIX, 231
WSM, 110, 180, 190, 194
WTVF, 156

Yamamoto, Tojo, 239
Yanes, Jamie, 80
Yardley, William Francis, 8, 20, 36, 219
yellow fever, 158, 175, 206, 219
Yellow Hammer's Nest, 128
Ying, Henry Wah, 126
York, Alvin C. *See* Medal of Honor, Tennessee recipients
York, Gracie, 198
York Grist Mill, 198
Young, John S., 180
Y-12 cyclotron (Oak Ridge), 35
Y-12 plant (Oak Ridge), 154

"Z" (writer), 80
Zenith, 96
Zenoff, David, 87
Zollicoffer, Felix K., 14, 51, 161–62, 248
Zollner, Lona Shope Wilhelmina Sutton, 241